MOON HANDBOOKS
Withdrawn

5/23/14
#16.99
B+T

DENVER

MINDY SINK

Contents

Maps

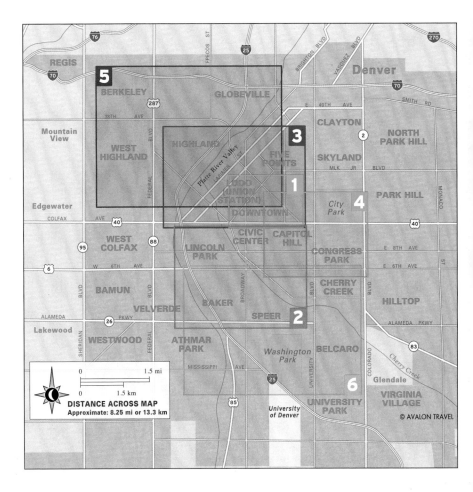

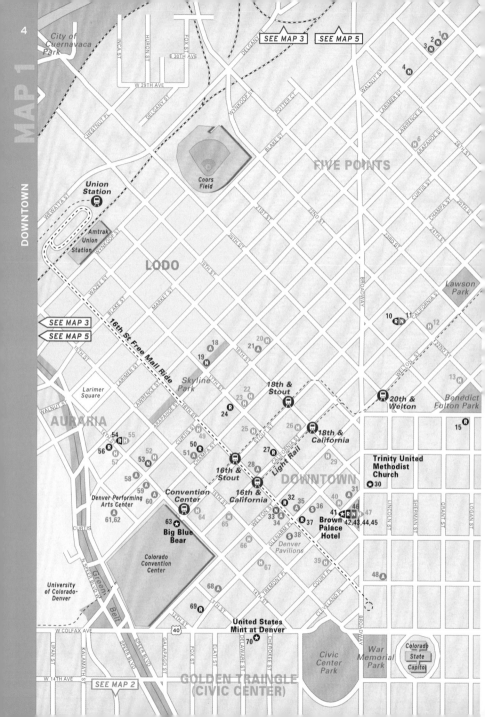

Curtis Park

30th & Downing

Black American West Museum 5

29th & Welton

27th & Welton

25th & Welton

Blair-Caldwell African American Research Library

Light Rail

NORTH CAPITOL HILL

CAPITOL HILL

St. Luke Hospital

SEE MAP 4

0   300 yds

0   300 m

DISTANCE ACROSS MAP
Approximate: 2.14 mi or 3.45 km

SEE MAP 4

SIGHTS
- 5 BLACK AMERICAN WEST MUSEUM
- 9 BLAIR-CALDWELL AFRICAN AMERICAN RESEARCH LIBRARY
- 30 TRINITY UNITED METHODIST CHURCH
- 41 BROWN PALACE HOTEL
- 63 BIG BLUE BEAR
- 70 UNITED STATES MINT AT DENVER

RESTAURANTS
- 8 TOM'S HOME COOKIN'
- 10 MERCURY CAFÉ
- 15 JONESY'S EATBAR
- 16 LAS DELICIAS
- 24 PANZANO
- 27 OLIVÉA
- 32 APPALOOSA GRILL
- 37 COOK'S FRESH MARKET
- 42 BROWN PALACE ATRIUM
- 43 ELLYNGTON'S
- 44 PALACE ARMS
- 45 SHIP TAVERN
- 50 MICI
- 54 EDGE RESTAURANT & BAR
- 56 RESTAURANT KEVIN TAYLOR
- 69 EMILY'S COFFEE

NIGHTLIFE
- 2 LARIMER LOUNGE
- 3 MEADOWLARK BAR
- 4 THE MATCHBOX
- 7 ROXY THEATRE
- 11 MERCURY CAFE
- 19 LANNIE'S CLOCKTOWER CABARET
- 33 JAZZ AT JACK'S
- 46 CHURCHILL BAR
- 53 CORNER OFFICE RESTAURANT AND MARTINI BAR

ARTS AND LEISURE
- 1 DENVER BCYCLE
- 14 CLEO PARKER ROBINSON DANCE
- 18 SOUTHWEST RINK AT SKYLINE PARK
- 21 FORZA FITNESS AND ATHLETIC CLUB
- 28 DIKEOU COLLECTION
- 31 AMERICAN MUSEUM OF WESTERN ART--THE ANSCHUTZ COLLECTION
- 34 UA DENVER PAVILIONS 15
- 35 PARAMOUNT THEATRE
- 48 YMCA
- 51 BOVINE METROPOLIS THEATRE
- 58 BOETTCHER CONCERT HALL
- 59 ELLIE CAULKINS OPERA HOUSE
- 60 GARNER GALLERIA THEATRE
- 61 HELEN BONFILS THEATRE COMPLEX
- 62 THE TEMPLE HOYNE BUELL THEATRE
- 68 DENVER ATHLETIC CLUB

SHOPS
- 17 CERAMICS IN THE CITY
- 36 I HEART DENVER STORE
- 38 DENVER PAVILIONS

HOTELS
- 6 THE GREGORY INN
- 12 MELBOURNE HOTEL AND INTERNATIONAL HOSTEL
- 13 QUEEN ANNE BED AND BREAKFAST INN
- 20 THE RITZ-CARLTON
- 22 DENVER MARRIOTT RESIDENCE INN CITY CENTER
- 23 HOTEL MONACO
- 25 MAGNOLIA HOTEL
- 26 MARRIOTT CITY CENTER
- 29 GRAND HYATT DENVER
- 39 SHERATON DENVER DOWNTOWN HOTEL
- 40 COMFORT INN
- 47 BROWN PALACE HOTEL
- 49 COURTYARD BY MARRIOTT DENVER DOWNTOWN
- 52 THE CURTIS
- 55 FOUR SEASONS HOTEL DENVER
- 57 HOTEL TEATRO
- 64 EMBASSY SUITES DENVER-DOWNTOWN /CONVENTION CENTER
- 65 HYATT REGENCY DENVER AT THE COLORADO CONVENTION CENTER
- 66 HAMPTON/HOMEWOOD SUITES HOTELS IN DOWNTOWN DENVER
- 67 CROWNE PLAZA DENVER DOWNTOWN HOTEL

© AVALON TRAVEL

MAP 2

GOLDEN TRIANGLE, LINCOLN PARK, AND SOBO

GOLDEN TRIANGLE
(CIVIC CENTER)

W COLFAX AVE

SEE MAP 3

W 14TH AVE PKWY

W 14TH AVE

W 13TH AVE

W 12TH PL

W 12TH AVE

W 12TH AVE

Lincoln
Park

W 12TH AVE

The Clyfford
Still Museum

W 11TH AVE

W 11TH AVE

10th &
Osage

W 10TH AVE

LINCOLN
PARK

Sunken
Gardens
Park

W 9TH AVE

Museo de
las Americas

W 8TH AVENUE VIADUCT

W 8TH AVE

Denver
General
Hospital

W 7TH AVE

W 7TH AVE

W 6TH AVE

W 6TH AVE

W 5TH AVE

W 4TH AVE

W 4TH AVE

W 3RD AVE

W 3RD AVE

W 2ND AVE

W 2ND AVE

BAKER

W 1ST AVE

W IRVINGTON PL

South Platte River

W ELLSWORTH AVE

Dailey
Park

W ARCHER PL

W BAYAUD AVE

W BAYAUD AVE

W MAPLE AVE

W CEDAR AVE

W BYERS PL

W ALAMEDA AVE

W NEVADA PL

SEE MAP 6

Alameda

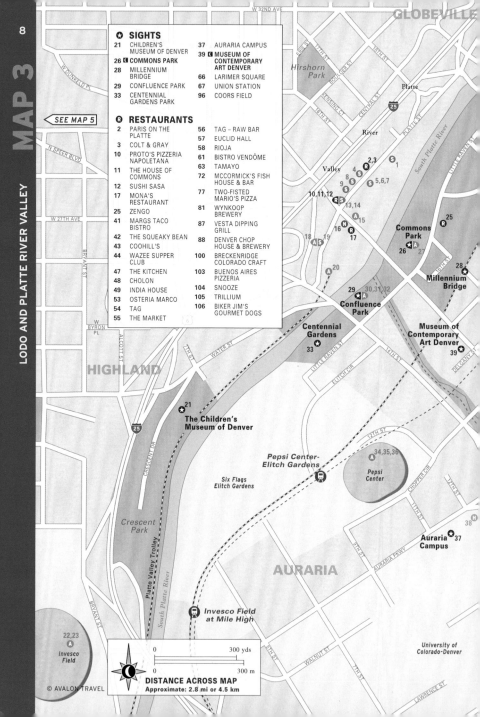

GLOBEVILLE

SEE MAP 5

✪ SIGHTS

21	CHILDREN'S MUSEUM OF DENVER	37	AURARIA CAMPUS
26	COMMONS PARK	39	MUSEUM OF CONTEMPORARY ART DENVER
28	MILLENNIUM BRIDGE	66	LARIMER SQUARE
29	CONFLUENCE PARK	67	UNION STATION
33	CENTENNIAL GARDENS PARK	96	COORS FIELD

ⓡ RESTAURANTS

2	PARIS ON THE PLATTE	56	TAG – RAW BAR
3	COLT & GRAY	57	EUCLID HALL
10	PROTO'S PIZZERIA NAPOLETANA	58	RIOJA
11	THE HOUSE OF COMMONS	61	BISTRO VENDÔME
12	SUSHI SASA	63	TAMAYO
17	MONA'S RESTAURANT	72	MCCORMICK'S FISH HOUSE & BAR
25	ZENGO	77	TWO-FISTED MARIO'S PIZZA
41	MARGS TACO BISTRO	81	WYNKOOP BREWERY
42	THE SQUEAKY BEAN	87	VESTA DIPPING GRILL
43	COOHILL'S	88	DENVER CHOP HOUSE & BREWERY
44	WAZEE SUPPER CLUB	100	BRECKENRIDGE COLORADO CRAFT
47	THE KITCHEN	103	BUENOS AIRES PIZZERIA
48	CHOLON	104	SNOOZE
49	INDIA HOUSE	105	TRILLIUM
53	OSTERIA MARCO	106	BIKER JIM'S GOURMET DOGS
54	TAG		
55	THE MARKET		

Hirshorn Park

Platte

River

Valley

Commons Park

Millennium Bridge

Confluence Park

Museum of Contemporary Art Denver

Centennial Gardens

HIGHLAND

The Children's Museum of Denver

Pepsi Center-Elitch Gardens

Pepsi Center

Six Flags Elitch Gardens

Crescent Park

AURARIA

Auraria Campus

Platte Valley Trolley

South Platte River

Invesco Field at Mile High

Invesco Field

University of Colorado-Denver

0   300 yds

0   300 m

DISTANCE ACROSS MAP
Approximate: 2.8 mi or 4.5 km

© AVALON TRAVEL

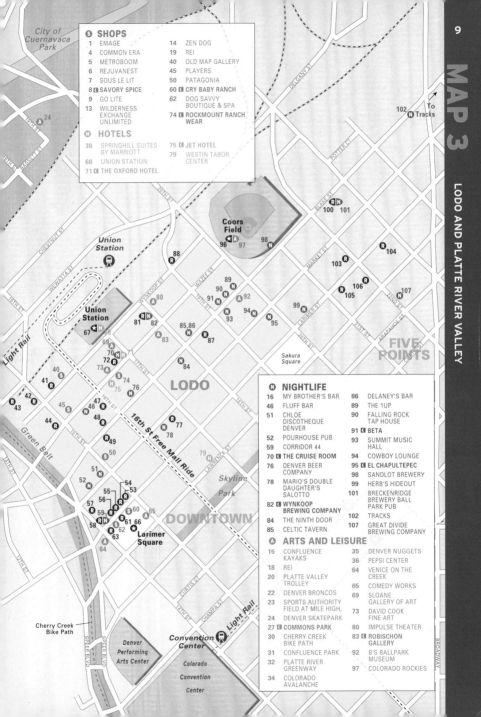

SHOPS
1 EMAGE
4 COMMON ERA
5 METROBOOM
6 REJUVANEST
7 SOUS LE LIT
8 SAVORY SPICE
9 GO LITE
13 WILDERNESS EXCHANGE UNLIMITED
14 ZEN DOG
19 REI
40 OLD MAP GALLERY
45 PLAYERS
50 PATAGONIA
60 CRY BABY RANCH
62 DOG SAVVY BOUTIQUE & SPA
74 ROCKMOUNT RANCH WEAR

HOTELS
38 SPRINGHILL SUITES BY MARRIOTT
68 UNION STATION
71 THE OXFORD HOTEL
75 JET HOTEL
79 WESTIN TABOR CENTER

NIGHTLIFE
16 MY BROTHER'S BAR
46 FLUFF BAR
51 CHLOE DISCOTHEQUE DENVER
52 POURHOUSE PUB
59 CORRIDOR 44
70 THE CRUISE ROOM
76 DENVER BEER COMPANY
78 MARIO'S DOUBLE DAUGHTER'S SALOTTO
82 WYNKOOP BREWING COMPANY
84 THE NINTH DOOR
85 CELTIC TAVERN
86 DELANEY'S BAR
89 THE 1UP
90 FALLING ROCK TAP HOUSE
91 BETA
93 SUMMIT MUSIC HALL
94 COWBOY LOUNGE
95 EL CHAPULTEPEC
98 SANDLOT BREWERY
99 HERB'S HIDEOUT
101 BRECKENRIDGE BREWERY BALL PARK PUB
102 TRACKS
107 GREAT DIVIDE BREWING COMPANY

ARTS AND LEISURE
15 CONFLUENCE KAYAKS
18 REI
20 PLATTE VALLEY TROLLEY
22 DENVER BRONCOS
23 SPORTS AUTHORITY FIELD AT MILE HIGH,
24 DENVER SKATEPARK
27 COMMONS PARK
30 CHERRY CREEK BIKE PATH
31 CONFLUENCE PARK
32 PLATTE RIVER GREENWAY
34 COLORADO AVALANCHE
35 DENVER NUGGETS
36 PEPSI CENTER
64 VENICE ON THE CREEK
65 COMEDY WORKS
69 SLOANE GALLERY OF ART
73 DAVID COOK FINE ART
80 IMPULSE THEATER
83 ROBISCHON GALLERY
92 B'S BALLPARK MUSEUM
97 COLORADO ROCKIES

SEE MAP 3

25th & Welton

Lawson Park

SEE MAP 1

Light Rail

FIVE POINTS

Benedict Fulton Park

18th & Stout

20th & Welton

18th & California

St. Luke Hospital

Presbyterian St. Luke Medical Center

E 22ND AVE

E 21ST AVE

E 20TH AVE

St. Joseph Hospital

16th St Free Mall Ride

Denver Pavilions

NORTH CAPITOL HILL

CITY PARK WEST

E 19TH AVE

E 18TH AVE

7

8

11

12

14 15

9

10

13

16

21

Cathedral Basilica of the Immaculate Conception

E 16TH AVE

22

27

28

40

E COLFAX AVE

24

25

26

War Memorial Park

Civic Center Park

23 Colorado State Capitol Building

Molly Brown House Museum

49

50

E 14TH AVE

CAPITOL HILL

GOLDEN TRIANGLE (CIVIC CENTER)

47 48

51

52

53

E 13TH AVE

E 12TH AVE

Cheesman Park

58

57

E 11TH AVE

56

55

E 10TH AVE

SEE MAP 2

E 9TH AVE

60

62

61

63

Governors Park

E 7TH AVE

SPEER

67

68

Denver General Hospital

© AVALON TRAVEL

64

66

65

E 6TH AVE

WHITTIER

E 25TH AVE
E 24TH AVE
E 23RD AVE

City Park
Golf Course

1

2
Denver Zoo

STEELE ST

DISTANCE ACROSS MAP
Approximate: 2.7 mi or 4.4 km

300 yds
300 m

Duck
Lake

Denver Museum of
Nature and Science
3   4

City Park
5

Ferril
Lake   6

E 20TH AVE

PARK PL

HIGH ST
RACE ST
VINE ST
GAYLORD ST
YORK ST

18
17 19
20

E 17TH AVE

E 17TH AVE

Mercy Medical
Center

CITY PARK ESPLANADE
CITY PARK ESPLANADE

DETROIT ST
ST BROWN ST
FILLMORE ST
MILWAUKEE ST
ST PAUL ST
STEELE ST
ADAMS ST
COOK ST
MADISON ST
MONROE ST
GARFIELD ST
HARRISON ST
COLORADO BLVD

E 16TH AVE

31
32   35   36

40   42,43,44   45

E COLFAX AVE

29   30   33   34

37 38   39

40

41   46

National Jewish
Medical Center

E 14TH AVE

JOSEPHINE ST
COLUMBINE ST
ELIZABETH ST
CLAYTON ST
DETROIT ST
FILLMORE ST
MILWAUKEE ST
ST PAUL ST

54

E 13TH AVE

CONGRESS PARK

E 12TH AVE

E 11TH AVE

Denver Botanic
Gardens
59

E 8TH AVE
E 8TH AVE

RACE ST
VINE ST
GAYLORD ST

E 7TH AVE PKWY
E 7TH AVE PKWY

HIGH ST

SEE MAP 6

✪ SIGHTS

2 DENVER ZOO
5 CITY PARK
3 ☪ DENVER MUSEUM OF NATURE AND SCIENCE
22 CATHEDRAL BASILICA OF THE IMMACULATE CONCEPTION

23 ☪ COLORADO STATE CAPITOL BUILDING
49 MOLLY BROWN HOUSE MUSEUM
59 ☪ DENVER BOTANIC GARDENS

🅝 RESTAURANTS

8 STEUBEN'S
9 THE AVENUE GRILL
10 MARCZYK FINE FOODS
11 ☪ WATERCOURSE FOODS
14 STRINGS
15 D BAR DESSERTS
16 PARALLEL 17
17 IL POSTO
19 ST. MARK'S COFFEEHOUSE
20 VINE STREET PUB & BREWERY
30 PETE'S KITCHEN
32 ☪ SAME CAFÉ
36 ☪ PINCHE TACOS
40 THE SHOPPE

41 THE CHURCH OF CUPCAKES
42 ATOMIC COWBOY
43 DENVER BISCUIT COMPANY
44 FAT SULLY'S
47 CITY, O' CITY
52 JELLY
54 LIK'S ICE CREAM
57 ☪ POTAGER
60 LUCA D'ITALIA
61 MIZUNA
62 BONES
63 BENNY'S RESTAURANT AND TEQUILA BAR
65 BROTHERS BBQ
68 FRUITION

🅝 NIGHTLIFE

18 THE THIN MAN
25 PROHIBITION
26 CHARLIE'S
33 LION'S LAIR

35 THE THREE LIONS
45 BLUEBIRD THEATER
46 ☪ MEZCAL
64 ☪ DON'S CLUB TAVERN

🅐 ARTS AND LEISURE

1 CITY PARK GOLF COURSE
4 IMAX THEATER AT THE DENVER MUSEUM OF NATURE AND SCIENCE
6 FERRIL LAKE
21 FILLMORE AUDITORIUM

27 OGDEN THEATRE
38 DENVER FILM CENTER/COLFAX
50 ☪ KIRKLAND MUSEUM OF FINE & DECORATIVE ART
58 CHEESMAN PARK
66 ESQUIRE THEATER
67 TROUT'S FLY FISHING

🅢 SHOPS

12 WOODHOUSE DAY SPA
13 TALULAH JONES
24 CAPITOL HILL BOOKS
28 THE COLORADO BEAD COMPANY

37 ☪ TWIST & SHOUT
39 ☪ TATTERED COVER BOOK STORE
48 BUFFALO EXCHANGE
53 WAX TRAX RECORDS

🅗 HOTELS

7 WARWICK HOTEL
29 THE HOLIDAY CHALET
31 CASTLE MARNE BED AND BREAKFAST INN
34 ADAGIO BED AND BREAKFAST

51 ☪ CAPITOL HILL MANSION BED AND BREAKFAST INN
55 BURNSLEY HOTEL
56 THE PATTERSON INN

DISTANCE ACROSS MAP
Approximate: 4.2 mi or 6.9 km

SEE MAP 3

● RESTAURANTS

2	TENN. ST. COFFEE	41	COMMON GROUNDS COFFEEHOUSE
3	PARISI ITALIAN MARKET & DELI	42	TRATTORIA STELLA
4	SWING THAI	43	PIZZA PUBLIC
6	BIG HOSS BBQ	44	PARK BURGER
8	AXIOS	45	SPUNTINO
10	CAFE BRAZIL	46	PATZCUARO'S
11	THAI BASIL	47	DUO RESTAURANT
13	BUCHI CAFÉ CUBANO	48	WOODEN SPOON CAFE & BAKERY
15	PAXIA	49	PASQUINI'S
16	LOU'S FOOD BAR	55	ROOT DOWN
17	TAMALES BY LA CASITA	58	Z CUISINE
18	LOS CARBONCITOS	60	LINGER
24	HIGHLANDS GARDEN CAFÉ	61	LITTLE MAN ICE CREAM
25	HIGHLAND PACIFIC	63	VITA
26	HAPPY CAKES	64	AMATO'S ALE HOUSE
36	BANG!	65	MASTERPIECE DELICATESSEN
38	CORAL ROOM		

● NIGHTLIFE

1	LOCAL 46	50	ZIO ROMOLO'S ALLEY BAR
9	TENNYSON'S TAP	54	WILLIAMS & GRAHAM
20	PATSY'S INN ITALIAN RESTAURANT	59	Á CÔTÉ
28	HAI BAR	62	LOLA
		67	FOREST ROOM 5

● ARTS AND LEISURE

12	THE DENVER PUPPET THEATER	21	THE BUG THEATRE
19	PIRATE: A CONTEMPORARY ART OASIS	23	SLOAN'S LAKE PARK
		53	VITRUVIAN FITNESS

● SHOPS

5	MOUTHFULS	34	ST. KILLIAN'S CHEESE SHOP
7	THE GIGGLING GREEN BEAN	35	WORDSHOP
22	THE BELLE ON COTTAGE HILL	37	STARLET
27	BABAREEBA THEN & NOW	39	HIGHLANDS SQUARE
29	REAL BABY	40	WILD YARNS
30	THE PERFECT PETAL	51	PERPETUAL CLOTHING
31	KISMET	52	INSPYRE BOUTIQUE
32	STRUT	66	MORE FLOWERS
33	DRAGONFLY		

● HOTELS

14	LUMBER BARON INN & GARDENS	57	HAMPTON INN & SUITES
56	MARRIOTT RESIDENCE INN		

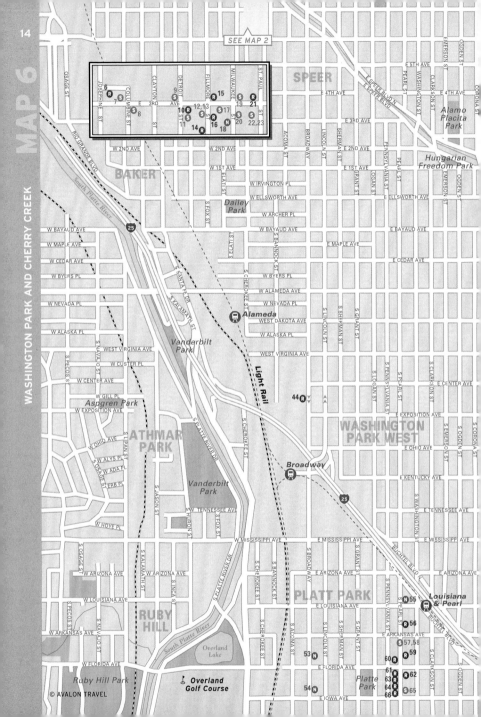

SEE MAP 2

SEE MAP 4

See Detail

DISTANCE ACROSS MAP
Approximate: 3.7 mi or 6 km

0   400 yds
0   400 m

COUNTRY CLUB

Denver Country Club Golf Course

Cherry Creek

Takayama Park

Cherry Creek Shopping Center

CHERRY CREEK

Pulaski Park

Burns Park

Brest Park

BELCARO

Bonnie Brae Park

Smith Lake

Washington Park

Grasmere Lake

NIGHTLIFE

| 18 | CHERRY | 54 | HERMAN'S HIDEAWAY |
| 53 | BLACK CROWN LOUNGE | 55 | THE VILLAGE CORK |

ARTS AND LEISURE

29	PISMO FINE ART GLASS	45	WASHINGTON PARK LAKES: SMITH LAKE
32	CHERRY CREEK ARTS FESTIVAL	46	WASHINGTON PARK
42	GATES TENNIS CENTER	47	WASHINGTON PARK LAKES: GRASMERE LAKE

SHOPS

1	NEST	31	WIZARD'S CHEST
2	THE STATIONERY COMPANY	33	CHERRY CREEK NORTH
4	DEJA BLUE	34	KAZOO & COMPANY
7	FIREFLY FURNISHINGS	35	LAWRENCE COVELL
8	REVAMPT	38	EDIT EURO SPA
9	ARTISAN CENTER	39	CHERRY CREEK FRESH MARKET
11	MAX	41	CHERRY CREEK MALL
12	ECCENTRICITY	49	POME
13	THE HERMITAGE BOOKSHOP	51	TROUT'S AMERICAN SPORTSWEAR
17	CREATOR MUNDI	57	OLD SOUTH PEARL STREET
19	GARBARINI	58	OLD SOUTH PEARL STREET FARMERS MARKET
20	LE SOUTIEN		
22	LITTLE ME'S	65	5 GREEN BOXES
23	SUGARLICIOUS		
27	HW HOME		
30	SOL		

HOTELS

| 24 | INN AT CHERRY CREEK | 28 | JW MARRIOTT |

RESTAURANTS

3	BAROLO GRILL	44	ASSIGNMENTS RESTAURANT
5	LITTLE OLLIE'S	48	BONNIE BRAE ICE CREAM
6	SYRUP	50	DEVIL'S FOOD BAKERY & COOKERY
10	CRÊPES N' CRÊPES	52	WASH PARK GRILLE
14	THE EGGSHELL OF CHERRY CREEK	56	DUFFEYROLL CAFÉ
15	SUSHI TAZU	59	STELLA'S COFFEEHAUS
16	PASTA PASTA PASTA	60	SUSHI DEN
21	CUCINA COLORE	61	BLACK PEARL RESTAURANT
25	CHERRY CRICKET	62	IZAKAYA DEN
26	SECOND HOME KITCHEN + BAR	63	GAIA BISTRO
36	BOMBAY CLAY OVEN	64	BUDAPEST BISTRO
37	ZAIDY'S DELI	66	PAJAMA BAKING COMPANY
40	ELWAY'S		
43	BASIL DOC'S PIZZA		

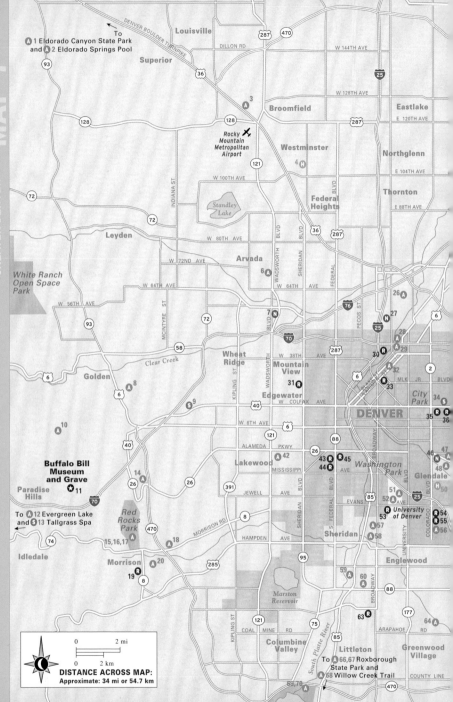

To Ⓐ1 Eldorado Canyon State Park
and Ⓐ2 Eldorado Springs Pool

93

DENVER BOULDER TURNPIKE

To

Louisville

Superior

287 470

DILLON RD

36

W 144TH AVE

25

128

Ⓐ3

Rocky
Mountain
Metropolitan
Airport

Broomfield

W 128TH AVE

Eastlake

E 120TH AVE

128

128

287

Westminster

4 Ⓝ

Northglenn

E 104TH AVE

72

121

W 100TH AVE

Standley
Lake

Federal
Heights

Thornton

E 88TH AVE

72

72

Leyden

W 80TH AVE

36

287

Arvada

W 72ND AVE

6 Ⓐ

WADSWORTH BLVD

SHERIDAN BLVD

FEDERAL BLVD

26 Ⓐ

White Ranch
Open Space
Park

W 64TH AVE

W 64TH AVE

PECOS ST

76

27 Ⓝ

25

6

W 56TH AVE

93

72

7 Ⓝ

28 Ⓐ

MCINTYRE ST

KIPLING ST

Ⓢ9

58

Clear Creek

Wheat
Ridge

W 38TH AVE

287

30 Ⓡ

29

2

Golden

6

Ⓐ8

Mountain
View

6

32

33 Ⓡ

MLK JR. BLVD

6

40

Edgewater

31 Ⓡ

City
Park

34 Ⓐ

Ⓐ10

40

W COLFAX AVE

DENVER

35 Ⓡ Ⓡ
36

Buffalo Bill
Museum
and Grave

W 6TH AVE

6

Paradise
Hills

★11

14 Ⓐ

121

ALAMEDA

Ⓐ42

Lakewood

26 Ⓐ

43 Ⓡ45
44Ⓡ

Washington
Park

46 Ⓐ

47 Ⓝ

Glendale

48

To Ⓐ12 Evergreen Lake
and Ⓢ13 Tallgrass Spa

26 Ⓐ

70

MISSISSIPPI

JEWELL   AVE

BROADWAY

50

Red
Rocks
Park

391

Ⓢ8

EVANS

85 Ⓡ

51 Ⓐ

52 Ⓐ

University
of Denver

54 Ⓡ

Idledale

74

15,16,17

470

MORRISON RD

HAMPDEN   AVE

SHERIDAN BLVD

S FEDERAL BLVD

53 Ⓡ

57 Ⓐ

58 Ⓐ

COLORADO BLVD

55 Ⓡ
56

19 Ⓐ 20 Ⓐ

Morrison

18 Ⓐ

285

Sheridan

95

59 Ⓐ

60 Ⓐ

Englewood

88

Ⓐ8

Marston
Reservoir

63 Ⓡ

177

64 Ⓐ

KIPLING ST

121

COAL   MINE   RD

75

85

ARAPAHOE

Greenwood
Village

Columbine
Valley

South Platte River

Littleton

To Ⓐ66,67 Roxborough
State Park and
Ⓢ68 Willow Creek Trail

COUNTY LINE

69,70 Ⓐ

470

N

0   2 mi

0   2 km

DISTANCE ACROSS MAP:
Approximate: 34 mi or 54.7 km

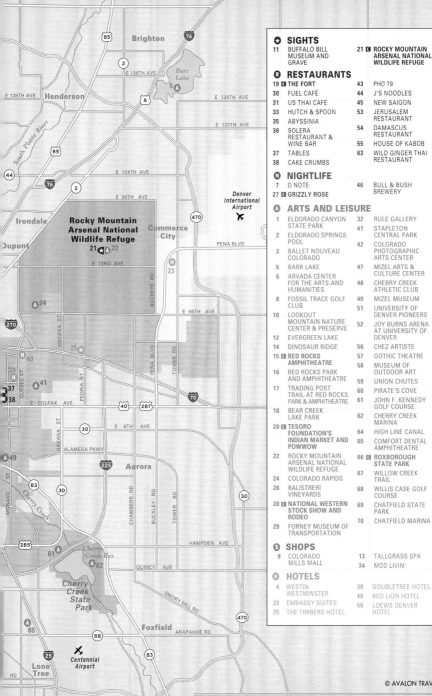

SIGHTS

11 BUFFALO BILL MUSEUM AND GRAVE

21 ROCKY MOUNTAIN ARSENAL NATIONAL WILDLIFE REFUGE

RESTAURANTS

19 THE FORT
30 FUEL CAFÉ
31 US THAI CAFÉ
33 HUTCH & SPOON
35 ABYSSINIA
36 SOLERA RESTAURANT & WINE BAR
37 TABLES
38 CAKE CRUMBS

43 PHO 79
44 J'S NOODLES
45 NEW SAIGON
53 JERUSALEM RESTAURANT
54 DAMASCUS RESTAURANT
55 HOUSE OF KABOB
63 WILD GINGER THAI RESTAURANT

NIGHTLIFE

7 D NOTE
27 GRIZZLY ROSE

46 BULL & BUSH BREWERY

ARTS AND LEISURE

1 ELDORADO CANYON STATE PARK
2 ELDORADO SPRINGS POOL
3 BALLET NOUVEAU COLORADO
5 BARR LAKE
6 ARVADA CENTER FOR THE ARTS AND HUMANITIES
8 FOSSIL TRACE GOLF CLUB
10 LOOKOUT MOUNTAIN NATURE CENTER & PRESERVE
12 EVERGREEN LAKE
14 DINOSAUR RIDGE
15 RED ROCKS AMPHITHEATRE
16 RED ROCKS PARK AND AMPHITHEATRE
17 TRADING POST TRAIL AT RED ROCKS PARK & AMPHITHEATRE
18 BEAR CREEK LAKE PARK
20 TESORO FOUNDATION'S INDIAN MARKET AND POWWOW
22 ROCKY MOUNTAIN ARSENAL NATIONAL WILDLIFE REFUGE
24 COLORADO RAPIDS
26 BALISTRERI VINEYARDS
28 NATIONAL WESTERN STOCK SHOW AND RODEO
29 FORNEY MUSEUM OF TRANSPORTATION

32 RULE GALLERY
41 STAPLETON CENTRAL PARK
42 COLORADO PHOTOGRAPHIC ARTS CENTER
47 MIZEL ARTS & CULTURE CENTER
48 CHERRY CREEK ATHLETIC CLUB
49 MIZEL MUSEUM
51 UNIVERSITY OF DENVER PIONEERS
52 JOY BURNS ARENA AT UNIVERSITY OF DENVER
56 CHEZ ARTISTE
57 GOTHIC THEATRE
58 MUSEUM OF OUTDOOR ART
59 UNION CHUTES
60 PIRATE'S COVE
61 JOHN F. KENNEDY GOLF COURSE
62 CHERRY CREEK MARINA
64 HIGH LINE CANAL
65 COMFORT DENTAL AMPHITHEATRE
66 ROXBOROUGH STATE PARK
67 WILLOW CREEK TRAIL
68 WILLIS CASE GOLF COURSE
69 CHATFIELD STATE PARK
70 CHATFIELD MARINA

SHOPS

9 COLORADO MILLS MALL

13 TALLGRASS SPA
34 MOD LIVIN'

HOTELS

4 WESTIN WESTMINSTER
23 EMBASSY SUITES
25 THE TIMBERS HOTEL

39 DOUBLETREE HOTEL
40 RED LION HOTEL
50 LOEWS DENVER HOTEL

© AVALON TRAVEL

Discover Denver

Welcome to Denver, where urban style and outdoor casual coexist and residents enjoy more sunny days year-round than cities in California or Florida. No longer heralded as the Queen City of the Plains, Denver is now called the Mile High City – a reminder of its 5,280-feet-above-sea-level status and its 140-mile vista of the Rocky Mountains to the west.

Denver has grown up a lot in recent years, and has finally found maturity by capitalizing on its natural assets and embracing its Western roots. No longer a cowtown, this diverse city includes neighborhoods rich in ethnic and local foods, cutting-edge architecture, one-of-a-kind historic sights, packed bars and nightclubs, and an abundance of open spaces.

With 20,000 acres of city parks and 200 miles of bicycling and jogging trails, Denver offers recreation as a way of life for the increasingly urban population. If you crave the grandeur and ski slopes of the mountains, you can get there quickly from downtown Denver or you can find a trail for hiking, snowshoeing, or cycling in the foothills of Golden or Boulder, less than one hour away by car.

Between the exciting attractions in the city, such as the Museum of Contemporary Art Denver, Commons Park, and the Red Rocks Amphitheatre, and the easy proximity to the mountains, the city has something to offer the weekend visitor, the university student, the snowboard enthusiast, the business traveler, and the newly relocated family. Revitalized, all grown-up, and still looking for ways to improve, this unique western metropolis reigns as the unofficial capital of the Rocky Mountain West.

Planning Your Trip

▶ WHERE TO GO

Downtown

The country's 10th-largest downtown is pedestrian-friendly with iconic sights like the Brown Palace Hotel and the modern Big Blue Bear sculpture. Major sights in adjacent neighborhoods, such as the Black American West Museum in Five Points, are also just steps away. The bulk of the city's hotels are located in the heart of downtown, and many visitors find that this is the perfect spot to stay since it is so close to many of the city's historic and cultural sights, upscale restaurants, and lively bars in adjacent neighborhoods.

Golden Triangle, Lincoln Park, and SoBo

With the Denver Art Museum as an anchor, the Golden Triangle has become a cultural destination; with several high-rise condominiums, it's also an up-and-coming residential urban neighborhood. Beyond the Golden Triangle, hip galleries, diverse restaurants, eclectic shops, and dynamic dance clubs and bars have brought vibrancy to the La Alma and Lincoln Park neighborhoods and the South Broadway corridor, popularly known as "SoBo." The main attractions in the Lincoln Park neighborhood are along or just off of Santa Fe Drive.

LoDo and Platte River Valley

LoDo (short for Lower Downtown) is known for many rescued historic buildings, most notably Union Station and Larimer Square, as well as a concentration of excellent bars and nightclubs. Now that the old LoDo warehouses have been turned into lofts, and green space has been added near the South Platte River, the entire Platte River Valley has exploded as an urban neighborhood and

destination. Major sights, such as the Museum of Contemporary Art Denver, Centennial Gardens, and Commons Park, are all found in the Platte River Valley area.

Capitol Hill and City Park

Filled with historic homes and mansions alongside apartment buildings, Capitol Hill is densely packed and always lively. The neighborhood is known for being gay and lesbian friendly, and is home to some of the city's best music venues along Colfax Avenue, including the Bluebird Theater and Ogden Theatre. Expansive City Park is large enough to be home to both the Denver Zoo and the Denver Museum of Nature and Science, plus many lakes, a golf course, and a new Mile High Loop jogging path.

Highlands

Denver's largest neighborhood has a unique blend of Latino culture and rejuvenated shopping and dining districts, such as Highlands Square and Tennyson Street. Historic homes are shoulder to shoulder with modern condominium developments, particularly in Eastern Highlands (called "LoHi," by some), which is linked to downtown by a pedestrian bridge that spans I-25 from Platte Street. Though there are not any major sights found in the Highlands neighborhood, it's a fun place to get a sense of local Denver culture.

Washington Park

The park itself is the big draw in this neighborhood, where charming bungalows on tree-lined streets surround large Washington Park. Locally referred to as "Wash Park," this family-friendly spot is popular for jogging, playing tennis, soccer, or a walk around the blooming flowerbeds. A few blocks away is the quaint shopping and dining block of South Gaylord Street, where locals stroll with their dogs. South Washington Park includes South Pearl Street, which draws people from beyond the neighborhood to its popular boutiques and restaurants and is accessible by light rail train.

Cherry Creek

The Cherry Creek neighborhood is associated with luxury, thanks to high-end clothing shops such as Max and Lawrence Covell, and specialty home decor stores that include Revampt and HW Home. The Cherry Creek

Bike Path meanders alongside the mellow waters below street level and ends near Cherry Creek's up-and-coming shopping district, which has added hotels and restaurants, including Elway's, to become more of a destination for travelers.

Greater Denver

The Greater Denver area extends at least 15 miles in any direction from downtown. Just beyond the edge of the suburbs are worthwhile parks, such as Roxborough State Park, Chatfield State Park, and Eldorado Canyon State Park, for hiking, boating, climbing, and more.

▶ WHEN TO GO

Denver is a draw for tourists year-round, but is generally more crowded in the summer, when road conditions for driving into the mountains are good. This is high season, when hotel rates tend to be at their peak.

Spring is the shoulder season, when flowers

are in bloom in the city, but in towns close to the Continental Divide, it's still snowing.

Fall is lovely in Denver, especially in the foothills, as the trees change from green to gold and light up the hillsides.

The low season in the city is winter, when hotels and attractions offer many discounts.

Cherry trees blossom along Cherry Creek.

Explore Denver

▶ THE TWO-DAY BEST OF DENVER

Day 1

▶ The best neighborhood in which to base your stay in Denver is LoDo (or Lower Downtown) at the Hotel Teatro, the Brown Palace Hotel, or The Oxford Hotel. From any of these, you can walk or take the free shuttle bus down the 16th Street Mall to start your morning with a hot cup of coffee and a pastry at The Market in historic Larimer Square. Outside seats are the best for local people-watching.

▶ After peeking in the shop windows at Larimer Square, walk a few blocks east up 14th Street, where you will pass the Denver Performing Arts Complex and walk under the glass-topped atrium that connects ten performance spaces, making it one of the largest complexes of its kind in the world. You'll spot Lawrence Argent's Big Blue Bear sculpture a block or two before you actually get to it.

▶ Take a stroll through Civic Center Park with its Greek-style amphitheater, fountains, and statues en route to the gold-domed Colorado State Capitol Building for a 45-minute tour of the building's architecture and artwork. After the tour, you are welcome to make the steep climb to the inside of the dome where there are spectacular views of the city and Rocky Mountains to the west.

▶ From the Colorado State Capitol Building it's just a short walk to the Denver Art Museum. Plan to spend a couple of hours viewing current or permanent exhibitions. Have lunch in the museum's Palette's restaurant, where the fishbowl windows provide a street-level view of the museum's public art outside.

▶ From the Denver Art Museum you can drive to Cherry Creek North in about five minutes. For the more adventurous, rent a bicycle from Denver B-cycle and ride along the Cherry Creek Bike Path to Cherry Creek's up-and-coming shopping district. Be sure to stop in Max, Garbarini, Lawrence Covell, and the Artisan Center.

▶ For dinner, drive or catch the light rail train to the 10th/Osage stop and experience The Buckhorn Exchange, where taxidermy meets fine dining. If you want to stay on foot, Rioja in Larimer Square or Zengo by Commons Park won't disappoint.

▶ Enjoy an after-dinner drink at The Cruise Room in The Oxford Hotel, live music at the Appaloosa Grill, or dance the night away at Beta nightclub.

Day 2

▶ Depending on the day of the week, there are some fabulous breakfast and brunch spots to try before seeing the sights. On the sophisticated end of the spectrum, you have Ellyngton's at the Brown Palace Hotel, which offers a champagne Sunday brunch. For more casual types, there's Snooze, An a.m. Eatery on the edge of LoDo, where diners can indulge in a seriously sweet stack of pancakes, such as the Pineapple Upside Down Pancakes or Red-Eye Velvet Pancakes.

WELCOME TO BEERTOWN

Beer is big business in Denver.

Denver is to beer what Napa is to wine. Forget about monikers like "Queen City of the Plains" and "Mile-High City" because nowadays Denver is being called "Suds City" and "The Napa Valley of Beer." According to VISIT DENVER, the Denver Convention and Visitors Bureau, there is more beer brewed per capita here than in any other U.S. city.

There are 15 brewpubs and microbreweries in downtown Denver. Colorado's governor, John Hickenlooper, was one of the founders of the **Wynkoop Brewing Company,** reportedly one of the largest brewpubs in the world.

For serious beer lovers, October is the time to visit. The celebration begins with **Denver Beer Fest** (www.denver.org/denverbeerfest), which kicks off the week before the three-day **Great American Beer Festival** (www.greatamericanbeerfestival.com). This is the Olympics of beer, where thousands of brews are sampled and gold, silver, and bronze medals are awarded.

Any time of year, there are brewery tours where visitors can see how vast quantities of their favorite ales are made; then they can sample a few. In Denver, there are tours at **Wynkoop Brewing Company, Breckenridge Brewery, and Great Divide Brewing Company.** Beyond Denver, there are brewery tours in Golden at the **MillerCoors Brewery Tour,** and also in Boulder and Fort Collins in what is called the "Denver Beer Triangle" by some.

Whether you're just passing through Denver International Airport (**Rock Bottom Brewery**), curious to find out if beer goes as well with cheese as wine does (**Great Divide Brewing Company Tap Room**), or if you want a classic beer at a Colorado Rockies baseball game (**Blue Moon Brewing Company**), you will find it here.

Red Rocks Amphitheatre

▶ After breakfast or brunch, walk or pick up the shuttle bus and take it to the end behind Union Station. The Millennium Bridge is just a block away, where you can walk up the stairs or take an elevator to the platform that affords city and mountain views before continuing on to the Platte River Valley district. Commons Park is right on the other side of the Millennium Bridge and, in fair weather, you can stand on one of the bridges over the South Platte River and watch kayakers practice in the rushing whitewater below. You may even want to walk over to Centennial Gardens, just south of Confluence Park, and see native plants in a formal garden. When it's too cold for walking, head straight to the Museum of Contemporary Art Denver instead.

▶ If you have a car, make the short drive up to Red Rocks Amphitheatre, where you can hike or hang out in the empty concert venue. In spring and summer, you might be able to catch a Colorado Rockies game at Coors Field.

▶ History buffs may be inclined to skip the sports and scenery and instead check out the Molly Brown House Museum in Capitol Hill or the Black American West Museum in Five Points.

▶ If you're in town on the first Friday of the month, plan to visit the Arts District on Santa Fe Avenue, where galleries are open late for the First Friday Art Walk.

▶ For dinner, try Cuba Cuba in the Golden Triangle or Domo in the Lincoln Park neighborhood.

10 PLACES TO GO ON A SNOW DAY (WITHOUT HEADING TO THE SLOPES)

Learn about the history of skiing at the History Colorado Center.

Skiing in the mountains isn't the only option when there is a big snowstorm. There is plenty to do in Denver on a cold, snowy day, whether you want to stay in or go play in the snow.

GET UP

- Sledding at **Commons Park** or **Stapleton Central Park**

- Cross-country skiing or snowshoeing in **Washington Park**

- Take a virtual ski jump at the **History Colorado Center.**

- Ice-skating at **Evergreen Lake,** in the foothills west of the city

- Try snowboarding at **Ruby Hill Rail Yard,** presented by Winter Park Resorts.

- Learn about mountain expeditions at the **Bradford Washburn American Mountaineering Museum** in nearby Golden.

WARM UP

- Sweat it out in the **Denver Botanic Gardens Boettcher Memorial Tropical Conservatory** or in the **Denver Zoo's** *Tropical Discovery.*

- Curl up next to the enormous fireplace in **REI** (and maybe start planning your next trip to the mountains). Kids can play at the indoor playground, and anyone can give the climbing wall a try when it's open.

FILL UP

- Have a casual soup-and-sandwich lunch at **Cook's Fresh Market,** where tables next to the huge windows offer a view of the snowfall and pedestrians on the 16th Street Mall.

- A leisurely dinner at **The Fort** in **Morrison,** with a view of the twinkling lights of the city against the fresh white snow

SIGHTS

The fact that Denver has the 10th-largest downtown in the country belies the city's quaint historic charms, but also highlights its world-class modern cultural offerings and abundant urban green spaces.

The city boasts over 800 miles of off-street biking, hiking, and jogging trails, which link the vibrant downtown to charming old neighborhoods buzzing with new energy. One of Denver's 200 parks, City Park has stunning views of the city's skyline and the Rocky Mountains, and is the home of the Denver Zoo and the Denver Museum of Nature and Science.

Denver's location 5,280 feet above sea level has become an attraction in itself, with many spots throughout the city physically marking a mile-high spot. Whether you're ambling through the Denver Botanic Gardens or just walking up and over the Millennium Bridge, it's a good idea to drink more water to lessen the effects of altitude sickness. Being one mile closer to the sun—especially in a city that gets over 300 days of sunshine annually—also means you should slather on the sunscreen before going out to see the sights.

Touring the sights in Denver might mean riding a bicycle past the white-water rapids on the South Platte River in Confluence Park, or meandering past the bronzed statues of Civic Center Park on the way to the Denver Art Museum's striking new addition. As wonderful as it is to sightsee in the fresh air, the city's

COURTESY OF HISTORY COLORADO

HIGHLIGHTS

© STEVE CRECELIUS, COURTESY OF VISIT DENVER

Kids love exploring the Denver Museum of Nature and Science.

❮ Best Public Art: At 40 feet tall, the whimsical **Big Blue Bear** is the city's most recognizable piece of public art. It's also the only piece of public art you can take with you: Much smaller models are available for sale at gift shops in the Denver Art Museum and Colorado History Museum (page 27).

❮ Best History Lesson: The **Black American West Museum** tells the rarely heard stories of pioneering African Americans throughout the West, with a special emphasis on those who lived in Colorado (page 27).

❮ Best Time Spent with Money: The only mint in the country that offers guided tours is the **United States Mint at Denver.** Free tours provide a chance to see coins being made and a peek at the elaborate interior of the original historic building (page 29).

❮ Best Museum: With a somewhat controversial wing designed by renowned architect Daniel Libeskind, the **Denver Art Museum** has remade itself into a sight to see inside and out (page 32).

❮ Best Park: Commons Park offers incredible views of downtown and Denver's surrounding mountain range. Enjoy the sounds of the South Platte River while strolling the park's paths, where signs describe the intriguing history of the land (page 38).

❮ Best Rooftop: On Friday nights, the **Museum of Contemporary Art Denver**'s rooftop, open-air bar is the best place to sit and enjoy a locally brewed beer or sip a glass of organic wine. Browse the museum's collections and end the night gazing at the stars (page 42).

❮ Best Use of Local Resources: The gold-domed **Colorado State Capitol Building** not only features gold mined from Colorado, but much of the building was created from marble, onyx, and granite quarried here as well. Rare rose onyx from Beulah, Colorado, was used extensively for interior panels (page 45).

❮ Best City Escape: The **Denver Botanic Gardens** has several nooks for peaceful contemplation, as well as extensive pathways for a stroll through the gardens (page 46).

❮ Best City Vista: For that postcard picture of the city's skyline framed by the snowcapped peaks of the Rocky Mountains, head to the Leprino Family Atrium of the **Denver Museum of Nature and Science.** Comfortable chairs and benches in the atrium make for more leisurely viewing (page 47).

❮ Best Wildlife Viewing: Only 10 miles from downtown you'll find bison, eagles, deer, and many other animals at the **Rocky Mountain Arsenal National Wildlife Refuge.** Hike the trails to see more than 300 species along the way (page 51).

downtown also offers a light rail train that quickly takes visitors from one sight to another, such as the Museum of Contemporary Art Denver or the Black American West Museum.

No matter how you get from Point A to Point B, it's always an adventure to explore Denver, learning about the city's rich past or discovering its latest additions.

Downtown   Map 1

◖ BIG BLUE BEAR
700 14th St., 303/228-8000,
http://denverconvention.com

Part whimsy, part serious artwork, with much left to personal interpretation, the 40-foot-tall Big Blue Bear peering into the windows of the Colorado Convention Center has become the most popular and recognizable piece funded by the city's public art program. First installed in 2005, the sculpture is officially titled *"I See What You Mean,"* and was designed and created by Denver artist and art professor Lawrence Argent. It is constructed from polymer concrete and a steel frame, covered in a bright blue that is evocative of the bluish hue of the nearby Rocky Mountains.

But like any bear you might meet in the mountains, you can't get too close. People so loved touching the bear and having their photograph taken right next to it that officials had to rope off the lawn around it to keep visitors at a safe distance.

◖ BLACK AMERICAN WEST MUSEUM
3091 California St., 720/242-7428,
www.blackamericanwestmuseum.com
HOURS: Thurs.-Sat. 10 A.M.-2 P.M., Sun. 1-4 P.M.
COST: $8 adult, $6 child, $7 senior

This tiny house is full of the little-known history of the West's African Americans, particularly those who made a life in Denver and Colorado.

For starters, the house itself is the former home of Justina L. Ford, the first female, African American licensed doctor in Colorado.

The house—now on the National Register of Historic Places—was saved from demolition and moved from its original location before being restored.

The museum's curator rattles off astonishing facts about African Americans in the West. For example, a third of all cowboys were black, and the only two stained-glass portraits of African Americans hanging in a U.S. state capitol building are at the Colorado State Capitol. And local businessman Barney Ford (a former slave)

© STEVE CRECELIUS, COURTESY OF VISIT DENVER

Artist Lawrence Argent's Big Blue Bear peeks in the windows of the Colorado Convention Center.

© MINDY SINK

The Black American West Museum showcases the history of black American cowboys.

opposed statehood for the territory because black men did not have the right to vote. The top floor of the museum has displays of Buffalo Soldier uniforms and rodeo memorabilia from the likes of "Deadwood Dick," whose real name was Nat Love and reputation was that of the greatest black cowboy, and Bill Pickett, a rodeo cowboy who was the first black honoree in the National Cowboy Hall of Fame.

The museum also owns a portion of Dearfield, Colorado, a ghost town northeast of Denver that was formerly a black township. There are plans for a

BLAIR-CALDWELL AFRICAN AMERICAN RESEARCH LIBRARY

2401 Welton St., 720/865-2401, www.denverlibrary.org

HOURS: Mon. noon-8 P.M., Wed. and Fri. 10 A.M.-6 P.M., Sat. 9 A.M.-5 P.M.

COST: Free

The Blair-Caldwell African American Research Library represents a lot of firsts for African Americans in Denver. The idea for a library focusing on all aspects of African American histories from Denver and beyond came from the city's first black mayor, Wellington E. Webb, and his wife, Wilma Webb. Opened in 2003, the library was intended to be part of a broad revitalization of the Five Points neighborhood and a gateway to the businesses on Welton Street. Five Points was historically a thriving African American neighborhood with great jazz clubs, soul food restaurants, and other businesses. The library is named after Omar Blair, the first African American to head the Denver School Board, and Elvin Caldwell, Denver's first black city councilman.

The first floor of the building is a typical lending library, but the second and third floors are more of a museum that tells of African Americans who came to the West and why, with artifacts on display. Visitors can sit in a replica barber shop and hear the story of how the shop's owner and his family fled a life of slavery and ended up in Denver, or hear the music that rocked Five Points in its heyday. The library also has rotating art exhibits by contemporary African American artists.

BROWN PALACE HOTEL

321 17th St., 303/297-3111, www.brownpalace.com

HOURS: Tours Wed. and Sat. 3 P.M.; private tours can be arranged for a fee at other times

COST: $10, free for hotel guests; reservations required

Unquestionably the city's most famous hotel, the Brown Palace Hotel offers enough history and architectural beauty to be visited even by those not staying the night. Ohio businessman Henry Brown came to Colorado in 1860 and bought up a few acres of land, including the triangular plot where the three-sided hotel opened in 1892. Working with architect Frank Edbrooke, who also worked on the design of the state capitol, Brown opted for a grand, Italian Renaissance style with a Tiffany

PUBLIC ART TOURS

The City of Denver has an ordinance requiring that 1 percent of any $1 million capital improvement project be spent on the acquisition of public art. As a result, the city has a considerable public art collection to show off that includes artwork from international artists as well as those who hail from Colorado. The work of Dale Chihuly, Herbert Bayer, Barbara Jo Revelle, Vance Kirkland, and many more artists is exhibited both outside and inside public buildings—including Coors Field, the Denver Center for Performing Arts, the Denver Art Museum, and others.

Even if your visit to Denver is so short that you never leave the airport, there is a large collection of public art on display there as well—much of it permanent, but with some temporary exhibits, too. Even the little windmills along the train tunnels are a public art installation. My personal favorite is Gary Sweeney's *America, Why I Love Her*, just off the main terminal. Sweeney's wall-size map of the United States is an homage to bizarre tourist sites around the country. Print out a brochure with a self-guided walking tour of the city's public art at www.denvergov.org or call 720/865-4307 to find out when guided tours of indoor public art are scheduled.

---

stained-glassed atrium that rises eight floors in the center of the building.

To this day, the hotel relies on its own artesian well, located beneath the hotel, for water. With so many famous guests over the years—from presidents to rock stars—the hotel took to naming some rooms after them. Now ordinary folks can spend a night in the Beatles or Eisenhower Suites.

In a long-held tradition, each January the hotel puts the National Western Stock Show's prize-winning steer on full display in the lobby, where anyone can be photographed with the bovine. Year-round, visitors can simply take in the ambience by dining in one of the hotel's three restaurants, going on a 45–60-minute tour with the hotel's historian, or sipping afternoon tea in the lobby.

TRINITY UNITED METHODIST CHURCH

1820 Broadway, 303/839-1493, www.trinityumc.org

HOURS: Mon.-Fri. 8 A.M.-5 P.M. for self-guided tours, Sun. noon for guided tours, Sun. worship services 8:15 A.M. and 11 A.M. and guided tours noon-1 P.M.

COST: Free

No matter what your denomination, a visit to the Trinity United Methodist Church in downtown is a must to hear the astoundingly clear sound of the church's Roosevelt Organ. Worshippers just see a glimpse of the organ's impressive pipes with 108 of them visible, but there are over 4,000 pipes in all. It took 18 months for New York's Roosevelt Organ Works to build the organ in the 1880s; it is the largest 19th-century-built working organ in the country.

The church also has music programs with several different choirs. On Sundays, choirs perform at the worship services; beautiful singing combined with awe-inspiring organ music resonates inside this remarkable building.

Trinity United Methodist Church was built in the Gothic style with a nearly 200-foot spire. The spire and much of the church's exterior is made from rhyolite, a volcanic rock from Castle Rock, Colorado.

The church offers free guided historical tours after the last worship service on Sundays.

◖ UNITED STATES MINT AT DENVER

320 W. Colfax Ave., 303/405-4761, www.usmint.gov

HOURS: Mon.-Fri. 8 A.M.-2 P.M. (tours)

COST: Free; reservations required

Perhaps inspired by the rebellious spirit of the West—or just naked entrepreneurial ambition—the United States Mint at Denver was originally founded as a private bank in the 1860s by an attorney who had the bright idea to mint coins from the gold and silver being mined in the mountains to the west. The mint was eventually sold to the government, and laws were made to prohibit private money-making. Today there are only four mints in the country, and the United States Mint at Denver is the only one with guided tours.

In 1906, the government opened the mint in Denver and the building is on the National Register of Historic Places. An example of elaborate Italian Renaissance architecture, the mint appears to be two stories tall but is actually five. Starting in 1935, several additions have been made to the building to accommodate increased coin production; making billions of coins each year, the mint now occupies an entire city block.

Tours begin at the entrance to one of the building's more modern additions. Security at the mint is tighter than at any airport, and visitors cannot bring in anything larger than a wallet.

Before the official tour begins, you can peruse *Money, Trade and Treasure,* a display of primitive money and the evolution of currency in the lobby. A tour guide and an armed security guard take groups into the coin production part of the plant, where you might see coins before they are pressed or as they are being sorted. It's not until the very end of the tour that you get to see the original shiny, marble hallways and unique Tiffany chandeliers of the 1906 building. Most fascinating about the tour are the facts—particularly the actual costs of making money and what materials are used to make coins. A visit here could be a last chance to see pennies being made; no one knows how much longer pennies will be produced given their low value and high cost to make.

The United States Mint at Denver can boast of never having been robbed, in part thanks to an original "machine-gun nest" or "sentry box" that was always manned until the 1960s. That relic is on display with a mannequin, and current security measures are top secret.

To get a few of your own state's quarters or other collectible coins, stop in at the gift shop located just outside of the mint. Even the change from each purchase is given in locally minted coins.

Golden Triangle, Lincoln Park, and SoBo   Map 2

BYERS-EVANS HOUSE MUSEUM
1310 Bannock St., 303/620-4933,
www.historycolorado.org
HOURS: House Gallery Mon.-Sat. 10 A.M.-3 P.M.; House Museum tours 10:30 A.M., 11:30 A.M., 12:30 P.M., 1:30 P.M., and 2:30 P.M.
COST: $6 adult, $5 senior and student (with ID), $4 child age 6-12, free for child under 6

A visit to the Byers-Evans House Museum is an opportunity to learn about Denver and Colorado history through the lives of two prominent families who once lived in this Italianate-style house. Visitors can see exactly how an upper-middle-class family lived in the early 1900s, as the house contains all original furnishings, including the family's Havilland china, Baccarat crystal, a 1760 Queen Anne highboy, and original artwork.

The house was built for William N. Byers in 1883. Mr. Byers was a prominent Denver citizen who printed the *Rocky Mountain News,* the city's first newspaper. After six years, Mr. Byers sold the house to William Evans, the son of the state's second territorial governor, John Evans. Today, there are mountain peaks named after both Byers and Evans because of their significant contributions to the state. The younger Mr. Evans made his own mark on the city and state as head of the Denver Tramway Company. The daughters of William Evans lived in the home with few modern modifications until 1981, as the neighborhood around them slowly fell away and changed. The house was added on to five times as the family grew over the years, and was lovingly restored to the 1912–1924 period; today it's worth visiting to see a well-furnished example of WWI–era style.

The house museum can only be seen on a guided tour. Each tour lasts about 45 minutes.

CIVIC CENTER PARK

101 W. 14th Ave. Pkwy., 720/913-1311, www.denvergov.org

HOURS: Daily 5 A.M.–11 P.M.

Listed on the National Register of Historic Places, Civic Center Park is today the reflection of years of input from various mayors, architects, and landscape architects. In 1904, Mayor Robert Speer was inspired by the City Beautiful movement and began to consult planners and designers for the project, but citizens rejected his request for funding for the park and, by 1912, Speer was out of office. The next mayor also hired experts to tinker with the park design, and when Speer was reelected in 1917, bits of each plan were incorporated with the new architect's design. The park was officially opened in 1919 and various statues and memorials have been added since.

Reflecting its name, Civic Center Park is flanked by government buildings, including the historic **City and County Building** (1437 Bannock St., 720/865-7840, www.denvergov.org)—home of Denver's mayoral offices today—to the west, and the **Colorado State Capitol Building** (200 E. Colfax Ave., 303/866-2604, www.colorado.gov) to the east. The **Greek Theater** (720/913-0700 for events and permitting) is the most distinctive structure within the park. It was used to hold public concerts as far back as 1920, and in modern times is often the staging area for a variety of

cultural and political events. Two bronze sculptures in the middle of the park represent the West, portraying both a cowboy and a Native American; Alexander Phimster Proctor created both *Bronco Buster* in 1920 and *On the War Trail* in 1922.

The park extends east across Broadway where the 45-foot-tall **Colorado Veterans Memorial** was dedicated in 1990. The memorial is made of Colorado red sandstone.

The entire neighborhood around Civic Center Park has undergone tremendous growth in recent years, leading to more interest in its use and future design plans. In the spring and summer, the flowerbeds in the center of the park are filled with vivid blooms. The Greek Theater and **Voorhies Memorial** (on the north or Colfax Ave. side of the park), which features murals by the artist Allen True on the ceiling, provide welcome shade on hot days. The park is used for a variety of free public events year-round, including a Cinco de Mayo celebration and the start of the Martin Luther King Jr. Day Parade.

CLYFFORD STILL MUSEUM

1250 Bannock St., 720/354-4880, www.clyffordstillmuseum.org

HOURS: Sat.-Thurs. 10 A.M.–5 P.M., Fri. 10 A.M.–8 P.M.

COST: $10 adult, $6 student and senior, $3 child age 6-17, free for child under 5

As someone who feels that Abstract Expressionism is, well, abstract, I have to say that my first visit to this museum brought me a long way toward appreciating if not the entire genre, then certainly this giant of the genre. Clyfford Still is considered to be one of America's most influential modern artists, and yet, like me, you might not have heard of him before. Still's peers became almost household names—Jackson Pollock, William de Kooning, and Mark Rothko, among them. At some point in his career, Still severed ties with commercial art galleries, and after his death in 1980, the

© RAUL J GARCIA, COURTESY OF THE CLYFFORD STILL MUSEUM

The Clyfford Still Museum is nestled next to the Denver Art Museum.

Clyfford Still Estate was sealed off from public and scholarly view. In his will, Still stipulated that his entire estate be given to an American city that would be willing to establish a permanent museum dedicated solely to his work. In 2004, Denver Mayor John Hickenlooper was able to secure the collection with the promise of a museum.

Practically under the eaves of the Denver Art Museum, the Clyfford Still Museum opened in late 2011. The architecture of this building is nearly as interesting as the 2,400 drawings, paintings, and prints of the single artist. Designed by Brad Cloepfil of Allied Works Architecture, the interior includes a unique, concrete, waffle-like ceiling that lets in natural light, which makes the paintings look slightly different at various times of the day or year. Note that the second floor consists of nine distinct galleries, each with different ceiling heights to emphasize different elements of the collection. At two points in the galleries,

visitors can step onto planted patios for a breath of fresh air.

The exhibits here will regularly change, as only a small fraction of Still's massive body of work can be displayed at one time. With the proximity to the Denver Art Museum, it is possible to cram in a lot of viewing in one day, but it is recommended to set aside half a day to thoroughly experience the work of this American artist.

◖ DENVER ART MUSEUM

100 W. 14th Ave. Pkwy., 720/865-5000, www.denverartmuseum.org

HOURS: Tues.-Thurs. 10 A.M.-5 P.M., Fri. 10 A.M.-8 P.M., Sat.-Sun. 10 A.M.-5 P.M.

COST: $10-13 adult, $3-5 child, $8-10 senior

Since opening in 2006, the Denver Art Museum's **Frederic C. Hamilton Building** has become an attraction in itself. Designed by architect Daniel Libeskind, the 146,000-square-foot building is all sharp angles and severe

© STEVE CRECELIUS, COURTESY OF VISIT DENVER

the Denver Art Museum

points—intended as an interpretation of rock crystals and of the jagged peaks of the Rocky Mountains. The building has had its fair share of criticism, being largely panned by national art critics, with visitors complaining of vertigo inside and questions about whether the art is enhanced or hampered by the architecture. Nonetheless, it's created a lot of exciting energy in the neighborhood and the city.

The Hamilton building is connected to the original Denver Art Museum building, a seven-story "castle" that has been home to the museum since 1971 and was also once controversial for its design. Now called the North Building, it was designed by Italian architect Gio Ponti.

Once inside either of the museum's buildings, visitors will discover more art and activities than can be seen in one day. The museum's **Institute for Western American Art** includes works by well-known masters, including Charles Deas's *Long Jakes, The Rocky Mountain Man,* as well as the work of local contemporary artists. Like much of the museum, the Western American art rooms include interactive areas, especially for children. In this room, visitors can make their own postcards using ink stamps with iconic Western images and colored pencils.

Other collections at the museum include African art, American Indian art, Oceanic art, and a Modern and Contemporary collections room with thousands of pieces by artists including Andy Warhol, Man Ray, and many others. The permanent collections are not all exhibited at one time, but on a rotation, though some public art pieces, such as the Mark di Suvero sculpture *Lao-Tzu,* are always on display outdoors.

There is a coffee shop, the **Celeste and Dick Callahan Café** (Tues.–Thurs. 11 A.M.–4 P.M., Fri. 10 A.M.–5 P.M., Sat.–Sun. 11 A.M.–4 P.M.), in the Hamilton Wing. Across Martin Plaza from the Hamilton Wing is the **MAD Beans**

FREE DAYS

In Denver, taxation equals free admission on specified days at many of the city's most popular sights. During a downturn in the economy in the 1980s, the state legislature eliminated funding for several of the city's main attractions, including the Denver Art Museum and the Denver Botanic Gardens. New admission fees did not provide enough financial support for these institutions, so a small sales and use tax of 0.1 percent (or $0.01 on every $10 purchase) was implemented in the surrounding seven-county area. The small tax adds up to millions, and that money is then distributed to scientific and cultural institutions throughout these seven counties. It's enough that the institutions can now afford to offer limited periods of free admission.

While the city's five largest facilities—the **Denver Center for the Performing Arts, Denver Art Museum, Denver Zoo, Denver Botanic Gardens,** and the Denver Museum of Natural History (now called the **Denver Museum of Nature and Science**)—get the lion's share of the $40 million in funds annually, much smaller theaters, art museums, and nature and science centers receive funding as well. Studies have shown that these millions invested in the city's cultural facilities equal billions spent in Denver in return.

The number of free days per year varies from one place to the next, but they are generally scattered so that not every institution has a free day on the same date. And free days are not a secret—show up early because each of these places fills up quickly, and it's first-come, first-served where seating is limited at the Ricketson Theatre and Stage Theatre in the Denver Center for the Performing Arts. Free days differ each calendar year. Go to www.scfd.org or pick up a bookmark listing the year's free days at any of the five major facilities.

---

and Wine Café (1200 Acoma St., 720/496-4158, www.madgreens.com, Mon.–Thurs. 7 A.M.–8 P.M., Fri. 7 A.M.–10 P.M., Sat. 8 a.m.–8 P.M., Sun. 8 A.M.–6 P.M., $10).

The parking garage for the museum is directly across the plaza from the Hamilton building. The Museum Residences, also designed by Mr. Libeskind, are above the garage. The glass "walls" of these private homes are meant to complement the titanium-skinned museum that they face.

DENVER CENTRAL PUBLIC LIBRARY

10 W. 14th Ave. Pkwy., 720/865-1111,

www.denverlibrary.org

HOURS: Mon.-Tues. 10 A.M.-8 P.M., Wed.-Fri.

10 A.M.-6 P.M., Sat. 9 A.M.-5 P.M., Sun. 1-5 P.M.

Denverites love their libraries; statistics show that the city has the highest number of library cardholders per capita in the country. But the Central Library of the Denver Public Library system is no ordinary library—it holds not just books, but also a large art collection, photograph archives, and genealogy data.

The Central Library was designed by well-known architect Michael Graves and opened in 1995 with 47 *miles* of books. Each section is roomy and huge windows bring in the natural light. Visit the fifth floor's Western Art Gallery and Gates Western Reading Room to see the library's Western art collection. Only a fraction of the entire 400 framed pieces—including works by Albert Bierstadt, Frederic Remington, and Thomas Moran, and thousands of sculptures, etchings, lithographs, and other artifacts dating back to the mid-1800s—can be on display at one time. While taking a peek at the art that is hung in an entryway hallway and set out between the stacks, you're bound to see people quietly conducting research, as this is also the Western History/Genealogy Department with a massive collection of digital photographs related to the history of the American West and Colorado.

SIGHTS

© STEVE CRECELIUS, COURTESY OF VISIT DENVER

Denver Central Public Library

If you still have time, the library's seventh floor has not just administrative offices, but also long hallways bedecked with a bit more Western art. The Vida Ellison Gallery hosts exhibits of artwork made by local artists (including library staff), and the gallery provides a nice view of Civic Center Park and downtown.

The library also hosts themed film series, guest lectures, book clubs, concerts, knitting and cooking classes, and more events throughout the year. Pick up the *Fresh City Life* magazine at any library for the current month's schedule.

HISTORY COLORADO CENTER

1200 Broadway, 303/866-3682, www.historycoloradocenter.org

HOURS: Mon.-Sat. 10 A.M.-5 P.M., Sun. noon-5:00 P.M.

COST: $10 adult, $8 senior and student with ID, $6 child age 6-12, free for child under 6

Ta–da! The History Colorado Center opened to the public in the spring of 2012 with exhibits of artifacts and lessons about the days of old. Already being called "the first great history museum of the 21st century" by Smithsonian Affiliations Director Harold Closter, the Center is years from being fully open. The 200,000-square-foot building was designed by Tryba Architects of Denver and will be opened in stages through 2014. The approach to history here is to feature high-tech, hands-on learning about the people and the environment that shaped the Centennial State. The experience begins with H. G. Wells–inspired "time machines" in the four-story atrium, where the mobile devices can be pushed around a terrazzo floor map of the state to learn about everything from the preservation of Mesa Verde to the tomato wars. While still in the atrium, look up to see a two-story media presentation. This six-minute video gives a taste of the historic places, first peoples, and traditions in Colorado. Step from this futuristic display into the past, where parts of the town of Keota,

COURTESY OF HISTORY COLORADO

A fort replica at the History Colorado Center teaches visitors about fur trading.

Colorado—inspiration for James Michener's novel, *Centennial*—are re-created and others have been salvaged. Inside this former agricultural town on the Eastern Plains, kids can gather eggs, slide in the barn, and "meet" town residents. Then it's time to head upstairs for a virtual ski jump, a mine tour, and to step into an old fort in the *Destination Colorado* exhibit, where eight significant stories about the state are told.

Plans for more history in the future include a *Denver A-Z* exhibit and an exhibit about how the harsh, dry environment shaped life in Colorado; there will also be temporary exhibits sprinkled in each year. A café and a gift shop are on the first floor: **Rendezvous Café** (303/447-8679, www.historycoloradocenter.org, Mon.–Sat. 10 A.M.–5 P.M., Sun. noon–5 P.M.) and **History Colorado Museum Store** (general admission not required; Mon.–Sat. 10 A.M.–5 P.M., Sun. noon–5 P.M.).

MUSEO DE LAS AMERICAS
861 Santa Fe Dr., 303/571-4401, www.museo.org
HOURS: Tues.-Fri. 10 A.M.-5 P.M., Sat.-Sun. noon-5 P.M.
COST: $5 adult, $4 senior, free for child under 13

In the heart of the Santa Fe Arts District is the Museo de las Americas, the first museum in the Rocky Mountain states devoted to the art, history, and culture of Latin America. The mission of the Museo de las Americas is to share the diverse art and culture of Latin America, from ancient to contemporary. While it seems more like a gallery than a museum with changing exhibits and artists, the museum offers art education and community programs in conjunction with each exhibition. Artists whose work is on display give talks about their art on special nights during the exhibit. There are also hands-on workshops and customized art tours for children.

Every third Friday of the month is Spanish Happy Hour, when people can come to have a drink and a snack and view the art, all while speaking Spanish.

Opened in 1994, the Museo de las Americas has helped this evolving neighborhood become a draw for new art galleries and other businesses. Be sure to visit their unique gift shop before leaving.

LoDo and Platte River Valley   Map 3

AURARIA CAMPUS
900 Auraria Pkwy., 303/556-3291, www.ahec.edu

The Auraria Campus on the outlying rim of LoDo is Colorado's largest campus, with about 38,000 students, and is home to three separate institutions: the Community College of Denver, the Metropolitan State College of Denver, and the University of Colorado at Denver. One addition to this commuter campus is the teaching hotel—a Springhill Suites which will be mostly operated by students as part of the hospitality program. As the campus was once a town of its own before merging with Denver in the 1860s, there are several historical sights worth visiting here.

The Ninth Street Historic Park is the oldest restored block in the city and includes 13 Victorian homes (now administrative offices) and a turn-of-the-20th-century grocery store (now a bagel and coffee shop). It's free to stroll along the block and read the small signs in front of each home, which tell a bit about the architecture and the people who originally lived there.

Not far from the historic park is the relocated and restored **Golda Meir House,** onetime home of the former Israeli prime minister. When she was a girl, Meir left her parents' home in Milwaukee to live with her sister and brother-in-law in Denver in their tiny duplex. She went to high school in the city and worked in the family laundry business. In literature describing Meir's time in Denver, she is quoted as saying, "It was in Denver that my real education began." One side of the duplex contains artifacts from Meir's life, while the other side is used for small conferences. Tours are available (303/556-3292).

The city's oldest church structure is now the **Emmanuel Gallery** (303/556-8337, www.emmanuelgallery.org, Tues.–Fri. 10 A.M.–6 P.M., Sat. 11 A.M.–5 P.M.), serving as an art gallery for the campus. The little stone chapel was built in 1876 for Episcopalians, then was converted into a Jewish synagogue in 1903, and eventually became an artist's studio until 1973. The gallery displays artwork by faculty and students in changing exhibits.

Still an active Catholic parish, **St. Elizabeth's Church** (also called St. Elizabeth of Hungary, 1060 St. Francis Way, 303/534-4014, http://stelizabethdenver.org) was founded by German immigrants in 1878. As the congregation grew too large, the original church was torn down and the current one constructed in 1898. The monastery was added in the 1930s. To learn more about the sometimes bizarre history of the church—a murdered priest, panhandling nuns—go to www.archden.org/noel.

St. Cajetan's (1190 9th St., 303/556-2755, www.ahec.edu), a Spanish colonial church, was built in 1925 for the Latino community. In 1973, the parish relocated and the church is now used for campus functions. Call ahead to schedule guided tours of these historic buildings (720/556-3291).

The most distinctive building on campus is the **Tivoli Student Union** (900 Auraria Pkwy., 303/556-6330, www.tivoli.org), which started out in 1866 as one of Denver's earliest breweries. The building had subsequent additions and uses, and today includes a multiplex movie theater where some screenings of the annual **Denver International Film Festival** are held. There are no tours offered of the Tivoli building; it is open to the public as a student union with various eateries and campus offices.

CENTENNIAL GARDENS PARK

1101 Little Raven St., 720/913-1311,
www.denvergov.org/parks

HOURS: Special permit only

In 2009, stewardship of this garden was transferred from the Denver Botanic Gardens to the city, and the city has since made it open only by permit for special events. The gardens can still easily be viewed, but unfortunately it is not currently possible to walk through them.

Centennial Gardens Park is a lovely little example of the transformation of the entire South Platte Valley from urban wasteland to dynamic neighborhood. People jogging, bicycling, or sauntering along the paths parallel to the South Platte River can detour into the gardens with dozens of carefully pruned topiary trees and smell the lavender plants, listen to the fountains trickling, or watch birds flit from trees to birdbaths.

Centennial Gardens Park is a formal garden, inspired by the gardens of Versailles in France. In the 1990s, former Denver mayor Wellington Webb and his wife, Wilma, visited Versailles and wanted to create a formal public garden in Denver. What makes this small garden unique is the use of only native plant species and drought-tolerant plants in the neatly patterned five-acre space. There is always a spot of brilliant color amongst the tidy green hedges; in the spring, yellow, purple, and white crocuses push up through native buffalo grass just before miniature irises and daffodils appear around deciduous trees and rows of junipers. A small pavilion with benches provides shade in the park on warm days.

CHILDREN'S MUSEUM OF DENVER

2121 Children's Museum Dr., 303/433-7444,
www.mychildsmuseum.org

HOURS: Mon.-Tues. 9 A.M.-4 P.M., Wed. 9 A.M.-7:30 P.M., Thurs.-Fri. 9 A.M.-4 P.M., Sat.-Sun. 10 A.M.-5 P.M.

COST: $8 adult age 2-59, $6 child age 1, $6 senior, free for child under 1

Whether you are traveling with a small child or are just tired of having the kids make a mess in your own house, the Children's Museum of Denver is a good place to explore. The museum offers several "playscapes" for a variety of ages—such as the "assembly plant" for ages four to eight, where kids use real tools and recycled materials to build whatever they want, or the "Center for the Young Child" for newborns to four-year-olds, where creepers can practice on carpeted slopes and toddlers can play house in a tree. The simplest play areas are the best here: a painting room, a small puppet theater, a mirrored wall to dress up and dance in front of, a real fire engine to "drive," and the outdoor playground near the bike path and South Platte River.

Every day of the week there is a story time at the museum, and the first Tuesday of each month the museum is open late with free admission. The museum also hosts temporary exhibits and shows such as the Blue Man Group. They also offer additional games and events for Easter, Halloween, and other holidays. Eat Street Café has grown-up and kid food with little tables and chairs for sitting inside. There are also picnic tables outside near the playground. The least crowded time to visit the museum is right when it opens or mid-afternoon.

◖ COMMONS PARK

15th and Little Raven Sts., 720/913-1311,
www.denvergov.org

HOURS: Daily 5 A.M.-11 P.M.

The broad and winding waters of the South Platte River have attracted dreamers since the earliest days of the city. In the late 1800s, this land was used for a castle and an amusement park, among other delights. Many years later, this broad expanse of land that sits roughly between LoDo's Union Station to the east and the South Platte River to the west was lost to the ravages of time and nature, and the river started being used as a dumping ground for old cars, refrigerators, and other debris. A severe flood along the river in 1965, in which lives, homes, and businesses were lost, led to long-needed changes all along the South Platte: a dam was built upstream and it was no longer used as an illegal garbage dump. Still, it took decades for new dreams to take shape and remake the land into a play area once again.

The Commons Park people visit today was years in the making as various government agencies and private organizations acquired funding and made plans. In 2001, the city unveiled the ambitious 20-acre park along the east side of the South Platte River. One portion of the park was designed to re-create how it would have looked before the settlers came, complete with native grasses, trees, and sand. Atop a constructed hill—popular for sledding in the winter and, in warmer weather, flying kites—there is a sunken black granite east–west directional sculpture that can't be seen from below. There are views of the Rocky Mountains and the city's skyline from the hilltop. One side of the park follows a street and looks up at condominiums and apartments, while the other drops down to foot and bike paths along the river. Bridges on either side of Commons Park lead to shopping and dining districts in historic neighborhoods. On any given day, depending on the season, you will see fitness classes, scrimmage games, skiers, sledders, and dog walkers or dogs in obedience classes. Public art inside the park is

© MINDY SINK

Snowboarders, skiers, pedestrians, kite fliers, and dog walkers are all drawn to Commons Park year-round.

user-friendly— it can all be walked in, sat on, and touched.

CONFLUENCE PARK

15th St. between Platte and Little Raven Sts., 720/913-1311, www.denvergov.org

HOURS: Daily 5 A.M.–11 P.M.

The point where Cherry Creek merges with the South Platte River is the approximate spot where gold was discovered by prospectors in 1858; thus, Denver was founded within the Kansas Territory. The confluence is still attracting people, but now it's a mecca for outdoor enthusiasts.

Rushing water carries kayakers through chutes and under bridges, as cyclists and runners whir past on riverside paths and families relax on the grassy knolls and sandy beaches throughout Confluence Park. A large deck on the side of a **flagship REI store** (1416 Platte St., 303/756-3100, www.rei.com, Mon.–Fri.

10 A.M.–9 P.M., Sat. 10 A.M.–7 P.M., Sun. 10 A.M.–6 P.M.) in the enormous former **Denver Tramway Building** invites people to sit and rest from all the activity or contemplate their next move while having a bite to eat. Inside REI, there are more indoor opportunities for recreation, such as the small playground in the children's section and a climbing wall.

Don't miss the historical signs posted along pedestrian paths in the park that tell the tragic story of the Native Americans who first called this spot home. Nearby Little Raven Street is named in honor of the Arapaho chief who struggled to coexist with white settlers.

COORS FIELD

2001 Blake St., 303/762-5437, http://colorado.rockies.mlb.com

HOURS: Tours April–Sept. Mon.-Sat. non-game days 10 A.M., noon, and 2 P.M.; evening game days 10 A.M. and

A sculpture outside of Coors Field commemorates the date of the stadium's ground breaking.

© MINDY SINK

noon; Oct.-Mar. Mon., Wed., Fri., and Sat. noon and 2 P.M.

COST: $7 adult, $5 child, $6 senior

Even in the off-season, there's a chance to tour Coors Field, home of the Colorado Rockies baseball team, and see parts of the field that are off-limits during games. The ballpark has been a major part of the redevelopment of LoDo from neglected warehouse district to hip, urban neighborhood with expensive condominiums and dozens of bars and restaurants.

Since opening in 1995, Coors Field has been noted for its modern yet classic architecture. The 75-minute tours at Coors Field include the field, going up to the higher deck where a purple row of seats marks 5,280 feet above sea level, the guest locker rooms, and suites. From the upper seats, there's a great view of the Central Platte Valley and the Rocky Mountains.

After the tour, you can walk around the stadium and check out some of the public art on display. To the north is Erick C. Johnson's *Bottom of the Ninth,* which shows a neon baseball figure sliding into home plate, and to the south is Lonnie Hanzon's *The Evolution of the Ball,* which is like an arched gateway to the stadium.

There is a large gift and souvenir shop on the Blake Street side of Coors Field, where just about anything in the team's purple and black can be found—blankets, hats, jackets, T-shirts, and more.

LARIMER SQUARE

Larimer St. between 14th and 15th Sts., 303/534-2367, www.larimersquare.com

Larimer Square is not really a square, but a preserved city block—the historic buildings along each side are now used for offices, restaurants, and shops. The history of this place goes back to the city's earliest days, when the area was inundated with people who wanted to strike it rich from gold found in the nearby

creek. General William H. Larimer Jr. arrived in 1858 and built a cabin on what is now Larimer Square. The city quickly grew and by the 1880s, there were 25 buildings on Larimer Street, including a bank, a drugstore, and a bookstore.

Over time, saloons and bars prospered here and this block became known as Denver's "skid row." In the 1960s, officials were ready to start anew, but preservationists gathered support to save the block from the wrecking ball. With 1870s and 1880s buildings fully restored, the block was listed on the National Register of Historic Places. Now it's the heart of LoDo, and draws people year-round. Stop in for coffee and a pastry at **The Market** (1445 Larimer St., 303/534-5140, www.themarketatlarimer.com, daily 6 A.M.–10:30 P.M.), buy a little something with cowboy flair for gals or little ones at **Cry Baby Ranch** (1421 Larimer St., 303/623-3979, www.crybabyranch.com, Mon.–Fri. 10 A.M.–7 P.M., Sat. 10 A.M.–6 P.M., Sun. noon–5 P.M.), or enjoy a sumptuous Mediterranean meal at **Rioja** (1431 Larimer St., 303/820-2282, www.riojadenver.com, Mon.–Tues. 4–10 P.M., Wed.–Thurs. 11:30 A.M.–2:30 P.M. and 4–10 P.M., Fri. 11:30 A.M.–2:30 P.M. and 4–11 P.M., Sat. 10 A.M.–2:30 P.M. and 4–11 P.M., Sun. 10 A.M.–2:30 P.M. and 4–10 P.M.).

During weekdays, the square is filled with students from the nearby Auraria Campus and businesspeople having lunch at one of the many restaurants. Evenings and weekends attract more tourists who come to shop, dine out, or have a laugh at the **Comedy Works** (1225 15th St., 303/595-3637, www.comedyworks.com, check calendar for hours) club.

Larimer Square is occasionally closed off to traffic for one of the handful of annual festivals the area hosts, such as June's **Denver Chalk Art Festival,** when artists paint murals on the blacktop.

For walking history tours of Larimer

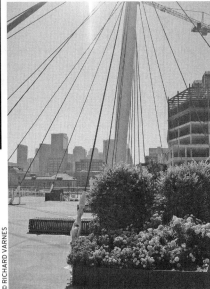

© RICHARD VARNES

Millennium Bridge connects LoDo to the Platte Valley and Commons Park.

Square, call 720/234-7929 or go to www.denverhistorytours.com.

Parking for Larimer Square is on Market Street, directly behind the square. Fees vary depending on parking duration.

MILLENNIUM BRIDGE
16th St. at Chestnut St.

Upon its 2003 opening, the Millennium Bridge became an instant landmark in Denver and an important part of the redevelopment of the Central Platte Valley.

The 16th Street Pedestrian Mall used to end at Wynkoop Street, where railroad tracks from behind Union Station dominated the landscape. Now 16th Street has extended beyond its old boundary in LoDo, and the Millennium Bridge brings people up and over the railroad tracks into the Platte Valley, the bustling Riverfront Park development area, and Commons Park. Up out of the flat prairie floor

rises a 200-foot white mast held in place on a wide deck by multiple steel cables. The bridge has stairs on either side as well as elevators, and is the most scenic walk from downtown to parks and the South Platte River. Additional bridges on the other side of Commons Park lead to restaurants and shops on Platte Street and then to the eastern edge of the Highlands neighborhood, which has a growing number of popular restaurants.

With the dramatic backdrop of the city's skyline and the distinctive architecture of the bridge, it has become a favorite spot for fashion shoots. In 2007, the inaugural Riverfront Fashion Series was held at the base of the bridge. As coal trains rattle below night and day, there are typically tourists and art students taking in the view from the bridge and trying to get a good shot of the mast.

◖ MUSEUM OF CONTEMPORARY ART DENVER
1485 Delgany St., 303/298-7554, www.mcadenver.org
HOURS: Tues.-Thurs. 10 A.M.-6 P.M., Fri. 10 A.M.-10 P.M., Sat.-Sun. 10 A.M.-6 P.M.
COST: $10 adult, $5 child, $5 senior

Not quite as talked about as the Denver Art Museum, but still an important aspect of the culture here, is the Museum of Contemporary Art Denver, also with a building designed by an internationally known architect.

The museum had humble beginnings in 1996 in a former fish market at downtown's Sakura Square block. Incredible success clashed with space limitations and the museum had to relocate. After hiring London-based architect David Adjaye, the museum reopened in late 2007 in a black, glass box of a building perched on the corner of 15th Street. At first glance, the minimalist modern building can seem as challenging as contemporary art itself—and the hidden front door adds to this perplexity—but inside it is full of welcome surprises where couples can meet

MODERN GREEN

The Museum of Contemporary Art Denver was designed and built as an environmentally sustainable building. The museum represents the first public building in the United States designed by African-born and London-based architect David Adjaye of Adjaye Associates. He also designed the Nobel Peace Center in Oslo, Norway, and The Idea Store in London. Here in Denver, Mr. Adjaye and the museum's curator, Cydney Payton, worked closely together to consider every possible environmentally friendly element.

From the use of recycled materials and wind power to the mechanical systems and exterior glass, every part of this building is eco-conscious. The green philosophy carries over into everyday life at the museum, where computer home pages use Blackle (an energy-saving search engine site) instead of Google and green cleaning products are used to mop the concrete floors. Employees and volunteers are encouraged to walk or ride the bus to work, and the food and drinks served in the café come from local sources.

Visitors who take public transportation (or just do not drive) to the museum receive $1 off admission.

for a cultural date and families can interact and be artistic.

Atop the museum is the **MCA Café** (Tues.–Fri. noon–9 P.M., Sat.–Sun. 10 A.M.–7 P.M.) inside a black glass cube and an outdoor bar. (Check the website for current hours, which differ from the museum.) There is also a rooftop garden, which itself is a piece of artwork, designed by Colorado landscape architect Karla Dakin. Ceramic sculptures inside the café were made by Kim Dickey, also a Colorado artist.

Children and families will find a small library with a selection of art books and the "Idea Box," where small tables and art supplies invite kids of all ages to get creative. Or, for a more laidback experience, simply lounge in an upper room full of bean bag chairs.

The museum was designed as an environmentally sustainable building and strives to reduce its carbon footprint—from offering locally grown food and drinks in the café to encouraging volunteers and staff to commute to work in an eco-friendly manner.

Exhibit space in the museum was designed as individual galleries so that video installations, photography, paintings, and other media are all displayed at once but separately. Past exhibitions have featured artists Jeff Starr, Chris Ofili, and many other internationally recognized artists. The exhibits here are often interactive for all ages, such as sculptures to walk through, light and sound that continuously change, or live carrier pigeons that can be brought home temporarily.

UNION STATION

1701 Wynkoop St., 303/534-6333,
www.denverunionstation.org
HOURS: Daily 6 A.M.-2 P.M.

Union Station anchors the Lower Downtown neighborhood, and this regal historic building is set to once again become a transportation hub for Denver. Land behind the train station has been developed into a bus and light rail station, and plans are underway to preserve and redevelop the original depot as well, making it a bustling center of activity.

Starting in the 1880s, over 60 trains arrived and departed the depot every day, and as late as 1958, there were more travelers through Union Station than the local airport. Today there are only two daily trains, plus the Ski Train that takes people to Winter Park ski resort on winter weekends. Inside, the huge wooden benches and grand high ceilings seem ready for hundreds of people to come streaming through

Union Station

the doors at any moment. But on most days, the train station is peaceful as people go to and from private offices within other parts of the building. In another time, Presidents Eisenhower, Taft, and Theodore Roosevelt traveled through this station.

Capitol Hill and City Park   Map 4

CATHEDRAL BASILICA OF THE IMMACULATE CONCEPTION
1530 Logan St., 303/831-7010,
www.denvercathedral.org
HOURS: Mon.-Sun. 6 A.M.-6 P.M.

The Cathedral Basilica of the Immaculate Conception looks as if it reaches up into the heavens—it is situated on a slight hill with its twin, 210-foot bell tower spires poking into the sky above. This Catholic church has both captivating history and architecture.

J. J. Brown, husband of Molly Brown, joined with a few investors to buy the land for the cathedral and, in 1902, ground was broken to start the new building. The building is French Gothic and made from limestone and granite. Italian marble was used for the altar, communion rail, statuary, and bishop's chair. The stunning interior features a 68-foot vaulted ceiling and 75 German-made stained-glass windows— more than any other Catholic church in the country. In 1912, lightning struck one of the church's spires and it toppled 25 feet off the top of the bell tower. Repairs were made before the church's dedication in 1912.

In 1993, the church was honored to have Pope John Paul II read mass here during World Youth Day.

This grand church is located on the corner of busy Colfax Avenue and Logan Street, just

© VISIT DENVER

a stone's throw from the state capitol. There is a small garden with statues and benches on the north side of the building.

There are three masses held daily at the cathedral, and six on weekends.

CITY PARK

3300 E. 17th Ave., 303/331-4113, www.denvergov.org

HOURS: Daily 5 A.M.-11 P.M.

The city's largest park (at 370 acres and a mile long) is City Park, located east of downtown. Denver's answer to New York's Central Park, City Park offers pretty much anything you could ask for in a park, sometimes in multiples. City Park has lakes, playgrounds, athletic fields, historic statues and fountains, running and cycling paths, a golf course, the **Denver Zoo,** and the **Denver Museum of Nature and Science.**

When the park was laid out in 1882, there was no surrounding neighborhood and downtown trolleys took people to this large patch of green. But it didn't take long for the city to grow around the park and beyond. The best time to visit the park is in summer, when paddleboats are rented by the hour on Ferril Lake and free jazz concerts are held in the park's historic pavilion.

The park is easily traversed by paved roads—some more like paths—but take note that from May through September, the roads are closed on Sundays. The park includes a Mile High Loop, a contour that is 5,280 feet above sea level, and a multi-use path that goes right by the Denver Museum of Nature and Science. Walk around during spring and enjoy a lilac garden, blooming trees, rows of tulips, and more.

◖ COLORADO STATE CAPITOL BUILDING

200 Colfax Ave., 303/866-2604, www.colorado.gov/capitoltour

HOURS: Mon.-Fri. 7:30 A.M.-5 P.M., tours Mon.-Fri. 10 A.M.-3 P.M.; check for holiday and renovation closures

COST: Free

A visit to the Colorado State Capitol is a history lesson in the making, especially when the legislature is in session (from January through May) and the governor and lawmakers are hard at work. Quiet visitors can watch the legislators in action just outside their respective chambers during sessions.

The story of the capitol building began in 1868, when Henry C. Brown, who also had the Brown Palace built a few blocks away, donated the land to the state of Colorado. Brown later tried to take it back, even going so far as to return grazing animals to the site because he was not pleased with construction delays. After a court battle, the state was able to keep the land. Two architects and 22 years later, the capitol building was completed.

Tours through the building highlight the use of native materials: marble, granite, sandstone, onyx, and gold. The original gold leaf used on the dome was a gift from Colorado miners. When standing on the first floor of the capitol, look 150 feet up to the rotunda ceiling. High up inside the rotunda is the stained-glass "Hall of Fame" that features portraits of 16 people who made a remarkable contribution to the state. There are other stained-glass portraits seen on the tour as well. Before ascending the 77 marble steps of the Grand Staircase, you'll learn about the Water Murals. Added in 1940, these murals are an artistic interpretation of the story of one of the state's most precious resources.

The true highlight of touring the capitol is the view from the dome's observation gallery. Like the hike up the 99 steps to the dome's interior, the views of the city and the mountains to the west from the dome are breathtaking. About halfway to the dome there is a small museum, Mr. Brown's Attic, in honor of Henry C. Brown's donation of the land. The museum includes a pop art replica of the capitol made from old soup cans by local engineering students.

© SCOTT DRESSEL-MARTIN, COURTESY OF VISIT DENVER

entrance to the Denver Botanic Gardens

On the west side steps of the capitol, you'll find the mile-high markers that indicate the point at which the city reaches 5,280 feet above sea level. This is a popular spot for tourist photos.

DENVER BOTANIC GARDENS

1005 York St., 720/865-3500, www.botanicgardens.org
HOURS: May-Sept. Daily 9 A.M.-8 P.M., Sept.-April 9 A.M.-5 P.M. (check for specific dates as daily hours change each year)
COST: $12.50 adult, $9.50 senior, $9 student, $9 child age 3-15, free for child under 3

The Denver Botanic Gardens was designed with all types of weather in mind, making it enjoyable year-round regardless of snow or blazing sun. The 23-acre gardens sit at the backside of Cheesman Park and are on the outer edge of the Capitol Hill neighborhood.

When the original site in City Park was repeatedly damaged, the city and local gardening enthusiasts agreed to transform an old cemetery into the new gardens. The 1960s addition of the Boettcher Memorial Tropical Conservatory, which houses tropical plants in a steamy hot dome, made the gardens more than a summer attraction.

While in recent years there has been a design emphasis and financial investment on making at least a portion of the gardens friendly to special events (such as weddings), the original mission to highlight thriving native plants remains obvious throughout the gardens. The Rock Alpine Garden, Water-Smart Garden, and Dryland Mesa in particular are a reminder of the arid climate of the region, and they show off what grows so well with so little water. Also check out the "green" roof of the gift shop as a progressive idea for environmental design.

Throughout the gardens, there are shaded benches and tables and chairs set up for enjoying a picnic—there is a small snack bar within the gardens—or taking a relaxing, pleasantly scented rest.

MILE-HIGH CITY

It's not enough for a city to just boast that it's a mile high, or 5,280 feet above sea level. People like to take home a souvenir, something to prove to the folks back home that they stood exactly one mile above sea level.

While it seems like a fantastic quirk of topography for the city to be located at exactly one mile above sea level, this elevation is not limited to one particular spot, but is actually reached in several places around the city. You can pinpoint that exact height by going to www.earthtools.org, and then go shutterbugging all over town, or visit the spots already designated by officials.

For a long time, the city's only 5,280-feet marker (pronounced "fifty-two eighty" by locals) was on the west steps of the **Colorado State Capitol Building,** although measurements were not always accurate. In 2003, when they discovered that someone had measured incorrectly years before, officials moved the

demarcation medallion from the 18th step to the 13th step. There are no plans to alter the 15th step, where the words "One Mile Above Sea Level" were carved in 1947.

Sports fans can head over to the home of the Colorado Rockies baseball team, **Coors Field,** where a row of purple seats rings the upper deck and marks that special seat a mile up. Invesco Field at Mile High, home of the Denver Broncos, has suites to honor the city and stadium's moniker.

The **Denver Museum of Nature and Science** in City Park is also believed to be on a mile-high spot. The museum has never had a marker that indicates where, or if, it sits at precisely 5,280 feet above sea level, but there is a 3.1-mile contour line that reaches 5,280 feet just outside the museum. This contour is now called the Mile High Loop, and is a multi-use pedestrian path through City Park.

In 2011, the Mordecai Children's Garden was opened atop the new parking garage across the street from the main gardens. With its own gift shop at the entrance, the garden itself includes various water features, bridges, caves, and, of course, plants.

During the summer, the Denver Botanic Gardens host a summer concert series with big-name bands, and tickets can be hard to come by. Membership to the gardens has many advantages (including discounts on those concert tickets) and members-only hours when the gardens have the ambience of a lovely backyard party.

◖ DENVER MUSEUM OF NATURE AND SCIENCE

2001 Colorado Blvd., 303/322-7009, www.dmns.org
HOURS: Daily 9 A.M.–5 P.M.
COST: $12 adult, $6 child age 3-18, $8 senior; additional fees for IMAX and the planetarium

With so many attractions, it is difficult to imagine the Denver Museum of Nature and

Science's humble beginnings as an oversized collection of treasured fauna specimens in the log cabin home of naturalist Edwin Carter. Features such as the Gates Planetarium, the Phipps IMAX Theater, and 215,000 square feet of exhibits all lend to the museum's current image. In 1908, the original stately Colorado Museum of Natural History opened on a hilltop on the eastern side of City Park. The building has been added on to considerably since then, and the variety and type of exhibits has increased. Some of the museum's oldest displays are of animals prepared by taxidermists and staged in large naturalistic settings behind glass windows—it's like a really quiet, clean zoo. Kids enjoy running through these wide halls and pushing the buttons to hear the sounds of cougars, buffalo, and other wildlife. Head up to the third level to learn about Colorado's variety of ecosystems (and the plants and animals that thrive in them). The *Prehistoric Journey* exhibit in the Explore Colorado section offers plenty of huge dinosaur skeletons, and it's the only place in the museum where visitors can watch what is typically behind-the-scenes work—preparing fossils for display. While the museum is one hands-on activity after another, particularly for children, a variety of educational programs are also offered off-site.

A family favorite is *Expedition Health* where people of all ages can learn about their own health by riding bikes, taking walks, breathing, and other seemingly ordinary things. Each gadget has a fun way to measure one's ability.

With its perch on the hill over City Park, the museum offers two places to catch the best view of the city—the Leprino Family Atrium and the Anschutz Family Sky Terrace, both on the building's west side.

Note that admission to the museum does not include tickets to special traveling exhibits or to the IMAX or Gates Planetarium shows (several daily). The museum can be especially crowded during morning school field trips; lines at the ticket windows are often much shorter in the afternoon.

DENVER ZOO

2300 Steele St., 303/376-4800, www.denverzoo.org
HOURS: March 1-Oct. 31 Daily 9 A.M.-5 P.M., Nov. 1-Feb. 29 Daily 10 A.M.-4 P.M.
COST: March 1-Oct. 31 $15 adult, $12 senior, $10 child age 3-11, free for child under 3; Nov. 1-Feb. 29 $12 adult, $10 senior, $8 child age 3-11, free for child under 3

The Denver Zoo is insanely popular with tourists and residents alike. Like many modern-day zoos, the Denver Zoo is trying to make its animal habitats look and feel more natural and its residents look less like caged wild animals. One exhibit addition is the $50 million Toyota Elephant Passage, which takes up 10 acres and is home to not only elephants, but also rhinos, tapirs, leopards, birds, and reptiles.

There are 29 primates found in the seven-acre Primate Panorama, and Predator Ridge offers 14 different animal species from Africa, including lions and hyenas. The African Kraal and Lorikeet Adventure are interactive animal exhibits where visitors can pet goats or feed the birds.

In addition to the 4,000 animals packed into this 80-acre park within City Park, the zoo is pulling in crowds with features beyond its residents and habitats. A huge annual draw during the holidays is ZooLights, when nearly half the zoo is illuminated with sparkling and colorful lights. Zoo-goers are treated to a glimpse of whatever nocturnal animals are out, as well as the sounds of choirs singing, a Kwanzaa performance, live ice-sculpture carving, and fire dancers.

The best time to visit the zoo is generally mid-afternoon, after school groups have come and gone. In winter, plan for time inside the hot and humid Tropical Discovery, where there are fish, turtles, snakes, bats, and Komodo dragons.

For a relaxing break from animal viewing, take a nostalgic ride on the zoo's Endangered Species Carousel. (Children and adults can choose from 48 hand-carved zoo animals or chariots; there is an additional cost of $2 to ride the carousel.) Look for the mother polar bear and two bear cubs to ride, which were made especially for the zoo in honor of its most famous animal residents, Klondike and Snow, two infant cubs that were hand-fed and raised by zoo staff and have since moved to another zoo.

MOLLY BROWN HOUSE MUSEUM

1340 Pennsylvania St., 303/832-4092, www.mollybrown.org
HOURS: Guided tours Tues.-Sat. 10 A.M.-3:30 P.M., Sun. noon-3:30 P.M.
COST: $8 adult, $6 senior, $4 child age 6-12, children under age 6 free

For being one of Denver's better-known residents, Molly Brown's fascinating life story sure isn't very well known. "The Unsinkable Molly

© DENVER ZOO

See elephants at the Denver Zoo.

Brown" is of course best known for surviving the 1912 sinking of the *Titanic,* but the tale of how she made it off the ship while valiantly trying to help others is just the tip of the iceberg.

In 1886, at age 19, Molly married 31-year-old miner J. J. Brown—*before* he struck it rich. After the Browns became wealthy from a gold mine, they moved to Denver in 1894 and eventually bought the Pennsylvania Street house that is now the museum. The Browns' renovations on the house are still evident today. Even during Molly Brown's lifetime, the house was rented out and became a run-down boarding-house. By the 1970s, it was barely saved from demolition and then painstakingly restored to its Victorian period of glamour.

The Molly Brown House Museum can only be viewed during guided tours, which are 30 minutes long and given on the hour and half-hour. The carriage house out back is where visitors sign up for tours. This is also the museum's large gift shop, filled with books

and movies about Molly Brown and other Victorian-era items. On the tours, visitors are led through the first floor, where rooms have been decorated to match photographs from when the Browns lived in the house. The tour then goes up to the second floor and back through the kitchen before ending on the home's back porch. Save time to watch a short movie about Molly Brown (included in the cost of the tour) and view artifacts on display on the porch.

Throughout her life, Molly Brown worked as a progressive social activist and was a tireless fundraiser and philanthropist. As visitors learn on the guided tours, the details of her full life are more than could be squeezed into a Broadway musical or Hollywood movie.

Tours do not include the home's third floor, but there are formal teas held there regularly. Check the website for details on annual teas such as the Harvest Tide Full Tea in the fall and the Mother's Day Full Tea in May.

NO, THE OTHER MR. BROWN

Tour guides at the Molly Brown House Museum and the Brown Palace Hotel, and now in Mr. Brown's Attic near the dome of the State Capitol Building, spend a fair part of their time explaining to visitors that the Brown Palace Hotel is not named after Mrs. Brown, nor was she married to the man it is named after, and she certainly did not own the hotel.

Molly Brown, born Margaret Tobin in Missouri, married J.J. Brown in Leadville, Colorado, in 1886. The couple moved to Denver in 1894, after Mr. Brown struck it rich in a gold mine. He worked as a mine supervisor, and so impressed his employers that they gave him a share of the profits when gold was discovered. Their Pennsylvania Street home—now a museum—was located just a few blocks from the capitol. As Molly Brown climbed the social ladder, her husband sought solitude while working in real estate and mining speculation. The couple legally separated in 1909, and Mr. Brown died in 1922.

Henry C. Brown was a wealthy businessman from Ohio who came to Denver in 1860 and purchased 160 acres of land, including the properties on which the Brown Palace Hotel was built and the land where the State Capitol Building now sits. As an honor to him and his gift to the people of Colorado, officials chose to name a small room after him in the capitol. Mr. Brown's Attic is a museum of artifacts from the building of the capitol, but, more practically, it's the room that visitors pass through before climbing the steep steps into the dome. There is also a portrait of him in the capitol. *This* Mr. Brown died in 1906.

Long after Henry Brown passed away, Molly Brown became a regular "resident guest" at the Brown Palace Hotel. She signed in for a month's stay in 1912 after surviving the sinking of the *Titanic*. During the Great Depression, Mrs. Brown's home was used as a boardinghouse, though she owned it until her death in 1932.

Greater Denver   Map 7

BUFFALO BILL MUSEUM AND GRAVE

987½ Lookout Mountain Rd., 303/526-0747, www.buffalobill.org

HOURS: May 1-Oct. 31 Daily 9 A.M.-5 P.M., Nov. 1-Apr. 30 Tues.-Sun. 9 A.M.-4 P.M.

COST: $5 adult, $4 senior, $1 child age 6-15, children age 5 and under free

Not too far from downtown is a view of both the plains and the mountains that so impressed frontiersman and showman William F. "Buffalo Bill" Cody that he asked to be buried on the spot. Over 20,000 people came to this site on Lookout Mountain in 1917, when Cody was laid to rest.

Relatively close to the grave is a 3,000-square-foot museum where visitors learn about the thrilling life and times of Buffalo Bill. Cody worked herding cattle and riding for the Pony Express, but earned his nickname from his skills as a buffalo hunter. He truly became a legend as a magnificent performer in his Wild West shows. On display at the museum are the costumes he wore in the shows, silent and talking movies, original posters, and guns from Cody's own collection. While the memorabilia is interesting enough, what many people come here for is the view. A breezy and scenic picnic spot is not far from the grave, and the **Pahaska Teepee Gift Shop** (May 1–Labor Day daily 8:30 A.M.–8:30 P.M., Labor Day–April 30 daily 9 A.M.–5 P.M., $4–10) between the museum and gravesite serves food such as buffalo burgers, buffalo chili, and ice cream.

The best route from downtown Denver is to go through Golden and follow 19th Street as it goes up into the mountains. You can also take I-70 west; just past the Lookout Mountain exit

SIGHTS

© BUFFALO BILL MUSEUM AND GRAVE

a photo of Buffalo Bill Cody with a group of Native Americans, from the Buffalo Bill Museum and Grave

there is a buffalo herd, most visible in winter and early spring.

◖ ROCKY MOUNTAIN ARSENAL NATIONAL WILDLIFE REFUGE

Havana St. and E. 56th Ave., Commerce City, 303/289-0930, www.fws.gov/rockymountainarsenal

HOURS: Visitor Center Tues.-Sun. 9 A.M.-4 p.m., refuge hours daily 6 A.M.-6 P.M.; tour times change monthly

COST: Free

It's an odd combination—nerve gas, natural beauty, and tourists—but somehow it works, and less than 15 miles from downtown, the Rocky Mountain Arsenal National Wildlife Refuge has become one of Denver's gems.

It's easy to spend the better part of a day at this oasis on a guided bus tour or walking through the miles of trails that traverse woodlands, wetlands, and prairie. Every season there is a chance to see some of the 300-plus

species that call this place home, and it's become a destination for bird-watchers. Summer is the best time to see burrowing owls and Swainson's hawks, while fall brings an opportunity to watch deer with their full antler racks. In winter, the bald eagles are more visible, and in spring, the migratory song birds and pelicans fly in. At any time of the year, you might spy coyotes, raptors, prairie dogs, and a variety of waterfowl. Over 20 bison (which were brought from Montana in 2007) live at the refuge and can be easily seen on most tours.

As the name suggests, this was not always a wildlife refuge. In the 1940s, the U.S. Army took possession of family farms to create a 27-square-mile chemical weapons facility, Rocky Mountain Arsenal. Mustard gas and napalm were manufactured here before the site was used to make agricultural pesticides. While the center of the arsenal has been described as one of the most polluted square

SIGHTS

© MICHAEL MAURO/USFWS

Eagles nest at the Rocky Mountain Arsenal National Wildlife Refuge.

miles on Earth, the buffer zone was attracting wildlife for decades. A 1989 *New York Times* headline about the Rocky Mountain Arsenal reads, "Nature Sows Life Where Man Brewed Death." In the 1990s, the wildlife was fenced in and work began to turn the arsenal into a wildlife refuge. Optimists talk of how nature has triumphed here, while skeptics point out soil contamination concerns.

The arsenal is closed sporadically for months at a time for ongoing clean-up efforts and federal holidays.

RESTAURANTS

Of course there's steak on the menu in Denver—but as the city has grown up and shed its cow town image, so have the restaurants. Food has become an important part of the city's culture: Local magazines write profiles about up-and-coming chefs, and national publications like the *New York Times, Food and Wine,* and *Bon Appétit* have featured articles about Denver's tantalizing fare and local celebrity chefs. For both locals and visitors, dining out can be an opportunity to explore world cuisine and local fare, and tempt your taste buds with something delectable.

On any night of the week, Denver restaurants offer mouth-watering comfort food, a selection of ethnic fare from Middle Eastern to Vietnamese, and contemporary seasonal cuisine that highlights produce and meats that thrive in Colorado. Every Denver neighborhood seems to have its favorite local hangout, whether it's a coffee shop, a spot for surprisingly fresh seafood and sushi, a microbrewery with classic pub food, a café for spicy Latin American eats, or an upscale, award-winning restaurant with a world-class wine list. And sprinkled around Denver for those special occasions in life, there are a number of excellent restaurants to choose from.

Still, when it comes to that steak for dinner, the options are limitless in Denver: Slice into a juicy cut amongst the kitschy animal decor of The Buckhorn Exchange, one of the

© MARC PISCOTTY

HIGHLIGHTS

© MINDY SINK

The comfort food at Bang never disappoints.

◖ **Best Carnivore Dining Experience:** You need a sense of humor and a hearty appetite to dine at **The Buckhorn Exchange,** where mounted animal heads adorn nearly every inch of wall space, and the menu offers a similar variety of game meats (page 58).

◖ **Best Ambience: Domo** is such a unique restaurant that it offers field trips for school children to visit its grounds. It specializes in country Japanese food, and features a traditional Japanese garden and folk art museum (page 60).

◖ **Best Ice Cream:** There are plenty of ice cream shops to choose from in the Mile-High City, and each has its own charm, but **Sweet Action Ice Cream** is just that much better with its creative flavors (page 61).

◖ **Best Menu with Local Produce: Potager** has a small garden on-site and a menu that features dishes made with ingredients grown at nearby farms and ranches (page 74).

◖ **Best Pay-What-It's-Worth Meal:** At **SAME Café,** or "So All May Eat," pay what you feel the meal was worth, or do a little work at the restaurant to pay for your food (page 75).

◖ **Best Street Tacos Off The Street:** Whether standing next to the exhaust pipe of the food truck or sitting inside the restaurant, **Pinche Tacos** are Denver's most delicious (page 76).

◖ **Best Vegetarian Meal: Watercourse Foods** offers the city's best vegetarian menu, with breakfast served all day (page 77).

◖ **Best Neighborhood Restaurant:** A simple lunch and dinner menu keep tiny **Bang** always packed with regulars who come for a salad or home-style meatloaf (page 78).

◖ **Best Spot for Your Sweet Tooth: Devil's Food Bakery & Cookery** offers an array of sweets to satisfy any sugar craving (page 89).

◖ **Unique Dining Experience:** It's worth the drive up to **The Fort** in Morrison to get the feel of being in an old fort and sampling the more exotic foods of the West (page 93).

PRICE KEY

💲 Most entrées less than $10
💲💲 Most entrées between $10-20
💲💲💲 Most entrées more than $20

city's oldest restaurants; savor tender beef, cooked to rare perfection and elegantly served, while a sommelier picks the best wine at the Palace Arms; or try buffalo steak in a re-created Western fort as your champagne is "tomahawked" with flair at The Fort.

Downtown   Map 1

AMERICAN

APPALOOSA GRILL 💲💲
535 16th St., 720/932-1700, http://appaloosagrill.com
HOURS: Daily 11 A.M.-2 A.M.

The Appaloosa Grill has a great story, nightly music, and good food. The Appaloosa is co-owned by a former waiter at the restaurant, who worked his way to the top and then mixed his new business with his old passion—music. Owner Johnny James Qualley is in a band, Oakhurst, and showcases lives music here nightly, with acts like the Clam Daddys and Go Go Lab. Music starts at 10 P.M. every night and there is no cover charge. The menu is typical bar food with an emphasis on bison in a variety of dishes, including chili, burgers, bratwurst, and meatloaf.

BROWN PALACE ATRIUM 💲💲
321 17th St., 303/297-3111, www.brownpalace.com
HOURS: afternoon tea daily noon-4 P.M., cocktails daily 4 P.M.-8 P.M., reservations highly recommended

The lobby of the Brown Palace doubles as one of the hotel's popular restaurants, serving a traditional English tea every afternoon with pastries and sandwiches, accompanied by the relaxing sounds of live piano or harp music. With the soaring, stained-glass atrium high above, the lobby offers the best seat in the house at any time of day. In the evening, it's time for cocktails here. During the holidays, reservations are required for teatime.

EDGE RESTAURANT & BAR 💲💲💲
1111 14th St., 303/389-3343,
www.edgerestaurantdenver.com
HOURS: Daily 6:30 A.M.-2:30 P.M. and 5-10 P.M.

The Edge may describe itself as an "American Progressive Steakhouse," but I find it to be more of a classic Colorado dining experience. Based in the Four Seasons, the Edge oozes class, and the large restaurant invites you to linger over a choice bison, steak, or lamb seasoned with its own signature rubs. The beef comes from Colorado ranches. Seating in the bar, which merges with the lobby, is also an option. On Sunday nights, the Edge has a terrific deal of $52.80 per couple for a three-course meal.

JONESY'S EATBAR 💲💲
400 E. 20th Ave., 303/386-7473, www.jeatbar.com
HOURS: Mon.-Thurs. 5-11 P.M., Fri. 5 P.M.-midnight, Sat. 10 A.M.-3 P.M. and 5 P.M.-midnight, Sun. 10 A.M.-3 P.M. and 5-11 P.M.

Jonesy's, you had me at grits. This often-overlooked Southern food staple is a personal favorite, but there is plenty more to love at Jonesy's. Here is upscale comfort food, such as meatloaf (also offered "meatless") with a "Colorado Cola glaze" and pork belly risotto. Get their "World Famous Fries" in a variety of flavors, like truffle and thai ginger.

SHIP TAVERN 💲💲
321 17th St., 303/297-3111, www.brownpalace.com
HOURS: Daily 11 A.M.-11 P.M., bar open until midnight

The Ship Tavern restaurant sits in one corner of

the Brown Palace's triangular footprint. With dark wood and stained-glass windows, the dimly lit room has an Old World pub atmosphere all of the time. Despite the large TV over the bar, it feels as if it's hardly changed since the hotel's opening in 1892. Offering lunch and dinner, the Ship Tavern's extensive menu includes burgers, prime rib, Rocky Mountain trout, seafood (including an exceptional lobster salad sandwich), pasta, and salads. On Wednesdays through Saturdays beginning at 8:30 P.M., there is live entertainment.

TOM'S HOME COOKIN' ⑤
800 E. 26th Ave., 303/388-8035
HOURS: Mon.-Fri. 11 A.M.-2:30 P.M.

Back in the day, the Five Points neighborhood had many authentic soul food restaurants. One of the remaining hole-in-the-wall spots is Tom's Home Cookin' with sweet tea, greasy friend chicken, cornbread, fried okra, and gumbo that satisfies a craving for Southern deliciousness. Save room for the peach cobbler and come on the early side to avoid possible lines. Be aware this is cash only—no credit cards—and a cell phone–free zone.

BREAKFAST AND BRUNCH
ELLYNGTON'S ⑤⑤⑤
321 17th St., 303/297-3111, www.brownpalace.com
HOURS: Mon.-Fri. 7-11 A.M. and 11:30 A.M.-2 P.M., Sat. 7-11 A.M., Sun. 7-10 A.M., Dom Pérignon Sunday Brunch 10 A.M.-2 P.M.

Ellyngton's is open for breakfast and lunch weekdays and attracts the city's power brokers, but what they are known for is their Dom Pérignon Sunday brunch buffet (reservations recommended). Like the rest of the Brown Palace's restaurants, Ellyngton's is in an elegantly appointed room and the service is exceptional. The brunch includes waffles, an omelet station, salads, seafood (including fresh sushi), and a choice of champagnes. The

brunch desserts are amazing, with crème brûlée as a standout.

MERCURY CAFÉ ⑤⑤
2199 California St., 303/294-9258, www.mercurycafe.com
HOURS: Breakfast Sat.-Sun. 9 A.M.-3 P.M., dinner Tues.-Sun. 5:30-11 P.M.

Just off the beaten path downtown, the Mercury Café is one of the city's most popular brunch hangouts. With an emphasis on organic and locally sourced ingredients, the menu offers a selection of hearty egg dishes, some with Colorado elk meat, as well as stuffed burritos—the "No More War Burrito" is a house favorite with green chile, polenta, and cheese. The café is also a nightclub with live music ranging from folk to swing bands and a variety of dance lessons offered, including tango, salsa, and belly dancing.

COFFEEHOUSES
EMILY'S COFFEE ⑤
1261 Glenarm Pl., 720/423-4797, www.emilyscoffee.com
HOURS: Mon.-Thurs. 7:30 A.M.-6 P.M., Fri. 7:30 A.M.-1 P.M., closed Sat. and Sun.

With coffee shops on almost every corner in downtown, does it really matter where you stop for a cup of joe? Yes! Emily's Coffee is part of the Emily Griffith Technical College (formerly Emily Griffith Opportunity School), where they teach job skills to immigrants and refugees. They also serve really good espresso. The pastries are baked by students in the school's baking program, and the coffee beans are locally roasted by Kaladi Brothers Coffee Company. Even the aprons worn here were made by women at the local African Community Center. Each cup of coffee bought here will have a community ripple effect.

CONTEMPORARY
OLIVÉA ❸❸❸
719 E. 17th St., 303/861-5050,
www.olivearestaurant.com
HOURS: Mon.-Fri. 5–10 P.M., Sat. 10 A.M.–2 P.M. and
5–10 P.M., Sun. 10 A.M.–2 P.M. and 5–9 P.M.
From the owners of Duo comes Olivéa, a restaurant with a touch of Spanish cuisine in most dishes. With award-winning chefs behind the scenes, a great meal is almost guaranteed at this standout on Restaurant Row in the Uptown neighborhood. Parts of the menu change seasonally to reflect available ingredients at their freshest. And on Mondays, the restaurant goes meatless, joining a nationwide trend to go vegetarian one night per week.

PALACE ARMS ❸❸❸
321 17th St., 303/297-3111, www.brownpalace.com
HOURS: Tues.-Sat. 5:30–9 P.M., closed Sun. and Mon.
It was only recently that the Palace Arms did away with their dinner jacket requirement, inviting a slightly more casual clientele. But the atmosphere here is still one of opulence, where the hotel's celebrity guests choose to dine in style. Everything here is top-notch, with chandeliers, French antiques, deep-red leather booths, and bone china. Service includes a tableside Caesar salad, bananas Foster, and martini cart. Foie gras is featured on the menu of the finest Colorado lamb, bison, and beef, all of which can be paired with a selection from the Palace Arms's award-winning wine list. Long considered one of Denver's very best restaurants, the Palace Arms is worth every extra penny spent.

RESTAURANT KEVIN TAYLOR ❸❸❸
1106 14th St., 303/820-2600,
www.restaurantkevintaylor.com
HOURS: Mon.-Sat. 5:30–10:30 P.M.
For a memorable night out in an elegant setting with spectacular food bursting with flavors, look no further than Restaurant Kevin Taylor in the Hotel Teatro. Taylor is one of Denver's preeminent chefs with a reputation for his creativity in the kitchen. At this namesake restaurant, the extensive menu is a fusion of French and New American with Southwestern and Asian twists. Restaurant Kevin Taylor can be a perfect pairing with a night at the theater; the Denver Center for the Performing Arts is only one block away.

ITALIAN
MICI ❸❸
1531 Stout St., 303/629-6424, www.miciitalian.com
HOURS: Mon.-Wed. 11 A.M.–9 P.M., Thurs.-Sat.
11 A.M.–10 P.M., Sun. noon–10 P.M.
The style at Mici is "quick-casual," where customers walk up to the counter and order and then get their food delivered to their table. However, don't expect the food to be fast food. This is quality Italian food in a stylish contemporary space. The pizza is always good and, like the rest of the menu, you can taste the house-made freshness. That might explain why Mici is over and over a "reader's choice" in local magazine surveys. This family-owned business is expanding and has two other Denver locations, one in Cherry Creek North (3030 E. 2nd Ave., 303/322-6424).

PANZANO ❸❸❸
909 17th St., 303/296-3525,
www.panzano-denver.com
HOURS: Mon.-Fri. 6:30–10 A.M.,
11 A.M.–2:30 P.M.; Mon.-Thurs. 5–10 P.M., Fri.-Sat. 5–11 P.M.;
Sat.-Sun. 8 A.M.–2:30 P.M., Sun. 4:30–11 P.M.
Panzano has not only been called one of Denver's best restaurants, but one of the best in America, and it has won numerous awards. Located adjacent to the Hotel Monaco in downtown Denver, Panzano offers a taste of the northern Italian countryside. In addition to the fine food, diners are made aware of the sustainable practices behind the scenes so that they can make true the saying, "chi manga

RESTAURANTS

bene, vive bene" (those who eat well, live well). And if you think Italian food is synonymous with pasta, think again—Chef Elise Wiggins has created gluten-free menus for both lunch and dinner.

LATIN AMERICAN
LAS DELICIAS ⑤
439 E. 19th Ave., 303/839-5675, www.delicias.net
HOURS: Mon.-Sat. 8 A.M.-9 P.M., Sun. 9 A.M.-9 P.M.

For some restaurants, the big appeal is how consistent the food and service are. Las Delicias, which has several Denver-area locations, is dependably decent Mexican food. There can be a wait for a table during lunch, when office workers from nearby downtown make the short walk over to "Las D," as it is referred to by locals. Red or green, smothered or not, for basic but filling burritos, tacos, and enchiladas, you will find something to fill you up here.

TAKEOUT
COOK'S FRESH MARKET ⑤
1600 Glenarm Pl., 303/893-2277,
www.cooksfreshmarket.com
HOURS: Mon.-Fri. 7 A.M.-8 P.M., Sat. 9 A.M.-6 P.M., closed Sun.

Downtown Denver's 16th Street Mall has finally been blessed with a gourmet deli that offers the city's growing urban population a place to grab a quick meal to go, or a place to get artisan cheeses, fresh seafood, and other groceries. With hot soups, made-to-order hot or cold sandwiches, and a salad bar, Cook's is very popular during the busy lunch hour. There is seating available inside the market, with huge windows perfect for people-watching. Call in an order and have it delivered curbside, or buy some groceries during your lunch hour and Cook's will hold them until you're ready to go home.

Golden Triangle, Lincoln Park, and SoBo   Map 2

AMERICAN
BEATRICE & WOODSLEY ⑤⑤
38 S. Broadway, 303/777-3505,
http://beatriceandwoodsley.com
HOURS: Mon.-Wed. 5-10 P.M., Thurs.-Fri. 5-11 P.M., Sat. 10 A.M.-4 P.M. and 5-11 P.M., Sun. 10 A.M.-4 P.M. and 5-10 P.M.

Beatrice & Woodsley—the emphasis is on the woods in décor here. It is meant to be an indoor wilderness with an inspired use of wood throughout the restaurant. (This can make for unexpected bumps in the dining tables, but the bathroom area is really a hoot.) And the ever-changing menu is for the adventurous eater, with choices such as a chicken-fried duck burger, crawfish beignets, and Cornish hen, to name a few. But a friend and I have plans to return soon for the brunch and share the grapefruit crisp and "monkey brains"—which are actually gooey cinnamon rolls.

◖ THE BUCKHORN EXCHANGE ⑤⑤⑤
1000 Osage St., 303/534-9505,
www.buckhornexchange.com
HOURS: Lunch Mon.-Fri. 11 A.M.-2 P.M., Dinner Mon.-Thurs. 5:30-9 P.M., Fri.-Sat. 5-10 P.M., Sun. 5-9 P.M.

Founded by one of frontiersman Buffalo Bill Cody's scouts, The Buckhorn Exchange has been open for business since 1893, serving all variety of beef and game meats. Over time, the walls of the Buckhorn were filled with a menagerie of hundreds of taxidermied animals to reflect some of the menu selections, such as bison and elk. The kitschy decor of taxidermy trophies is done with a sense of humor—such as the "herd" of antelope heads near the front door. To round out the Old West feel, there is cowboy music in the upstairs lounge on weekends. With a light rail stop practically at the front door, the Buckhorn is more accessible from downtown than ever.

© MINDY SINK

The décor at Beatrice & Woodsley is woodsy, as the name suggests.

DELUXE $$$

30 S. Broadway, 303/722-1550,
www.deluxedenver.com

HOURS: Tues.-Thurs. 5-9 P.M., Fri.-Sat. 5-10 P.M., closed Sun. and Mon.

Tucked in amongst hip boutiques and within walking distance of an art-house cinema and nightclubs along South Broadway, Deluxe is a perfect choice for a casual date night in a cozy booth or at the bar with a view of the kitchen. Entrées include improved-upon classics like roasted chicken, pork chops, and steak, and there is a small, eclectic wine list. Save room for comfort-food desserts, such as the ice-cream sandwich made with frozen chocolate mousse. Deluxe is named in a lot of local "best of" lists in Denver, such as "Best Chef's Counter in 2011" and "Best Bouillabasse."

DOUGHERTY'S RESTAURANT & PUB $$

5 E. Ellsworth Ave., 303/777-5210,
www.doughertysrestaurant.com

HOURS: Daily 11 A.M.-2 A.M.

Just a few steps from the hectic pace of South Broadway's burgeoning nightclub and restaurant scene is the welcome calm of Dougherty's. With every square inch painted seafoam green and decorated with quaint landscape paintings of the Irish countryside, Dougherty's seems heavy on the Irish, but it's mostly in the decor. The menu is appetizing salads, stuffed burgers, and divine desserts, with a small wine list and excellent service. The place is divided with the restaurant in one room and a small bar with TV and pool tables on the other side.

THE HORNET $$

76 Broadway, 303/777-7676,
www.hornetrestaurant.com

HOURS: Mon.-Fri. 11 A.M.-2 A.M., Sat. 10 A.M.-2 A.M., Sun. 10 A.M.-midnight

The Hornet seems an unlikely fusion restaurant with pool tables and a bar, but there are some tasty (if unusual) Latin American/Asian/American combinations here. Assuming there are no calories to count, try the lobster and bacon shells and cheese, the honey-stung chicken with mashed potatoes and stir-fry veggies, or bacon brie home fries. A table by the window is a perfect fishbowl spot to watch people head off to nearby clubs or the movies.

MAD GREENS $

1200 Acoma St., Ste. B, 303/464-7336,
www.madgreens.com

HOURS: Daily 10 A.M.-6 P.M.

Mad Greens is located on the ground floor of the Museum Residences, which were designed by architect Daniel Libeskind in conjunction with his addition to the Denver Art Museum. Mad Greens is primarily a casual salad restaurant, with specialty salads as well as "build your

RESTAURANTS

own" options. There is a cafeteria-style line for ordering; the set up—and decor—are nearly identical to many burrito joints, where diners watch their food being made behind glass and give instructions as to which ingredients get piled on. The restaurant has a sleek, clean style that attracts businesspeople from the neighborhood on weekdays. In addition to the salad options, they also have panini sandwiches, soup, and a kids menu that includes mac 'n' cheese and grilled cheese. This is a quick, healthy, and pretty affordable place for lunch—and even a glass of wine.

PALETTE'S ❸❸❸
100 W. 14th Ave. Pkwy., 303/534-1455, www.ktrg.net
HOURS: Tues.-Thurs. 11 A.M.-3 P.M., Fri. 11 A.M.-8:30 P.M., Sat.-Sun. 10 A.M.-3 P.M., closed Mon.

All that walking around the Denver Art Museum can make you hungry, and the museum's Palette's restaurant is the perfect place to recharge. Windows wrap around the dining room and offer a view of the museum's new wing, the Hamilton Building, and outdoor sculptures. Billed as "contemporary cuisine," lunch and dinner are sophisticated takes on steak, lobster, salads, and sandwiches, with a menu for kids as well. Palette's is also a great place to bring the in-laws, with a little something for everyone on the menu and plenty of art to look at and discuss before or after a meal. During special exhibitions, plan your visit to include a meal here with a themed menu that matches the current exhibit.

ASIAN
❖ DOMO ❸❸❸
1365 Osage St., 303/595-3666, www.domorestaurant.com
HOURS: Daily 11 A.M.-2 P.M. and 5-10 P.M.

Authentic Japanese peasant food is a rarity not only in Denver, but probably in the rest of the country, too. Not far from the edge of downtown is this Japanese garden oasis, with its small ponds, burbling fountains, blossoming trees, and a unique menu of fresh seafood and "sea vegetables," along with a menu of artisan sake. On one side of the garden is a folk art museum, which rounds out the field trips hosted here for children. Domo has a tea menu as well, for anyone who just wants to get away from the city and sip tea in this little garden. The restaurant's sushi presentations are works of art, and the goal is to give customers a very authentic experience (so forget about special orders or having soy sauce on your table to reseason your food).

COFFEEHOUSES
STUDIO 6 COFFEE ❸
910 Santa Fe Dr., 303/534-8900, http://studio6coffee.com
HOURS: Tues.-Fri. 8:30 A.M.-7 P.M., Sat. 10 A.M.-5 P.M.

Hidden in the Studio 910 Arts building in the Art District on Santa Fe Drive is a little boutique coffee shop that allows art patrons to take a quick break. This brightly colored space has a short menu of sandwiches and salads along with pastries and ice cream (and, yes, coffee and tea). If you get the right barista, even your latte can be made into a work of art here.

CONTEMPORARY
BITTERSWEET ❸❸❸
500 E. Alameda Ave., 303/942-0320, http://bittersweetdenver.com
HOURS: Tues.-Sat. 5-10 P.M., closed Sun. and Mon.

After a chemical cleanup at this former gas and service station, Bittersweet has become one of Denver's hottest restaurants with rave reviews from local and national press. The concept is a seasonally influenced menu of traditional foods with a modern twist. Think pork with rhubarb gastrique in the spring, for example. Given the word-of-mouth and terrific press, it's best to make reservations to dine here, as the small space can only accommodate so many diners on a busy night.

FOLLOW THAT FOOD TRUCK!

Food trucks converge on Civic Center Park during summer for Civic Center Eats.

Food trucks are the new fad in dining, or more accurately, eating out. Here in Denver, there are restaurants with a food truck that serves as a mobile extension of the brick-and-mortar business (Denver Cupcake Truck, Denver Biscuit Company, Steuben's), as well as great advertising, and then there are the businesses that started as a food truck and became so popular that they added a restaurant, too (Pinche Tacos, Biker Jim's). Someone had the brilliant idea to round up all the food trucks weekly in a central location and make it possible to sample from as many as you like. **Civic Center Eats** (www.civiccenterconservancy.org) takes place in Civic Center Park on Tuesdays and Thursdays during the lunch hour in the summer months. Look for the longest lines and you'll know you have found the best street food truck in town.

CHARCOAL ❸❸❸

43 W. 9th Ave., 303/454-0000,
www.charcoaldining.com

HOURS: Mon.-Fri. 11 A.M.-2 P.M.; Sat.-Sun. 10 A.M.-2 P.M.;
Mon.-Thurs. 5-10 P.M., Fri.-Sat. 5-11 P.M., Sun. 5-9 P.M.

Denver diners can now choose between their Scandinavian-inspired restaurants. Opened in 2011, Charcoal quickly made the top new restaurant lists, and its menu spells out the country of origin when a dish differs enough from American fare. Try the Swedish pancakes or Swedish meatballs for brunch, or find out what mustard herring is for lunch or dinner. The menu does change depending on seasonal availability of ingredients.

DESSERTS

◖ SWEET ACTION ICE CREAM ❸

52 Broadway, 303/282-4645, www.
sweetactionicecream.com

HOURS: Sun.-Thurs. 1-10 P.M., Fri.-Sat. 1-11 P.M.

Making the SoBo neighborhood just that much more hip is the Sweet Action Ice Cream shop, with its creative flavors, vegan options, and

© STEVE CRECELIUS, COURTESY OF VISIT DENVER

locally sourced ingredients. Try the Molasses Cornbread, Stranahan's Whiskey Brickle, or Thai Iced Tea—or better yet, try them in an enormous ice cream sandwich. The flavors change daily, so you might find something surprising as well as cool and refreshing.

ETHIOPIAN
ARADA ❸❺
750 Santa Fe Dr., 303/329-3344,
www.aradarestaurant.com
HOURS: Tues.-Sat. 11:30 A.M.-3 P.M. and 5-10 P.M.

Although Santa Fe Drive is known for mostly Latin American restaurants, Arada relocated to this increasingly popular street after years in another neighborhood. In a larger space with a new bar, Arada still offers diners classic Ethiopian food, with various spiced meats, vegetables, and sauces served on *injera,* a sourdough flatbread. Arada also offers Ethiopian

coffee (along with a traditional coffee ceremony) and honey wine.

LATIN AMERICAN
CUBA CUBA CAFÉ & BAR ❸❺
1173 Delaware St., 303/605-2822,
www.cubacubacafe.com
HOURS: Mon.-Thurs. 5-10 P.M., Fri.-Sat. 5-10:30 P.M., closed Sun.

Before stepping inside Cuba Cuba, you get a sense of the colorful and playful Caribbean vibe. The restaurant occupies two little Victorian houses joined together and painted blue with yellow trim. It's mellow and even cozy inside, where the night gets off to a perfect start with a smooth mojito and a bowl of plantain chips while listening to some live music. The entrées at Cuba Cuba are traditional Cuban favorites done to perfection, such as a Sandwich Cubano or Ropa Vieja. In the summer, the

COURTESY OF SWEET ACTION ICE CREAM

Sweet Action Ice Cream scoops up some cool treats.

back patio is adorned with lanterns and it feels like an island vacation in the city.

EL NOA NOA $

722 Santa Fe Dr., 303/623-9968,
http://denvermexicanrestaurants.net
HOURS: Mon.-Sat. 9 A.M.-10 P.M., Sun. 9 A.M.-9 P.M.
Drawing repeat customers long before the bustling Santa Fe Arts District developed along this strip, El Noa Noa has been serving icy margaritas and smothered burritos for decades. On weekends in the summer, a mariachi band plays music on the patio, where umbrella-sheltered tables make this the ideal place to nosh on reasonably priced chiles rellenos, fajitas, enchiladas, or tacos during the First Friday Art Walk. Although the patio is popular and fills up in nice weather, there is rarely a wait for a table inside. There is also live music on Thursday nights.

EL TACO DE MEXICO $

714 Santa Fe Dr., 303/623-3926,
www.eltacodemexico.com

HOURS: Sun.-Thurs. 7:30 A.M.-10 P.M., Fri.-Sat. 7:30 A.M.-11 P.M.
Next door to El Noa Noa is El Taco de Mexico, an almost roadside stand of a restaurant that takes cash only. The average customer at El Taco orders a traditional shredded beef taco and an *horchata* (cinnamon-flavored rice milk) for a quick, satisfying meal, but those in search of "authentic" Mexican food are thrilled to find tongue and brain on the menu as well.

SEÑOR BURRITOS $

12 E. 1st Ave., 303/733-0747,
http://senorburritos.blogspot.com
HOURS: Mon.-Sat. 8 A.M.-9 P.M., closed Sun.
Running late for a movie at the Mayan Theatre? Just around the corner is Señor Burrito, a simple Mexican food joint that serves up great, no-fuss food in a hurry. Señor Burrito is often busy just before showtimes, and they also pack in the breakfast crowd in the mornings. Order at the counter, then find a table in the small restaurant. There is limited metered parking on the street.

LoDo and Platte River Valley   Map 3

AMERICAN
BIKER JIM'S GOURMET DOGS $

2148 Larimer St., 720/746-9355,
www.bikerjimsdogs.com
HOURS: Sun.-Thurs. 11 A.M.-10 P.M., Fri.-Sat. 11 A.M.-3 A.M.
Biker Jim's story is the quintessential American Dream, if that dream involves a jalapeño cheddar elk dog in a bun. Once a car repo man, Biker Jim fulfilled his dream of making gourmet hot dogs with exotic and unusual meats, like elk, Alaskan reindeer, rattlesnake, wild boar, pheasant, and duck. It's a place where a buffalo dog seems like the most normal item on the menu. The toppings are equally outrageous—as in, "harissa roasted cactus." Jim's dogs have been featured on shows like Anthony

Bourdain's *No Reservations*. The restaurant includes a kids' menu and beer.

COLT & GRAY $$$

1553 Platte St., 303/477-1447, www.coltandgray.com
HOURS: Tues.-Thurs. 5-10 P.M., Fri.-Sat. 5-11 P.M., Sun. 5-9 P.M.
At the foot of the 16th Street pedestrian and bicycle bridge is one of Denver's best-reviewed restaurants. As cyclists whiz past the patio en route to the bike paths along the South Platte River one block away, waiters at Colt & Gray are serving sophisticated dishes of pig trotters, sautéed sweetbreads, rabbit, and more. Named one of Denver's 25 best restaurants by *5280 Magazine*, Colt & Gray is a place for serious foodies.

RESTAURANTS

RESTAURANTS

EUCLID HALL ❶❸

1317 14th St., 303/595-4255, http://euclidhall.com
HOURS: Mon.-Thurs. 11:30 A.M.-1 A.M., Fri.
11:30 A.M.-2 P.M., Sat. 2 P.M.-2 A.M., Sun. 2 P.M.-1 A.M.

The team from Rioja and Bistro Vendôme has branched out into comfort pub food with this new restaurant. For the overflow crowds from the nearby Auraria campus, Pepsi Center, and tourists visiting Larimer Square, there are cheese curds, chicken and waffles, and pad thai pig ears—and no, this is not your mom's comfort food! Also on the menu are "fresh hand cranked sausages" and that Midwestern favorite, poutines.

THE KITCHEN ❶❸❸

1530 16th St., 303/623-3127,
www.thekitchencommunity.com
HOURS: Sun.-Tues. 11 A.M.-9 P.M., Wed.-Sat.
11 A.M.-10 P.M.

Almost as exciting as learning that there will be a Trader Joe's coming to Colorado was finding out that the popular Boulder restaurant, The Kitchen, had opened a Denver location. In other words, there's a loyal fan base for this food. The menu is slightly different than the Boulder original, with a large selection of seafood. The ample starters can make for a fun sampling with friends (definitely order the Goat Gouda Gougére) before selecting an entrée (you cannot go wrong with the Wisdom Farm Chicken Char Grilled). The sticky toffee pudding is so good that people seem to favor it over the *pot au chocolat*. Community Hour (3–6 P.M. daily) is a chance to try the "nibbles" at discounted rates.

THE MARKET ❶

1445 Larimer St., 303/534-5140,
http://themarketatlarimer.com
HOURS: Mon.-Thurs. 6 A.M.-11 P.M., Fri.-Sat. 6 A.M.-midnight, Sun. 6 A.M.-10 P.M.

For a quick bite to go or a no-frills lunch, The Market is an old Denver favorite. In good weather, the outdoor café tables along the storefront and perched on the curb across the sidewalk are always occupied. The Auraria campus is a couple of blocks away, and The Market's clientele is a blend of students, businesspeople, and tourists. As Larimer Square has evolved into more of a tourist destination in the past 20 years, The Market has stayed the same. They offer hot and cold deli items, sandwiches, and ample-sized sweets all day long—their Spring Fling cake is a favorite.

ASIAN

CHOLON ❶❸

1555 Blake St., 303/353-5223,
www.cholon.com/denver
HOURS: Mon.-Fri. 11 A.M.-10 P.M., Sat. 5-10 P.M.

Ask anyone if they have eaten at ChoLon, a modern Asian bistro, and the answer is invariably, "Yes. I had the onion soup dumplings!" This explosion of flavor is just one example of the exciting tastes found at ChoLon, where the presentation is just as thrilling as the food itself. I don't even really like eggs, but I really wanted a dish with an "egg cloud" (kind of like French toast, it is a spicy custard-like egg mixture on toast points) and was also curious about "Chow Fun" (a noodle bowl with fresh, house-made tapioca rice noodles, shrimp, lobster, and black bean sauce) on a dish of short ribs. For those on a dining budget, come for the happy hour menu, with small plates at $5 each starting at 2 P.M. on Saturdays.

SUSHI SASA ❶❸

2401 15th St., 303/433-7272, www.sushisasa.com
HOURS: Mon.-Thurs. 11:30 A.M.-2:30 P.M. and
5-10:30 P.M., Fri.-Sat. 11:30 A.M.-2:30 P.M. and 5-11:30 P.M.,
Sun. 5-10:30 P.M.

It would be pretty hard to just stumble across Sushi Sasa while out looking for a bite to eat. The acclaimed sushi restaurant's entrance is practically the back door of a large, historic building, just as the sidewalk ends before 15th

Street heads over I-25. But inside, it is calm serenity, with bamboo and white decor and a perfectly balanced menu of Japanese dishes beyond just sushi. Noodle bowls, tempura, vegetarian plates, and a variety of salads with or without seafood—all are on offer alongside the extensive sushi list.

BREAKFAST AND BRUNCH
MONA'S RESTAURANT ❸
2364 15th St., 303/455-4503,
www.monasrestaurant.com
HOURS: Mon.-Fri. 7 A.M.-2 P.M., Sat.-Sun. 7 A.M.-3 P.M.

Mona's is named after the Mona Lisa portrait painted on the exterior of the building by New York artist Stefano Castronovo in the '80s, when this space was an art gallery. The restaurant has an artistic flair which starts with the extra-large spoon that serves as a doorknob and the wall of curved chalkboards for diners to leave a quick review of their dining experience or to doodle on while they wait for their meal. Most weekends, there is a long line out the door of this small establishment, where people happily wait for blueberry flapjacks, huevos rancheros, and sandwiches and salads.

SNOOZE ❸
2262 Larimer St., 303/297-0700,
www.snoozeeatery.com
HOURS: Mon.-Fri. 6:30 A.M.-2:30 P.M., Sat.-Sun. 7 A.M.-2:30 P.M.

It's no wonder that the pancakes at Snooze have developed a loyal following: With options such as caramel glazes and shameless amounts of chocolate, they are somewhere between breakfast and dessert. There's even a Pineapple Upside Down Pancake. The menu also features several savory egg dishes and sandwiches on the lunch side, though breakfast is served all day. The *"Jetsons*-meets-*Happy Days* colorful and unique decor makes Snooze fun, too. Located near the ballpark in LoDo, Snooze is still in a slightly rough part of downtown. There are several Snooze locations around Denver and Colorado.

BREWPUBS
BRECKENRIDGE COLORADO CRAFT ❸❸
2220 Blake St., 303/297-3644, www.breckbrew.com
HOURS: Mon.-Sat. 11 A.M.-1 A.M., Sun. 11 A.M.-midnight

Just a couple of blocks from Coors Field is the cavernous Breckenridge Colorado Craft (formerly Breckenridge Brewery & Pub), ready to hold most of the crowd leaving a baseball game on a warm summer night. With five Colorado locations under various names, Breckenridge Brewery offers beers that are unique to each location or the season, such as Ball Park Brown and 2220 Red at this Denver location, or the Summerbright Ale served only during summer months. Avalanche Ale is their most popular brew year-round. The menu is typical brewpub fare—burgers, salads, Tex-Mex appetizers—but read closely and look for those items mixed with the brew itself, such as the Southwestern green chili made with Avalanche Ale or any of the "Beer-B-Que" sandwiches. The brewery also has several large TV screens for watching a game.

DENVER CHOP HOUSE & BREWERY ❸❸❸
1735 19th St., 303/296-0800, www.chophouse.com
HOURS: Mon.-Thurs. 11 A.M.-11 P.M., Fri.-Sat. 11 A.M.-midnight, Sun. 11 A.M.-10 P.M.

Across the street from Coors Field, where there is no shortage of sports bars and steak houses to choose from, the Denver Chop House & Brewery has loyal regulars—including professional athletes—who don't mind paying a bit more. In addition to the classic steak and seafood menu, the Chop House has pizza (try the Bourbon Beef Pizza) and salads. The theme here is 1940s' steak house, complete with period music, cigars, scotch, and freshly brewed ales.

BEER FOOD

There's beer, and then there's food made with beer. Denver has become known as a beer town, with several original microbreweries and brewpubs, and as host of the annual Great American Beer Festival. Cooking with beer isn't a new idea, but it can be a fun way to try more of those original flavors of ambers, lagers, porters, and pilsners. In addition to drinking a cold one, why not try the "Beer-B-Q sauce" or Vanilla Porter milkshake at Breckenridge Colorado Craft? Or sample the beer-battered fish-and-chips or stout-braised pot roast at the Wynkoop Brewery.

WYNKOOP BREWERY $$

1634 18th St., 303/297-2700, www.wynkoop.com

HOURS: Daily 11 A.M.-2 A.M.; Mon.-Thurs. kitchen closes at 11 P.M., Fri.-Sat. kitchen closes at midnight, Sun. kitchen closes at 10 P.M.

The Wynkoop Brewing Company was founded by Colorado Governor and former Denver Mayor John Hickenlooper and his business partners in the 1980s, when the LoDo neighborhood was just beginning its transformation from vacant warehouse district to hip, urban hot spot. Occupying a few floors of a historic mercantile building across the street from Union Station, the Wynkoop is a great place for a game of pool and a beer—the second floor is devoted to billiards—or a meal. The brewery has a traditional pub menu with shepherd's pie and pot roast, complemented by its line of beers brewed on-site.

CAFÉS AND TEAHOUSES

THE HOUSE OF COMMONS $

2401 15th St., 303/455-4832, www.houseofcommonstea.com

HOURS: Daily 10 A.M.-6 P.M.

More than just another sandwich shop, The House of Commons will satisfy any Anglophile's need for a cup of freshly brewed, proper English tea in the afternoon. Much of the tea comes from Taylors of Harrogate in Yorkshire, England, and there is a selection of over 30 flavors. There's also Devonshire cream, buttery scones, fresh lemon curd, and cucumber sandwiches on the menu. Brightly lit and with a couple of outdoor tables, The House of Commons is a cheery place to share a spot of tea with a friend.

PARIS ON THE PLATTE $

1553 Platte St., Ste. 102, 303/455-2451, www.parisontheplatte.com

HOURS: Mon.-Thurs. 7 A.M.-1 A.M., Fri. 7 A.M.-2 A.M., Sat. 8 A.M.-2 A.M., Sun. 8 A.M.-1 A.M.; Sun.-Thurs. kitchen closes 10 P.M., Fri.-Sat. kitchen closes 11 P.M.

The scent of clove cigarettes being smoked by pierced, tattooed, and vaguely Goth-styled young people has defined Paris on the Platte for decades. This was the late-night place to be for young clubgoers after the bars and clubs closed, or the spot for those too young to even get into a bar to hang out. As the neighborhood on and near Platte Street has been developed with expensive apartments, condominiums, and a lot more shops, the clientele at Paris on the Platte has also changed—with a wine bar next door, it's become a bit more sophisticated. Now smoking is only allowed outside and the location is a popular place to plug in the computer for a few hours. There is also a menu of yummy sandwiches and snack platters.

CONTEMPORARY AND NEW AMERICAN

THE SQUEAKY BEAN $$

1500 Wynkoop St., 303/623-2665, http://thesqueakybean.net

HOURS: Daily 5:30-10 P.M.

Now located in the old saddlery building in LoDo, The Squeaky Bean has improved in every way since moving from LoHi in 2012. The space has lots of natural light, tables that allow enough privacy (and noise levels) for people to hold a conversation, and quirky touches here and there, such as the cookbooks attached to the menus that make great conversation pieces. Diners can partake of the cheese cart that gets wheeled around the dining room and order by the ounce. There is an expansive cocktail, wine, and beer list. The menu, which changes seasonally, is a modern take on things like fried chicken (the skin comes in sheets).

TAG ❸❸❸

1441 Larimer St., 303/996-9985,
http://tag-restaurant.com

HOURS: Mon.-Fri. 11:30 A.M.-2 P.M., Mon.-Thurs. 5-10 P.M., Fri.-Sat. 5-11 P.M., Sun. 5-9 P.M.

Chef Troy Guard specializes in creativity in the kitchen, providing diners with something unexpected. Caramelized butterfish, anyone? How about the Skuna Bay Salmon with pickled watermelon *rind*? It would be easy to fill up on a variety of small plates here, but don't overlook the "principal" plates either. Plan ahead with the "Omakase," which is a multi-course meal created by the chefs (24-hour advance notice strongly recommended) to get a full sense of all that the menu has to offer.

TAG RAW BAR ❸❸

1423 Larimer St., 303/996-2685, http://tagrawbar.com

HOURS: Tues.-Thurs. 11:30 A.M.-9 P.M., Fri. 11:30 A.M.-10 P.M., Sat. 5 A.M.-10 P.M., closed Sun. and Mon.

Kangaroo meat. That's right—there is kangaroo loin on the menu here. For those who think of raw food as limited to salad and sushi, think again. TAG Raw Bar serves *almost* an entire menu of raw foods. Rounding out the rawness are cooked noodles and the "almost raw meat" selection that includes kangaroo. For the most part, though, it is sushi prepared in a most creative way. Stop in for a quick bite or stay for a several-course dinner.

TRILLIUM ❸❸❸

2134 Larimer St., 303/379-9759,
www.trilliumdenver.com

HOURS: Tues.-Sat. 5-10 P.M., Sun. 10 A.M.-2 P.M. and 5-9 P.M.

There is more to food from Northern Europe than the meatballs from IKEA, and with the Scandinavian and American cuisine at Trillium, diners can learn—and taste!—more. From climates with long winters come cold-water fish and root vegetables, expertly seasoned and presented. Small plates feature a roasted carrot pudding, toast "skagen," and sockeye salmon raaka, and turnips and radishes pop up in unexpected dishes. With huge front windows and 14-foot-high ceilings, the large space feels open and airy. The kitchen is "exhibition style," which allows diners to observe the chefs at work.

VESTA DIPPING GRILL ❸❸❸

1822 Blake St., 303/296-1970, www.vestagrill.com

© STEVE CRECELIUS, COURTESY OF VISIT DENVER

Zengo has an Asian-Latin fusion menu.

HOURS: Sun.-Thurs. 5-10 P.M., Fri.-Sat. 5-11 P.M.

Named after a beautiful goddess, and designed with sensuous curves in the bar and large booths, Vesta is a sexy place, and great for a romantic date night. At Vesta, diners order an entrée accompanied by three sauces—the menu includes suggestions to complement each dish, but there are dozens to choose from and sample. The entrées themselves are almost as varied as the sauces, with steak, venison, tuna, duck, chicken, and vegetables. Portions are large, but much like eating fondue (with each bite dipped and flavored individually), it's fun to eat a lot or share family-style. Dipping sauces are also part of the desserts.

ZENGO ❸❸

1610 Little Raven St., 720/904-0965, www.richardsandoval.com

HOURS: Sun.-Thurs. 5-10 P.M., Fri.-Sat. 5-11 P.M.

Just a few steps from the base of the Millennium Bridge and looking over Commons Park, Zengo is in a great location as the Platte River Valley neighborhood continues to grow. With its large and vibrantly colored dining room, Zengo is fun with a group for family-style dining, or come alone to sit at the bar and enjoy a bowl of noodles. The Asian-Latin fusion works in just about every dish, such as Won Ton Tacos or Chipotle-Miso Soup. A personal favorite is the Achiote-Hoisin Pork Arepas for an appetizer.

FRENCH
BISTRO VENDÔME ❸❸❸

1416 Larimer St., Ste. H, 303/825-3232, www.bistrovendome.com

HOURS: Mon.-Thurs. 5-10 P.M., Fri.-Sat. 5-11 P.M., Sun. 5-9 P.M.; brunch Sat.-Sun. 10 A.M.-2 P.M.

Tucked in behind the shops of Larimer Square in the historic Sussex building is the charming Bistro Vendôme, with the feel of being off the beaten path in Paris or New York. Owned by the same women who started the restaurant Rioja across the street—chef-owner Jennifer Jasinski and manager-owner Beth Gruitch—Bistro Vendôme is one of Denver's most romantic date restaurants, with seating inside or outside on the small patio, and complimentary champagne for anyone celebrating a special event. Their weekend brunch features fresh croissants and crepes.

COOHILL'S ❸❸❸

1400 Wewatta St., 303/623-5700, http://coohills.com

HOURS: Mon.-Thurs. 5-9 P.M., Wed.-Fri. 11:30 A.M.-1:30 P.M., Fri.-Sat. 5-10 P.M., Sun. 10 A.M.-2 P.M.

Dine creekside above Cherry Creek at Coohill's, where the menu is "French-influenced, but it's Colorado grown." There is a variety of seafood—including blue crab and octopus (that surely is not Colorado grown or raised)—as well as rack of lamb, steak, and salads. Appetizers include a cheese plate and a patô plate. Plan ahead and reserve a tasting menu for four, five, or seven courses. There is outdoor patio seating as well as indoor space with floor-to-ceiling windows.

INDIAN
INDIA HOUSE ❸❸

1514 Blake St., 303/595-0680, www.indiahouse.us

HOURS: Lunch Mon.-Fri. 11 A.M.-2:30 P.M., Sat.-Sun. noon-2:30 P.M.; dinner Sun.-Thurs. 5:30-10 P.M., Fri.-Sat. 5:30-11 P.M.

If you're craving tandoori and other traditional Indian foods, India House is a good place for lunch or dinner. In one of LoDo's historic buildings, India House is like a loft, with exposed brick walls and wooden beams, and traditional Indian musical instruments on display. It's American bistro meets home-style Indian food. Try the mango chicken or chicken tikka masala for dinner. During lunch, there is a set-price buffet.

© MARC PISCOTTY

Dine out at Bistro Vendôme in Larimer Square.

ITALIAN
BUENOS AIRES PIZZERIA ❶❺

1319 22nd St., 303/296-6710, www.bapizza.com

HOURS: Tues.-Sat. 11:30 A.M.-10 P.M., Sun. noon-8 P.M.

For those who can't make it to Argentina to try the pizza, there is Buenos Aires Pizzeria. What makes Argentine pizza special is the uniqueness of its toppings—like the signature pie with ham, hearts of palm, hard-boiled egg, and more; a bacon and corn pizza; or one with blue cheese. The pizzeria also serves empanadas, sandwiches, and gelato. There are two entrances here because the business is divided into two sides by another shop in between—one for takeout and ordering gelato or pizza by the slice, and one for sit-in dining. The restaurant is cute, with checkered tablecloths and distinct trattoria ambience, whereas the take-out and gelato side is so casual, it feels like you're in the back room. The staff is friendly and service is prompt.

OSTERIA MARCO ❶❺

1453 Larimer St., 303/534-5855, http://osteriamarco.com

HOURS: Sun.-Thurs. 11 A.M.-10 P.M., Fri.-11 A.M.-11 P.M.

In the subterranean space beneath Larimer Square's The Market is Osteria Marco (which also includes patio seating on the sidewalk), with a casual but sophisticated take on Italian food from local chef and restaurateur Frank Bonnano. These pizzas are not overly complicated just for the sake of it; they are for a grown-up palate, with prosciutto instead of pepperoni and goat cheese rather than just mozzarella. There are also *paninis,* salads, and hearty entrees, all accompanied by an excellent wine list.

PROTO'S PIZZERIA NAPOLETANA ❶❺

2401 15th St., 720/855-9400, www.protospizza.com

HOURS: Daily 11 A.M.-10 P.M.

After moving to Colorado, Pam Proto craved the thin-crust Italian-style pizza of her childhood—in Connecticut. She opened her first pizzeria in Longmont, Colorado, and now has five locations. A few months after starting her business, Pam Proto visited Italy for the first time and was thrilled to discover that she was serving authentic Italian pizza in Colorado. At this Platte Street location, the colorful bar top made of broken tile pieces is the centerpiece of a tiny restaurant that fills up just about every night. Proto's does not deliver, but offers takeout. Friday nights are all about clam pizza, which is a surprisingly popular pie.

RIOJA ❶❺❸

1433 Larimer St., 303/820-2282, www.riojadenver.com

HOURS: Wed.-Fri. 11:30 A.M.-2:30 P.M., Mon.-Thurs. 4-10 P.M., Fri.-Sat. 4-11 P.M., Sat.-Sun. 10 A.M.-2:30 P.M., Sun. 4-10 P.M.

For an evening of sophisticated dining, visit Rioja in Larimer Square to try some delectable Mediterranean-inspired seasonal cuisine. The muted earth tones and copper-topped bar

RESTAURANTS

set off against exposed brick are reminiscent of the colors of the Spanish wine country, Rioja. The wine list, of course, features wine from the Rioja region. The dinner menu includes a memorable artichoke tortellini, unexpectedly light gnocchi, and hearty entrées, some made with handmade pastas. The bar menu, always available, has a few items under $5, and the pastas are available as appetizers, too. Rioja's patio is open when weather permits for lunch and dinner.

TWO-FISTED MARIO'S PIZZA ⑤
1626 Market St., 303/623-3523,
www.twofistedmarios.com
HOURS: Sun.-Wed. 11 A.M.-2 A.M., Thurs.-Sat.
11 A.M.-3 A.M.

For lunch or a very late-night snack of lip-smacking good pizza by the slice or pie, try Two-Fisted Mario's in LoDo. The pizza shop and the bar next door, **Double Daughters**

a picnic plate at Rioja in Larimer Square

Salotto (1632 Market St., 303/623-3523, www. doubledaughters.com), are owned by the same people. This means that you can either hang out in the brightly colored Two-Fisted Mario's, where they play fairly loud music, or order some pizza while taking it easy at Double Daughters. During the lunch hour, the bar ambience is less obvious, and kids really like the chaotic energy of this place as much as the pizza.

WAZEE SUPPER CLUB ⑤⑤
1600 15th St., 303/623-9518,
www.wazeesupperclub.com
HOURS: Mon.-Sat. 11 A.M.-2 A.M., Sun. noon-midnight

Freshly renovated in 2012, the Wazee Supper Club is back in business, serving beer, pizza, and sandwiches to a mix of regulars that might include local politicians and businesspeople, nearby loft residents, and, increasingly, tourists. The Wazee has been around since the 1970s—the building a lot longer—and they have a selection of locally brewed beers on tap, along with *strombolis* and salads.

LATIN AMERICAN
MARGS TACO BISTRO ⑤⑤
1519 Wynkoop St., 303/534-6274,
www.margstacobistro.com
HOURS: Mon.-Thurs. 11 A.M.-11 P.M., Fri. 11 A.M.-midnight, Sat. noon-11 P.M., Sun. noon-10 P.M.

The name and the large, tacky margarita glass that adorns the front of this restaurant might mislead some patrons expecting a rowdy bar. Inside, it's all about the global flavors stuffed in fresh-pressed flour tortillas. (Gluten-free options are corn tortillas or lettuce wraps.) Choose from Moroccan, Korean, and Jamaican (and... Ninja?) flavors, as well as more traditional *carnitas* and *pescado* for your tacos. Order by the platter and make it a sampler with friends, too. The service here is quick and friendly, even on busy weekend nights.

© MARC PISCOTTY

TAMAYO $$$
1400 Larimer St., 720/946-1433,
www.richardsandoval.com
HOURS: Lunch Mon.-Fri. 11 A.M.-2 P.M.; dinner Sun.-
Thurs. 5-10 P.M., Fri.-Sat. 5-11 P.M.

On the southeast corner of Larimer Square, Tamayo has great views of the mountains from inside the main restaurant or, better yet, up on their rooftop deck. Tamayo is part of Richard Sandoval Restaurants, which has several different restaurants in Denver, all with a similar theme of sophisticated Latin American food. The best way to experience Tamayo is from the rooftop, watching the sun set over the mountains while you enjoy a sangria or mango mojito and a few appetizers.

SEAFOOD
MCCORMICK'S FISH HOUSE & BAR $$$
1659 Wazee St., 303/825-1107,
www.mccormickandschmicks.com
HOURS: Mon.-Thurs. 7 A.M.-midnight, Fri.-Sat.
7 A.M.-1 A.M., Sun. 7 A.M.-11:30 P.M.

In the historic Oxford Hotel, McCormick's Fish House & Bar is like two separate restaurants separated by a hallway. The main dining room offers fairly private booth seating and reservations are recommended. In the corner bar, it's a combination of benches and chair seating at tables along the windows. A lovely stained-glass panel behind the antique bar is a reminder of the hotel's lavish past. Just about every kind of seafood imaginable is flown in fresh daily here, with over 30 varieties available. The happy hour menu in the bar is the best bargain in town, with items for $3–6.

Capitol Hill and City Park   Map 4

AMERICAN
ATOMIC COWBOY $$
3237 E. Colfax Ave., 303/377-7900,
www.atomiccowboy.net
HOURS: Mon.-Fri. 4 P.M.-2 A.M., Sat.-Sun. 11 A.M.-2 A.M.

The Atomic Cowboy is located in Colfax's Bluebird district, next to the Bluebird Theater. Space-age Western decor make the Atomic feel like a 1950s' boy's bedroom, with humorous artwork—cowboy meets alien—and an assortment of games, from pinball and pool to board games and poker night. The set up here is unconventional: the Atomic Cowboy is a bar with two restaurants in the same space that are open at slightly overlapping and then different times. These restaurants are **Fat Sully's NY Pizza** (303/333-4440, www.fatsullyspizza.com) and the **Denver Biscuit Company** (303/377-7900, www.denbisco.com).

THE AVENUE GRILL $$
630 E. 17th Ave., 303/861-2820, www.avenuegrill.com
HOURS: Mon.-Thurs. 11 A.M.-11 P.M., Fri.-Sat. 11 A.M.-
midnight, Sun. 10 A.M.-10 P.M.

For years a staple of Uptown dining on 17th Avenue, The Avenue Grill has a solid reputation as a power-lunch spot for businesspeople, as well as a place for a casual family dinner, and now brings in a brunch crowd on weekends. The menu here includes steak, but also has San Francisco, Asian, and Italian influences. The bar at The Avenue Grill is also a draw, with friendly bartenders mixing up what has been consistently voted "Best Martini" in local surveys for sticking to the classic version.

BROTHERS BBQ $
568 Washington St., 720/570-4227,
www.brothers-bbq.com
HOURS: Daily 10 A.M.-10 P.M.

When it comes to barbecue, often one restaurant

RESTAURANTS

will have the best sauce, while another has the best sides. At Brothers BBQ, it's a home run all around, with just the right balance of tangy to sweet in the sauce and beans and coleslaw good enough to buy extra for later. (Would you believe the founders of this award-winning barbecue joint are two brothers from England?) Brothers BBQ has five locations in the greater Denver metro area, and they also offer delivery. From the outside, this location just off 6th Avenue still looks a bit like the convenience store it once was, but inside, it's all chrome and modern, with table-and-barstool seating available.

STEUBEN'S ❺❸

523 E. 17th Ave., 303/830-1001, www.steubens.com
HOURS: Mon.-Thurs. 11 A.M.-11 P.M., Fri. 11 A.M.-midnight, Sat. 10 A.M.-midnight, Sun. 10 A.M.-11 P.M.

After successfully creating sophisticated contemporary food with Vesta Dipping Grill, owners Josh and Jen Wolkon went retro and opened Steuben's as an homage to 1950s' style and food. The menu at Steuben's is all comfort food: mac 'n' cheese, fried cheese, fried chicken with mashed potatoes and gravy, root beer floats, cheeseburgers, and hot dogs. Booth seating inside adds to the nostalgic feel, and the

RESTAURANT WEEK

Every year, Denver hosts a citywide "Restaurant Week," when over 200 participating restaurants offer multi-course dinners for two for $52.80—a "Mile-High Price" to match the city's elevation of 5,280 feet above sea level. (Single diners aren't left out; they get the meal for half-price at $26.40.) Go to www.denver.org to find out the dates for the next Restaurant Week, get a list of participating restaurants, and review the menus on offer. All restaurants still serve their regular menus during Restaurant Week. Reservations are strongly recommended.

patio on the side of the restaurant is modern and delightful. Easy curbside takeout is also available—and you might need it if you come for weekend brunch when lines stretch outside.

STRINGS ❺❺❺

1700 Humboldt St., 303/831-7310, www.stringsrestaurant.com
HOURS: Mon.-Fri. 11 A.M.-10 P.M., Sat. 5-10 P.M., Sun. 10 A.M.-3 P.M. and 5-9 P.M.

Long one of Denver's most beloved restaurants for the consistently excellent food and service, Strings does not disappoint. Strings was an Uptown restaurant before there was a Restaurant Row in Uptown. The menu here is upscale American, with entrees of lamb, sea bass, steak, burgers, and pasta for dinner and lunch. Strings attracts a well-to-do clientele, but there is no dress code and, as in other parts of town, casual works as well as fancy.

VINE STREET PUB & BREWERY ❸

1700 Vine St., 303/388-2337, www.mountainsunpub.com
HOURS: Mon. 4 P.M.-1 A.M., Tues.-Sun. 11 A.M.-10 P.M.

A spinoff of the popular Mountain Sun Pub & Brewery in Boulder, Vine Street opened as a neighborhood pub in Denver, where, surprisingly, there wasn't one already; it quickly became a fixture of the 17th Street Restaurant Row. Much like Mountain Sun, Vine Street offers a more "hippified" version of a pub—board games instead of TVs tuned to sports channels, and wholesome pub fare paired with award-winning beers and great service. Note that they do not accept credit cards.

ASIAN
BONES ❺❺

701 Grant St., 303/860-2929, www.bonesdenver.com
HOURS: Mon.-Fri. 11 A.M.-2 P.M., Daily 5-10 P.M.

Noodles. Asian. Fusion. That sums up what Bones is all about. What you think you know about these things will be enhanced by what you actually eat here. Certainly the ramen noodles will be a surprise if your only experience is with the store package variety, as these are cooked in lobster broth. But maybe plum-soy broth with the udon noodles is more to your liking. A farm-fresh poached egg can be added to any of the noodle bowls, too.

PARALLEL 17 ❷❸

1600 E. 17th Ave., 303/399-0988,
www.parallelseventeen.com
HOURS: Lunch Mon.-Fri. 11:30 A.M.-3 P.M.; dinner Sun.-Thurs. 3-10 P.M., Fri.-Sat. 3-11 P.M.; brunch Sat.-Sun. 10 A.M.-3 P.M.

Parallel 17 is a French-Vietnamese fusion restaurant with an ultra-cool vibe and popular bar. The food here is best enjoyed family-style, with several small plates shared among the table. Try the Hanoi curry or *pho*—with or without oxtail. In addition to its reputation for excellent modern Vietnamese food, Parallel 17 is known for its Vietnamese Coffeetini and other specialty cocktails.

BREAKFAST AND BRUNCH
DENVER BISCUIT COMPANY ❸

3237 E. Colfax Ave., 303/377-7900, www.denbisco.com
HOURS: Daily 8 A.M.-2 P.M.

What makes biscuits so darn good is that they can be turned into a breakfast, lunch, or dessert with a few simple toppings. The Denver Biscuit Company has it covered with the basic biscuits and gravy (platter, no less!) and strawberry shortcake biscuits; then it goes to the next level with over-the-top biscuit sandwiches, a biscuit cinnamon roll, and the requisite Southern side dishes for mopping up a selection of jams, butters, and honey, or eggs and grits.

JELLY ❸

600 E. 13th Ave., 303/831-6301,
http://eatmorejelly.com
HOURS: Daily 7 A.M.-3 P.M.

The name is misleading: There are plenty of typical breakfast and lunch items on the menu at Jelly that have nothing do with the fruity spread. In fact, it only shows up on toast or biscuits or as the center of a doughnut. The cute décor, booths, and counter seats make Jelly feel like a retro diner with simply tasty meals of pancake stacks, scrambles, hashes, and lots more.

CAFÉS AND TEAHOUSES
ST. MARK'S COFFEEHOUSE ❸

2019 E. 17th Ave., 303/322-8384,
www.stmarkscoffeehouse.com
HOURS: Daily 6:30 A.M.-midnight

The theme at St. Mark's is Venetian—from name to artwork—while the vibe is urban and original. St. Mark's offers Espresso Roma coffee from the San Francisco Bay Area and a selection of teas, tasty sandwiches, and too many yummy cookies, pastries, and desserts. An old garage door is yanked open on warm days, making the coffee shop feel even larger. With late hours and the Thin Man bar located right next door, St. Mark's can be a nice place to chill out before calling it a night.

CONTEMPORARY AND NEW AMERICAN
FRUITION ❷❸❸

1313 E. 6th Ave., 303/831-1962,
www.fruitionrestaurant.com
HOURS: Mon.-Sat. 5-10 P.M., Sun. 5-8 P.M.

If awards matter to you when choosing a restaurant, then look no further than Fruition, which garners local and national awards annually for best chef, best farm-to-table cuisine, traveler's choice, and many more. Foodies can't stop raving about Chef Alex Seidel's contemporary take on comfort food that emphasizes locally grown and seasonal ingredients. This small and cozy restaurant, where meals are paired with the perfect wine, is ideal for a special date night. In winter, there's fanciful chicken noodle soup; in summer, there are crisp, flavorful salads plus

Potager specializes in using locally-grown organic ingredients.

more extravagant entrées that include duck breast, pork belly, and pastas. Reservations are recommended.

MIZUNA ❸❸❸

225 E. 7th Ave., 303/832-4778, http://mizunadenver.com

HOURS: Tues.-Sat. 5-10 P.M., closed Sun. and Mon.

Mizuna is a must for anyone serious about food and gourmet dining. It's been voted Denver's number one restaurant by *Zagat* and chef-owner Frank Bonanno has received nods from many other publications. Bonanno is known for delectable lobster mac 'n' cheese, as well as artfully presented ostrich loin and beef tenderloin. The seasonal menu is changed monthly, and the service is as impeccable as the food, with servers somehow attending to every need, but not aggressively so. Mizuna has published its own cookbook, available on the website. Reservations are strongly

recommended, especially given the small size of the restaurant.

◖ POTAGER ❸❸❸

1109 Ogden St., 303/832-5788, www.potagerrestaurant.com

HOURS: Tues.-Thurs. 5:30-10 P.M., closed Sun. and Mon.

Potager was on the cutting edge of seasonal, locally grown ingredients long before those ideas became mainstream. Across the street from a launderette and a grocery store in the thick of the Capitol Hill neighborhood, Potager stands out as a simply elegant restaurant in the clatter of the city. There are tables out back, where the chef grows a few herbs and small vegetables, and inside, crisp white tablecloths stand out against the pock-marked concrete walls. The menu changes frequently to keep up with what is seasonally available; some examples include spinach and nettle soup in spring, and Colorado lamb and beef, fresh garden salads, and summer desserts with Colorado-grown peaches, rhubarb, strawberries, and more. No reservations are accepted, and the best time to come is early or on a weeknight. There is limited free parking behind the restaurant.

DESSERTS
THE CHURCH OF CUPCAKES ❸

1489 Steele St., Ste. C, 720/524-7770, http://churchofcupcakes.com

HOURS: Tues.-Fri. 11 A.M.-6:30 P.M., Sat. 10 A.M.-5 P.M., Sun. 11 A.M.-5 P.M.

Between Capitol Hill and City Park, The Church of Cupcakes (formerly Lovely Confections Bakery) has an emphasis not only on making moist and yummy cupcakes, but also on using organic and locally grown ingredients. It would be easy to plan your week around the available flavors that include five staples during the weekdays—vanilla, lemon, coconut, chocolate, and carrot, each with its own special frosting—and on weekends, it's time to be surprised by additional flavors and cupcake and frosting combinations.

D BAR DESSERTS ❸

1475 E. 17th Ave., 303/861-4710,
www.dbardesserts.com
HOURS: Sun.-Mon. 5-10 P.M., Tues.-Thurs.
11 A.M.-10 P.M., Fri.-Sat. 11 A.M.-midnight

When D Bar first opened up, people were drawn to the celebrity owner, Keeghan Gerhard, from *Food Network Challenge*. Gerhard, the booming-voiced host of the cooking competition show, opened D Bar with his wife, Lisa Bailey, who is also a pastry chef. Now people come for the food first, whether it's the crazy-good desserts, or the savory small(ish) plates. The space is about the size of a petit four, so the wait for a seat can be long at night. But it's always worth the wait when the "Southernfried Belgian" (fried chicken and waffles) or "Not Quite a Cobb" (salad with a twist) arrives. Do leave room for dessert because you do not want to miss the liquid-center chocolate cake (aka "Molten Cake Thingy Everybody Has...but simpler!") and other sugary delights.

LIK'S ICE CREAM ❸

2039 13th Ave., 303/321-2370, www.liksicecream.com
HOURS: Daily noon-10 P.M.

The location of Lik's on the corner of busy 13th Avenue does not excite me, but their freshly churned ice cream does. Like any food that you are accustomed to eating not-fresh—maybe berries, for example—once you've had freshly picked or made, it's hard to go back. These small-batch ice cream flavors are worth driving across town for in any season. And you'll need to come often to taste their many flavors—there are more than 15 banana variations alone!

THE SHOPPE ❸

3103 E. Colfax Ave., 303/322-3969,
www.theshoppedenver.com

HOURS: Tues.-Thurs. 9 A.M.-11 P.M., Fri.-Sat. 9 A.M.-2 A.M., Sun.-Mon. 11 A.M.-6 P.M.

The best or worst time for a cupcake, depending on your perspective, is late at night. The Shoppe has found its sweet-tooth niche by staying open late amongst the live music venues, bars, and restaurants of Colfax Avenue. Certainly The Shoppe attracts the young and hip because of their location and hours, but maybe also for their eccentric cupcake flavors, like "Shirley Temple" and "Root Beer Float." (Old favorites like red velvet and chocolate appeal to anyone and everyone.) They even offer cupcake delivery.

DINERS

PETE'S KITCHEN ❸

1962 E. Colfax Ave., 303/321-3139,
www.petesrestaurants.com

HOURS: Daily 24 hours

There are very few places open 24 hours in Denver, and Pete's Kitchen has 'em lined up out the door and waiting in any weather after the bars have closed and on weekends for breakfast. The food and ambience is classic diner with a Greek flair. Breakfast basics like eggs, pancakes, and hash browns are always available, as are gyros and souvlaki and burgers and burritos. Driving along East Colfax, look for the neon sign of a chubby chef flipping burgers.

◖ SAME CAFÉ ❸

2023 E. Colfax Ave., 720/530-6853,
www.soallmayeat.org

HOURS: Mon.-Sat. 11 A.M.-2 P.M.

The idea at SAME Café is simple: There are no prices, but the food is not free. Customers are expected to pay what they can, or what they feel their meal is worth, by dropping cash in a can by the door. The goal here is in the name: So All May Eat (SAME). And not eat just any food, but food made from fresh, organic ingredients. The menu changes daily, based on the availability of what's in season, but it generally includes soups, salads, pizzas, and a selection of desserts. If people cannot afford to pay anything for their meal, they are asked to do work at the restaurant as payment. Inside and outside seating is available at about 10 tables. The ambience is as casual and laidback as its diners, who can chat with the friendly owners when it is slow.

ITALIAN

FAT SULLY'S ❺❺

3237 E. Colfax Ave., 303/333-4440,
www.fatsullyspizza.com
HOURS: Daily 11 A.M.-2 A.M.

It can be a bit confusing to have two different restaurants sharing the same space in a bar. Fat Sully's is in the Atomic Cowboy, and serves New York-style pizza where the Denver Biscuit Company also makes delectable biscuit dishes. The idea here is simple pizza: Pick your sauce, red or white? Pick your toppings, regular or premium? Pick your size, slice or pie? Delivery is also available.

IL POSTO ❺❺❺

2011 E. 17th Ave., 303/394-0100,
www.ilpostodenver.com
HOURS: Lunch Mon.-Fri. 11 A.M.-2 P.M.; dinner Sun.-Thurs. 5-10:30 P.M., Fri.-Sat. 5-11 P.M.

Discriminating diners quickly became regulars at Il Posto shortly after it opened. The Italian food here is made in part with organic produce from Colorado farms and the menu changes daily. Guests appreciate that some of the servers have sommelier status and can offer wine pairings with any dish. Chef-owner Andrea Frizzi can be seen working in the open kitchen or out in the dining room greeting customers at their tables. Open a bit later than many Denver restaurants, Il Posto offers the chance for a late-night supper. Reservations are recommended.

LUCA D'ITALIA ❺❺❺

711 Grant St., 303/832-9357, www.lucadenver.com

HOURS: Tues.-Sat. 5-10 P.M., closed Sun. and Mon.

With Luca D'Italia, it's another success for chef-owner Frank Bonanno of Denver's spectacular Mizuna. Named after Bonanno's son, Luca has the same attention to detail and fantastic service as Mizuna. But the menu here is strictly Italian with a personal touch: handmade pastas, housemade cured meats, hand-packed sausages, mozzarella made in-house, and fresh, locally grown ingredients in every dish. Luca is at least twice the size of Bonanno's Mizuna just around the corner, but the crisp white tablecloths on perfectly square tables are identical. The richly colored walls are adorned with simple but personal oil paintings that give the restaurant a homey touch. The servers are very knowledgeable about the wine and food and how best to pair them. Reservations are recommended.

LATIN AMERICAN

BENNY'S RESTAURANT AND TEQUILA BAR ❺

301 E. 7th Ave., 303/894-0788,
www.bennysrestaurant.com
HOURS: Mon.-Thurs. 11 A.M.-10 P.M., Fri. 11 A.M.-11 P.M., Sat. 9 A.M.-11 P.M., Sun. 9 A.M.-10 P.M.

For Tex-Mex–style food, you cannot go wrong with Benny's, a Capitol Hill institution. The menu here is combination plates of enchiladas, tacos, chile rellenos, and smothered burritos. The place gets packed on weekend nights and the bar area can get loud and rowdy with TVs turned up. For a quieter atmosphere, aim for the dining room or patio.

▣ PINCHE TACOS ❺

1514 York St., 720/475-1337, www.pinchetacos.com
HOURS: Mon. 3-10 P.M., Tues.-Sat. 11 A.M.-10 P.M., Sun. 11 A.M.-9 P.M.

One of the city's most popular food trucks has become a favorite restaurant, too, with street food on the menu. Order tacos one at a time or like donuts—by the dozen—depending on your favorite. Just be sure to order *quesa a la plancha, rajas con crema y maiz,* and the *carnitas,* as well. The restaurant also has a dizzying selection of tequilas. Desserts here are part of the fun—churros dipped in chocolate or a frozen ice cream taco. One tip: Because the word *pinche* translates to both something inoffensive (kitchen help) and something offensive (Shhh!), the name does not appear on the business at all...yet strangely remains plastered across the food truck seen in public parks. Come at off-times to avoid crowds and a long wait for a table.

TAKEOUT
MARCZYK FINE FOODS 🟢
770 E. 17th Ave., 303/894-9499,
www.marczykfinefoods.com
HOURS: Mon.-Sat. 8 A.M.-8 P.M., Sun. 10 A.M.-6 P.M.

Walk into Marczyk Fine Foods and it's likely one of the owners will greet you and offer to help you find whatever you need. This boutique grocery store and deli, located in the Uptown neighborhood between downtown and Capitol Hill, is all about a family-friendly atmosphere. Marczyk is known for featuring products—from beef to fruit—from Colorado companies, and for making killer take-out food and sandwiches on request. There is limited outdoor seating available and a small wine store as well. In the summer, Niman Ranch burgers are grilled outside every Friday; in the fall, Marczyk hosts Denver's only urban pig roast. In 2011, a second location of Marczyk Fine Foods was opened at 5100 E. Colfax Ave., 303/243-3355, and they maintain the same standards and delicious selection of foods.

VEGETARIAN
CITY, O' CITY 🟢🟢
210 E. 13th Ave., 303/318-9844,
www.cityocitydenver.com
HOURS: Daily 7 A.M.-2 A.M.

Denver's two best known vegetarian restaurants have the same owner, but different names and menus. City, O' City is a pizza place, a coffee shop, a sandwich shop, and a bar all in one, where any eating and drinking needs throughout the day and into the night can be met. Its central location on the southern edge of the Capitol Hill neighborhood makes it walking distance from downtown and the Golden Triangle, and it attracts everyone, from lawmakers from the state capitol a block away to tattooed and pierced hipsters who call the neighborhood home.

🄲 WATERCOURSE FOODS 🟢🟢
837 E. 17th Ave., 303/832-7313,
www.watercoursefoods.com
HOURS: Mon.-Thurs. 11 A.M.-10 P.M., Fri.-Sun. 8 A.M.-10 P.M.

Since moving to a bigger and brighter space, Denver's premier vegetarian restaurant, WaterCourse Foods, has become even more popular. There's now a bar, patio seating, and plenty of tables inside, so the wait for a table isn't too long. The all-day menu at WaterCourse specializes in creative ways to eat tofu, salad, tempeh, pasta, and, of course, vegetables. Try the tamales for breakfast or dinner and design your own salad. There's also a wine and beer list, a variety of teas, and fresh smoothies.

RESTAURANTS

Highlands   Map 5

AMERICAN

(C) BANG $$

3472 W. 32nd Ave., 303/455-1117,
www.bangdenver.com
HOURS: Tues.-Fri. 11 A.M.-9 P.M., Sat. 10 A.M.-9 P.M.,
closed Sun. and Mon.

Neighborhood favorite Bang is the kind of place where owners are on a first-name basis with their regulars, but still attract new customers all the time for their dependable, simple food, such as meatloaf and mashed potatoes, a shrimp po'boy, or a crisp salad. Their gumbo was featured on the Food Network's *Diner's, Drive-In's and Dives* in 2011. Located in an old house in Highland Square, Bang put its kitchen on the street side, and diners walk through a narrow corridor to get into the dining room and patio around back. Parts of the menu change seasonally, but don't miss the gingerbread with whipped cream for dessert and, when available, the red velvet cake or coconut cream pie.

BIG HOSS BBQ $$

3961 Tennyson St., 720/855-3061,
www.bighossbarbq.com
HOURS: Daily 11 A.M.-11 P.M.

Situated on Tennyson St. in the Highlands neighborhood (or, more specifically, the Berkeley section of the Highlands neighborhood), Big Hoss BBQ always has at least a few tables full of people chowing down on tangy barbeque sandwiches and ribs. Side dishes are exactly right, with cheesy corn, Grandma's slaw, and baked beans. There is even a kids' menu to make this a family place. The sauce that started it all is sold at Whole Foods Markets as well as here at the restaurant.

HIGHLANDS GARDEN CAFÉ $$$

3927 W. 32nd Ave., 303/458-5920,
www.highlandsgardencafe.com
HOURS: Tues.-Sat. 11 A.M.-2 P.M. and 5-9 P.M.

Highlands Garden Café, located just up the street from Highlands Square in two joined Victorian homes, is a great place for a special dinner. The lovely patio on the side of one house, with shade trees, herbs, and blooming flowers, is perfect in summer. Because the café is in two old houses, dining here can be very private depending on which room you are seated in. The extensive menu includes seafood, lamb, duck, chicken, beef, and more.

LOU'S FOOD BAR $$

1851 W. 38th Ave., 303/458-0336,
www.lousfoodbar.com
HOURS: Mon.-Thurs. 11 A.M.-10 P.M., Fri. 11 A.M.-11 P.M.,
Sat.-Sun. 10 A.M.-11 P.M.

Chef Frank Bonnano, known in Denver for Mizuna and Luca D'Italia, has opened Lou's with "American food with a French twist" in the Highlands neighborhood. Though one does not typically think of Paris when gobbling up fried chicken and whipped potatoes, the housemade sausages don't seem out of line with a picnic lunch in the French countryside. The name in neon along busy 38th Avenue tells diners that this a place to get a bite to eat, not plan a romantic night out. You can't go wrong for lunch or dinner at Lou's.

MASTERPIECE DELICATESSEN $

1575 Central St., 303/561-3345,
www.masterpiecedeli.com
HOURS: Mon.-Fri. 8 A.M.-8 P.M., Sat.-Sun. 9 A.M.-8 P.M.

A sandwich seems so simple to make, but there is more skill required to make it a meal worth having repeatedly. Denver restaurant veterans and owners of Masterpiece Delicatessen Steve

RESTAURANTS

Lou's Food Bar is all about sophisticated comfort food.

Allee and Justin Brunson definitely have the skill to make some of the best sandwiches in Denver. Just steps from the pedestrian bridge that links 16th Street to the Lower Highlands (or Highlands) neighborhood, Masterpiece Delicatessen was an instant hit with locals who keep coming back. The simple salad and sandwich menu has some dynamite standouts, like the Cubano sandwich and the vegetarian sandwich with manchego cheese. Start the day here with a sandwich on a bagel and a cup of coffee. The indoor seating is limited, and outdoor seating is best in the late afternoon, after the sun has shifted behind the building. The deli is good for takeout and delivery, too.

PARK BURGER ❶

2643 W. 32nd Ave., 303/862-8461,
http://parkburger.com
HOURS: Sun.-Thurs. 11 A.M.-9 P.M., Fri.-Sat. 11 A.M.-10 P.M.

Craving a basic meal? Look no further than Park Burger for a burger, hot dog, and fries. Of course, what makes Park Burger worth a stop is the fact that the burgers are not that basic. Along with never-frozen beef burgers, there is a turkey burger, veggie burger, and buffalo burger; turn one of those into a specialty burger with cheese, onions, egg, guacamole, and more. Then wash it all down with a milkshake, beer, wine, or cocktail. There are two Park Burger locations in Denver.

BREWPUBS
AMATO'S ALE HOUSE ❶❶

2501 16th St., 303/433-9734,
http://alehousedenver.com
HOURS: Sun.-Thurs. 11 A.M.-midnight, Fri.-Sat. 11 A.M.-1 A.M.

In what was for decades a garden statuary shop, there is now Amato's Ale House, one of the Breckenridge Brewery restaurants. (Amato's was the name of the previous shop.) With over 42 craft beers on tap that change daily, many from Colorado, Amato's has developed a steady stream of regulars since opening in 2010. The menu consists of salads, burgers, and generous appetizers that can fill you up before the entrée arrives. Parking is a challenge here, so take advantage of the restaurant's location next to the 16th Street pedestrian and bicycle bridge and walk or ride over from downtown.

CAFÉS AND TEAHOUSES
BUCHI CAFÉ CUBANO $

2651 W. 38th Ave., 303/458-1328,
www.buchicafecubano.com
HOURS: Mon.-Wed. 8 A.M.-6 P.M., Thurs.-Sun.
8 A.M.-9 P.M.

Cuban coffee has its followers, and they come faithfully to Buchi Café Cubano in the Sunnyside neighborhood of Highlands. Owner Emmet Barr is a native of Key West, Florida, where he grew up with traditional Cuban coffee shops almost within sight of Cuba itself. He's transplanted those tastes to the Mile-High City, and locals dine on tostone, empanadas, and panini-pressed sandwiches while sipping their *café con leche*.

COMMON GROUNDS COFFEEHOUSE $

3484 W. 32nd Ave., 303/458-5248,
www.commongroundscoffeehouse.com
HOURS: Mon.-Fri. 6:30 A.M.-10 P.M., Sat.-Sun.
6:30 A.M.-11 P.M.

In the heart of Highlands Square, Common Grounds is a neighborhood institution for people to chat or sit quietly and read while sipping a cup of hot coffee. With large tables set up in a few rooms, Common Grounds makes for a good local meeting place. They offer pastries, sandwiches, and salads, as well as wine and beer. There is a second location in LoDo (1550 Wazee St., 303/296-9248); both locations have free Wi-Fi. A bulletin board in the back of the coffeehouse holds notices about local events and property for rent or sale.

TENN. ST. COFFEE $

4418 Tennyson St., 303/455-0279,
www.tennstreetcoffee.com
HOURS: Mon. 6:30 A.M.-6 P.M., Tues.-Fri.
6:30 A.M.-9 P.M., Sat. 7 A.M.-9 P.M., Sun. 7 A.M.-6 P.M.

Right along buzzing Tennyson Street is sweet little Tenn. St. Coffee, appealing to those with some budget leisure time on their hands. The shop is made up of two rooms—one with small tables where Dazbog coffee and quick bites are on offer (Bluepoint Bakery pastries, Udi's Deli sandwiches, fresh smoothies), the other with stacks of used books to browse or purchase while listening to the relaxing sounds of a local musician. When the weather is just right, grab a seat on the patio out front.

WOODEN SPOON CAFÉ & BAKERY $

2418 W. 32nd Ave, 303/999-0327,
www.woodenspoondenver.com
HOURS: Tues.-Fri. 7 A.M.-2 P.M., Sat.-Sun. 8 A.M.-2 P.M.

After being open for about two seconds, the Wooden Spoon became a neighborhood favorite for their scrumptious breakfast pastries (apple tarts, blueberry scones, croissants, and more) and hearty sandwiches. Located in a historic building filled with other restaurants along this block, the Wooden Spoon feels like a European shop. Or perhaps it's the strict rules on no screens—no laptops or phones allowed—that make it feel old-fashioned, as people talk and read actual newspapers and books here.

CONTEMPORARY
CORAL ROOM $$$

3489 W. 32nd Ave., 303/433-2535,
www.coralroom.com
HOURS: Mon.-Thurs. 9 A.M.-2 P.M. and 4-10 P.M., Fri.-Sat. 9 A.M.-2 P.M. and 4-10:30 P.M., Sun. 9 A.M.-2:30 P.M. and 4-9:30 P.M.

The Coral Room's location in a strip mall within Highlands Square can be deceiving, but this little restaurant makes simple, elegant

CAFFEINE AND BLOG BUZZ

Coffee and blogs seem like a match made in heaven, so it's no surprise that one caffeine-lover started www.milehighbuzz. com, where readers can find opinions on seemingly every independently owned coffeehouse in Denver, and even visit the coffeehouse "cemetery" to find out who is no longer buzzing. Visitors can view photos of coffeehouses, read descriptions of what is served, and, of course, find out about the quality of the coffee and who has free Wi-Fi.

contemporary Asian fusion dishes full of flavor. A table inside or out front is great for people-watching at night. Bargain-hunting families take note that kids 10 and under eat free from the children's brunch menu. Reservations are recommended for dinner; the small space can fill up fast, especially on weekends. The service is quick and friendly and the vibe is sophisticated—just like the menu.

DUO RESTAURANT ❸❸❸

2413 W. 32nd Ave., 303/477-4141, www.duodenver.com

HOURS: Mon.-Sat. 5-10 P.M., Sun. 5-9 P.M., Sat.-Sun. 10 A.M.-2 P.M.

As the Highlands neighborhood has exploded in popularity, niche neighborhoods have sprung up here and there with great restaurants and boutiques. Duo Restaurant at 32nd Avenue and Zuni Street has helped to establish this intersection as a destination. The owners are up front to greet diners, and the open kitchen offers a glimpse of the chefs hard at work on seasonal dishes for dinner or brunch. Duo is on the ground floor of a large historic building that has been renovated and filled with shops and restaurants. Pick a seat next to one of the large windows and watch the people stroll by, or sit at one of the tables along the exposed brick walls for a more intimate evening.

LINGER ❸❸

2030 W. 30th Ave., 303/993-3120, www.lingerdenver.com

HOURS: Lunch Tues.-Fri. 11:30 A.M.-2:30 P.M., happy hour Tues.-Fri. 5-6:30 P.M., dinner Tues.-Sat. 5:30-10 P.M.

Linger is yet another business that has found a way to turn a piece of the historic Olinger mortuary into a hot spot. This time it's a multi-level restaurant in the mortuary's former hearse garage. In case you haven't noticed, the name is Linger (dropped the O). Chef Justin Cucci has created a menu of eclectic world tastes. Translation: Come here with a group of friends and order lots of small plates to sample dishes evocative of Asia, Africa, the Middle East, America, Europe, and Eurasia. The drink menu is nearly as extensive, with beers from as far as China and Missouri, wines from Colorado and Austria, and cocktails with curious names like "Corpse Reviver." There is even a kids' menu (American-style with chicken tenders and mac 'n' cheese). Reservations are a must since there can be a line down the block *before* Linger even opens for dinner.

ROOT DOWN ❸❸

1600 W. 33rd Ave., 303/993-4200, www.rootdowndenver.com

HOURS: Mon.-Thurs. 5-10 P.M., Fri.-Sat. 5-11 P.M., Sun. 5-9 P.M., Sat.-Sun. 10 A.M.-2:30 P.M.

Playing off the theme of the building's former incarnation as a car repair garage, Root Down staffers don mechanics shirts and some of the old signs (like one reading "Tires") remain. The theme of the food is global, inspired by local ingredients. Above all, Root Down strives to please the customer with options to make some entrees gluten-free or vegan, and a promise that a majority of the ingredients are organic. My personal fave here is the veggie burger sliders with scrumptious sweet potato fries on the side. Try to get a seat on the patio that overlooks downtown on the east side of the restaurant.

VITA $$$

1575 Boulder St., 303/477-4600, www.vitadenver.com

HOURS: Lunch Mon.-Fri. 11 A.M.-3 P.M.; dinner Sun. 4-10 P.M., Mon.-Thurs. 3-10 P.M., Fri. 3-11 P.M., Sat. 4-11 P.M.; brunch Sat.-Sun. 10 A.M.-2 P.M.

A former mortuary in the über-hip eastern Highlands neighborhood (also called LoHi, HiDo, and East Highlands) is now home to a handful of restaurants, including Vita in the mortuary's former florist shop. The menu at Vita is modern American, with dishes that burst with flavor and creativity. A rooftop patio is an added bonus for bar seating and dining on small plates.

DESSERTS

HAPPY CAKES $

3434 W. 32nd Ave., 303/477-3556, www.happycakesdenver.com

HOURS: Mon.-Sat. 10 A.M.-6 P.M., closed Sun.

There's just room for cupcakes and one or two eager customers in tiny Happy Cakes in Highlands Square. Not only is it a petite place, they sell itty-bitty gourmet cupcakes in addition to regular and jumbo size. Gluten-free cupcakes are available in limited flavors daily, and there is a vegan flavor on Fridays. The main cupcake flavors rotate daily, so check their website for the line-up and make a date to try the French Toast on Wednesday, the Cherry Limeade on Friday, or the Dirt Cake on Saturday. On Tuesdays, the cupcakes are a bargain $2.

LITTLE MAN ICE CREAM $

2620 16th St., 303/455-3811, www.littlemanicecream.com

HOURS: Daily 11 A.M.-midnight

Seriously, you would think people had never tasted ice cream before this shop came along. Built on the site of the Olinger Mortuary in the Lower Highlands neighborhood, Little Man

There are many creative cupcake flavors at Happy Cakes bakeshop.

© LAURA REYNOLDS

© MINDY SINK

Little Man Ice Cream has lines down the block in the summer.

Ice Cream is a giant replica of a silver milk can, and named after its founders nickname. People gaze at the Denver skyline as they wait in the line that stretches up the block all summer. Little Man Ice Cream runs out of the favorite flavors early every day, but cross your fingers for the salted Oreo because it is the best. There are also gelato flavors and milkshakes.

FRENCH
AXIOS ❶❸
3901 Tennyson St., 720/328-2225,
http://axiosdenver.com
HOURS: Mon.-Thurs. 11 A.M.-9 P.M., Fri. 11 A.M.-10 P.M., Sat. 10 A.M.-10 P.M., Sun. 10 A.M.-9 P.M.
In 2011, Axios opened in a space that was previously a French bistro and, before that, a natural foods store. The Greek menu was a welcome change in the neighborhood, with the restaurant's friendly service and affordable menu items. For lunch and dinner, stick to the Greek

basics, which are all delicious. The feta cheese omelet on the brunch menu took me back to a childhood trip to a tiny Greek island, but there are also pancakes and French toast for those in the mood for a more traditional meal in the morning.

Z CUISINE ❶❸
2245 W. 30th Ave., 303/477-1111,
www.zcuisineonline.com
HOURS: Wed.-Sat. 5-10 P.M., closed Sun.-Tues.
On a small, residential side street in the eastern part of the Highlands neighborhood is the popular French bistro Z Cuisine. Each day, a chalkboard displays the authentic French menu chef-owner Patrick DuPays has created using fresh, seasonal ingredients from local growers. The cramped space adds to the ambience, as you hear people at neighboring tables chatter in French and English. Two doors down, Dupays also has a wine bar that offers a smaller menu selection.

ITALIAN
PARISI ITALIAN MARKET & DELI ❶❸
4401 Tennyson St., 303/561-0234,
www.parisidenver.com
HOURS: Mon.-Thurs. 11 A.M.-9 P.M., Fri.-Sat. 11 A.M.-9 P.M., closed Sun.
Parisi is a modern take on a traditional neighborhood pizzeria and market, with wonderful sandwiches, wood-oven baked pizzas, and salads for lunch or dinner. This is casual dining where customers line up to place their order, then take their number to a table. While waiting for their food, they can browse the Italian market, deli, gelato, and other pastry desserts for something to take home. Downstairs is **Parisi's Firenze a Tavola** (Florence at Your Table, 303/561-0234), a more formal restaurant with a full bar that is perfect for a private party or special date night. The downstairs is only open Wednesday–Saturday, 5:30–10 P.M.

RESTAURANTS

PASQUINI'S ❶❸

2400 W. 32nd Ave., 303/477-4900,
www.pasquinis.com

HOURS: Sun.-Thurs. 11 A.M.-11 P.M., Fri.-Sat. 11 A.M.-
midnight

With a distinctive, vintage neon sign blazing above the front door on the corner of 32nd Avenue and Zuni Street in the Highlands, Pasquini's anchors the busy intersection of restaurants here. It's a family-friendly atmosphere: All kids are given pizza dough to play with while they wait for their food, and on Tuesday night, there's free pizza for kids and very affordable wines—under $12—for their harried parents. The menu includes calzones, big salads, pasta, and pizzettas. Takeout and delivery are available. Check their website often for coupons.

PIZZA PUBLIC ❸

3109 N. Federal Blvd., 720/524-8885,
www.thepizzapublic.com

HOURS: Sun.-Thurs. 11 A.M.-10 P.M., Fri.-Sat. 11 A.M.-2 A.M.

Once you get past the not-so-appealing exterior of Pizza Public, you'll be glad you went inside. Opened in 2012, Pizza Public offers gourmet pizzas with names to honor its neighborhood. Try "The Highland" or "The Tejon" or "The Federal," all of which reference a street or the neighborhood here. Pizzas can also be made gluten-free.

SPUNTINO ❸

2639 W. 32nd Ave., 303/433-0949,
www.spuntinodenver.com

HOURS: Mon. 11 A.M.-3 P.M., Tues.-Thurs. 11 A.M.-9 P.M.,
Fri.-Sat. 11 A.M.-10 P.M., Sun. 10 A.M.-8 P.M.

In a short time, this space has evolved from an ice cream shop (The Red Trolley Cake and Cone) to an Italian eatery with gelato to an Italian eatery with gelato, but with a new chef and a different menu. And in no time at all, Sputino has become the go-to lunch spot with neighborhood friends. Perfect sandwiches and

salads with a gelato to share (the chocolate salted caramel is the remaining bit from Red Trolley) or a gourmet Popsicle on a hot day. The emphasis is not so much on Italian as it is on impeccably made food with fresh ingredients in ideal portions.

TRATTORIA STELLA ❶❸

3470 W. 32nd Ave., 303/458-1128,
http://trattoriastella.squarespace.com

HOURS: Mon., Wed.-Sat. 11 A.M.-2 P.M. and 5-10 P.M.,
Sun. 10 A.M.-2 P.M. and 5-9 P.M., closed Tues.

In a snug Victorian home in the hub of Highlands Square is the darling Trattoria Stella. The restaurant inside has just a handful of tables, but also a large outdoor patio that is covered and heated in cold months. In warm weather, this is the best patio in the Highlands for enjoying a weekend brunch of a big frittata or cheesy scrambled eggs. The menu is Italian with Mediterranean influences, and each dish is rich and filling. Trattoria Stella is open for happy hour 2–5 P.M. on Monday and on Wednesday through Saturday. A second location is in the Capitol Hill area (3201 E. Colfax Ave., 303/320-8635).

LATIN AMERICAN

CAFE BRAZIL ❶❸

4408 Lowell Blvd., 303/480-1877,
www.cafebrazildenver.com

HOURS: Tues.-Sat. 5-10 P.M.

Off the beaten path of Highlands hot spots, Cafe Brazil remains a perennial favorite for their South American fare. With orange walls and blue tablecloths, it has a playful and casual feel. My personal favorites here include *palmito* (hearts of palm in a white wine cream sauce) and the Feijoada Completa, a Brazilian black bean stew with fried bananas, collard greens, sausages, and oranges. Housemade desserts change daily. Reservations are recommended.

LOS CARBONCITOS 🄢

3757 Pecos St., 303/458-0880,
www.loscarboncitos.com
HOURS: Sun.-Wed. 9 A.M.-11 P.M., Thurs.-Sat.
9 A.M.-1:30 A.M.

As someone who prefers Tex-Mex over true Mexican, I must defer to the many people in Denver who just rave about Los Carboncitos. According to my sources, the tongue at Los Carboncitos is amazing. They also rave about the *carboncitos* and the huaraches. And consider the orange flames painted on the building's exterior to be a warning: The hot salsa is *extremely* hot. The chips are served with a quartet of salsas that are fun to sample and pick a favorite.

PATZCUARO'S 🄢

2616 W. 32nd Ave., 303/455-4389,
www.patzcuaros.com
HOURS: Daily 11 A.M.-9 P.M.

As Denver's Highlands neighborhood has changed, it has lost some of the Mexican restaurants that filled the storefronts for years. But Patzcuaro's has held its ground and remains a favorite for locals still craving pork smothered with green chile, and platters of enchiladas or burritos for less than $10. Menudo is served on weekends only. The favorite drink here is a *liquado*, which is a very sweet fruit juice loved by adults and children.

PAXIA 🄢🄢

4001 Tejon St., 720/583-6860, www.paxiadenver.com
HOURS: Sun.-Thurs. 11 A.M.-10 P.M., Fri.-Sat. 11 A.M.-midnight

From the owners of the neighborhood favorite Los Carboncitos comes Paxia, with a spiffier restaurant and menu. Unlike a plate of small tacos at Los Carboncitos, an appetizer of a trio of tamales can fill up one person before the entrée arrives. Some of the dishes here come with a story about their connection to Mexico, from where the chefs/owners hail. For example, the

Chiles en Nogada got its name from nuns who served it to a Mexican emperor. Who knew? Since opening in 2011, Paxia has built a loyal customer base of locals who like to walk over for lunch or dinner.

TAMALES BY LA CASITA 🄢

3561 Tejon St., 303/477-2899,
www.tamalesbylacasita.net
HOURS: Mon.-Fri. 7 A.M.-7 P.M., Sat. 9 A.M.-7 P.M., closed Sun.

Long considered home of Denver's best tamales, La Casita has both dine-in and takeout. But even if you've never set foot in this informal café, it's possible you've eaten a La Casita tamale—they supply several restaurants and vendors around town with their green chile and cheese or red chile pork tamales. This is a great takeout place for a very inexpensive, spicy meal—just over $1 for a single tamale—and service is ridiculously fast. La Casita is busiest in the morning; note that they close just when most people are heading out for dinner.

SEAFOOD

HIGHLAND PACIFIC 🄢🄢

3934 W. 32nd Ave., 303/477-6644,
www.highlandpacific.net
HOURS: Mon.-Fri. 11 A.M.-10 P.M., Sat.-Sun. 5 P.M.-1 A.M.

Up the street from the cluster of shops and restaurants in Highlands Square is a small, more sedate business strip that includes Highland Pacific. Owned by a neighborhood family, Highland Pacific attracts the locals with its cool, simple, and clean atmosphere. The specialty is fresh seafood—try the shrimp and grits or sea scallops—but the non-seafood fare is also very good. Don't miss the carrot fritters as a healthy appetizer. There is live, mellow acoustic music on Wednesday, Friday, and Saturday evenings starting at 9:30 P.M.

RESTAURANTS

THAI

SWING THAI $$

4370 Tennyson St., 303/477-1994, www.swingthai.com

HOURS: Sun.-Thurs. 11 A.M.-9 P.M., Fri.-Sat. 11 A.M.-10 P.M.

Denver has a fair amount of Thai restaurants to choose from, but Swing Thai stands out for their dependably good food, appealing decor, and fast service. This location at 44th and Tennyson Streets is one of their larger locations in Denver, with a bar, banquette, and tables inside, as well as a patio out back. In an effort to be more health-conscious, Swing Thai offers gluten-free and vegan menu items, as well as all-natural beef and chicken and organic tofu. Takeout and delivery are available.

THAI BASIL $$

3301 W. 38th Ave., 303/433-2888, www.thaibasil.co

HOURS: Mon.-Thurs. 11 A.M.-10 P.M., Fri.-Sat. 11 A.M.-10:30 P.M., Sun. 4:30-10 P.M.

Thai Basil is an Asian fusion restaurant, with an emphasis on Thai specialties. The Highlands location in a former florist shop is one of six in the Denver metro area. The decor is heavy wooden chairs and Bali-esque touches, putting diners in the mood for lemongrass chicken, Vietnamese slaw, crispy duck with peanut sauce, and Thai curry lime beef. The prices are very reasonable for the portions. Takeout and delivery are also available.

Washington Park and Cherry Creek   Map 6

AMERICAN

ASSIGNMENTS RESTAURANT $$

675 S. Broadway, 303/778-6625, www.artinstitutes.edu/denver

HOURS: Mon.-Fri. 11:30 A.M.-1:30 P.M. and Tues.-Fri. 6-9 P.M.

Hungry for homework? If you are willing to take a chance with pretty much every aspect of dining out, then try Assignments. The name is literal: The restaurant is affiliated with the International Culinary School at the Art Institute of Colorado, and it is essentially run by the students, who are practicing their homework. The prices are reasonable and the meals are usually tasty—and this is a place where your feedback is truly wanted. Call ahead to find out when the final-exam formal dinners are scheduled and make a reservation.

CHERRY CRICKET $$

2641 E. 2nd Ave., 303/322-7666, www.cherrycricket.com

HOURS: Daily 11 A.M.-2 A.M.

Before the Cherry Creek neighborhood was synonymous with all things swanky, its biggest retailer was the Sears store and it had neighborhood bars like the Cherry Cricket. What people like about the Cherry Cricket is that it hasn't changed much, if at all, with the rest of the neighborhood. Year after year, this is the place to go in Denver for a green chile burger—or any burger. They also serve Mexican food, sandwiches, and salads. There is free parking in the lot behind the building.

ELWAY'S $$$

2500 E. 1st Ave., 303/399-5353, www.elways.com

HOURS: Mon.-Thurs. 11 A.M.-10 P.M., Fri.-Sat. 11 A.M.-11 P.M., Sun. 11 A.M.-9 P.M.

A former Super Bowl–winning quarterback for the Denver Broncos, John Elway is one of Denver's biggest celebrities. For years he put his name on car dealerships, but he has now switched to restaurants. Elway's is a brightly lit, modern steak house with lots of windows and a piano bar that offers seafood, steak, and a few surprises, like tacos for an appetizer and s'mores for dessert. Certainly the restaurant draws a lot of sports fans hoping for a glimpse of Elway himself as well as other celebrities. A second

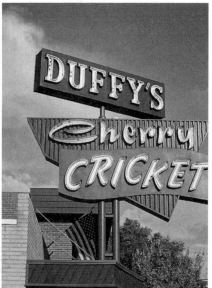

© MINDY SINK

Cherry Cricket is a local favorite for green chile burgers.

location is downtown at the Ritz-Carlton Hotel (1881 Curtis St., 303/312-3107).

SECOND HOME KITCHEN + BAR ❸❸❸

150 Clayton Ln., 303/253-3000,
www.secondhomedenver.com

HOURS: Daily 6:30 A.M.–11 P.M.

The JW Marriott in Cherry Creek North has a surprise inside, just past the lobby—it's a restaurant with dependably delicious food all day long. Personally, I have found this to be a great spot for the whole family with a big enough menu to please everyone. There are brick oven pizzas, burgers, pasta, and much more. The pajama brunch on weekends is fun for the kids because they can wear their pj's to the restaurant (and if they are eight or under and wearing their pj's, they eat for free, too!). The outdoor patio with a fire pit is a pleasant place for drinks and appetizers in winter or summer.

ASIAN
IZAKAYA DEN ❸❸

1518 S. Pearl St., 303/777-0691, www.izakayaden.net

HOURS: Lunch Sat.–Sun. 11:30 A.M.–2:30 P.M.; dinner Tues.–Thurs. 5–10 P.M., Fri.–Sat. 5–11 P.M., Sun. 5–10 P.M.

An offshoot of Sushi Den, one of the most well-established sushi restaurants in Denver, comes in the form of Izakaya Den. Certainly this serene restaurant benefits from the overflow crowd at Sushi Den across the street, but Izakaya Den has been gaining a reputation of its own for its delicate and flavorful small plates. In addition to sushi and sashimi, Izakaya has a Japanese-Mediterranean fusion tapas menu featuring combinations like Kobe beef with edamame and watermelon.

LITTLE OLLIE'S ❸

2364 E. 3rd Ave., 303/316-8888,
http://littleolliescherrycreek.com

HOURS: Mon.–Thurs. 11 A.M.–9:30 P.M., Fri. 11 A.M.–10 P.M., Sat. 11:30 A.M.–10 P.M., Sun. 11:30 A.M.–9:30 P.M.

On the fringe of Cherry Creek North is Little Ollie's, which offers Chinese food in a bright and comfortable space. Windows open to the wraparound patio in good weather, and patio seating is also available in colder months, when it is covered and heated. The miso soup and kung pao chicken keep regulars coming back for more. Only on-street parking is available and it can be hard to find near the restaurant, but there is delivery in the evenings.

SUSHI DEN ❸❸❸

1487 S. Pearl St., 303/777-0826, www.sushiden.net

HOURS: Mon.–Thurs. 11:30 A.M.–2:30 P.M. and 4:45–10:30 P.M., Fri. 11:30 A.M.–2:30 P.M. and 4:45 P.M.–midnight, Sat. 4:30 P.M.–midnight, Sun. 5–10:30 P.M.

Sushi Den has a consistently long wait, but no one is complaining—it's see and be seen here among a young, good-looking clientele in the cramped waiting area and bar. Pull up a chair to watch and listen as the sushi chefs make their beautiful creations, or grab a table and start

RESTAURANTS

RESTAURANTS

© STEVE CRECELIUS

Steak and lamb are on the menu at Elway's.

ordering sushi or another of the house specialties. Then sink your teeth into what many consider to be the city's best sushi. Chefs here will also take custom orders.

SUSHI TAZU ❸❸❸
300 Fillmore St., Ste. G, 303/320-1672, www.denver-sushi.net
HOURS: Mon.-Thurs. 11:30 A.M.-2:30 P.M. and 4:30-10 P.M., Fri.-Sat. 11:30 A.M.-2:30 P.M. and 4:30-11 P.M., Sun. noon-10 P.M.

This Japanese restaurant offers daily specials along with an extensive menu of fresh sushi and cooked entrées. Sushi Tazu is often a "reader's choice" vote for best sushi in Denver in local magazines' annual surveys. They are also recognized for their many vegetarian selections, including veggie sushi. Their daily happy hour (4:30–6 P.M.) includes half-price sushi and discounted sake. Because the restaurant is small, it fills up fast on weekend evenings. There is some parking behind the restaurant.

BREAKFAST AND BRUNCH
CRÉPES N' CRÉPES ❸
2816 E. 3rd Ave., 303/320-4184, www.crepesncrepes.com
HOURS: Tues.-Fri. 9 A.M.-10 P.M., Sat. 8:30 A.M.-10 P.M., Sun. 8:30 A.M.-3 P.M., closed Mon.

It's crepes for breakfast, lunch, and dinner at Crépes N' Crépes, and still people can't seem to get enough of them. Perhaps it's because this is a true French *crêperie,* with French sweet or savory ingredients filling the thin pancakes cooked on hot French griddles—even the menu is in French (with English translation). Crépes N' Crépes feels like a find even if you've been here before, with tables squeezed up to the walls so there is just enough room to walk by between the well-stocked bar and each table. Inside, and in the adorable patio out back, it feels like a trip to Europe. It's a great little dessert stop after a movie or dinner elsewhere, too. There is a second location in LoDo's Writer Square (1512 Larimer St., 303/534-1620, Mon.–Tues. 10 A.M.–3 P.M., Wed.–Sun. 10 A.M.–10 P.M.).

THE EGGSHELL OF CHERRY CREEK ❸
235 Fillmore St., 303/322-1601, www.theeggshell.com
HOURS: Mon.-Fri. 6:30 A.M.-2 P.M., Sat. 7 A.M.-3 P.M., Sun. 7:30 A.M.-3 P.M.

Long a staple for breakfast in the Cherry Creek North neighborhood, The Eggshell has a big variety of omelets—including the classic Denver omelet or the build-your-own option. Given the name, the bulk of the offerings are some take on eggs, but there are also pancakes and waffles. On weekdays, it's easy to get a table, but on weekends, there can be a wait. Though known for breakfast, The Eggshell also has a lunch menu with sandwiches and salads.

PAJAMA BAKING COMPANY ❸
1595 S. Pearl St., 303/733-3622, www.pajamabakingcompany.com
HOURS: Sun.-Thurs. 7 A.M.-8 P.M., Fri.-Sat. 7 A.M.-10 P.M.
Once upon a time, what is now the Platt Park

neighborhood was actually a separate town called South Denver. The vestiges of a single business district to support that town remain along South Pearl Street with shops and restaurants. The Pajama Baking Company has become a modern version of the community hub, with a garage door rolled up to relieve the roomy space where neighborhood families can stroll in for breakfast, a sandwich, or a treat. Check their website for daily bread flavors.

SYRUP ◐

300 Josephine St., 720/945-1111, www.syrupdenver.com

HOURS: Mon.-Fri. 6:30 A.M.-2:30 P.M., Sat.-Sun. 7:30 A.M.-3 P.M.

It's a slightly different spin on how you usually order breakfast (although it sounds vaguely familiar, like the old International House of Pancakes updated): Select a pancake, waffle, or French toast first, then figure out which signature syrup you want with it. This is about the sweet tooth breakfast with chocolate syrup, strawberry, blackberry, cinnamon apple, and maple-vanilla. Those who prefer a savory breakfast have plenty of syrup-free options with eggs, potatoes, and oatmeal.

ZAIDY'S DELI ◐

121 Adams St., 303/333-5336, www.zaidysdeli.com

HOURS: Mon.-Fri. 6:30 A.M.-7 P.M., Sat.-Sun. 7:30 A.M.-7 P.M.

When it comes to Jewish deli food, Zaidy's is the place to go in Denver. This Cherry Creek mainstay has a loyal clientele—including me, especially when I am in need of matzo-ball soup. Every table is given a bowl of pickles to munch on before ordering. There are a variety of sandwiches to choose from, as well as latkes, knishes, corned beef hash, and large slices of cake for dessert.

CAFÉS
◖ DEVIL'S FOOD BAKERY & COOKERY ◐

1024 S. Gaylord St., 303/733-7448, www.devilsfoodbakery.com

HOURS: Mon.-Fri. 7 A.M.-9 P.M., Sat.-Sun. 7 A.M.-3 P.M.

It started out as a place for sweets and just kept growing until Devil's Food Bakery turned into an all-day restaurant for every meal. Whether you're in the mood for a full breakfast, lunch, brunch, or supper, or simply an afternoon tea or just something sinfully sweet, Devil's Food Bakery & Cookery can fill your craving. I think if I lived around the corner from this place, I wouldn't need a kitchen. Decorated with random windows hanging like artwork, and artwork by local artists hung on the deep-red walls, Devil's Food is a cute and clean café. Try the grapefruit tart, vanilla-bean cream puffs, or double-chocolate "doughnut." There can be a wait for brunch on weekends.

© MINDY SINK

Devil's Food Bakery & Cookery has divine sweets as well as hearty breakfasts.

RESTAURANTS

DUFFEYROLL CAFÉ ●

1290 S. Pearl St., 303/953-6890, www.duffeyrolls.com

HOURS: Mon.-Fri. 6 A.M.-3 P.M., Sat. 6 A.M.-4 P.M., Sun. 7 A.M.-3 P.M.

It all started with a really good cinnamon roll. Now there are six gooey glaze toppings to choose from and two sizes of cinnamon rolls, along with a full menu of sandwiches, soups, and salads. All sandwiches come with a free mini cinnamon roll. The original Duffeyroll Café is near the light rail stop at Pearl and Louisiana Streets, where there are a few cute shops just around the corner. Outdoor seating and free Wi-Fi make Duffeyroll a place to hang out, too. There are three locations in metro Denver, and they also deliver.

STELLA'S COFFEEHAUS ●

1476 S. Pearl St., 303/777-1031, www.stellascoffee.com

HOURS: Sun.-Thurs. 6:30 A.M.-11 P.M., Fri.-Sat. 6:30 A.M.-midnight

As you walk into Stella's, you'll pass a covered patio filled with people and their dogs, and once inside, it appears there is no more seating. Don't worry, keep walking: This old house has several rooms with sofas and chairs in the rear—and since they added Wi-Fi, it looks like several people set up office here all day, sipping their Pablo's coffee. The menu is small, with burritos, pastries, and quiche available. Local artists not only display their artwork on the walls of Stella's, but sell it here as well. Stella's has live acoustic music on Friday and Saturday nights. Wednesdays bring coffee discounts.

CONTEMPORARY AND NEW AMERICAN

BLACK PEARL RESTAURANT ●●●

1529 S. Pearl St., 303/777-0500, www.blackpearldenver.com

HOURS: Lunch Mon.-Fri. 11:30 A.M.-3 P.M.; dinner Sun. 5-9 P.M., Mon.-Sat. 5-10 P.M.; brunch Sat.-Sun. 10 A.M.-3 P.M.

Black Pearl Restaurant is an intriguing mix of the owners' East Coast roots and the seasonal availability of fresh, organic ingredients here in Colorado. Set in a small building in South Pearl Street's dining and shopping district, Black Pearl is sleek and simple in design and menu. Out back, there is a stone communal table, which sits around a fire pit. The "contemporary American" dinner menu at this award-winning restaurant includes raw oysters, mussels, crawfish, steaks, duck, and pasta. At weekend brunch, the bottomless mimosas mean a bit of a wait for a table. In addition to the lunch, dinner, and brunch menus and times, there are also happy hour and late night menus and hours.

GAIA BISTRO ●●

1551 S. Pearl St., 303/777-5699, www.gaiabistro.com

HOURS: Tues.-Fri. 7 A.M.-2 P.M., Sat.-Sun. 8 A.M.-2 P.M., Wed.-Thurs. 5-8:30 P.M., Fri.-Sat. 5-9 P.M., closed Mon.

Gaia Bistro describes itself as being "earth friendly" by using organic ingredients grown in the backyard of this Victorian house. And while being green is certainly an appeal to many customers, what really keeps them coming back are the crepes and large patio out front. Expect a wait for a table outside if the weather is nice. In addition to their crepes—both savory and sweet with a huge variety of possible fillings—Gaia offers sandwiches, soups, and salads that have also helped it establish a devoted crowd of regulars. Gluten-free crepes are available on request.

DESSERTS

BONNIE BRAE ICE CREAM ●

799 S. University Blvd., 303/777-0808, www.bonniebraeicecream.com

HOURS: Sun.-Thurs. 11 A.M.-10:30 P.M., Fri.-Sat. 11 A.M.-11 P.M.

Bonnie Brae has long been Denver's favorite ice cream. Located on the edge of the Washington Park neighborhood and not far from the Cherry Creek area, Bonnie Brae Ice Cream has lines

RESTAURANTS

© MINDY SINK

Bonnie Brae Ice Cream is locally made and very popular.

out the door on summer nights for their specialty flavors made on-site. The list of flavors is a bit mind-boggling—how does one choose between butterscotch custard, malted milk ball, cappuccino crunch, and on and on?

HUNGARIAN
BUDAPEST BISTRO $$

1585 S. Pearl St., 303/744-2520,
www.budapestbistro.com
HOURS: Tues.-Sat. 5-10 P.M., closed Sun. and Mon.

Goulashes, schnitzels, and paprikash are the heart of the Eastern European menu, and so are the featured dishes at the Budapest Bistro. When people think of "ethnic food," they do not immediately crave Hungarian, but this is a unique culinary experience in an old-fashioned and charming restaurant on a vibrant historic block. Where else are you going to find Transylvanian Beef and Kraut?

INDIAN
BOMBAY CLAY OVEN $$

165 Steele St., 303/377-4454,
www.bombayclayoven.com
HOURS: Daily 11 A.M.-9:30 P.M.

At Bombay Clay Oven, diners can choose to sit at regular tables and chairs or try divan seating, where shoes are removed and chairs are replaced with pillows around a low table. The menu includes vegetarian options, as well as lamb, chicken, and seafood dishes. On weekends, when there is live music to accompany the food, dining here becomes an experience.

ITALIAN
BAROLO GRILL $$$

3030 E. 6th Ave., 303/393-1040,
www.barologrilldenver.com
HOURS: Tues.-Sat. 5:30-10:30 P.M., closed Sun. and Mon.

Everyone who works at Barolo Grill is an expert on northern Italy, since the owner takes the entire staff there each year to experience the inspiration for the restaurant's food and wine. This firsthand knowledge equals first-class service that matches the excellent menu, which changes seasonally with the exception of a single dish: the braised duckling with kalamata olives. Barolo also offers a five-course tasting menu with optional wine pairing. The grill has a warm and inviting atmosphere year-round, but a table next to the fireplace is especially cozy in winter. Reservations are recommended on weekends.

BASIL DOC'S PIZZA ⑤⑤

2107 E. Virginia Ave., 303/778-7747,
www.basildocspizzeria.com
HOURS: Daily 4:30-10 P.M.

When Basil Doc's first opened in Washington Park, people would drive across town to pick up one of their East Coast–style pizza pies. Basil Doc's has expanded to meet the demand,

and there are now four locations in Colorado. Every pizza is made to order, and there is a long list of possible combinations to choose from. The crust is thin, but not too crunchy. If you just want a quick meal, you can run in and eat perched on one of the stools, but it feels like eating in the kitchen; it's best to just take your pie back home. All locations are "takeout only"—they don't deliver.

CUCINA COLORE ⑤⑤⑤

3041 E. 3rd Ave., 303/393-6917, www.cucinacolore.com
HOURS: Sun.-Thurs. 11 A.M.-10 P.M., Fri.-Sat. 11 A.M.-11 P.M.

On the corner of a quiet block in Cherry Creek North is one of the neighborhood's best restaurants. Cucina Colore offers upscale, contemporary Italian food and a pleasant wine list for both lunch and dinner. Try the *pollo e orzo* salad or a crisp pizza with the house sangria for lunch. Patio seating at umbrella-sheltered tables is available on both sides of the restaurant, and indoor tables are bathed in natural light from the many windows.

PASTA PASTA PASTA ⑤

2800 E. 2nd Ave., 303/377-2782,
www.pastapastapasta.us
HOURS: Mon.-Fri. 10:30 A.M.-5:30 P.M., Sat. 10:30 A.M.-4 P.M., closed Sun.

One of Cherry Creek North's best dining secrets is a little find of a café, Pasta Pasta Pasta, offering simple and always tasty Italian food. Customers walk up to the counter and see what's available that day—such as a slice of salmon, chicken Milanese, ravioli, spaghetti, and salads—and order and pay before seating themselves at one of the small tables. The walls are adorned with ornate, Italian ceramic plates and bowls (all for sale). Pasta Pasta Pasta is a cheery and unpretentious spot to take a shopping break.

Pasta Pasta Pasta actually serves more than just pasta.

WASH PARK GRILLE ❸❸❸
1096 S. Gaylord St., 303/777-0707,
www.washparkgrille.com

HOURS: Daily 4:30-10 P.M.

While the Wash Park Grille describes its cuisine as "Italian With a Twist," it seems more like a standard American menu with a slightly expanded pasta selection. Either way, it is a good neighborhood restaurant on charming South Gaylord Street where the whole family can find something to eat. The Sunday buffet brunch attracts a crowd—mostly large families—and kids love to get a treat from the chocolate fondue fountain.

Greater Denver   Map 7

AMERICAN
❰ THE FORT ❸❸❸
19192 Hwy. 8, Morrison, 303/697-4771,
www.thefort.com

HOURS: Mon.-Fri. 5:30-9:30 P.M., Sat.-Sun. 5-9:30 P.M.

For a one-of-a-kind dining experience in the West, The Fort is the place to go. Inspired by a drawing of a historic fort, Sam Arnold bought the land in the 1960s and hired a crew to build (or re-create) a true 1840s' fort. When it wasn't feasible as a private home, Mr. Arnold decided to make it a restaurant and studied cooking so that he could provide only the best ingredients and menu. Today, with Mr. Arnold's daughter Holly Arnold Kinney at the helm, The Fort offers what can only be described as exotic Western, with a large variety of game meats, trout, Rocky Mountain oysters, Southwestern spices, and other unexpected culinary delights. There is a gift shop on-site, and annual Western-themed events, such as a powwow, are held here.

FUEL CAFÉ ❸❸
3455 Ringsby Ct., 303/996-6988,
www.fuelcafedenver.com

HOURS: Mon.-Wed. 11 A.M.-3 P.M., Thurs.-Fri. 11 A.M.-3 P.M. and 5-9 P.M., Sat. 5-9 P.M., closed Sun.

Off the beaten path, but only a five-minute drive from downtown in the River North Arts District, Fuel Café feels like a real find of a restaurant. Located just off the South Platte River and down the road from a bus depot, Fuel is part of the TAXI development (a modern arts colony). The restaurant and its environs have an industrial feel, and that is part of its charm. Fuel is a place for foodies, with octopus and duck gizzards on the appetizer menu, but even picky eaters can find something to love for lunch or dinner because the food is so well prepared with fresh and local ingredients.

HUTCH & SPOON ❸
3090 Larimer St., 303/296-2317,
www.hutchandspoon.com

HOURS: Mon.-Fri. 7 A.M.-4 P.M., Sat. 8 A.M.-2 P.M.

In a relatively far corner of the Five Points neighborhood is a breakfast and lunch eatery worth checking out. Although the menu can change, I hope to catch the watermelon, feta, and black olive salad or the grilled cheese with peach chutney, simply out of curiosity. It's like that—surprising flavor combinations abound here. The homemade sodas are also delicious. As a bonus, be sure to enjoy the spoon collection on display.

SOLERA RESTAURANT & WINE BAR ❸❸❸
5410 E. Colfax Ave., 303/388-8429,
www.solerarestaurant.com

HOURS: Tues.-Thurs. 5-10 P.M., Fri.-Sat. 5-11 P.M., Sun. 5-9 P.M., closed Mon.

A neighborhood favorite that also attracts foodies willing to make a pilgrimage, Solera is a special place with an unforgettable menu

RESTAURANTS

of unique dishes. Using fresh seasonal ingredients, Chef Christian "Goose" Sorensen creates mouthwatering "Spanish farmhouse" specialties. Somehow, this includes a Thai-style calamari appetizer and sea scallops over a bed of truffle mac 'n' cheese, which are big favorites here. The wine list and excellent service round out a perfect dining experience. Enjoy dinner at a table on their lush patio in the summer.

TABLES $$$

2267 Kearney St., 303/388-0299,
http://tablesonkearney.com
HOURS: Tues.-Sat. 5-9:30 P.M., closed Sun. and Mon.
As lovely a neighborhood as Park Hill is, it is not known as a dining destination. One of the few restaurants in this neck of the woods is Tables, which is worth the drive over from downtown. The menu is simultaneously simple and sophisticated, with fresh, crisp salads before hearty entreés of pork chops, trout, lamb loin, steak, and pasta. The upscale wine list rounds out an exquisite meal in a quaint neighborhood.

ASIAN
J'S NOODLES $

945 S. Federal Blvd., Ste. E, 303/922-5495,
www.jsnoodlesnewthai.blogspot.com
HOURS: Mon.-Thurs. 11 A.M.-9 P.M., Fri.-Sat.
11 A.M.-10 P.M., Sun. noon-9 P.M.
Denverites have been known to crave the curry from J's Noodles, with a thick sauce and just the right amount of meat and veggies. And J's must rely on its delicious food to keep customers coming because this hole-in-the-wall lacks ambience. But the service is always friendly, and even when it's elbow-to-elbow with the next table, customers do not feel rushed. J's delivers, too.

NEW SAIGON $

630 S. Federal Blvd., 303/936-4954,
www.newsaigon.com
HOURS: Tues.-Sun. 11 A.M.-9:30 P.M., closed Mon.
Gritty Federal Boulevard southwest of downtown is known for authentic Asian food, particularly Vietnamese and Thai. New Saigon is the perennial favorite in a crowded field (or strip mall) of many no-frills diners. The extensive menu here includes dozens of rather exotic specials (for a landlocked Western city) that feature shark fin, mussels, clams, and other seafood, in addition to menu items with chicken, lamb, beef, tofu, shrimp, pork, duck, and much more.

PHO 79 $

781 S. Federal Blvd., 303/922-2930,
www.pho79restaurant.com
HOURS: Daily 9 A.M.-9 P.M.
For *pho* lovers, Pho 79 is a sure winner every time, with its seasoned-just-right broth and noodle bowls. Like many South Federal Boulevard dining establishments, the clientele returns time and again for the delicious food and not the atmosphere. It's cramped and very informal, and the menu is rather small. Still, the *pho* is addictive and people swear by it as a hangover cure. Pho 79 can also be a fun and affordable dining-out experience with kids.

US THAI CAFÉ $$

5228 W. 25th Ave., Edgewater, 303/233-3345,
www.usthaicafe.com
HOURS: Tues.-Thurs. 11 A.M.-9 P.M., Fri. 11 A.M.-9:30 P.M.,
Sat. noon-9:30 P.M., Sun. noon-9 P.M.
Denver has a lot of Thai restaurants to choose from, but what sets US Thai apart is the heat. It has earned a reputation for authentic and *spicy* Thai food that is consistently very good-but with the emphasis on spicy, maybe don't choose to have your dishes "hot" on the first visit. This small eatery is just west of the Highlands neighborhood in Edgewater.

WILD GINGER THAI RESTAURANT ❸❸

399 W. Littleton Blvd., Littleton, 303/794-1115,
www.wildginger.info

HOURS: Lunch Mon.-Fri. 11 A.M.-3 P.M., Sat. noon-3 P.M.
and 5-10 P.M.; Dinner Mon.-Thurs. 5-9 P.M., Fri. 5-10 P.M.,
closed Sun.

The suburb of Littleton isn't exactly known for
its ethnic restaurants, but Wild Ginger is the
exception-it has built a solid reputation with
Thai basics like chicken *satay,* green curry,
and coconut ice cream. Wild Ginger is regularly voted "best Thai" restaurant in many
local surveys, with the curry receiving much
of the attention. In contrast to the Thai restaurants found on South Federal Boulevard, Wild
Ginger is positively swanky, with a full bar and
a variety of seating options more than an arm's
length from the nearest table.

DESSERT

CAKE CRUMBS ❸

2216 Kearney St., 303/861-4912,
www.cake-crumbs.com

HOURS: Mon.-Sat. 6 A.M.-7 P.M., Sun. 7 A.M.-4 P.M.

To be honest, I'd never heard of the Cake
Crumbs bakery until I started following the
Denver Cupcake Truck on Facebook. I imag-
ined the owners baking up those tasty little
cakes in the truck, frosting between stops.
Then I wised up and actually went to their
shop, where they have coffee, pies, and, in addition to the cupcakes, make specialty cakes.
With free Wi-Fi, Cake Crumbs has established
itself not just as a spot for a sweet treat on the
go, but also a place to hang out and enjoy a
nibble.

ETHIOPIAN

ABYSSINIA ❸

4116 E. Colfax Ave., 303/316-8830

HOURS: Wed.-Mon. 11:30 A.M.-10 P.M., closed Tues.

Start with the honey wine, then explore a variety of lamb, beef, chicken, and vegetarian
dishes, all made with unique Ethiopian spices.

And I should mention this place is a real bargain. The tiny space is decorated with traditional Ethiopian crafts. Reservations are a must
for dinner here, maybe in part because of the
size of the place, but also because the friendly
service can be on the slow side.

MIDDLE EASTERN

DAMASCUS RESTAURANT ❸

2276 S. Colorado Blvd., 303/757-3515

HOURS: Daily 11 A.M.-11 P.M.

Chances are that you will drive right by
Damascus the first time, as its inconspicu-
ous storefront in an aged strip mall along busy
Colorado Boulevard blends right in. Once you
do find it and step inside, the music and decor
will make you feel as if you have left Denver for
a taste of Syria. A friend described it as "quaint
and charming in a dive-y kind of way." The
smooth hummus and baba ghanoush will have
you coming back. Make a night of it and stop at
Damascus before going to a movie at the Chez
Artiste theaters.

HOUSE OF KABOB ❸

2246 S. Colorado Blvd., 303/756-0744,
www.houseofkabobrestaurant.com

HOURS: Daily 11 A.M.-11 P.M.

Dinner and a show, Middle Eastern style!
House of Kabob might strike some as a little
touristy with its weekend-night belly dancers, but it's fun to try something so different from the typical restaurant. Besides, the
food is good. Try the lamb, beef, or chicken
kabob entrées, or the Kobeideh, which blends
them all together. For a little more fun of a
different sort, step into their Hookah Palace
next door.

JERUSALEM RESTAURANT ❸

1890 E. Evans Ave., 303/777-8828,
www.jerusalemrestaurant.com

HOURS: Sun.-Thurs. 9 A.M.-4 A.M., Fri.-Sat. 9 A.M.-5 A.M.

Middle Eastern restaurants tend to be south of

RESTAURANTS

downtown and in the vicinity of the University of Denver, and this is no exception. Jerusalem Restaurant is only a block away from the campus, and is popular with college students who crave falafel and kabobs in the wee hours. The service at Jerusalem is lacking, but for a late-night bite of authentic Middle Eastern food, this place fits the bill.

NIGHTLIFE

Given that a saloon was reportedly Denver's first building, the city has long had a rich nightlife to offer and the options just keep growing. Whether it's for music, drinks, or dancing, Denver has impressive credentials. One of the city's more popular microbreweries, the Wynkoop Brewing Company, was cofounded by Governor John Hickenlooper; the newest and hottest nightclub, Beta, was started by the founders of Beatport, the world's leading online source for electronic music downloads; and there is a handful of fantastic jazz clubs—El Chapultepec, Dazzle, and Jazz at Jack's—which all attract nationally renowned jazz musicians who play at the venues regularly.

Get to know the locals by spending an evening on a barstool, whether it be at a dive bar like Don's Club Tavern, authentic Parisian bar À Côté, or just sitting in a club chair at the Churchill Bar in the Brown Palace Hotel. Each of these places offers a chance to relax and talk to a friendly stranger.

Of course there is the requisite country-and-western music night out, stomping through a line dance in pointy cowboy boots and tight jeans, and in Denver, there are plenty of options. The Grizzly Rose is a traditional country venue with well-known Nashville musicians playing live; the Cowboy Lounge is the lower-downtown version of the Rose, with more college students than cowboys; and there's also Charlie's, the gay and lesbian bar for the country crowd.

HIGHLIGHTS

© VISIT DENVER

playing pool at Wynkoop Brewing Company

◖ **Best Jazz Bar: El Chapultepec** refuses to give itself a glossy makeover to match the changes in LoDo, and that's part of the charm. Well-known musicians have been known to drop in to jam with the regulars (page 99).

◖ **Best Country Music Bar:** Whether or not you wear your cowboy boots, you can join a line dance at the **Grizzly Rose** (page 100).

◖ **Best Dance Club: Beta** is one of the best clubs in the city, with world-class DJs in the main room and the Beatport Lounge (page 103).

◖ **Best French Bar and Bistro: À Côté** is the closest thing Denverites have to a true Parisian bar and bistro; it's full of Old World charm (page 106).

◖ **Best Historic Bar:** Step into the glorious art deco **Cruise Room** in the historic Oxford Hotel and you'll feel as if you're aboard a cruise ship. The bar was modeled after a lounge on the *Queen Mary* (page 107).

◖ **Best Dive Bar: Don's Club Tavern** is a simple dive bar that offers just drinks and pool, with no fancy cocktails, seating, or music. This unaffected quality is what makes Don's a local favorite year after year (page 107).

◖ **Best Margarita:** Bigger is better at **Mezcal,** where pint-glass margaritas rule, made with fresh lime juice instead of bottled sweet-and-sour mix (page 110).

◖ **Best Wine Bar:** Sample wines recommended by experts and nosh on some tasty food at **The Village Cork** (page 112).

◖ **Best Disguised Bar: Williams & Graham** has intrigues patrons with its clever speakeasy front: a bookstore hiding a well-stocked bar (page 112).

◖ **Best Drinks with Geeks:** Beer is usually associated with depleting brain cells, but Café Scientifique gatherings at the **Wynkoop Brewing Company** offer a way to enjoy both fresh brew and smart ideas (page 116).

Beyond country-and-western music, Denver's thriving music scene has helped launch a few acts that have received national acclaim, such as Big Head Todd and the Monsters, Slim Cessna's Auto Club, and DeVotchka. Though they've gone on to the big time, you can still catch some of these bands at venues like the Gothic Theatre, the Bluebird Theater, or Red Rocks Amphitheatre.

Other clubs include the Hi-Dive, where you can dance to intense alternative rock music; the Skylark Lounge, where you can bop to some rockabilly tunes; and Lannie's Clocktower Cabaret offers everything from burlesque to showtunes.

Most bars and clubs close at 2 A.M., but you can find a few after-hours spots, such as the aptly named Two A.M., where dancing lasts until 5 A.M.

Live Music

BLUEBIRD THEATER

3317 E. Colfax Ave., 303/377-1666, www.bluebirdtheater.net

HOURS: Vary

COST: Varies

`Map 4`

The Bluebird Theater was originally built in 1913 and used as a movie house. After many incarnations and a bit of neglect, it was turned into one of Denver's most popular concert venues in 1994. All shows at the Bluebird are 16 and over, though anyone under 21 is restricted to the balcony during a concert while alcohol is served on another level. There is a wide range of acts that play at the Bluebird—from Shelby Lynne to Oasis to Slim Cessna's Auto Club to less well-known groups still getting their start.

DAZZLE RESTAURANT AND LOUNGE

930 Lincoln St., 303/839-5100, www.dazzlejazz.com

HOURS: Mon.-Thurs., Sat. 4 P.M.-2 A.M., Fri. 11 A.M.-2 A.M., Sun. 9:30 A.M.-2 A.M.

COST: Varies

`Map 2`

Consistently chosen as a Denver favorite for jazz in local surveys and by music magazines, Dazzle Restaurant and Lounge offers live music nightly from local, national, and international musicians. Dazzle has two rooms, the Dazzle Showroom and the Dizzy Room,

each featuring a different band or event every night of the week. The lineup changes daily here—one night might be a mix of Latin Jazz, the next night a CD release party, followed by torch singers—and each act is locally or nationally recognized. There are jazz brunches on Sundays, a Friday Lunch Club, and happy hour and dinner are nightly.

D NOTE

7519 Grandview Ave., 303/463-6683, www.dnote.us

HOURS: Mon.-Thurs. 3 P.M.-12 A.M., Fri.-Sun. 11 A.M.-2 A.M.

COST: Varies

`Map 7`

Located in charming Olde Town Arvada, the D Note is a unique blend of a family-friendly, gourmet pizza place and a live music venue. The acts vary here from local acoustic musicians to folk, jazz, blues, and zydeco groups who play on a stage against one wall of the large, open room. The exposed brick walls are perfect for displaying art by local artists, which is all for sale. Check the calendar in advance as the variety of shows includes Baby Boogie, community events, and different bands.

EL CHAPULTEPEC

1962 Market St., 303/295-9126, http://thepeclodo.com

HOURS: Daily 11 A.M.-1 A.M.; music starts at 9 P.M. nightly

NIGHTLIFE

NIGHTLIFE

SMOKING BAN

In 2006, Colorado joined a dozen other states with a statewide smoking ban inside bars, restaurants, and workplaces. Cigar bars are the lone exemption, so not much changed at the Brown Palace Hotel's Churchill Bar, where there is a selection of 60 cigars kept fresh in a humidor.

On the flip side, some bars claim that the ban drove them out of business when customers had to leave their favorite barstool to smoke outdoors. For the most part, though, many wait-resses, bartenders, and other people who work inside these establishments expressed appreciation for no longer having to work in clouds of smoke.

If you drive by a nightclub or bar and see what looks like a line to get in, look again—it's likely nicotine addicts legally smoking just outside their favorite establishment. The ban also means that the air on some bars' rooftop patios and street-front seating areas is often thick with smoke.

COST: $2 cover on Friday and Saturday nights

Map 3

Once on the edge of downtown in a seedy locale, El Chapultepec hasn't bothered to change its appearance since the neighborhood has become a thriving nightlife scene near Coors Field. That gritty, dive-bar quality is part of the appeal, though. Note this is a cash-only bar—no credit cards. Stop in for a cold beer and a burrito at the bar anytime, or come by later to hear local jazz musicians and even some jazz greats play nightly. Opened in 1951, El Chapultepec has hosted Tony Bennett, Frank Sinatra, and even the Rolling Stones. If it's too crowded, head to the Highlands and check out **Chapultepec Too** (3930 W. 38th Ave., 303/480-9406).

◖ GRIZZLY ROSE

5450 N. Valley Hwy., 303/295-2353,
www.grizzlyrose.com
HOURS: Tues.-Sun. 11 A.M.-1:30 A.M.
COST: Varies

Map 7

For the total Western cowboy/cowgirl experience—line dancing and riding on the mechanical bull—the Grizzly Rose is the place to go. The Rose has been around for decades as a celebration of Denver's cow town reputation, where Wrangler jeans and cowboy boots are in style all the time. No worries if you are new

to dancing; the Rose offers free introductory classes so that, in no time, you'll kick up those heels and shout "Yee-haw!" with the crowd in 40,000 square feet of room. More advanced students can pay for series of dance lessons. Cover charges vary depending on live music acts, which have included Delbert McClinton and the Marshall Tucker Band, but with an emphasis on regional acts.

HERMAN'S HIDEAWAY

1578 S. Broadway, 303/777-5840,
www.hermanshideaway.com
HOURS: Vary
COST: Varies

Map 6

For a casual, up-close night out listening to rock 'n' roll music, head to Herman's Hideaway. This small bar has been hosting local and national bands for a quarter century, and is known as the place where Big Head Todd and the Monsters got their start. There is a dance floor as well as seating with a view of the stage. Shows at Herman's range from the band the Subdudes to a regular New Talent Showcase night.

HI-DIVE

7 S. Broadway, 720/570-4500, www.hi-dive.com
HOURS: Shows typically begin at 8 or 9 P.M.; closes at 2 A.M.

© STEVE STALZLE

Listen to live jazz at Dazzle Restaurant and Lounge.

COST: Varies

`Map 2`

Since 2004, Hi-Dive has been one of Denver's best punk and indie rock dive bars to see bands like the Thermals, Why?, the Ya Ya's, and many more nationally known and local acts. The venue holds less than 300 people, so it gets packed quickly for the really popular shows. Hi-Dive offers both 16-and-over and 21-and-over shows about five nights a week. The club is connected to Sputnik, where they serve food and drinks.

JAZZ AT JACK'S

500 16th St., Ste. 320, 303/433-1000, www.jazzatjacks.com

HOURS: Daily 5 P.M.–1 A.M.

COST: Varies

`Map 1`

Jazz at Jack's is part-owned by local jazz band Dotsero, which performs at the club every Saturday night. On Tuesday, it's funk night;

there is no cover for Sunday happy hour; and the rest of the week is filled in by a selection of well-known jazz artists on tour, such as Steve Cole, Dave Grusin, and many more. And you never know who might drop in and play with the band. To find Jack's, look for the neon saxophone in the Denver Pavilions on the 16th Street Mall. The name comes from the first location, which was on Platte Street in the old Jack's Carpet Warehouse building; this new spot is a big improvement over that cramped and hot room. Here there is ample seating and even a year-round patio.

LANNIE'S CLOCKTOWER CABARET

1601 Arapahoe St., 303/293-0075, http://lannies.com

HOURS: Doors usually open at 7 P.M. on show nights

COST: Varies

`Map 1`

Local music legend Lannie Garrett has found her groove with cabaret in the basement of the landmark D & F Clocktower on the 16th

Street Mall. This purple, red, and gold room hosts a wide range of entertainers, including drag queens, burlesque performers, nationally known bands, and singers like Erica Brown, in a variety of shows, like Lannie's own long-running country-western spoof, "The Patsy DeCline Show." Every Tuesday night is open-mike night, where anyone can come and show off their vaudeville talents.

LARIMER LOUNGE

2721 Larimer St., 303/291-1007, www.larimerlounge.com
HOURS: Mon.-Fri. 4 P.M.-2 A.M., Sat. 6 P.M.-2 A.M.; call for Sun. hours
COST: Varies
Map 1

A popular stop for indie bands, the Larimer Lounge is a good blend of hip and gritty. The space is intimate, which can also mean pretty loud. Bands usually don't go on until about 9 P.M. or later. Past shows here have included Thurston Moore, ManCub, So-Gnar, and many others.

LION'S LAIR

2022 E. Colfax Ave., 303/320-9200
HOURS: Mon.-Fri. 3 P.M.-2 A.M., Sat.-Sun. 2 P.M.-2 A.M.
COST: Varies
Map 4

This hole-in-the-wall is a great little place to stop in for a cold beer, with no worries about style or who's who. Live music at the Lair can be extremely loud, with the band right in the center of the small room. The bands tend to be punk and hard rock, and sometimes alt-rock. Drinks are always reasonably priced, and seating at the bar is the best in the house.

MEADOWLARK BAR

2701 Larimer St., 303/293-0251,
www.meadowlarkbar.com
HOURS: Mon.-Fri. 4 P.M.-2 A.M., Sat.-Sun. 6 P.M.-2 A.M.
COST: Varies
Map 1

If you like your live music up close and

personal, almost as if you are getting a private concert in your basement, then welcome to Meadowlark, a basement space of cellar proportions, but with stylish ambience. *Westword* has dubbed Meadowlark Denver's "best place to learn to be a rockstar," among other accolades. In summer, an outdoor patio and performance space makes the bar twice as appealing (and twice the size). Rocker wannabes should be there for Open Stage Night on Tuesdays.

MERCURY CAFE

2199 California St., 303/294-9281,
www.mercurycafe.com
HOURS: Tues.-Sun. 5:30 P.M.-1 A.M., closed Mon.
COST: Varies
Map 1

The Mercury Cafe has a little something for everyone, depending on the night of the week. Their all-ages shows range from blues and swing to tango and acoustic, and dancing classes are offered as well. The entertainment doesn't stop with these specialty bands though—there's also "open stage" Wednesday for magicians, comics, and musicians, and poetry readings on Friday. The Mercury revels in its reputation as a "hippie" hangout for bohemian types, but anyone who enjoys dancing and live music will feel at home. Service can be spotty, so allow extra time for a night out here. No credit cards are accepted, but there is an ATM on-site.

ROXY THEATRE

2549 Welton St., 720/429-9782,
www.theroxydenver.com
HOURS: Tues.-Sun. 5:30 P.M.-1 A.M., closed Mon.
COST: Varies
Map 1

The historic Roxy Theatre in the Five Points neighborhood has owners intent on making it a hip place once again. The 500-seat theatre was once a movie house and has changed hands over the years as a music venue. Although there is an emphasis on hip-hop music, there is a wider variety than that on the calendar. The history of the theater is explored down the street at the Blair-Caldwell African American Research Library.

SKYLARK LOUNGE

140 S. Broadway, 303/722-7844,
www.skylarklounge.com
HOURS: Mon.-Fri. 4 P.M.-2 A.M., Sat.-Sun. 2 P.M.-2 A.M.
COST: Varies
Map 2

Rockabilly and honky-tonk music dominate weekends at the Skylark Lounge on South Broadway. The Skylark Lounge has been around since 1943, but new owners relocated it to the current location in the 1990s. Still, the Skylark has a 1950s' vibe with a yellow-and-black-tiled dance floor, a jukebox, and pool tables. Downstairs is where bands play on weekends, and the occasional Thursday night as well; upstairs is a bit quieter for conversation and games like shuffleboard and pinball. This is a 21-and-over club.

SUMMIT MUSIC HALL

1902 Blake St., 303/487-0111, www.lodolivemusic.com
HOURS: Box office is open Mon.-Fri. 11 A.M.-5 P.M. and on show nights

COST: Varies
Map 3

Named "Best New Venue-2011" by the *Westword* magazine, the Summit Music Hall is a 12,500-square-foot space for punk, metal, hip-hop, and industrial music shows. When the former dance club isn't filled up with concert-goers for these big acts, the venue can shrink to host local bands still building an audience. Many of the shows here are all ages, but some are for 18 and over only. Some of the bands that played in 2012 included Balkan Beat Box, Tycho, and Bouncing Souls. All shows here are general admission.

3 KINGS TAVERN

60 S. Broadway, 303/777-7352,
www.3kingstavern.com
HOURS: Daily 5 P.M.-2 A.M.
COST: Varies
Map 2

Along the bar and restaurant strip of South Broadway that has grown significantly in recent years, 3 Kings Tavern stands out with its mix of live country, rock, blues, and punk rock on weekends and DJs on weeknights. Before the shows start or for a diversion from the music, 3 Kings also has several pool tables, pinball, and video games. This is a 21-and-over club.

Dance Clubs

BAR STANDARD

1037 Broadway, 303/832-8628, www.coclubs.com
HOURS: Fri.-Sat. 9 P.M.-2 A.M., closed Sun.-Thurs.
COST: Free-$10
Map 2

What sets Bar Standard apart from many Denver clubs is its retro art deco decor and ambience. The music is Afropop, indie-electric, house, and "nujazz," with different themes and guest DJs each night, as well as burlesque dancers. While the music and dancing are great at Bar Standard,

comfy booths and a reasonable volume make this a place for chatting with friends and hanging out for the evening. This is a 21-and-over club.

(BETA

1909 Blake St., 303/383-1909, www.betanightclub.com
HOURS: Thurs.-Sat., closed Sun.-Wed.; call for specific times
COST: Varies
Map 3

Denver's world-class nightclub is Beta; since its

NIGHTLIFE

Sip cool drinks at Chloe Discotheque.

opening in 2008, it has become the city's most popular dance club, and in 2012, it was named one of the top 25 clubs in the world by DJ Mag. Internationally known and local DJs have played here, including Steve Bug, Modeselektor, Danny Tenaglia, Wyatt Earp, and DJ Foxx. Within Beta is the Beatport Lounge, a separate club with its own Funktion One sound system (the main floor has one, too). The patio area is more of a lush summer garden with abundant flowers and grass. But the grass isn't the only thing green at Beta: The club was designed with environmental awareness and features acoustic panels made from recycled blue jeans. They have a recycling program and energy-efficient lightbulbs are used throughout the club.

CHERRY
231 Milwaukee St., 303/362-1145,
www.cherrydenver.com
HOURS: Wed.-Fri. 5 P.M.-2 A.M., Sat.-8 P.M., closed Sun.-Tues.

COST: No cover
Map 6

For those looking to boogie, a slightly upscale "dance parlor" is on offer in the Cherry Creek North neighborhood. The music here is a mix of pop, funk, soul, and rock to get everybody on the dance floor at least once during their night out. Check the calendar for "54 Friday" every fourth Friday of the month in a retro nod to the 1970s and NYC's Studio 54; it's Girls Night Out every Third Thursday with complimentary drinks and fabulous drawings and prizes.

CHLOE DISCOTHEQUE DENVER
1445 Market St., 720/383-8447,
http://chloe-denver.com
HOURS: Discotheque: Thurs.-Sat. 10 P.M.-2 A.M., Mezze Lounge: 4 P.M.-2 A.M., dinner 4 P.M.-10 P.M.
COST: No cover
Map 3

Chloe Discotheque is just one of three parts: a restaurant, garden patio, and disco. Come for drinks, have some dinner, and end the night with dancing. The vibe here is one designed to attract celebrities, scenesters, and others who like to "dress to impress" on a night out. In other words, leave your sports-bar look and attitude at home when you come to Chloe. Chloe has grown a reputation around special event nights, such as a sexy Halloween weekend, and the colored LED lights on the dance floor's ceiling make a great disco-ball effect.

THE CHURCH
1160 Lincoln St., 303/832-2383, www.coclubs.com
HOURS: Thurs.-Sun. 9 P.M.-2 A.M., closed Mon.-Wed.
COST: No cover
Map 2

The name of this Denver nightclub is literal: The Church is a beautiful historic church that has been transformed into a nightclub that highlights the original architecture with colorful lights illuminating the Gothic windows and immense ceilings. The Church has three dance floors, each with different reverberating dance music, several bars scattered throughout three floors, and a sushi bar. The Church is a bit of a singles scene for young, urban professionals, but fun for anyone in the mood to dance.

COWBOY LOUNGE

1941 Market St., 303/226-1570,
www.tavernhg.com/cowboy_lounge
HOURS: Thurs.-Sat. 8 P.M.-2 A.M., closed Sun.-Wed.
COST: $5; free on Thursday
Map 3

If you are in LoDo and not in the mood for the typical dance club, try the Cowboy Lounge for some country-and-western tunes and traditional dancing on the spacious dance floor. On Thursdays, ladies get in free and enjoy drink specials. A large patio out front with tables and chairs is perfect for smokers and those needing to cool off after dancing. Private parties

here can pull out all the Western stops, with two-step and line dancing lessons, a mechanical bull, a shoot-out game, and lots of other clichés that make the night memorable.

LA RUMBA

99 W. 9th Ave., 303/572-8006,
www.larumba-denver.com
HOURS: Thurs.-Sat. 9 P.M.-2 A.M.
COST: Varies
Map 2

This local institution for salsa dancing has a loyal fan base because it offers dependable music from both DJs and live salsa bands rocking the house. You don't have to be a pro—La Rumba is for rookie salsa dancers as well as the experts. It's all about sensuous dancing to beautiful and fun music.

TWO A.M. AFTERHOURS

1144 Broadway, 303/830-9325, www.coclubs.com

NIGHTLIFE

© BRITT CHESTER

The Church is one of Denver's most popular nightclubs.

HOURS: Fri.-Sat. 1-5 A.M., closed Sun. -Thurs.

COST: $10-15

Map 2

Not ready to call it a night? The place to go is Two A.M., where electronic dance music is still rocking the house until dawn. The basement-level club is all about dancing, with minimal furnishings and no alcohol served. Two A.M. is near a handful of other hot clubs that are all owned by the same organization, and is part of the South of Colfax nightlife district along Broadway. There is a discount on admission to Two A.M. for patrons who have been at any of the related clubs earlier in the evening.

Bars

❰ À CÔTÉ

2245 W. 30th Ave., 303/477-1111,
www.zcuisineonline.com

HOURS: Tues. 5-10 P.M., Wed.-Sat. 5 P.M.-midnight, closed Sun. and Mon.

COST: No cover

Map 5

Not willing to settle for having one of Denver's best French restaurants, if not *the* best, Patrick DuPays opened À Côté, a Parisian wine bar, two doors down from Z Cuisine. Just like the restaurant, the bar was an instant success. Both places have the feel of a true bistro—small, warm, personable, simple, and fresh—and feature art and fixtures made by local artisans (don't miss the chandeliers by Tracey Barnes). The bar also offers a scaled-down menu of the French fare found at Z.

ADRIFT

218 S. Broadway, 303/778-8454

HOURS: Daily 5 P.M.-2 A.M.

COST: No cover

Map 2

I often hear people say that Denver would be perfect if it only had a beach. Good news for those folks! Adrift is Denver's tiki bar, with a Polynesian island theme in decor (puffer fish lanterns, for one thing), cocktails, staff attire, and menu. The drink names alone are worth a visit—there are the Zombie, Paralysis, and Painkller, in addition to daiquiris and mai tais. The patios are perfect for playing beach "staycation" in the summer.

CHURCHILL BAR

321 17th St., 303/297-3111, www.brownpalace.com

HOURS: Daily 11 A.M.-11 P.M.

COST: No cover

Map 1

Since a 2006 state law was passed to prohibit smoking in bars and restaurants, about the only place it is legal to smoke inside is a cigar bar, such as the Churchill Bar in the Brown Palace Hotel. The Churchill Bar has the feel of an old gentleman's club, with large, brown leather chairs in a quiet room tucked away from the bustle of the hotel lobby and other restaurants. They offer a selection of 60 cigars, as well as scotches, bourbons, and cocktails.

CORNER OFFICE RESTAURANT AND MARTINI BAR

1401 Curtis St., 303/825-6500, www. thecornerofficedenver.com

HOURS: Daily 6 A.M.-close

COST: No cover

Map 1

The Curtis Hotel is hooked on themes, and that includes the decor and everything else at its Corner Office Restaurant and Martini Bar. The design is unabashedly 1970s, for better or worse, and beyond that, it's about the nine-to-five life. Every clock in the Corner Office is set at 5 P.M.—time to leave the office for a drink. And some of the specialty cocktails and martinis carry on the concept with names like "Working Stiff" and "The Secretary." The bottom line is that the Corner Office is best for a drink after a night at the theater. If you're in the mood for something sweet, make sure to try the surprising desserts, such as the wispy cotton candy and the "psychedelic boat trip." Closing hours vary depending on how busy the restaurant is.

CORRIDOR 44

1433 Larimer St., 303/893-0044, www.corridor44.com

HOURS: Daily 4 P.M.-2 A.M.

COST: No cover

`Map 3`

Denver's only champagne bar offers a small-plates menu to complement the selection of bubbly. Located in historic Larimer Square next to Rioja, Corridor 44 is cleverly named

COURTESY OF THE CRUISE ROOM

Step into the past at The Cruise Room inside the Oxford Hotel.

after the 44-foot-long hallway that links the bustling front bar to the more intimate dining room in the rear. The small plates range from oyster shooters to mini sandwiches and salads to a caviar tasting plate. Champagnes are available by the glass or full or half bottle.

◖ THE CRUISE ROOM

1600 17th St., 303/825-1107, www.theoxfordhotel.com

HOURS: Sun.-Thurs. 4:30-11:45 P.M., Fri.-Sat. 4:30 P.M.-12:45 A.M.

COST: No cover

`Map 3`

Step back in time, to about the 1930s or so, in the pink-hued, art deco Cruise Room on the first floor of the historic Oxford Hotel in LoDo. It's hard to get up and leave The Cruise Room once you've settled into one of their cushy booths and ordered a few of their fabulous martinis from the excellent bartenders. The Cruise Room, which opened the day after Prohibition ended in 1933, is modeled after a cruise ship lounge on the *Queen Mary*. The bar is great for a romantic date night or just a casual night out for drinks with friends.

◖ DON'S CLUB TAVERN

723 E. 6th Ave., www.donsclubtavern.com

HOURS: Mon.-Fri. 2 P.M.-2 A.M., Sat.-Sun. 11 A.M.-2 A.M.

COST: No cover

`Map 4`

There's a reason Don's Club Tavern doesn't have a phone: "Don used to say, 'You can't sell beer over the phone,'" explains a friendly bartender on a slow night. In keeping with the anti-modernization attitude, there is one pay phone in a booth. Don's has been around since 1947, and nobody wants it to change. It is routinely named the city's best dive bar for its simple qualities: a few pool tables, worn-out booths, threadbare carpet, and beer and cocktails without pretension.

NIGHTLIFE

FLUFF BAR

1516 Wazee St., 720/295-3583, http://fluffbar.com

HOURS: Tues.-Thurs. 11 A.M.-11 P.M., Fri.-Sat. 11 A.M.-2 A.M., Sun. noon-7 P.M., closed Mon.

COST: No cover

Map 3

When I first heard of Fluff Bar, I could not imagine drinking gaily and allowing someone to cut my hair. However, I've been set straight; people primarily come here to have their hair styled more than cut (though cuts and colors are also on the menu). And it's not just about fluffing up one's hair—you can also get a shave (gentlemen), brows contoured, and makeup done, all while sipping on a "Spa-tini," a "Fluff-arita," or simply a glass of champagne.

FOREST ROOM 5

2532 15th St., 303/433-7001, www.forestroom5.com

HOURS: Mon.-Sat. 4:30 P.M.-2 A.M.

COST: No cover

Map 5

At the place where the Highlands neighborhood begins on 15th Street is Forest Room 5, where patio seats offer a view of the city lights. With flickering candles and large windows in the front room, Forest Room 5 is a hip, little neighborhood bar that offers more than a few drinks and tapas. Forest Room 5's back room features dance music and is perfect for private parties.

HAI BAR

3600 W. 32nd Ave., Ste. D, 720/855-0888, www.sushihai.com

HOURS: Wed.-Sun. 8 P.M.-1 A.M., closed Mon. and Tues.

COST: No cover

Map 5

Past the busy sushi chefs on display near the entrance in Sushi Hai and past diners seated on black leather banquettes, stairs lead to the Hai Bar, a cool underground room with exposed rock walls and mellow lighting. Named in reference to its home, the Highlands (Hai-lands, get it?), the Hai Bar is an inviting place for late-night sushi and specialty martinis and sake. Kick back and watch some TV or a pool game from the cushy lounge seating. The sushi bar serves until midnight and happy hour begins at 10 P.M.

HERB'S HIDEOUT

2057 Larimer St., 303/299-9555, www.herbsbar.com

HOURS: Daily 7 P.M.-2 A.M.

COST: $5 Fri.-Sat. after 10 P.M.

Map 3

In the mix with LoDo's mega-sports bars and brewpubs, all walking distance from Coors Field, is Herb's Hideout, a classic, old drinking bar. The result of location and history is an intriguing mix of committed barflies and hipsters either lost or looking for something off the beaten track. There is live jazz and blues music at Herb's every night of the week. Reasonable prices, decent barbecue, and friendly bartenders keep people coming back for more. The sign outside reads "Herb's," but locals know it as Herb's Hideout.

THE LIVING ROOM

1055 Broadway, 303/339-6636, www.coclubs.com

HOURS: Tues.-Thurs. 4-11 P.M., Fri.-Sat. 4 P.M.-2 A.M., closed Sun. and Mon.

COST: No cover

Map 2

Wine on tap? That's kind of the idea at The Living Room, a wine bar on the fringe of the Golden Triangle neighborhood. An Enomatic machine allows you to sample up to two dozen wines by the ounce by simply pushing a button. The concept is similar to a copy machine: Buy a $10 card, then each sample gets deducted from the total. They also have beer and small plates so you can lounge about in the booths. Check their calendar for various music and film nights.

Sample wines using the Enomatic machine at The Living Room.

LOCAL 46

4586 Tennyson St., 720/524-3792,
www.local46bar.com
HOURS: Mon.-Thurs. 3 P.M.-2 A.M., Fri. 2 P.M.-2 A.M., Sat.-Sun. noon-2 A.M.
COST: No cover
Map 5

Tennyson Street is being revitalized, and that means new businesses are bringing spark to neighborhood business strip. Local 46 opened in 2012 in a building that has been a beauty salon, a convenience store, and, more recently, the Music Bar (until rent shot up with the revitalization underway). Check the entertainment page of Local 46's website to find out if it's karaoke night, game night, a battle of the bands, open mic or some other live music playing.

LOLA

1575 Boulder St., 720/570-8686, www.loladenver.com
HOURS: Mon.-Thurs. 4-11 P.M., Fri. 4-midnight, Sat. 10 A.M.-midnight, Sun. 10 A.M.-10 P.M.

COST: No cover
Map 5

While Lola is a Mexican food restaurant, what it's really known for is its bar and, specifically, its tequila selection. Judging by the almost daily overflow crowds on the outdoor patio, people come here to drink together. It's happy hour at Lola all night on Mondays, from 4-6 P.M. on Tuesdays through Fridays, and 2:30-5 P.M. on Saturdays and Sundays. There is also live music on Sundays.

THE MATCHBOX

2625 Larimer St., 720/437-9100,
www.matchboxdenver.com
HOURS: Mon.-Fri. 4 P.M.-2 A.M., Sat.-Sun. noon-2 A.M.
COST: No cover
Map 1

On the edge of what has recently become known as the River North Arts District, a neighborhood of creative businesses (it's where the artists fled to when LoDo became popular, trendy, and expensive), is The Matchbox. The name of this place was in part inspired by a fire that gutted the building in 2009. Now it's been reborn, with an open beer garden and bocce ball court out back, and a narrow but large interior with exposed brick that reveals a historic-sign mural. This is a place for drinking, not eating, but local food trucks make a stop on special nights.

◖ MEZCAL

3230 E. Colfax Ave., 303/322-5219,
www.mezcalcolorado.com
HOURS: Mon.-Fri. 11 A.M.-1 A.M., Sat.-Sun. 10 A.M.-2 A.M.
COST: No cover
Map 4

The hundreds of tequilas to choose from at Mezcal make it the place to come for margaritas or shots. The place is done up in a Mexican movie madness theme, with posters of bodacious Latinas on the walls and Mexican church candles flickering. Across the street from the Bluebird Theater, Mezcal attracts concertgoers as well as neighborhood locals. Check their calendar for the annual taco-eating contest and for live music nights. Note that there is both an early *and* late happy hour here. Parking can be very limited on nearby side streets and along Colfax Avenue.

MY BROTHER'S BAR

2376 15th St., 303/455-9991
HOURS: Mon.-Sat. 11 A.M.-2 A.M., closed Sun.
COST: No cover
Map 3

My Brother's Bar is best known for being a one-time hangout of writer Jack Kerouac's Denver buddy, Neal Cassady, who was a well-known barfly. It is one of Denver's oldest bars, and not much seems to change here year after year. The main reason people eat here are the hamburgers, but also try the vegetarian Nina (a cheese sandwich named after a former waitress). The patio out back is a great place to spend a

summer evening drinking a cold beer before or after a football or baseball game nearby. Brother's does not have any kind of sign out front, but you can't miss it. It's right on the corner of Platte and 15th Streets, and there is always classical music playing on its outdoor speakers.

THE 1UP

1925 Blake St., 303/779-6444, www.the-1up.com
HOURS: Oct.-March Mon.-Thurs. 3 P.M.-2 A.M., Fri.-Sat. 11 A.M.-2 A.M.; April-Sept. daily 11 A.M.-2 A.M.
COST: No cover
Map 3

Games and drinking go together like salt and pepper, yet The 1Up is a fairly unique concept for Denver: Classic arcade games such as Pac-Man, Donkey Kong, Tron, and lots more line the walls, and there are also pinball machines, Skee-ball, and Giant Jenga to play while drinking beer or cocktails. To complete

JACK KEROUAC AND NEAL CASSADY

Jack Kerouac was drawn to Denver to spend time with his friend Neal Cassady, who enjoyed drinking at many Denver bars. Kerouac's classic *On the Road* is partially set in Denver, and Neal Cassady was renamed Dean Moriarty as a character in the novel. One of Cassady's favorite haunts was **My Brother's Bar** (then called Paul's Place), which is walking distance from the railroad tracks and steps from the South Platte River.

Long before the two men met, Neal Cassady had some minor run-ins with the law and spent some time in jail. A letter he wrote to a friend asking for help paying off his bar tab of "3 or 4 dollars" is framed and on display near the restrooms. Years later, when Kerouac visited Cassady in Denver, the two often enjoyed drinking in what is now called My Brother's Bar.

the time-machine feel, hit the jukebox for some classic tunes.

PATSY'S INN ITALIAN RESTAURANT
3651 Navajo St., 303/477-8910, www.patsysinn.com
HOURS: Mon.-Thurs. 11 A.M.-9 P.M., Fri. 11 A.M.-10 P.M., Sat. 5-9:30 P.M., Sun. 4-8 P.M.
COST: No cover
Map 5

Patsy's is a throwback to the Highlands neighborhood days as an Italian immigrant enclave. The bar and restaurant were opened in 1921, and not much has changed at Patsy's in that time, from menu to decor (the murals of the old country are charming). But the block has changed to include a handful of art galleries, making Patsy's the perfect place to have a drink and discuss art before or after cruising the latest gallery openings. The drinks and good food are very reasonably priced.

PROHIBITION
504 E. Colfax Ave., 303/832-4840, www.prohibitiondenver.com
HOURS: Mon.-Tues. 5 P.M.-2 A.M., Wed.-Fri. 2 P.M.-2 A.M., Sat. 11 A.M.-2 A.M., Sun. 10:30 A.M.-2 A.M.
COST: No cover
Map 4

Think back to a time when drinking was not almost universally accepted and celebrated, but unlawful and unacceptable—a time of prohibition. At this establishment in the Capitol Hill neighborhood, prohibition seems kind of stylish, with an ancient bar anchoring the refurbished space that includes banquettes and tables with framed, vintage newspaper headlines about the real time of prohibition. Some cocktails of the era are even served in a tin cup. The food is a mix of burgers, salads, pot pie, and bar snacks. In this still-rough patch of Colfax Avenue, Prohibition is aiming for a more upscale and trendy crowd.

NOTHING TO WINE ABOUT

While not exactly Napa Valley, there are Colorado vineyards and wineries, and a great place to sample their products is right here in Denver.

Colorado Winery Row is a small collective of four artisanal Colorado wineries (www.coloradowineryrow.com): Bonacquisti Wine Company, Cottonwood Cellars, Garfield Estates Vineyard & Winery, and Verso Cellars. Located just of I-70, Colorado Winery Row makes itself a destination and not just someplace to stop.

While most Colorado grapes are grown on the Western Slope four hours from Denver, the **Balistreri Vineyards** (1946 E. 66th Ave., 303/287-5156, www.balistrerivineyards.com) grows them just northeast of downtown. The winery is open for tours and tastings daily noon-5 P.M.

The Infinite Monkey Theorem (931 W. 5th Ave., 303/736-8376, www.infinitemonkeytheorem.com) is the least conventional of these urban wineries, as it is located in a Quonset hut on an alley. Visitors are invited to visit the hut for a tasting or a winemaking tour. Try the IMF wine from a can or a bottle.

SPUTNIK
3 S. Broadway, 720/570-4503, www.sputnikdenver.com
HOURS: Mon.-Fri. 10:30 A.M.-2 A.M., Sat.-Sun. 10 A.M.-2 A.M.
COST: No cover
Map 2

Sputnik is the satellite bar right next door to the concert venue Hi-Dive. Sputnik features DJs six nights a week, playing everything from 1960s' garage rock to punk to the latest releases by bands that have played or will play at Hi-Dive. The bar also has a rather wild bingo night on Mondays. In addition to a menu of eclectic comfort food, Sputnik has a full espresso and liquor bar. The music and clientele match the

NIGHTLIFE

Williams & Graham is a modern speakeasy.

Hi-Dive for the most part—loud, young, a bit grunge, and up for a very late night.

TENNYSON'S TAP

4335 W. 38th Ave., 303/455-4269,
www.tennysonstap.com
HOURS: Daily 8 A.M.-2 A.M.
COST: No cover
Map 5

It's a bar! It's an art gallery! It's a recording studio! And speaking of what's on tap, the emphasis is on Colorado spirits and brews. Patrons can come in and drink Stranahan's Colorado Whiskey, Zebra Vodka, Lefthand Milk Stout, or some other Colorado-made beer, while listening to local musicians who specialize in jazz, blues, funk, and rock. There is also a comedy night. Tennyson's Tap was voted one of Denver's best new bars by *Westword* magazine in 2012.

THE THIN MAN

2015 E. 17th Ave., 303/320-7814,
http://thinmantavern.com
HOURS: Daily 3 P.M.-2 A.M.
COST: No cover
Map 4

This narrow bar with dark red lighting is a decent place to start an evening or grab a drink while waiting for a table at a nearby restaurant. The only drawback to The Thin Man is its success as the anti-LoDo place to be—it can be challenging to find a barstool or table in the packed bar, especially on a weekend, and it's also very loud. But the terrific bartenders and tasty appetizers keep regulars happily squeezed in.

◖ THE VILLAGE CORK

1300 S. Pearl St., 303/282-8399, www.villagecork.com
HOURS: Mon.-Thurs. 4-10:30 P.M., Fri. 4 P.M.-midnight, Sat. 5 P.M.-midnight, Sun. 10:30 A.M.-2:30 P.M.-
COST: No cover
Map 6

Not necessarily for oenophiles, but for regular people who might want to learn more about wine or sample wines not typically available by the glass, The Village Cork is a neat little Washington Park nook for a romantic date. Local magazines voted this "Best Wine Bar" and "Best Rising Chef" in 2012. Not far from the Louisiana–Pearl Street light rail stop, this can be the ideal after-dinner spot for a sweet treat and a glass of wine. Try the three sample wines for $10 before committing to a glass or bottle.

◖ WILLIAMS & GRAHAM

3160 Tejon St., 303/997-8886,
www.williamsandgraham.com
HOURS: Daily 5 P.M.-1 A.M.
COST: No cover
Map 5

People have not been this excited about a speakeasy since there were, well, speakeasies. Opened in 2011 in the increasingly popular

LoHi neighborhood, Williams & Graham was quickly welcomed by locals for its unique faux bookstore entrance, which cleverly hides the bar behind a velvet curtain. Staff members are dressed for the era in 1920s' garb, but it's not costumey. The extensive liquor selection and tasty small plates have led this bar to the top of many lists. Reservations are recommended.

ZIO ROMOLO'S ALLEY BAR

2400 W. 32nd Ave., 303/477-0395,
www.pasquinis.com

HOURS: Mon.-Thurs. 4 P.M.-midnight, Fri. 4 P.M.-2 A.M., Sat. 11 A.M.-2 A.M., Sun. 11 A.M.-midnight

COST: No cover

Map 5

Before this historic building was added on to long ago in what used to be a working alley is the art deco Zio Romolo's Alley Bar. The bar includes an "exterior" wall with the original Coca-Cola sign painted on it. The 1950s-style neon signs and pressed-tin ceiling make Zio Romolo's a place to see as well as stop for a drink. Located in the evolving LoHi section of Highlands, Zio's is a friendly bar for locals and tourists.

Breweries and Pubs

BRECKENRIDGE BREWERY
BALL PARK PUB

2220 Blake St., 303/297-3644, www.breckbrew.com

HOURS: Sun.-Thurs. 11 A.M.-midnight, Fri.-Sat. 11 A.M.-1 A.M.

COST: No cover

Map 3

Beer lovers are not just limited to Denver; many towns throughout Colorado have spawned terrific brewpubs of their own. Breckenridge Brewery became a staple of its namesake town before adding another location near the ballpark in LoDo. This immense space offers basic pub food and hand-crafted ales. It is a favorite on Colorado Rockies game days, and there are numerous TVs showing sports at any time of year.

BULL & BUSH BREWERY

4700 Cherry Creek Dr., 303/759-0333,
www.bullandbush.com

HOURS: Mon.-Fri. 11 A.M.-2 A.M., Sat.-Sun. 10 A.M.-2 A.M.

COST: No cover

Map 7

A re-creation of the famous London pub, Bull & Bush is a cozy place with wood beam ceilings and a fireplace, but with one big difference: TVs tuned to a variety of sports. There's always a selection of their own microbrews on tap to pair with the traditional pub food, including smoked-cheddar bacon burgers, steaks, fish and chips, and shepherd's pie. Bull & Bush is just a stone's throw from the Cherry Creek neighborhood.

CELTIC TAVERN

1801-1805 Blake St., 303/308-1795,
www.celtictavern.com

HOURS: Mon.-Fri. 11 A.M.-midnight, Sat. 5 P.M.-2 A.M., Sun. 5 P.M.-midnight

COST: No cover

Map 3

The Celtic Tavern is that rare Irish pub that does not serve Guinness. Instead, the bartenders pour Murphy's Irish Stout, which is brewed in Ireland, and a long list of other beers brewed nowhere near Ireland. The tavern also has an impressive selection of single-malt scotches and whiskeys. The scene here is a mix of regulars who enjoy the leather easy chairs and volumes of books, and LoDo barhoppers. Locals might be confused that this is a non-smoking bar, but take a breath because they've simply made a separate bar next door for cigar lovers.

NIGHTLIFE

DELANEY'S BAR

1801-1805 Blake St., 303/308-1795,
www.theceltictavern.com

HOURS: Mon.-Fri. 11 A.M.-midnight, Sat. 5 P.M.-2 A.M.,
Sun. 5 P.M.-midnight

COST: No cover

Map 3

Part of what seems like the Celtic Tavern compound is Delaney's Bar, a cigar bar with an ambience separate from the Celtic. There is dark wood, exposed brick, and, in private rooms, comfy upholstered chairs for time to spend leisurely smoking, drinking, or perhaps browsing through a book while enjoying the fireplace. This claims to be "the only place in North America" where you can smoke a cigar *and* go bowling. It's a full service bar with a full menu, plus a selection of whiskeys and other drinks.

DENVER BEER COMPANY

1695 Platte St., 303/433-2739,
http://denverbeerco.com

HOURS: Mon.-Thurs. 3-11 P.M., Fri.-Sat. noon-midnight,
Sun. noon-9 P.M.

COST: No cover

Map 3

Opened in 2011, the Denver Beer Company has a bit of the essence of some guys coming up with new brews in their garage—just like the founders once did. The beers here change seasonally, and this constant reinvention has led to some award-winning brews. As a result, this is the place to come to try something new, not necessarily tried and true.

FALLING ROCK TAP HOUSE

1919 Blake St., 303/293-8338,
www.fallingrocktaphouse.com

HOURS: Daily 11 A.M.-2 A.M.

COST: No cover

Map 3

Beer aficionados are repeat customers at the Falling Rock Tap House, one block from Coors Field. There are about 70 local,

national, and international beers on tap to sample here, as well as some bottled brews. This bar is the favorite hangout during the annual Great American Beer Festival in October. There are billiard tables and dartboards for fun and games. While this is a friendly bar, it's not really a place for the family to come after a game.

GREAT DIVIDE BREWING COMPANY

2201 Arapahoe St., 303/296-9460,
www.greatdivide.com

HOURS: Sun.-Tues. 2-8 P.M., Wed.-Sat. 2-10 P.M.

COST: No cover

Map 3

At the Great Divide Brewing Company, beer is nearly celebrated, not just consumed. Choose between seasonal, year-round, or barrel-aged brews. Plan to come for a beer and cheese pairing night, a "Hop Disciples" night to discuss "all things beer related," or take a tour of the place. Don't forget to shop! They have clothing and bottle openers adorned with the company logo, and, of course, beer to go.

PINT'S PUB

221 W. 13th Ave., 303/534-7543, www.pintspub.com

HOURS: Mon.-Sat. 11 A.M.-midnight, Sun. 11 A.M.-8 P.M.

COST: No cover

Map 2

Pint's Pub is a traditional British pub that screams that fact from the curbside with cheery, red, old-fashioned telephone booths and the flag of England flying (or emblazoned) on the sign. Just down the street from the Denver Art Museum and Byers-Evans House Museum, Pint's is a welcoming place to stop in for a pint and fish-and-chips for lunch or dinner. The pub is known for its cask-conditioned ales and single-malt whiskeys.

POURHOUSE PUB

1435 Market St., 303/623-7687,
www.pourhousepubdenver.com

BREWING 101

With Denver's reputation as a sudsy Napa Valley of sorts, it's worthwhile to learn more about where and how the local beer is made. Tours are on tap at a few local breweries, with free samples along the way. Start with the **Great Divide Brewing Company** in LoDo (2201 Arapahoe St., 303/296-9460, www.greatdivide.com). Great Divide offers free tours six days a week (Mon.-Fri. 3 P.M. and 4 P.M., Sat. on the hour 2-7 P.M.). The tours start in the Tap Room and include four (free!) tastings along the way. Opened in 1994, Great Divide has become an award-winning brewpub with beers named after the region, such as Denver Pale Ale and Ridgeline Amber Ale.

Also check in with the **Wynkoop Brewing Company** (1634 18th St., 303/297-2700, www.wynkoop.com), **Breckenridge Brewery** (2220 Blake St., 303/297-3644, www.breckbrew. com), and **Bull & Bush Brewery** (4700 Cherry Creek Dr., 303/759-0333, www. bullandbush.com) to schedule tours of their facilities.

HOURS: Daily 2 P.M.-2 A.M.
COST: No cover
Map 3

In the midst of the swanky nightclubs and lounges of LoDo is a comfy pub with the feel of a neighborhood bar. The barstools are the best seats in the house at the Pourhouse Pub, but also check out the heated roof deck, a great spot year-round. The music at Pourhouse does not drown out conversations, and the bartenders are friendly and fun to talk to. While not a typical sports bar, Pourhouse does have TVs tuned to sports channels.

RACKHOUSE PUB

208 Kalamath St., 720/570-7824,
www.rackhousepub.com
HOURS: Daily 11 A.M.-midnight

COST: No cover
Map 2

What makes the Rackhouse Pub worth a visit are its close ties with Stranahan's Colorado Whiskey Distillery (200 S. Kalamath St., 303/296-7440, www.stranahans.com). This popular whiskey is the foundation for a menu of local spirits, local beers, and dishes that incorporate the whiskey, too. The Rackhouse is in the vicinity of the Santa Fe Arts District and can—possibly should—be included during an art-walk night there. There are tours of the distillery, and reservations are highly recommended.

RENEGADE BREWING COMPANY

925 W. 9th Ave., 720/401-4089,
http://renegadebrewing.com
HOURS: Mon.-Thurs. 3-9 P.M., Fri.-Sat. 2-10 P.M., Sun. 1-6 P.M.
COST: No cover
Map 2

You know a neighborhood has reached a tipping point from up-and-coming to found when it gets its own brewery. Now the Santa Fe Arts District has the Renegade Brewing Company—craft beer among the arts and crafts of the area. Renegade partners with local food truck vendors, so if you're hungry as well as thirsty, check the website to find out which truck is there on each day of the week.

SANDLOT BREWERY

2161 Blake St., 303/298-1587
HOURS: Only open on Colorado Rockies game days
COST: Ticket required for access
Map 3

Coors didn't just put their name on the Colorado Rockies' home field, they also set up a brewery and restaurant at Coors Field. Sandlot Brewery—or Blue Moon Brewery at Sandlot, as it is also called—features the Coors Brewing Company's Blue Moon label and other award-winning beers. The atmosphere at Sandlot is

NIGHTLIFE

family-friendly, with a kids' menu, too. This is like an exclusive club with the only access from inside the stadium.

THE THREE LIONS

2239 E. Colfax Ave., 303/997-6886,
www.threelionsdenver.com
HOURS: Mon.-Fri. 11 A.M.-2 A.M., Sat.-Sun. 7 A.M.-2 A.M.
COST: No cover
Map 4

Like football? A lot? For lovers of world football (according to this bar's website, there are over 6 billion such fans), this is a place to watch, cheer, and drink. The fare here is American-style pub food with chicken wings alongside fish and chips; wash it down with local or European ales. The theme here is to embrace the British way of things in as many ways as possible.

◖ WYNKOOP BREWING COMPANY

1634 18th St., 303/297-2700, www.wynkoop.com
HOURS: Daily 11 A.M.-2 A.M.
COST: No cover
Map 3

Denver's first brewpub remains one of the city's favorites year after year. At the corner of 18th and Wynkoop Streets, the Wynkoop Brewing Company was one of the pioneer businesses in transforming the LoDo neighborhood. One of the co-founders of the Wynkoop is John Hickenlooper, Denver's governor. The brewery offers free tours every Saturday to see its

BRAINS AND BEER

A night out with good conversation and drinks can be an intellectual experience in Denver, if you know where to go.

For several years, the **Wynkoop Brewing Company** has hosted monthly Café Scientifique meetings in the Mercantile Room. Based on French philosophy clubs that meet in cafés, **Café Scientifique** (www.cafescicolorado.org) is an informal gathering where a guest speaker presents a topic and then opens it up to questions from the audience. Topics range from vaccinations to black holes and all kinds of other scientific matters. The meetings are free and begin at about 6:30 P.M. Beer is served, but food must be enjoyed in the restaurant before or after meetings.

If science isn't your thing, a group of local writers and classical musicians share their crafts in various cafés and bars in Denver, such as the **Mercury Cafe. Telling Stories** (www.tellingstoriesmusic.org) night at the Mercury is a chance to listen to original essays and solo classic music selections.

signature line of beers being made on-site. On the first floor of this historic mercantile building is the main bar, restaurant, and patio seating. The second floor has a bar, 22 pool tables, and a few dart lanes.

Lounges

BLACK CROWN LOUNGE

1446 S. Broadway, 720/353-4701,
www.blackcrownlounge.com
HOURS: Mon.-Thurs. 4 P.M.-midnight, Fri. 4 P.M.-2 A.M.,
Sat. 11 A.M.-2 A.M., Sun. 11 A.M.-midnight
COST: No cover
Map 6

Situated in an old house along Antique Row on South Broadway, the Black Crown Lounge's decor of antique sofas, chairs, chandeliers, and draped curtains inside make it stand out. But what makes it a pleasant place to hang out and drink are the exterior patios with slightly more modern furnishings, fountains, eclectic gardens, and statuary. By day, this is a piano bar and retail shop for the antiques; by night, there are happy hours, live music and entertainment, and dinner.

FUNKY BUDDHA LOUNGE

776 Lincoln St., 303/832-5075, www.coclubs.com
HOURS: Tues.-Fri. 5 P.M.-2 A.M., Sat. 7 P.M.-2 A.M., closed
Sun. and Mon.
COST: No cover
Map 2

The Funky Buddha Lounge has one of the best rooftop bars and lounges in Denver, with views of the Rocky Mountains and the city lights. The semi-enclosed space has limited heat, so it can even be enjoyed on chilly nights. Inside the narrow space, with leather booths on one side of the room and barstools on the other, the Funky Buddha can quickly become packed and loud. DJs play hip-hop and house music as the young, good-looking regulars mingle.

MARIO'S DOUBLE DAUGHTER'S SALOTTO

1632 Market St., 303/623-3505,
www.doubledaughters.com
HOURS: Daily 5 P.M.-2 A.M.

COST: No cover
Map 3

With Tim Burton–esque decor in dimly lit reds, blacks, and purples, Mario's Double Daughter's Salotto is typically described as LoDo's only "goth" bar. Named after fictitious conjoined twins, the Double Daughter's Salotto embraces all things freakish, with drinks named "Six-Toed Kitten" and "Rabid Monkey." There is always a DJ playing the best hip-hop and electronica music, and excellent pizza is available from Two-Fisted Mario's Pizzeria next door. The crowd is a mix of young and old, tattooed and buttoned-up, and it can be hard to snag one of their curvy red booths on a busy weekend night.

MILK

1037 Broadway, 303/832-8628, www.coclubs.com
HOURS: Thurs.-Sat. 9 P.M.-2 A.M., closed Sun.-Wed.
COST: Varies
Map 2

For something a bit more laid-back than the many dance clubs and live music venues along Broadway, step into Milk. Downstairs from Bar Standard, the pillow-festooned seating invites patrons to sit and sip while listening to DJs play everything from goth to 1980s' to industrial music. Milk-white booths with sheer curtains allow a bit more privacy than the main room. The club attracts a young and trendy crowd.

THE NINTH DOOR

1808 Blake St., 303/292-2229, www.theninthdoor.com
HOURS: Mon.-Fri. 4:30-10:30 P.M., Sat.-Sun.
4:30-11 P.M.
COST: No cover
Map 3

The Ninth Door brings some unique ideas to Denver's bar and restaurant scene: The emphasis here is on Spain and South America in decor,

NIGHTLIFE

COURTESY SOUTH OF COLFAX NIGHTLIFE DISTRICT

Rock out to music from the '80s and '90s at Milk.

food, and wine. The wine list—with sparkling wines, whites, and reds all from Spain, Argentina, Chile, and Portugal—changes seasonally. The menu includes true Spanish tapas and paella, which can be served at the community table made from old Spanish doors. The name is a reference to a bar favored by expatriate writers in a Spanish town. On Tuesday nights, there is live, flamenco guitar music and on weekends, there is a DJ.

Gay and Lesbian Venues

THE BAR
554 S. Broadway, 303/733-0122, www.itsthebar.com
HOURS: Mon.-Fri. 3 P.M.-close, Sat.-Sun. 2 P.M.-close
COST: Varies
`Map 2`

The Bar, which used to be The Atrium Bar & Grill, has a mix similar to that of a casual neighborhood bar, with a clientele of straight, gay, and lesbian customers. The website describes it as "The (Best) Most Schizophrenic Bar in Denver." Perhaps that explains the odd array of live music nights, "Big Drag Poker," open mic comedy night, a burlesque variety show and...goldfish races?

CHARLIE'S
900 E. Colfax Ave., 303/839-8890,
www.charliesdenver.com
HOURS: Daily 11 A.M.-2 A.M.
COST: No cover
`Map 4`

Before there was *Brokeback Mountain,* there were many gay cowboys and cowgirls looking for a dance partner, even in the wilds of Denver. Charlie's in Capitol Hill is the city's gay and lesbian country-and-western dance club. There are free dance lessons, and for those not into the country scene, a separate dance floor with a DJ playing house and disco music creates a different vibe. Charlie's is the home of the Colorado Gay Rodeo Association.

COMPOUND

145 Broadway, 303/722-7977,
www.compounddenver.com
HOURS: Daily 7 A.M.-2 A.M.
COST: No cover
Map 2

Denver's anti-smoking laws led a staple on the gay and lesbian nightclub scene to significantly improve. In 2007, Compound added a smoking patio out behind the building and expanded its dance floor as part of its $600,000 renovation. During the day, the club is a friendly bar; after 6 P.M. on Wednesdays through Sundays, it is a wild dance party for mostly gay men and lesbian women (though not exclusively), with DJs playing the latest music. Compound's bartenders are also known for their generous pours on all drinks.

TRACKS

3500 Walnut St., 303/863-7326,
www.tracksdenver.com
HOURS: Sun.-Tues. 8 P.M.-1 A.M., closed Wed., Thurs.-Sat. 9 P.M.-2 A.M.; Women only first Fri. of the month 9 P.M.-2 A.M.
COST: $5-7
Map 3

In the 1980s, Tracks was Denver's premier gay and lesbian nightclub, where a mixed crowd mingled for sweaty, fun-filled nights on the dance floor. But when the land was sold in 2001 to make way for new development along the old railroad tracks, the club was shuttered. In June 2005, Tracks reopened in a new location and resumed its status as one of the city's best dance clubs for all. On Thursday night, the club is open to those 18 and over, and on Saturday nights, it is 21 and up only.

NIGHTLIFE

ARTS AND LEISURE

If you fly into Denver International Airport, you'll immediately catch a glimpse of the Denver arts scene—many permanent exhibits by local artists are on view in the main terminal. Once downtown, you will begin to notice even more public art on display in the most unexpected spaces.

As Denver has been forming an identity beyond its cow town image, the two qualities that civic leaders have truly invested in are culture and recreation. Beyond the established Denver Art Museum and Museum of Contemporary Art Denver, Denver museums are diverse, boasting eclectic art collections, such as the Kirkland Museum of Fine & Decorative Art and the Forney Museum of Transportation,

which holds the world's largest steam locomotive. In 2010, Denver hosted its first international contemporary art biennial.

The arts are routinely celebrated throughout Denver. There are monthly First Friday events when galleries around the city open their doors for a casual evening of browsing and cocktails, the city boasts a full Arts Week in the fall, and the Cherry Creek Arts Festival is one of the city's biggest annual events.

Whether you're gallery-hopping or touring public art, you'll see many reminders that recreation is part of everything Denverites do. Rather than inhibit activity, the thinner air at 5,280 feet above sea level encourages it, since the body is working that much harder and

HIGHLIGHTS

© STEVE CRECELIUS, COURTESY OF VISIT DENVER

The National Western Stock Show and Rodeo is one of Denver's oldest and biggest annual events.

(Best Art Collection: The **Dikeou Collection** shows off the private international pop art collection of artist Devon Dikeou (page 123).

(Best Art Studio Turned Museum: Vance Kirkland's artwork and decorative arts collection are on display at one of Denver's cultural treasures, the **Kirkland Museum of Fine & Decorative Art** (page 123).

(Best Art Gallery: The art at **Robischon Gallery** is always appealing for looking at, talking about, and even buying (page 127).

(Best Theater: The **Ellie Caulkins Opera House** is an elegant venue for Opera Colorado, the Colorado Ballet, and touring musicals (page 129).

(Best Outdoor Concert Venue: Red Rocks Amphitheatre is famous for its acoustics as well as the surrounding scenery. It is worth seeing even when there is not a performance (page 134).

(Best Powwow: Listen to the ancient sounds of tribal drums and chants at the **Tesoro Foundation's Indian Market and Powwow** (page 137).

(Best Arts Festival: Artists sell their wares during the Fourth of July weekend at the **Cherry Creek Arts Festival** (page 137).

(Best Cowboy Parade: Every January during the **National Western Stock Show and Rodeo,** cowboys herd longhorn cattle through downtown streets to lead the truly Western parade (page 142).

(Most Spectacular Scenery: The hikes around **Roxborough State Park** are easy to moderate, and the red rock scenery is breathtaking (page 143).

(Best Sledding: The hill at **Commons Park** has the perfect contours for sledding. It's free and near light rail stops, so you don't have to drive in the snow to get there (page 158).

ARTS AND LEISURE

burning calories much more efficiently. Denver ranks as one of the country's "fittest" cities, according to a 2012 *Men's Fitness* magazine article, and in their 2008 survey, the magazine found that 83 percent of Denver adults are physically active. It's easy to be motivated to get fit when there are more sunny days here than in Miami, Florida, and the area holds more than 4,000 acres of traditional parks and parkways. This isn't just playtime though: Denverites run, bike, or walk to work on over 200 miles of jogging and cycling paths. Nearby parks in the foothills of the Front Range mean that city dwellers and visitors can get their mountain fix by driving 30 minutes or less to a trailhead for a day hike amid forests and wildflowers. Spectator sports are also a popular pastime in Denver, and there is a professional team or two for every season of the year. The fans in Denver are as legendary as the teams they love, so taking in a Colorado Rockies baseball game or a Denver Broncos football game can get your pulse racing.

The Arts

MUSEUMS

AMERICAN MUSEUM OF WESTERN ART– THE ANSCHUTZ COLLECTION

1727 Tremont St., 303/293-2000, www.anschutzcollection.org

HOURS: Mon. and Wed. 10 A.M. and 1:30 P.M. for curated tours, or by appt. for larger groups on Tues. and Thurs.

COST: $10 adult, $7 senior and student

Map 1

Directly across the street from the Brown Palace Hotel is the historic Navarre Building, built in 1880, which has served as a school, hotel, brothel (which may have once included a tunnel to bring "clients" over from the Brown), and a dining and jazz club. In 1997, it was bought by the Anschutz Corporation and refurbished for its private offices and to become the American Museum of Western Art from the corporation's private collection. This is serious art that has been previously on loan for exhibits around the world, so viewing is limited to the two-hour tours twice a week, with no children under age eight permitted; children under 16 must be accompanied by an adult. Artists in the collection of 400 paintings on display include Georgia O'Keefe, Albert Bierstadt, Thomas Moran, Ernest Blumenschein, Frederic Remington, and many more.

ARVADA CENTER FOR THE ARTS AND HUMANITIES

6901 Wadsworth Blvd., Arvada, 720/898-7200, www.arvadacenter.org

HOURS: Mon.-Fri. 9 A.M.-6 P.M., Sat. 9 A.M.-5 P.M., Sun. 1-5 P.M. (museum only)

COST: Free

Map 7

Deep within the large Arvada Center in the suburbs west of downtown Denver is a small historical museum. The showpiece and bulk of the museum is a tiny log cabin over a century old that was saved and relocated to this property in the 1970s and 1980s. The additional artifacts tell the unique history of this town and its agricultural past. The surrounding center includes art galleries, theaters that host concerts and plays, and space for art workshops and camps, as well as an outdoor amphitheater and public art always on display.

B'S BALLPARK MUSEUM

1940 Blake St., 303/974-5835, www.ballparkmuseum.com

HOURS: Mon.-Fri. two hours before Colorado Rockies home games, Sat. noon-6 P.M.

COST: $5 (free for military and child under 2)

Map 3

Enhance your ballpark experience by visiting

The American Museum of Western Art—The Anschutz Collection is housed in the historic Navarre Building.

B's Ballpark Museum before you see the game. This is an impressive private collection that goes beyond the Colorado Rockies. Did you know there was a Denver baseball team before the Rockies? Come see what the team was called and when it played. Bits and pieces of other stadiums are part of the collection—bricks, light fixtures, pieces of bats, a telephone, uniforms, and lots more.

◖ DIKEOU COLLECTION

1615 California St., Ste. 515, 303/623-3001,
www.dikeoucollection.org
HOURS: Wed.-Fri. 11 A.M.-5 P.M., or by appt.
COST: Free
Map 1

The Dikeou Collection is an unknown art treasure to even most Denverites, but it should not be missed by anyone with a curiosity about contemporary art. This is the private art collection of Devon Dikeou, an artist who divides her time between Denver and New York, where she also publishes *Zing Magazine.* Not far from the architecturally famous museum buildings in downtown, the Dikeou Collection is housed on the fifth floor of a historic office building (just a few doors down from the Jamba Juice on the corner of the 16th Street Mall), with giant, pink inflatable bunnies by artist Momoyo Torimitsu greeting visitors in the first of many rooms.

FORNEY MUSEUM OF TRANSPORTATION

4303 Brighton Blvd., 303/297-1113,
www.forneymuseum.com
HOURS: Mon.-Sat. 10 A.M.-4 P.M.
COST: $8 adult, $4 child, free for child under 3, $6 senior
Map 7

The Forney Museum is an odd but interesting collection of trains, cars, bicycles, and buggies. The big attraction here is the world's largest steam locomotive on display in the cavernous space. Cars and trains are animated with dressed-up mannequins, which give a sort of creepy and humorous feel to the museum. A few of the displays can be climbed on or sat in, but for the most part, it's just a chance to view the vehicles.

◖ KIRKLAND MUSEUM OF FINE & DECORATIVE ART

1311 Pearl St., 303/832-8576,
www.kirklandmuseum.org
HOURS: Tues.-Sun. 11 A.M.-5 P.M.
COST: $7 adult, $6 senior and student; no child under 13 allowed; child 13 to 17 must be accompanied by an adult
Map 4

The Kirkland Museum of Fine & Decorative Art is one of Denver's cultural gems. This space began as artist Vance Kirkland's studio, and it has been preserved as if the man himself might reenter and hang from his special harness to

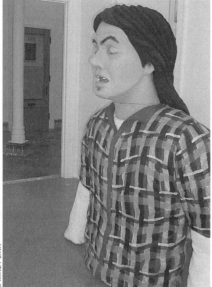

© MINDY SINK

The Dikeou Collection includes works by Lawrence Seward and many other contemporary artists.

begin another dot painting. After his death, the museum was established and took over the fried chicken building next door to open in 2002. In 2003, the collection of over 3,000 examples of arts and crafts, art nouveau, pop art, art deco, and more could be seen on the first and basement floors of the museum. In addition to the modernist decorative works that date from 1880 to 1980, Mr. Kirkland's impressive body of work and rotating exhibits of Colorado artists are on display. Check the website for current special tours.

MIZEL ARTS & CULTURE CENTER
350 S. Dahlia St., 303/316-6360, www.maccjcc.org
HOURS: Singer Gallery only Mon.-Fri. 9 A.M.-4 P.M., Sun. 1-4 P.M.
COST: Free
Map 7

The Mizel Arts & Culture Center is on the campus of the Robert E. Loup Jewish Community Center and includes a variety of cultural events and spaces. The Singer Gallery hosts photography and art exhibits, with an emphasis on national and international Jewish artists and Jewish life. The annual Jewish Film Festival and Jewish Book Festival are also held at the MACC. Check the website to find out about current and upcoming shows as they change every few months.

MIZEL MUSEUM
400 S. Kearney St., 303/394-9993, www.mizelmuseum.org
HOURS: Mon.-Wed. 9 A.M.-4:30 P.M., Thurs. 9 A.M.-8 P.M., Fri. 9 A.M.-4:30 P.M., Sun. 11 A.M.-4:30 P.M.
COST: $7 adult, $3 child age 6-18, free for child 5 and under, $4 senior and student
Map 7

The Mizel Museum should not be confused with the Mizel Arts & Culture Center, with which it was briefly merged. The Mizel Museum hosts various exhibitions throughout each year that reflect on and celebrate Judaism, such as 2008's *Israel at 60*, which included paintings, slide shows, and musical revues. The museum also started the New Israeli Cinema, held weekly in July, and in August 2012, it held its first annual World Kugel Day Festival.

MUSEUM OF OUTDOOR ART
1000 Englewood Pkwy., Englewood, 303/806-0444, www.moaonline.org
HOURS: Indoor gallery Tues.-Thurs. 9 A.M.-5 P.M., Fri. 9 A.M.-4 P.M., Sat. 11 A.M.-4 P.M., closed Sun. and Mon.; Outdoor collection daily (24 hours)
COST: Free
Map 7

The Museum of Outdoor Art is an award-winning museum recognized for its integration of art and environment. There are both indoor and outdoor art spaces, with a permanent collection on display in Greenwood Plaza. The work is displayed in a handful of public

INTERIOR VIEW OF KIRKLAND MUSEUM BY RON RUSCIO.
COURTESY OF KIRKLAND MUSEUM OF FINE & DECORATIVE ART

A table designed by Frank Lloyd Wright is flanked by the work of artist Vance Kirkland at the Kirkland Museum of Fine & Decorative Art.

parks throughout Englewood and Greenwood Village. Artists include Robert Mangold, Todd Siler, Patrick Dougherty, and many others. There are regular additions and acquisitions to the outdoor collection.

GALLERIES
CENTER FOR VISUAL ART

965 Santa Fe Dr., 303/294-5207,
www.metrostatecva.org

HOURS: Tues.-Fri. 11 A.M.–6 P.M., Sat. noon–5 P.M.; Open until 8 P.M. on first and third Fridays during exhibitions

Map 2

The Metropolitan State College's Center for Visual Art is a reminder that downtown Denver is home to a large college campus. (Metro State is on the Auraria Campus, which can be seen from Larimer Square.) The off-campus gallery seems just like another high-end gallery along Santa Fe Drive, with its expansive exhibit space and crisp white walls. This nonprofit is not just

a place for students; it also hosts unique contemporary art exhibits, such as an exhibition of prints and objects by Christo and Jeanne-Claude and a group show of female Vietnamese artists.

COLORADO PHOTOGRAPHIC ARTS CENTER

445 S. Saulsbury St., Lakewood, 303/837-1341,
www.cpacphoto.org

HOURS: Tues.-Sat. noon–5:30 P.M., closed Sun. and Mon.

Map 7

In the heart of suburban Lakewood's Belmar mall is a photography gallery and school worth a visit. The workshops here—mainly digital photography classes—are taught by professional photographers and are primarily at the Belmar location, but for any old-school photographers who want to learn more than digital photography, the school's Silver Print

FIRST FRIDAY ART WALK

First Fridays have become a citywide event. Every neighborhood that has art galleries and cultural institutions is getting into the act. The first Friday of each month, art galleries stay open late and it's as festive as a typical art opening, with wine and hors d'oeuvres offered at most stops. Oh, and it's free.

Some of the more organized First Fridays are in the Golden Triangle and along Santa Fe Drive. There are over a dozen galleries in just a couple of blocks, mixed in with many delightful restaurants. The **River North Art District** (www.rivernorthart.com) galleries are also open late on First Fridays. Try the **Art Bus shuttle** (303/534-0771, www.gtmd.org) that takes patrons from one gallery to the next; check out the website to see which galleries are participating. There are free drinks at most galleries, so if you're driving on your own, it's a good idea to have that designated driver. And at www.artsdistrictonsantafe.com, there is also information about a shuttle bus that brings visitors to Santa Fe Drive to alleviate parking on the busy street that popular night.

With a smaller concentration of galleries, other neighborhoods have their shops and gallery doors open 5-9 P.M. on the first Friday of each month. Try Tennyson Street between 38th and 44th Avenues or 37th Avenue and Navajo Street in Highlands, Wazee Street near 17th Street in LoDo, and Cherry Creek North.

First Fridays have become such a success that legislation was approved by the governor authorizing galleries to legally serve complimentary wine, beer, and spirits up to 15 times per year.

Darkroom (Capitol Hill, 709 Clarkson St., 303/837-0872, ext. 308) offers weekend classes. The gallery displays and sells some of the best student work.

DAVID COOK FINE ART

1637 Wazee St., 303/623-8181, www.davidcookfineart.com
HOURS: Tues.-Sat. 10:30 A.M.-6 P.M., closed Sun. and Mon., or by appt.
`Map 3`

The emphasis at David Cook Fine Art is on American regional art, including Native American pieces such as drums, jewelry, sculptures, fetishes, and other items. Certainly the West and Southwest are well represented here, but artifacts from tribes all over can be found here, too. Gustave Baumann, Vance Kirkland, George Biddle, and dozens of other familiar and lesser-known artists' work is for sale at David Cook. The gallery is located around the corner from the historic Oxford Hotel in LoDo.

GALLERY 910ARTS

910 Santa Fe Dr., 303/815-1779, www.910arts.com
HOURS: Thurs.-Sat. 11 A.M.-5 P.M.; Open until 9 P.M. on first and third Fridays, closed Sun.-Wed.
`Map 2`

The gallery 910Arts is part of an artist colony along Santa Fe Drive where the green-built and colorfully painted building provides live/work space, artist studios, a coffeehouse, and a small courtyard garden. The gallery showcases visual as well as performing arts at the gallery, often by 910 studio artists. A mission of 910 Arts is to foster discussion about art, so, in conjunction with exhibits, there are gallery talks scheduled each month.

GILDAR GALLERY

82 S. Broadway, 303/993-4474, www.gildargallery.com
HOURS: Wed.-Sat. noon-6 P.M.
`Map 2`

Previously the Illiterate Gallery, the Gildar Gallery opened in 2012 and maintains the same commitment to local artists just getting their start in the art world. This is the place to spot young new talent in Denver, and there is no telling what's next at this contemporary art hot spot. Make a night of it on a First Friday and include Gildar on your route as you check out the restaurants, shops, and other galleries of SoBo.

PIRATE: A CONTEMPORARY ART OASIS

3659 Navajo St., 303/458-6058,
www.pirateartonline.org
HOURS: Fri. 6-10 P.M., Sat.-Sun. noon-5 P.M., closed Mon.-Thurs.

Map 5

The Pirate has given many fledgling Denver artists their start, and this contemporary artist cooperative has changed little since it began. Only recently did the Pirate lose a bit of the old grittiness that was part of its charm, getting a makeover with big windows and a neon sign out front. Longtime members Phil Bender and Louis Recchia have gone on to have their work collected by the Denver Art Museum, and alumni include other well-known artists such as Dale Chisman. This little corner is an art hot spot in the Highlands.

PISMO FINE ART GLASS

2770 E. 2nd Ave., 303/333-2879, www.pismoglass.com
HOURS: Mon.-Sat. 10 A.M.-6 P.M., Sun. 11 A.M.-5 P.M.

Map 6

Dale Chihuly is the name that comes to mind when anyone mentions glass art, but you'll discover a huge array of styles and artists in the medium for sale at Pismo Fine Art Glass in Cherry Creek. It is simply fascinating to look at all of the fragile vessels, objets d'art, and light fixtures in multicolored hues on display. Pismo also has jewelry and beads, with an annual bead invitational to show off even more of these tiny works of art.

◖ ROBISCHON GALLERY

1740 Wazee St., 303/298-7788,
www.robischongallery.com

HOURS: Tues.-Fri. 11 A.M.-6 P.M., Sat. noon-5 P.M., closed Sun. and Mon.

Map 3

The only problem with the exhibits at the Robischon Gallery in LoDo is that they do not stay up long enough. Jim Robischon and his wife Jennifer Doran select such exquisite artists that it is tempting to visit more than once. The gallery hosts about seven shows per year with a variety of mediums—photography, painting, prints, and installations. Well-known artists whose work has been shown here include Richard Serra, Robert Motherwell, and Judy Pfaff, to name just a few. Other artists whose work has been displayed here include Colorado's Jack Balas, Wes Hempel, Jae Ko, and Manuel Neri, and group shows of contemporary Chinese art.

RULE GALLERY

3340 Walnut St., 303/777-9473, www.rulegallery.com
HOURS: Tues.-Sat. noon-5 P.M., closed Sun. and Mon.

Map 7

Robin Rule manages a lovely balance of local modern and contemporary artists with national artists in her gallery. Rule has a long history with the Denver art scene, and this is just her latest business name and location. Local standouts here include abstract painter Dale Chisman, Clark Richert, and Jeff Starr, among others. Rule also represents the work of Sandy Skoglund and Barbara Takenaga. Rule moved to the River North Arts District neighborhood in 2010, just as the area was exploding with potential and growth as more bars, restaurants, and galleries opened.

SLOANE GALLERY OF ART

1612 17th St., 303/595-4230,
www.artnet.com/sloane.html
HOURS: Tues.-Sat. noon-7 P.M., closed Sun. and Mon., or by appt.

Map 3

While names of the hottest, contemporary

RIVER NORTH ART DISTRICT

Artists are pioneers in urban neighborhoods, fearlessly moving into old warehouses and transforming them into art havens. The latest, funky, art enclave in Denver is the River North Art District, now being called RiNo, where many artists have colonized old warehouses near the train tracks and the Platte River north of downtown.

The best way to understand and experience RiNo is to go to the website www.rivernorthart. com and print out the field guide that has a list of the nearly 50 members in the greater Denver area. These include specialty furniture shops, artist studios, galleries, architect offices, and a lot more.

RiNo includes a few key live/work spaces in the greater district. One of these is the **TAXI development** (3457 Ringsby Ct., 303/573-0781, www.taxibyzeppelin.com), a distinctive new building that provides live/work space with its own café and easy access to mass transit and bike paths along the river.

Ironton Studios (3636 Chestnut Pl., 303/297-8626, www.irontonstudios.com) is home to 13 artist studios, a gallery, and a garden. Ironton hosts events other than just the First Fridays each month, so be sure to check the calendar for upcoming openings.

The **Dry Ice Factory** (3300 Walnut St., www. dryicefactory.org) is a renovated old—yes—ice factory with 22 artist studios, a common ceramics studio, two art galleries, and a coffee shop.

Russian artists may not be on the lips of most people, some of the best can be found right in Denver at the Sloane Gallery, located on the ground floor of the Oxford office building adjacent to the Oxford Hotel. The Sloane Gallery of Art has been in business since 1981 and represents artists whose work is found in major museum collections around the world. These include Russian-born and Russian American artists, as well as some from republics of the former Soviet Union. The subject matter in the paintings on display and for sale at Sloane tends to range from darkly humorous to starkly political.

VAN STRAATEN GALLERY

760 Santa Fe Dr., 303/573-8585,

www.vanstraatengallery.com

HOURS: Tues.-Fri. 10 A.M.-6 P.M., Sat. 11 A.M.-4 P.M., closed Sun. and Mon.

Map 2

One of the art gallery staples on Santa Fe Drive was The Sandy Carson Gallery, which was suddenly acquired by the van Straaten Gallery in 2008. Sandy Carson stayed on as a consultant so that the transition was seamless. The van Straaten's reputation was established with its gallery in Chicago, but it continues here as the gallery represents artists such as John Baldessari, Jim Dine, Andrea Modica, Barbara Shark, and many more. This remains one of the highlights of the First Friday Art Walk along Santa Fe Drive each month.

WALKER FINE ART

300 W. 11th Ave., 303/355-8955,

www.walkerfineart.com

HOURS: Tues.-Sat. 11 A.M.-5 P.M., First Fridays 6-8 P.M., closed Sun. and Mon., or by appt.

Map 2

Given the loft-style space of Walker Fine Art, local artists such as Roland Bernier, Robert Delaney, and Munson Hunt are given ample room to display their two-dimensional and three-dimensional sculptures and large canvas works. The gallery is on the ground floor of a modern condominium building in the Golden Triangle, just four blocks from the Denver Art Museum. Even if you miss an opening or First Friday Art Walk, there is always an exhibit of new work in the rear of the gallery.

ARTS AND LEISURE

WILLIAM HAVU GALLERY
1040 Cherokee St., 303/893-2360,
www.williamhavugallery.com
HOURS: Tues.-Fri. 10 A.M.-6 P.M., Sat. 11 A.M.-5 P.M., First Fridays 6-9 P.M., closed Sun. and Mon., or by appt.
`Map 2`

Among the handful of art galleries in the Golden Triangle, within walking distance of the Denver Art Museum, the William Havu Gallery stands out as one of the best for contemporary art. Havu represents a significant number of well-known Denver artists, many of whom choose to paint or photograph or sculpt the city and surrounding landscape. Artists include Tracy Felix, Homare Ikeda, Stephen Dinsmore, and many others.

THEATERS
THE BUG THEATRE
3654 Navajo St., 303/477-9984, www.bugtheatre.org
HOURS: Vary
`Map 5`

The corner of 37th and Navajo Streets is a little arts colony of mostly visual arts galleries, as well as The Bug Theatre, where emerging filmmakers are showcased and original or little-seen plays are produced. The Bug started out in 1912 as a nickelodeon theater, before many other uses, and finally was neglected until being rescued by local artists who renovated it and found it easy to fill with popular productions like the annual *Santaland Diaries* or amateur night with *Freak Train*. It's always an affordable night out at The Bug.

THE DENVER PUPPET THEATER
3156 W. 38th Ave., 303/458-6446,
www.denverpuppettheater.com
HOURS: In summer: Wed.-Fri. 10 A.M., Sat. 1 P.M.; Closed September; In winter, Thurs.-Fri. 10 A.M., Sat.-Sun. 1 P.M.
COST: $7
`Map 5`

An old-fashioned puppet theater has been enhanced by **Zook's,** a coffee-and-treats shop, and a courtyard with a fountain. The Denver Puppet Theater offers marionette shows based on classic children's stories, such as "Little Red Riding Hood," "Aesop's Fables," "Jack and the Beanstalk," and more. The shows are geared for ages three and up, and children are expected to sit quietly during showtime. Before and after shows, kids can make a souvenir puppet ticket and play with puppets, and their parents can buy a variety of puppets to bring home.

EL CENTRO SU TEATRO
721 Santa Fe Dr., 303/296-0219, www.suteatro.net
HOURS: Vary
`Map 2`

The third-oldest Chicano theater in the country was started as a 1970s' student group for those interested in the Chicano civil rights movement. Today, it remains a community-based Chicano/Latino Cultural Arts Center where visual and performing arts can be seen as well as learned in workshops. In 2010, El Centro Su Teatro purchased the historic Denver Civic Theater and became part of the vibrant arts scene on Santa Fe Drive.

◖ ELLIE CAULKINS OPERA HOUSE
14th and Curtis Sts., 303/357-2787,
www.denvercenter.org
HOURS: Box office Mon.-Sat. 10 A.M.-6 P.M.
`Map 1`

The Ellie Caulkins Opera House opened in 2005 and is the jewel in the crown of the Denver Performing Arts Complex (DPAC). The 1908 grand theater, formerly called the Auditorium Theatre, was completely renovated and can seat 2,268 for opera or other musical performances. Both the Opera Colorado and the Colorado Ballet perform at the "Ellie," as it is called locally. The theater is included on tours of the DPAC, when performance schedules allow. Visit http://operacolorado.org for information on upcoming shows, buy tickets at the administrative offices at 695 South

ARTS AND LEISURE

Colorado Boulevard, or call 303/778-1500 or 303/468-2030.

GARNER GALLERIA THEATRE
14th and Champa Sts., 303/893-4000, www.denvercenter.org
HOURS: Box office Mon.–Sat. 10 A.M.–6 P.M.
Map 1

Within the Denver Performing Arts Complex is the little, 210-seat Garner Galleria Theatre for cabaret-style shows. The Galleria is home to Denver's longest-running musical, *I Love You, You're Perfect, Now Change,* which is up and running again after a hiatus. Shows typically run about four to six months at the Galleria, and if you're just passing through or spontaneously going out on the town, it's the best place at the complex to get a last-minute ticket any time of year. There is a bar in the theater, so drinks are served during the show, too.

HELEN BONFILS THEATRE COMPLEX
1101 13th St., 303/893-4000 or 303/893-4100, www.denvercenter.org
HOURS: Box office Mon.–Sat. 10 A.M.–6 P.M.
Map 1

The Helen Bonfils Theatre Complex is part of the larger, city-owned Denver Performing Arts Complex (DPAC) at 13th and Arapahoe Streets. There are four separate theaters in the Bonfils complex—the Stage, with 770 seats; the Space, a theater-in-the-round with over 400 seats; the Ricketson Theatre, with 250 seats; and the Jones Theatre, with just 200 seats. It's in one of these theaters that patrons are likely to see an original production by the Denver Center Theatre Company. The DPAC is the second-largest performing arts center in the United States, with 10 venues connected by an 80-foot-tall glass ceiling. Tours of the complex and various theater spaces are offered every week. Call 303/893-4100 or 303/446-4829 to schedule a tour.

THE TEMPLE HOYNE BUELL THEATRE
1101 13th St., 303/893-4000, www.denvercenter.org
HOURS: Box office Mon.–Sat. 10 A.M.–6 P.M.
Map 1

The Buell Theatre at the Denver Performing Arts Complex has 2,830 seats and is typically the venue for big, traveling Broadway shows and the crowds they draw. The theater is acoustically designed for musicals, but also hosts dramatic plays and comedies. The city-owned and -run Buell is a former sports arena that was gutted and renovated to become the theater it is today. It is the second-highest-grossing theater in North America with less than 5,000 seats.

DANCE
BALLET NOUVEAU COLORADO
3001 Industrial Ln., Broomfield, 303/466-5685, http://bncdance.com
Map 7

Although based in the suburb of Broomfield, Ballet Nouveau Colorado (BNC) has made a name for itself in Denver with its contemporary style—one performance was a dance to the music of David Bowie, Queen, and INXS. The company describes its style as "innovative," and they hold an annual "Disco Dance Off" fundraiser. Shows are held at a variety of venues in Denver and other suburbs, as well as at Ballet Nouveau's own theater. The BNC was founded in 1992, but really blossomed in 2007 with the arrival of artistic directors Garrett Ammon and Dawn Fay. **Dance Magazine** named BNC one of "25 to Watch" in 2011.

CLEO PARKER ROBINSON DANCE
119 Park Ave. W., 303/295-1759 ext. 13, www.cleoparkerdance.org
Map 1

Led by founder, artistic director, and choreographer Cleo Parker Robinson, the dance company of her name is known for its cross-cultural programs with African American traditions. The company is based in Five Points at the historic Shorter A.M.E. Church, but it performs at other locations in the city and around the world. This is also home to a dance school and various dance classes for children and adults. Like the performances, classes offered include a huge variety of styles, from ballet to tap to West African dance.

COLORADO BALLET

1278 Lincoln St., 303/837-8888, www.coloradoballet.org

HOURS: There are no box office services at the Colorado Ballet headquarters at 1278 Lincoln St. Tickets can be purchased online at www. coloradoballet.org, by phone at 303/837-888 ext. 2, and two hours before each performance at the Ellie Caulkins Box Office at 14th and Curtis Sts.

Map 2

The Colorado Ballet has the dependable annual performance of the *The Nutcracker* during the holidays that reliably draws sold-out crowds. Otherwise, each season is a surprise, with a small handful of other dances running for limited engagements. The company performs at the Ellie Caulkins Opera House, as well as doing onetime performances at other venues, such as the Arvada Center. Some students at the Academy of Colorado Ballet become principal dancers who perform regularly with this company.

COMEDY

BOVINE METROPOLIS THEATRE

1527 Champa St., 303/758-4722, www.bovinemetropolis.com

HOURS: Check website for latest listings; closed Tues. and Wed.

COST: $8-16

Map 1

For anyone who has ever played Mad Libs, the Bovine takes it a step further with their regular "On the Spot" night, during which audience members make suggestions to the cast and a moderator for songs, games, and scenes that will basically create the show. Shows remain on the schedule for weeks to months, with titles like "Improv Hootenanny," "But Wait! There's More!," and other silly names. But that doesn't mean it's the same thing each week, since the nature of improv is to make it up as you go along. Because the Bovine does not serve alcohol, most shows are all ages, but be sure to double-check all of the details on the website for the most current rules, as there can be adult-only ribald humor late into the night.

COMEDY WORKS

1226 15th St., 303/595-3637, www.comedyworks.com

HOURS: Check website for latest listings; closed Mon.

COST: $12-45

Map 3

Roseanne Barr is perhaps more famous than this club where she got her start, but Comedy Works is still the best-known comedy place in town, often with lines out the door. Comedy Works is where you are likely to see big-name comedians—the ones who have made it to TV, like Wanda Sykes and George Lopez. On Tuesday night, it's a chance to try out or catch up-and-coming jokesters on New Talent Night. The seating can be a bit cramped in this basement space, and there is a two-drink minimum. Parking can be found at the Larimer Square Parking Garage on Market Street or at metered spots on the street. Note that there are two locations for Comedy Works, and its online calendar lists both locations. Shows are 18 and over and 21 and over.

IMPULSE THEATER

1634 18th St., 303/297-2111, www.impulsetheater.com

HOURS: Thurs. 8 P.M., Fri.-Sat. 7:30 P.M. and 9:45 P.M., closed Sun.-Wed.

COST: $18

Map 3

True improvisational comedy can be found at the Impulse Theater, located in the lower level of the Wynkoop Brewing Company. Three

ARTS AND LEISURE

THE LAUGHS KEEP COMING

Sometimes the funniest comedy teams aren't found in a comedy club. Denver's own **The Grawlix** (www.fiveunicorns.com/grawlix) performs at places like the **Bug Theatre** (3654 Navajo St., 303/477-9984, www.bugtheatre.org) when in town. Families can enjoy *Rodents of Unusual Size* (www.coloradoimprov.com) at the **Denver Puppet Theater** (3156 W. 38th Ave., 303/458-6446, www.denverpuppettheater.com) in the Highlands neighborhood twice a month. Think you're funny? Then sign up for one of the improv classes here, too.

nights a week, the players manage to create 90 minutes of very funny skits, in a style that is adult, but not vulgar or lewd. The shows are considered appropriate for all ages, though anyone under 21 must be accompanied by a parent or guardian. It's a whole evening out in one place, with dinner and beer upstairs and comedy with cocktails downstairs. There are also "all ages" nights when no alcohol is served.

CONCERT VENUES

BOETTCHER CONCERT HALL
1000 14th St., 303/623-7876,
www.coloradosymphony.org
Map 1

Located in the Denver Performing Arts Complex, Boettcher Concert Hall is the home of the Colorado Symphony Orchestra. When it was built in 1978, Boettcher was the first symphony hall-in-the-round in the United States. About 80 percent of the hall's 2,634 seats are within 65 feet of the stage. There are no true vertical or horizontal surfaces in Boettcher, so that the sound is evenly dispersed.

COMFORT DENTAL AMPHITHEATRE
6350 Greenwood Plaza Blvd., Englewood,
303/220-7000, www.livenation.com
Map 7

The largest outdoor amphitheater in the Denver metro area features 7,500 fixed seats, plus a general admission lawn area to give it a total capacity of 18,000. Formerly Fiddler's Green, then Coors Amphitheatre, and now called Comfort Dental Amphitheatre, this is the place to see mega-shows like Lollapalooza (there have been six held here, under the various name changes). Headline musicians like Stevie Wonder and Dan Fogelberg have also played at Fiddler's. The amphitheater is south of downtown Denver in the suburb of Greenwood Village. There is public and private parking available.

FILLMORE AUDITORIUM
1510 Clarkson St., 303/837-1482,
www.fillmoreauditorium.org
HOURS: Vary
Map 4

The Fillmore Auditorium is a wonderfully refurbished former ice rink that hosts nationally touring acts such as Erykah Badu, Widespread Panic, George Clinton, and Rufus Wainwright. Located on the corner of Clarkson Street and Colfax Avenue in Capitol Hill, the Fillmore is walking distance from downtown. With a seating capacity of about 3,000, the Fillmore is the ideal space for audiences slightly smaller than those hosted at larger venues like Red Rocks Amphitheatre.

GOTHIC THEATRE
3263 S. Broadway, Englewood, 303/788-0984,
www.gothictheatre.com
HOURS: Vary
Map 7

On the cutting edge in the early 1990s as a host to alternative rock bands including Nirvana, the Gothic is now one of a handful of midsize

© STEVE CRECELIUS, COURTESY OF VISIT DENVER

The Pepsi Center hosts basketball and hockey, as well as concerts.

concert venues in historic theaters around Denver. Located just over the city boundary in the suburb of Englewood, the beautiful, art deco theater has great sound. This onetime favorite of heavy metal bands now has concerts that range from reggae to punk rock, featuring local musicians as well as national acts like the B-52s. Shows vary from 16 and up to 21 and up.

OGDEN THEATRE

935 E. Colfax Ave., 303/830-2525,
www.ogdentheatre.net

HOURS: Vary; box office opens before shows

Map 4

One of Denver's premier concert venues for small to midsize shows is the Ogden Theatre. The Ogden is on the National Register of Historic Places, and ornate detail and interesting architectural touches can be seen throughout the building. With a capacity of about 1,200 people, the theater hosts smaller shows than the Fillmore down the street. The Smashing Pumpkins, the Hives, Jimmy Cliff, and the Goo Goo Dolls have all played at the Ogden.

PARAMOUNT THEATRE

1621 Glenarm Pl., 303/825-4904,
www.paramountdenver.com

Map 1

Right off the 16th Street Mall in downtown is the historic Paramount Theatre, a relatively small 1,870-seat venue. Listed on the National Register of Historic Places, the Paramount was originally a movie theater in the 1930s and still has original art deco touches. The original Wurlitzer organ that was installed to accompany silent movies is still played; along with a sister organ at Radio City Music Hall, it's one of the last remaining organs like it in the country. The Paramount has a somewhat sporadic schedule and hosts a wide variety of entertainment, including comedy, ballet, and music.

ARTS AND LEISURE

PEPSI CENTER

1000 Chopper Cir., 303/405-1100,
www.pepsicenter.com
Map 3

Home to two of Denver's major league sports teams—the Colorado Avalanche hockey team and the Denver Nuggets basketball team—the Pepsi Center is also a concert venue for big-name acts like Madonna, Bruce Springsteen, Coldplay, and Celine Dion. When Red Rocks Amphitheatre is closed for the season, the Pepsi Center is the place for big concerts. (The Pepsi Center was also the site of the Democratic National Convention in 2008.)

RED ROCKS AMPHITHEATRE

18300 W. Alameda Pkwy., Morrison, 303/697-4939,
www.redrocksonline.com
HOURS: May–Sept. Daily 8 A.M.–7 P.M., Oct.–Apr. Daily 9 A.M.–4 P.M.; box office opens two hours before doors open, showtimes vary
Map 7

Given its worldwide reputation as a premier outdoor concert venue, Red Rocks Amphitheatre hardly needs any introduction. The Beatles, U2, the Grateful Dead, and many more big names in music have played here over the years, even immortalizing the shows in concert movies. Red Rocks has a summer concert lineup that includes some annual events, such as Reggae on the Rocks and 1964: The Beatles Tribute Band, as well as whoever is touring that year, such as James Taylor or Florence & The Machine. Plan to come early on concert days to be able to park and walk around a bit.

CINEMA

CHEZ ARTISTE

2800 S. Colorado Blvd., 303/352-1992,
www.landmarktheatres.com
Map 7

Located in a worn-down strip mall well south of downtown, Chez Artiste is the least architecturally interesting of the Landmark Theatres chain's local theaters. It's most conveniently located for people from the nearby University of Denver neighborhood, or the suburbs of Littleton and Englewood. Still, it's worth the extra drive if they're showing a great little movie that can't be found anywhere else in town. It's also just down the street from a handful of Middle Eastern restaurants worth checking out before or after the flick.

DENVER FILM CENTER/COLFAX

2510 E. Colfax Ave., 303/595-3456,
www.denverfilm.org
Map 4

The Lowenstein Theatre Complex has become a mini cultural hub on East Colfax Avenue, with the Tattered Cover Bookstore in the historic theater building and the Denver Film Society setting up in the addition next door. The Denver Film Center/Colfax has become the new home to the annual Denver Film Festival, which has screenings at other locations around town, too. There are three main screens, plus a café seating area in the lobby. In 2012, **Westword** magazine voted this the best theater in town because of the free refills on fountain drinks and better-than-average popcorn.

ESQUIRE THEATER

590 Downing St., 303/352-1992,
www.landmarktheatres.com
Map 4

Capitol Hill's art house movie theater has two screens devoted to independent and foreign language films. The Esquire, the Mayan, and the Chez Artiste theaters are all operated by the Landmark Theatres company, which runs historic movie houses throughout the country. This is the kind of theater where you can get herbal tea with your popcorn. There is a small parking lot adjacent to the theater, but otherwise, on-street parking in this residential neighborhood can be tricky.

© MINDY SINK

The historic Mayan Theatre shows movies on three screens.

building dams, or humans scaling mountain peaks. Admission to the museum and planetarium are not included in IMAX ticket prices.

MAYAN THEATRE

110 Broadway, 303/744-6799, www.landmarktheatres.com

Map 2

The theater itself is worth a visit at the unique art deco–style Mayan, which has three screens—one large theater on the main level, and two smaller theaters upstairs. When the glorious building was saved from the wrecking ball in the 1980s, there wasn't much of a scene on this strip of Broadway. Now this neighborhood has its own trendy moniker, SoBo (as in, South Broadway), and there are many wonderful restaurants, bars, and shops within walking distance of this neighborhood hot spot. Fans of foreign and independent cinema love the Mayan with good reason.

IMAX THEATER AT THE DENVER MUSEUM OF NATURE AND SCIENCE

2001 Colorado Blvd., 303/322-7009, www.dmns.org

COST: $8-13

Map 4

For thrilling, really-big-screen movie adventures, go to the IMAX Theater at the Denver Museum of Nature and Science. Perhaps it's just the nature of IMAX films, or the fact that the theater is part of the museum, but the movies shown at this IMAX seem to always have a connection to the museum's theme. Viewers can visually explore coral reefs, beavers

UA DENVER PAVILIONS 15

500 16th St., Ste. 10, 303/454-9086, www.denverpavilions.com

Map 1

On the top level of the 16th Street Mall is a United Artists multiplex movie theater that shows all the latest blockbuster movies several times each day. There are 15 screens to choose from, in rooms of various sizes and seating capacities. The lobby itself is an entertainment zone, with video games and snacks galore at the immense concession stand. You can't beat the variety of showtimes here, including weekday matinees.

ARTS AND LEISURE

Festivals and Events

SPRING

CINCO DE MAYO

Civic Center Park, 100 W. 14th Ave. Pkwy.,
303/534-8342, www.cincodemayodenver.com

Map 1

One of the largest Cinco de Mayo celebrations in the United States is held in Denver every spring in a two-day event. It's a chance to eat Mexican food and enjoy Mexican music while learning more about the culture. There is a parade, live music, dancing, and a green chili cook-off. The organized festival takes place at Civic Center Park, but the Highlands neighborhood, where there is a significant Latin American population, is also a hot spot for the weekend of or near May 5 every year. This often translates to streets clogged with cruisers waving Mexican and American flags.

DENVER MARCH POWWOW

Denver Coliseum, 4600 Humboldt St., 303/934-8045, www.denvermarchpowwow.org
HOURS: Daily 10 A.M.-10 P.M.

Map 7

Denver's largest powwow—one of the largest in the nation—is held for three days every March at the coliseum just beyond downtown. A powwow is essentially a gathering of Native American tribes; the focus is on different dance performances done in elaborate costumes to the beat of live drums. To watch any of the dances—men's or women's, fancy or traditional—is to learn about a particular tribe, region, or history. There are also a lot of vendors selling Native American jewelry, food, artwork, and fetishes. Different activities and performances take place daily.

HIGHLANDS SQUARE STREET FAIR

32nd Ave. and Lowell St., www.highlands-square.com

Map 5

What started as a small, neighborhood fair in the 1980s has exploded into one of the bigger annual festivals, with several blocks around Highlands Square closed off for a full day in mid-June. There is live music on three stages, over 100 vendors set up on the blacktop, and parking lots filled with kids' games and activities. The quality of the festival depends a lot on the weather—it can be scorching hot in mid-June, cold and rainy, or just right. It's best to arrive early before 32nd Avenue becomes too crowded to walk through. There is no admission fee to attend the fair.

SPRING BEAR POWWOW

Regis University, 3333 Regis Blvd.,
www.ravendancers.org

Map 7

While the Spring Bear Powwow at the Regis University Field House has a traditional grand entry performance, drumming, and dancing, it is a no-contest event. This one-day community gathering, with free admission to all, is typically held in mid-May. Native American foods and crafts are sold, and dancers and drummers are all invited to perform. The Regis campus is located just north of the Highlands neighborhood.

ST. PATRICK'S DAY PARADE

Starts at 27th and Blake Sts.,
www.denverstpatricksdayparade.com

Map 3

It's not like events in Chicago or Boston, but Denver's St. Patrick's Day Parade is huge and very popular. The parade winds its way through a portion of LoDo-where, conveniently, there are many brewpubs and bars—with a variety of things Irish or not, like bagpipers and beauty queens riding in convertibles and little dogs doing tricks. The weather can sometimes be downright wintry in March, but people still dye their hair green to match their outfits and come out for a day of celebration. The parade is held on the weekend closest to March 17 on any given year.

◖ TESORO FOUNDATION'S INDIAN MARKET AND POWWOW

The Fort Restaurant, 19192 Hwy. 8, Morrison, 303/839-1671, www.tesoroculturalcenter.org

Map 7

What makes the Tesoro Foundation's Indian Market and Powwow worth the drive up to Morrison is the location. The market is held on outdoor patios of The Fort restaurant, where artisans display their wares in individual tents and booths. The powwow takes place in an open field behind the restaurant. The setting, combined with the sounds of Native American drumming and chanting, transports visitors to another time and place to truly absorb the unique experience that is a celebration of the West, Southwest, and Native American cultures. This is usually a two-day event in mid-May, with performances scheduled at different times each day.

SUMMER

CHERRY BLOSSOM FESTIVAL

Sakura Square, between Lawrence, Larimer, 19th, and 20th Sts., www.tsdbt.org/cherryblossom

Map 3

Just beyond the bars and nightclubs of LoDo is a relatively small, high-rise building and shopping complex, Sakura Square. This quiet, serene city block stands out with its little bonsai garden and Japanese public art on display. While one can go to the Asian food market or restaurants at the square year-round, the best time to come is during the Cherry Blossom Festival in June, to celebrate Japanese-American culture and hear traditional music, watch dancers, tour the temple, and sample authentic Japanese food.

◖ CHERRY CREEK ARTS FESTIVAL

Cherry Creek North, between 1st and 3rd Aves., and Clayton and Steele Sts., 303/355-2787, www.cherryarts.org

Map 6

Every Fourth of July weekend, the streets of Cherry Creek North's shopping district are barricaded for three days to host a huge, outdoor celebration of the arts. The emphasis is on the artwork to be sure, but there is also live music and a whole street devoted to culinary creations. Wander the various booths until something catches your eye, then duck inside the tent, where you might find yourself having a one-on-one chat with one of the artists. The free festival includes local artists as well as those who have come from around the world to participate.

CITY PARK JAZZ

City Park, 3300 E. 17th Ave., 303/744-1004, www.cityparkjazz.org

Map 4

Sunday evenings in the summer (June–early August) are the perfect times to mellow out with some live jazz music and a few thousand fellow citizens in City Park. There are 10 concerts in all, featuring local jazz musicians playing in the bandstand near Ferril Lake or closer to the Denver Museum of Nature and Science in the Meadows. The concerts are free, and blankets and chairs are not provided, but some food is available for sale on-site. Parking is limited, so biking or walking to the weekly concerts is encouraged. Concerts are held rain or shine.

DENVER CHALK ART FESTIVAL

Larimer Square, Larimer St. between 14th and 15th Sts., 303/685-8143, http://denverchalkart.com

Map 3

Just before the heat of summer settles in, Larimer Square transforms its blacktop into a sort of piazza for one weekend in June.

ARTS AND LEISURE

© STAN OBERT COURTESY OF VISIT DENVER

The Denver Chalk Art Festival is held in Larimer Square each June.

Amateur and professional artists use chalk to make beautiful and detailed murals on the city street. Those not drawing can watch the process while enjoying Italian foods, such as gelato and pizza, and step into the wine-tasting tent to sample Italian wines. There's even a special spot for kids to practice their chalk expertise. By Sunday night, all of the art is washed away and Larimer Square returns to normal.

DRAGON BOAT FESTIVAL
Sloan's Lake Park, corner of Stuart St. and 23rd Ave., 303/722-6852, www.cdbf.org
Map 5

Boat racing meets cultural recognition and celebration at the annual Dragon Boat Festival. This has become the largest Pan-Asian festival in the region, with crowds of about 100,000 gathered to learn more about Asian American and Pacific Islander communities. The main draw at this two-day event in July is the boat

racing across the lake—and the competition gets more fierce every year, as racers learn from the previous year and more types of races are offered. "Explore Asia" is one aspect of the festival where local ethnic groups—Hmong, Filipino, Mongolian, and others—can demonstrate cultural traditions. Admission to the festival is free; it's best to consider the shuttle service options for getting there.

PRIDEFEST
Civic Center Park, 100 W. 14th Ave. Pkwy., http://glbtcolorado.org
Map 1

The Gay, Lesbian, Bisexual, and Transgender Community Center of Colorado hosts the annual Pridefest each June. The two-day event includes a parade (in sign of how far this community has come, it is now called the Coors Light Pridefest Parade) that starts in Capitol Hill's Cheesman Park and is the highlight of the festival, with outrageous floats and

© STEVE CRECELIUS, COURTESY OF VISIT DENVER

Denver's annual Pridefest includes a wild parade.

costumes. At Civic Center Park, there is a dance stage and booths with everything from food to crafts to health-awareness information. There is always a huge turnout for the festival, so plan accordingly when it comes to parking. This has become the third-largest pride festival in the country.

A TASTE OF COLORADO

Civic Center Park, 100 W. 14th Ave. Pkwy., 303/295-6330, www.atasteofcolorado.com

Map 1

Labor Day weekend in Denver is a chance to sample various Colorado culinary specialties and gourmet favorites in a three-day eating extravaganza. Chefs do demonstrations, and attendees can enjoy a full meal or just snack throughout the day at every little booth. Over the years, the food has become just one part of the festival; there's also live music, arts and crafts, and other special exhibits. At this time of year, be on the lookout for fresh melons and peaches, though any kind of barbecue seems to always be the favorite. Parking can be a problem, so be prepared to walk off whatever you eat on the way back to the car.

FALL
DENVER ARTS WEEK

www.denverartsweek.com

Denver Arts Week is a way for the entire city to celebrate its culture, super-sized for one week each year. The week usually starts off on a Friday, with free admission to all museums, which have extended hours and shuttle service between each facility. Art galleries host the First Friday Art Walk, and there are special artistic activities for kids at the Denver Zoo and Denver Botanic Gardens. The week also overlaps with the Denver International Film Festival, and it's not just about visual art, but also performance art and more.

ARTS AND LEISURE

DENVER INTERNATIONAL FILM FESTIVAL

303/595-3456, www.denverfilm.org

Map 3

Yes, the stars do come out to walk the red carpet at the annual Denver International Film Festival, with famous directors and actors in attendance and giving special talks. The big gala nights are typically held at the Denver Performing Arts Complex, with the majority of films shown at the Denver Film Center/Colfax. Be sure to check the schedule for any local filmmakers who might be showcasing their latest work. It's wise to buy tickets in advance instead of at the door, as shows can sell out fast.

GREAT AMERICAN BEER FESTIVAL

Colorado Convention Center, 700 14th St., 303/477-0816, www.greatamericanbeerfestival.com

Map 1

Thirsty? Check out the three-day Great American Beer Festival where a ticket to just a single day of the event is a pass to try as many one-ounce samples of over 2,200 beers as possible in one evening. It might sound like a bad frat-party idea, but this is a truly serious beer competition held every October. It's basically the Beer Olympics, and the brewers and tasters mean business. Though the festival is only three days, there is a whole week of related activities around town. The festival, which takes place at the Colorado Convention Center, is now featured in the book *1,000 Places to See Before You Die.*

JUNETEENTH

24th-28th and Welton Sts., 720/276-3693, www.juneteenthmusicfestival.org

Map 1

After dwindling participation and interest effectively killed the long-standing Juneteenth celebration in the historically African American neighborhood of Five Points, the festival was reborn in 2008. A lot has changed in Five Points over the years as the community has been gentrified; much of its intriguing past—soul food restaurants, jazz clubs—is on display in the galleries of the Blair-Caldwell African American Research Library. The two-day Juneteenth festival, which celebrates the end of slavery in the United States, includes a parade, live music, and food. The festival takes place in June every year, but the exact date of the event changes annually.

ROCK 'N' ROLL DENVER MARATHON

Starts at the Colorado State Capital Building, 200 Colfax Ave., http://runrocknroll.competitor.com/denver

Map 4

Before the winter weather creeps in and while fall colors are on display, runners take to the streets over one weekend in September for the Rock 'n' Roll Denver Marathon. (Until 2010, it was simply the Denver Marathon.) The event includes a half marathon and a marathon. This Boston Marathon–qualifying race begins and ends at the Colorado State Capitol Building, and is a sightseeing tour of many of Denver's best sights, including Larimer Square, Coors Field, and City Park.

SPANISH COLONIAL & WESTERN ART MARKET AND 1830S RENDEZVOUS

The Fort Restaurant, 19192 Hwy. 8, Morrison, 303/839-1671, www.tesoroculturalcenter.org

Map 7

Learn about and experience the rugged life in this part of the world before it was Colorado, with mountain men and women in historically accurate camps and trading posts ready to answer questions about "their" life. It's not so much "cowboys and Indians" as it is frontiersmen and Native Americans, with Spanish heritage to boot. During the two-day annual event in late September, sit inside tepees, chat with fur trappers, and check out Spanish Colonial artwork.

COURTESY OF VISIT DENVER

The Denver City and County Building lights up for the holidays.

WINTER
BLOSSOMS OF LIGHT AT
DENVER BOTANIC GARDENS
1005 York St., 720/865-3585,
www.botanicgardens.org

`Map 4`

When the gardens are sleeping for the winter and most of the color is evergreen shrubs, brown dirt, or brilliant-white, fresh snowfall, the annual holiday Blossoms of Light is a welcome burst of color. For about six weeks through December and part of January, the Denver Botanic Gardens puts up over one million lights (with energy-efficient bulbs), draped across evergreen trees or shaped into luminescent flowers. On select nights, there are carolers or other special events. The exact dates, times, and costs vary each year.

DOWNTOWN DENVER'S
GRAND ILLUMINATION
Union Station, 16th Street Mall and Larimer Square, 303/534-6161, www.downtowndenver.com

`Map 3`

In one festive night every year, downtown streets and buildings go from just lit up at night to brightly lit with thousands of colorful holiday lights. Things kick off at Union Station in LoDo, where carolers sing and officials count down to the flip of the switch, when a large tree made of strings of lights and the building itself suddenly glow. The 16th Street Mall (where energy-efficient LED lights are used), Larimer Square, and the Denver City and County Building all turn on their yellow, red, green, and blue lights as huge crowds gather to watch and take part in the festivities.

ARTS AND LEISURE

◖ NATIONAL WESTERN STOCK SHOW AND RODEO

National Western Complex, 4655 Humboldt St.,
303/297-1166, www.nationalwestern.com
COST: $2-14
Map 7

Like it or not, Denver becomes a cow town each January when the National Western Stock Show is held for over three weeks. One major highlight is the cattle drive right through the middle of downtown as long-horn steers are guided up 17th Street from Union Station to the Brown Palace. The event schedule at the complex is packed with 4-H competitions, horse shows, bull riding, and other rodeo shows, as well as an array of special performances, like the popular Mexican Rodeo Extravaganza and Martin Luther King Jr. African American Heritage Rodeo. Overall attendance at the stock show in 2011 was over 644,000 during the 16-day event. (The high watermark was in 2006 during the 100th anniversary when over 700,000 people came.)

ZOO LIGHTS

Denver Zoo, 2300 Steele St., 303/376-4800,
www.denverzoo.org
HOURS: 5:30 P.M.-9 P.M.
COST: $8 adult, $4 child, free for child under 2, $6 senior
Map 4

Usually, the Denver Zoo is a quiet place at night as most of the animals slumber, but during the holiday season, it becomes a festive gathering place for people and animals with lights blazing through about half of the zoo. It's more than just lights shaped like zoo animals and sparkling trees, though—there are ice sculptures made on-site, a Kwanzaa celebration, dances, and carolers. It's a busy time as families enjoy being outside in the crisp winter air and take the chance to see the zoo at a different time of day.

Sports and Recreation

PARKS

CHEESMAN PARK

Franklin and 8th Sts., 720/913-1311, www.denvergov.org
HOURS: Daily 5:30 A.M.-11 P.M.
Map 4

Where the Capitol Hill neighborhood blends into the Congress Park neighborhood is Cheesman Park, which abuts the Denver Botanic Gardens' south end. The large Parthenon-like pavilion in Cheesman Park is popular for wedding pictures, with a stunning view of the Rocky Mountains as a backdrop. Many high-rise apartment buildings overlook the park, an oasis of green in the densely packed neighborhood. There is a large playground and a gravel running path in Cheesman. Due to the sizable gay and lesbian population in Capitol Hill, Cheesman is known as an LGBT hangout and is the place where the annual Pridefest parade begins.

RED ROCKS PARK AND AMPHITHEATRE

18300 W. Alameda Pkwy., Morrison, 303/697-4939,
www.redrocksonline.com
HOURS: May-Sept. Daily 8 A.M.-7 P.M., Oct.-Apr. Daily 9 A.M.-4 P.M.
COST: Free
Map 7

Red Rocks is known for its phenomenal open-air acoustics and live concerts-with past acts including the Beatles, U2, the Grateful Dead, Elvis, John Denver—but the scenery can be enjoyed here anytime, even without music. This nearly upright ring of red sandstone cliffs to the west of Denver is surprisingly close to the city and offers more than just great concerts.

OFF-LEASH DOG PARKS

Dogs are welcome at all Denver parks, but they usually need to remain on a leash or their owners risk tickets and fines. The city has set aside off-leash parks adjacent to a handful of city parks. Go to www.denvergov.org/parks for a list of these 11 dog-friendly zones.

In the Platte Valley, a group of dog-lovers created the **Railyard Dog Park** (www.railyarddogs.org), directly across the street from the Denver Skatepark and very near Commons Park.

Earthdog (370 Kalamath St., 303/534-8700, www.earthdogdenver.com, Mon.-Fri. 6:30 A.M.-7 P.M., Sat. 8 A.M.-7 P.M., Sun. 2-7 P.M.), a doggy daycare, offers public use of its off-leash park and doggy swimming pool for only $5 per dog.

Depending on the weather, visitors can either choose a hiking trail around the red rocks, where wildlife such as deer can be seen wandering about, or check out the visitors center at the top of the amphitheater to see photos of previous concerts. This is also a popular place for mountain biking and cycling. On days when there are no shows scheduled, visitors are allowed to roam the amphitheater for free. There is no climbing allowed on the rocks anywhere in the park, however, as they can be slippery and fragile.

◖ ROXBOROUGH STATE PARK

4751 Roxborough Dr., Littleton, 303/973-3959, http://parks.state.co.us/parks
Map 7

Roxborough State Park is like a little taste of Utah's red rock country just a short drive from downtown Denver. This is one of my personal favorite places to get the feeling of a mini-vacation and still make it home for supper. There are very easy trails for hiking with views of the jutting red rocks, and places to enjoy a picnic on an overlook bench. The easier trails, such as Fountain Valley Loop, are pretty shadeless, so it's best to arrive early in the day. Also note that Roxborough is at a slightly higher elevation than the city, rising over 6,000 feet.

SLOAN'S LAKE PARK

Sheridan Blvd. and W. 26th Ave., www.denvergov.org
HOURS: Daily 5 A.M.-11 P.M.
Map 5

Though the greater Highlands neighborhood has numerous small parks and is also close to downtown parks (such as Commons Park), the gem in this part of town is Sloan's Lake Park. The park is primarily the lake itself, which is encircled by a mile-or-so-long running and biking path. There are two playgrounds, tennis and basketball courts, and athletic fields. Boating, waterskiing, and fishing are all permitted on the lake. It rarely feels crowded at Sloan's Lake, except during the very popular **Dragon Boat Festival** each summer.

STAPLETON CENTRAL PARK

Martin Luther King and Central Park Blvds., 303/355-9600, www.stapletondenver.com
HOURS: Daily 5 A.M.-11 P.M.
Map 7

Where there were once airport runways and an airport, there are now homes and an 80-acre park in the new infill community of Stapleton, east of downtown. Central Park is Denver's third-largest park, with a "forest" (it's planted) and wetlands just beginning to develop, picnic areas, walking and cycling paths, and views. A state-of-the-art playground for young children can be a blast, but certainly the trees still need to grow up to create more shade and ambience. In the winter, the sledding hill is quite popular.

WASHINGTON PARK

S. Downing St. and E. Louisiana Ave., 303/698-4962, www.denvergov.org

ARTS AND LEISURE

HOURS: Daily 5 A.M.–11 P.M.
Map 6

With two lakes, tennis courts, jogging and bicycle paths, playgrounds, a soccer field, a recreation center, flower gardens, and more within 165 acres, Washington Park is one of the city's most popular parks. People are drawn to this neighborhood for the historic bungalows that surround the park as much as for the active lifestyle of the park. Poet and journalist Eugene Field lived in Denver for two years in the late 1800s and is remembered in Washington Park with a statue of "Wynken, Blynken and Nod," named after his most well-known poem. Rent a boat or go fishing in the summer to get a different perspective from the water in this park. Views of the mountains can be seen from various spots in the park, too.

HEALTH CLUBS
CHERRY CREEK ATHLETIC CLUB
500 S. Cherry St., 303/399-3050,
www.cherrycreekclub.com
Map 7

Just a short drive (or bike ride or jog down the Cherry Creek Bike Path) from Cherry Creek North is the Cherry Creek Athletic Club. This is a club for the family who wants to play and swim indoors or outdoors, as well as individuals who want to get fit anywhere inside this 100,000-square-foot full-service athletic club. After working up a sweat, check in to the Sanctuary Day Spa for the ultimate reward of a massage, facial, or pedicure. No need to leave as there is a small restaurant and a poolside grill when you get hungry. Non-members can sign up for Pilates classes and pay a guest fee for use of any facilities for a single day.

DENVER ATHLETIC CLUB
1325 Glenarm Pl., 303/534-1211,
www.denverathleticclub.cc
Map 1

The Denver Athletic Club is as much a social club as a place to work out, and it is also home to the Denver Petroleum Club, which was established in 1948 for members of the oil and gas industries to schmooze. Founded in 1884, the Denver Athletic Club is one of the oldest private clubs in the country. The club is walking distance from the Colorado Convention Center and many hotels. Situated in a landmark historic building, the interior of the club is completely modern with a swimming pool, racquetball and squash courts, volleyball and basketball courts, exercise studios, and a bowling alley. The 125,000-square-foot club has the latest fitness equipment and is open 24 hours a day, 365 days a year.

FORZA FITNESS AND ATHLETIC CLUB
1849 Curtis St., 303/294-9494, www.forzadenver.com
Map 1

Forza is a state-of-the-art fitness club in the heart of downtown. Ritz-Carlton guests have access to the club during their stay. Co-owner and founder Steve Hess trains professional athletes, so the equipment and programs at Forza were selected with triathletes and the like in mind. Wow factors at Forza include a 24-foot climbing wall and fixed stairs modeled after the ones at Red Rocks Amphitheatre. There is strength training, yoga and Pilates classes, a lap pool, basketball courts, and much more.

VITRUVIAN FITNESS
3212 Tejon St., 303/455-0437, www.vmfit.com
Map 5

Vitruvian Fitness is a pretty tiny fitness studio in the Highlands neighborhood. Inside this brightly colored space, you will find dedicated instructors for indoor cycling, TRX, strength and conditioning, and personal training for all levels and abilities. The motto here is "Play Hard. Eat Well. Be Happy." IT sounds simple, and so is getting into a fitness routine here.

YMCA

25 E. 16th Ave., 303/861-8300, www.denverymca.org

Map 1

The YMCA just off the end of the 16th Street Mall is a nice, affordable place to work out for people who live and/or work downtown. The only downside is that there is no pool at this location, though a membership at this YMCA location is valid at other locations in the city with pools. At the downtown location, there are treadmills, indoor cycling, weight machines, and fitness classes. There is a chance to relax in the sauna or steam room, or with a massage.

SPECTATOR SPORTS
Baseball
COLORADO ROCKIES

Coors Field, 2001 Blake St., 303/762-5437, http://colorado.rockies.mlb.com

Map 3

Even after losing the World Series in 2007, the Colorado Rockies continue to attract committed fans to home games at Coors Field. The team played its first game in 1993 at the original Mile High Stadium (now Sports Authority Field at Mile High, previously Invesco at Mile High, and rebuilt) to such huge success that architects working on the new Coors Field expanded the seating capacity to over 50,000 for the 1995 opening game. The "rockpile" cheap seats and attractive stadium keep the fans donning the purple-and-black team colors, even when the Rockies aren't winning a lot of games. An on-site playground and Buckaroo snack bar make the baseball field popular with families.

There are 75-minute tours of Coors Field offered throughout the year. Call ahead to join a tour that goes down into the locker rooms and up to the "mile high" seats.

© STAN OBERT, COURTESY OF VISIT DENVER

ARTS AND LEISURE

Artist Lonnie Hanzon's "Evolution of the Ball" greets sports fans as they enter Coors Field.

Basketball
DENVER NUGGETS
Pepsi Center, 1000 Chopper Cir., 303/405-1100,
www.nba.com/nuggets
`Map 3`

Certainly a number of big-name basketball players have been on the Denver Nuggets team over the years, but the team has had a fairly bad losing streak for a long time. Things seemed to be turning around with the addition of Carmelo Anthony, but he went to the New York Knicks in 2011, and a championship win still eludes the Nuggets despite making it to the playoffs each year. The Nuggets' home games are almost more entertaining during breaks in the game itself, with cheerleaders and various contests. This National Basketball Association team plays at the Pepsi Center in LoDo.

Football
DENVER BRONCOS
Invesco Field at Mile High, 1701 Bryant St.,
720/258-3333, www.denverbroncos.com
`Map 3`

The Broncos have just not been the same since quarterback John Elway retired in 1999 after his two Super Bowl victories, but now that Elway is back as executive vice president of the team, there is hope for another big win soon. This is a football kind of town, and Broncos fans will brave the coldest weather to cheer on their team. The venerable Mile High Stadium has been replaced by the more modern Sports Authority Field at Mile High, though the location is the same. No matter where the team plays, Broncomania lives on: Bumper stickers around town read, "If God Isn't a Broncos Fan, Why Are Sunsets Blue and Orange?"

Hockey
COLORADO AVALANCHE
Pepsi Center, 1000 Chopper Cir., 303/405-7646,
http://avalanche.nhl.com
`Map 3`

After relocating from Canada and being renamed, the Colorado Avalanche was the team to beat in the National Hockey League. The 1996 and 2001 Stanley Cup dream team has changed as players have retired, but a handful of those original players remain, making the Avalanche a very solid team that is exciting to watch. And some former star players, such as Joe Sakic, have become team executives to help oversee this next generation. Like the Nuggets, the Avalanche plays its home games at the Pepsi Center in LoDo.

Lacrosse
THE OUTLAWS
Sports Authority Field at Mile High, 1701 Bryant St.,
303/688-5297, www.denveroutlaws.com
`Map 2`

The Outlaws, Denver's own Major League Lacrosse team, have been setting attendance records since their inaugural game in 2006 and make it to the playoffs each year. Although lacrosse players are not as well known as football, basketball, and baseball players in this country, for those in the know, it is impressive to have Brian Langtry, Brendan Mundorf, Matt Bocklet, Jesse Schwartzman, and Lee Zink on this home team. And it helps that the team color of orange is already so familiar here.

Soccer
COLORADO RAPIDS
Dick's Sporting Goods Park, 6000 Victory Way,
Commerce City, 303/727-3500,
www.coloradorapids.com
`Map 7`

With so many professional sports teams in one city, locals are still finding room in their hearts and wallets to support the soccer team. So far, Rapids players have hardly become household names and likely won't be opening any eponymous restaurants, but the team still has a strong following with enthusiastic fans. The Colorado Rapids play at Dick's Sporting Goods

Park in Commerce City, which is just north of downtown.

UNIVERSITY OF DENVER PIONEERS

Magness Arena, 2240 Buchtel Blvd., 303/871-7403, www.denverpioneers.com

Map 7

When the National Hockey League was on strike in the 2004–2005 season, hockey fans turned to college teams for their ice action. It helped that the Pioneers won back-to-back championships in 2004 and 2005, making it even harder to get tickets to the games. Numerous Pioneer alums have gone on to join the National Hockey League. The team plays at the campus's Magness Arena, which also doubles as a concert venue.

GUIDED AND WALKING TOURS

BALISTRERI VINEYARDS

1946 E. 66th Ave., 303/287-5156, www.balistreriwine.com

HOURS: Daily noon–5 P.M.

Map 7

Unusual and surprising, right in the middle of Denver, there is not only a winery, but a vineyard. The Balistreri Vineyards make some of their wines from grapes grown on Colorado's Western Slope, where there is a growing wine industry, but they also squeeze enough out of their own Denver vineyard to produce their cabernet sauvignon, muscat, and merlot. The winery produces 4,500 cases annually. Tours include complimentary tastings and visits to the wine cellar and winemaking facilities.

COLORADO ADVENTURE SEGWAY TOURS

866/642-4919, www.coloradoadventuresegwaytours.com

It's a rare thing to see a Segway rolling along the streets of the Mile High City, where people prefer to get exercise by simply walking

from point A to point B. Nonetheless, there is a tour company that offers the opportunity to see the city's historical high points without wearing oneself out too much. Instead of walking alongside the South Platte River through Confluence Park, you get to "glide." Tours are guided and helmets are required (and provided) for everyone.

DENVER HISTORY TOURS

720/234-7929, www.denverhistorytours.com

There's a theme for every kind of tour, and a range of ways to tour, with Denver History Tours. There are haunted-house tours, a visit to historic Littleton, and a look back at the seamy side of the city when bordellos and saloons thrived. Many of these are guided walking tours that usually last about two hours. There are also bus tours that can take an entire day and go well beyond the downtown environs to everywhere from local infill projects to Victorian towns in the foothills. Prices vary. Call ahead to make reservations.

DINOSAUR RIDGE

16831 W. Alameda Pkwy., Morrison, 303/697-3466, www.dinoridge.com

Map 7

Overlooking Denver is a view into the past, where you can clearly see dinosaur footprints left in what was once a swamp and is now a slanted rock. Dinosaur Ridge can be walked for free—though consider that it is a steep, exposed road—or experienced with a guide on a small bus tour. Also on site are a gift shop and museum (separate buildings) on a historic ranch homestead. The "Trek Through Time" exhibit hall is a thrill for little kids.

LODO HISTORIC WALKING TOURS

303/628-5428, www.lodo.org/lodo-walk-tour.html

Lower Downtown has a rich history, from the first encampments along the South Platte River to the first buildings—and including all of the

ARTS AND LEISURE

© MINDY SINK

At Dinosaur Ridge, view dinosaur footprints right where they once roamed.

colorful characters along the way. There are three different walking tours, each departing from a different locale with a unique schedule and itinerary. The LoDo Historic District's two-hour tour is a chance to learn about the businesses that first occupied many of the beautiful buildings, or that still do, such as the Oxford Hotel. It's adults only on the late-afternoon tour from Gold Camp to Paris on the Platte, which includes alcoholic beverages and appetizers.

PLATTE VALLEY TROLLEY

15th and Platte Sts., 303/458-6255, www.denvertrolley.org
HOURS: Memorial Day–Labor Day Fri.–Mon. noon–4 P.M., Apr.–Oct. Fri.–Sun. noon–4 P.M.
COST: $5 adult, $2 child age 4-13, children under 4 free

`Map 3`

Departing from behind REI, just off of 15th and Platte Streets, the Platte Valley Trolley is a

quirky tour of Confluence Park and the businesses along this stretch of the South Platte River, including the Children's Museum. Perhaps more interesting than the actual sights is the history of this open-air car, a "breezer," and the fact that there used to be an entire trolley-car system throughout the city. The trolley serves as a shuttle ride to Broncos games during the football season. The trolley schedule has been cut back each year, so double-check the website for the most current days and times.

VENICE ON THE CREEK

Creekfront Plaza, 303/893-0750, www.veniceonthecreek.com
HOURS: June–Aug. Thurs.–Sun. 5–10 P.M., Wed. 10 A.M.–4 P.M. (charter rides only)
COST: $15-75

`Map 3`

It's not so much what you see on the punt boat rides south of Larimer Square along the

BIKE TO WORK MONTH

June is Bike to Work Month, with a Bike to Work Day at the end of the month. The **Denver Regional Council of Governments** (DRCOG, www3.drcog. org/biketowork) promotes the event, and on its website, cyclists can register (as well as find out where breakfast stations are set up throughout the city), win prizes, and plan their biking route to and from work. Each year, thousands of people participate—at least 23,000 people rode their bikes to work on the designated day in 2011, according to the DRCOG—and that means fewer cars on the road.

Cherry Creek as it is just the experience of riding on the water so serenely. (A punt is very similar to a gondola.) This is strictly a summertime activity and mainly in the evenings, 5–10 P.M., with candlelight rides starting at dusk. The rides are round-trip, unless otherwise arranged in advance. Reservations are recommended, though there is sometimes a chance of availability for walk-up service at the kiosk on Larimer Street between Speer Boulevard and 14th Street. The boat rides went on hiatus in 2012 for repairs. Check the website for the latest schedules and prices.

BICYCLING
Trails
CHERRY CREEK BIKE PATH
Confluence Park to University Blvd.
Map 3

The Cherry Creek Bike Path is one of the most popular off-street recreation paths in the city. There is a concrete path along either side of Cherry Creek, with one side designated for wheels and the other for pedestrians. Starting at Confluence Park, the creek and paths run below the street level

of busy Speer Boulevard all the way to the Cherry Creek shopping district, where Speer Boulevard intersects with University Boulevard. There are ramps at intervals on the paths to climb up to street level and see the nearby sights. Down below the streets, it's a world away from traffic and urban life, with greenery and the sounds of the water to listen to instead. It's 4.4 miles from Cherry Creek to University Boulevard, but the trail continues on to the Cherry Creek Reservoir (another nine miles from University Blvd.).

HIGH LINE CANAL
University Blvd. to Hwy. C-470,
www.denverwater.org/recreation
Map 7

The High Line Canal is flanked by a crushed gravel path along most of its length through a handful of counties, parks, residential neighborhoods, and commercial districts. An 8.1-mile leg of the trail starts at Big Dry Creek Trail and winds through neighborhoods and open space with a few chances to glimpse the mountain range and peaks up ahead. After intersecting with the Columbine Memorial Trail, you can detour onto a new trail or continue on the High Line Canal Trail into Douglas County.

PLATTE RIVER GREENWAY
Confluence Park to Bear Creek Trail
Map 3

The bike paths along the South Platte River are truly appealing, with lots of cottonwood trees and other greenery along the way. Leaving from Confluence Park in either direction, there are some stretches through industrial sites that are less attractive. Heading south from the park, the concrete path goes out to the nearby suburbs and affords views of the Front Range at different intervals. To go all the way to Bear Creek Trail is an easy ride of 8.6 miles.

ARTS AND LEISURE

THE ROADS LESS TRAVELED

The Cherry Creek Bike Path and Platte River Greenway are the main activity paths within the city, but each extends beyond the county lines with offshoots to many other popular paths for bicycling, running, and other sports.

For more about where and when to bicycle around the Denver metro area, go straight to the local experts who have conveniently established websites with loads of helpful information.

On www.bikepaths.com, there is a great top 10 list of less-traveled trails, a calories-burned calculator, and a list of regional cycling events. There are links and a list of nearly every bike shop in the metro area, too.

For more general information about advocacy for bicycling in Denver, ordinances, and maps, try www.denvergov.org/bikeprogram or www.bikedenver.org. Both of these websites portray bicycling not as just a sport but a movement—and a way of life. The website http://bicyclecolo.org offers free online cycling maps and also sells hard copies.

Resources
BICYCLE DOCTOR
860 Broadway, 303/831-7228, www.bicycledr.com
HOURS: Mon.-Fri. 10 A.M.-7 P.M., Sat. 10 A.M.-5 P.M.; call for Sun. hours
Map 2

Bikes need regular maintenance just like automobiles. Schedule a tune-up at the Bicycle Doctor and get the wheels aligned and the tires checked, along with other advice on fixing up your bike. The shop also sells lots of cycling gear and rents quality bicycles. Unlike the city's popular bike rental program, here there is a large selection of bikes to rent with a friendly staffer to offer advice and tips on where to go and the best routes for bikes.

DENVER BCYCLE
2737 Larimer St., 303/825-3325,
http://denver.bcycle.com
Map 1

Rent a bike to ride around Denver at your convenience. Denver Bcycle provides red bicycles from dozens of docking stations around the city. There is a fee to check out the bikes and, like a taxicab, there are rates being added on as long as you keep the bike checked out after the first 30 minutes. This was the first, large-scale, municipal bike-sharing system in the United States, and it has now spread to many other cities. Fun features of each bike include a front basket and the hidden computer system that can track the distance ridden, the calories burned, and the carbon offset from riding instead of driving.

DENVER BICYCLE TOURING CLUB
303/756-7240, www.dbtc.org

Cycling can be a solo or group sport. For those who like to mingle, there is the Denver Bicycle Touring Club, which offers a large variety of weekday and weekend rides throughout the metro area. The idea is to bike at least 15 miles along bike paths and neighborhood streets, either with the intention to socialize and share a meal at the end of the ride or to just get fit. The club also offers extended tours beyond the city and state. There is an annual membership fee to join, but it's free to tag along once and see what it's all about first.

BOATING
BARR LAKE
13401 Piccadilly Rd., Brighton, 303/659-6005,
http://parks.state.co.us/parks
Map 7

Barr Lake is divided into two sections: the southern half is a wildlife refuge for birds, and the northern half permits boating. Canoeing, sailboarding, and other boating with electric

The reservoir at Chatfield State Park is popular for boating.

or gas motors of 10 horsepower or less are allowed. Barr Lake is irrigation storage and can therefore have fluctuating water levels. There is no swimming or wading allowed. Although the birds have their own half of the lake, one of the pleasures of boating here is getting a chance to see some of the 300 species of birds that flock here.

BEAR CREEK LAKE PARK

15600 W. Morrison Rd., 303/697-6159, www.lakewood.org/bclp
HOURS: May -Sept. 6 A.M.-10 P.M., Mar.-Apr. and Oct. 7 A.M.-8 P.M., Nov.-Feb. 8 A.M.-6 P.M.
Map 7

Within Bear Creek Lake Park are the Bear Creek Reservoir, Big Soda Lake, and Little Soda Lake, and each has different boating rules. Only Bear Creek Reservoir allows motorized boats; Big Soda Lake is open only to non-motorized craft, and Little Soda Lake does not allow private boats. The location is nearly at the foot of the foothills, with views both back to downtown and of the mountains up close. Double-check the website for the most updated boat ramp hours. The boat ramps are closed November 15–March 15 annually.

CHATFIELD MARINA

Chatfield State Park, 11500 N. Roxborough Park Rd., Littleton, 303/791-5555, www.parks.state.co.us
Map 7

So that everyone can enjoy their preferred on-the-water activity, the reservoir at Chatfield State Park is divided: There are "no wake zones" for more relaxed fishing and canoeing, while in the "power zone," general boating and waterskiing are permitted. Chatfield, south of Denver in Littleton, is very popular during the summer. There is an off-season, when boating is still allowed and it's fairly peaceful and calm, until the water ices over.

ARTS AND LEISURE

© MICHAEL ALOSI; HTTP://PARKS.STATE.CO.US/PARKS/CHATFIELD

CHERRY CREEK MARINA

4800 S. Dayton, Cherry Creek State Park,
303/779-6144, www.cherrycreekmarina.com

Map 7

The Cherry Creek State Park includes a lake where just about any kind of boat can be rented by the hour. Rentals include pontoon boats, fishing boats, paddleboats, and sailboats, starting for as little as $15 per hour. The marina on the west side has slips and water access. The Cherry Creek Yacht Club is both a restaurant and a special events center at the lake, so it is used for private parties and weddings.

FISHING
Lakes
BEAR CREEK LAKE PARK

15600 W. Morrison Rd., 303/697-6159,
www.lakewood.org/bclp
HOURS: May-Sept. 6 A.M.-10 P.M., Mar.-Apr. and Oct.
7 A.M.-8 P.M., Feb.-Nov. 8 A.M.-6 P.M.

Map 7

Bear Creek Lake is open year-round for fishing, which means there is ice fishing here, as well. The lake is stocked monthly in summer with rainbow trout, smallmouth bass, walleye, and more. Bear Creek River can also be fished with artificial flies and lures only. All state fishing regulations do apply here.

FERRIL LAKE

City Park, 3300 E. 17th Ave., www.denvergov.org/parks
HOURS: Daily 5 A.M.-11 P.M.

Map 4

At 25 acres, Ferril Lake is the largest lake in City Park. It allows fishing in a fairly serene setting, considering that it is in the middle of the city and walking distance from downtown. Ferril Lake has yellow perch, sunfish, and carp stocked in the fall, and rainbow trout stocked in the spring. Only rented novelty paddleboats are allowed in Ferril Lake, and fishing is only permitted from piers or platforms.

FISHING RULES

There are ample opportunities to go fishing at city and state park waterways in and around Denver, but everyone must have a license first. Start with the **Colorado Division of Wildlife** (www.wildlife.state.co.us/fishing) to learn more about rules, regulations, and even buy a license online. Numerous sporting-goods stores throughout the greater metro area sell fishing licenses. Every year, the first weekend in June is the only time that licenses are not required as part of "Colorado Free Fishing Days."

The rules about catch-and-release or catch-and-carry vary from place to place, so be sure to look for posted signs at each site before you get started.

WASHINGTON PARK LAKES

Washington Park, S. Downing St. and E. Louisiana Ave., www.denvergov.org/parks
HOURS: Daily 5 A.M.-11 P.M.

Map 6

Smith Lake is just one of three lakes at Washington Park where there are many recreational options, including fishing. The 19-acre Smith Lake is stocked with carp, catfish, largemouth bass, and rainbow trout. Smith Lake also allows sailboats, canoes, kayaks, and rowboats, and it has a fishing pier. Willow trees provide a bit of shade on hot days, and a boathouse at the lake can be rented out for private parties. Grasmere Lake is also 19 acres with a similar selection of fish to catch, but the difference is that this lake is a little less busy than Smith, which has the boathouse on one side. Lily Pond is a mere one acre and is designated for children under 16 to practice their fishing skills.

Resources
TROUT'S FLY FISHING

1303 E. 6th Ave., 877/464-0034,
www.troutsflyfishing.com

Golfers playing on the City Park Golf Course enjoy a view of downtown.

HOURS: Mon.-Wed. 10 A.M.-7 P.M., Thurs.-Fri.
10 A.M.-8 P.M., Sat. 9 A.M.-6 P.M., Sun. 11 A.M.-5 P.M.

Map 4

While 6th Avenue may seem a long way from a perfect fly-fishing spot, Denver is just a couple of hours' drive from some great rivers ideal for hooking a big one. Trout's not only sells gear and flies, but also teaches the important skills in its outfitting and education center. Visit the store or the website to find out about fishing events in the area and to get local fishing reports, along with a list of the best places in Colorado to fish.

GOLF
CITY PARK GOLF COURSE
2500 York St., 303/295-2096,
www.denvergov.org/denvergolf

Map 4

The location of the 18-hole regulation City Park Golf Course is pretty great, given its proximity to downtown and views of the skyline and mountain peaks beyond. Tree-lined fairways can make the course a little challenging. There is also a pro shop, a driving range, and the pleasant Bogey's on the Park restaurant at the golf course. The golf course is part of City Park, but a road separates it from the main park and attractions, such as the Denver Zoo and the Denver Museum of Nature and Science.

FOSSIL TRACE GOLF CLUB
3050 Illinois St., Golden, 303/277-8750,
www.fossiltrace.com

Map 7

A stunningly beautiful golf course designed by golf course architect Jim Engh lies just west of Denver in Golden. Here the 18-hole course is highlighted by rocks with dinosaur fossils still visible. This completely unique course is consistently ranked number one by golf experts from ESPN.com to *Golf Digest* and more. Another bonus is that it's a short drive from downtown

ARTS AND LEISURE

IT'S ALL ABOUT ALTITUDE

The Mile-High City is more than a moniker—it's an altitude that affects everything from the speed of baseballs to the ability to breathe, especially when exercising.

Experts say that a baseball can travel up to 9 percent faster at 5,280 feet than it does at sea level. Air pressure gets lower as the elevation increases, meaning that a ball has less friction when flying through the air (and possibly on up over the fence). But the good news ends there, as the batter is slowed by getting less air in his lungs while he runs for the bases.

Running, cycling, and even walking can seem more difficult in the Mile-High City. While exploring the city, and especially nearby mountain parks, be aware of possible increases in elevation.

Though true altitude sickness typically affects people who are unaccustomed to elevations over 8,000 feet, it's a good idea to drink extra water when just visiting Denver. Even at 5,280 feet high, visitors may feel mild symptoms of altitude sickness that include headache, dizziness, fatigue, and disrupted sleep.

---

to get here and you are surrounded by the natural beauty of the foothills.

JOHN F. KENNEDY GOLF COURSE

10500 E. Hampden Ave., Aurora, 303/755-0105, www.denvergov.org/denvergolf

Map 7

Southeast of downtown, Kennedy Golf Course is one of the city's larger and more varied courses. This is a place where the whole family can have some fun. Kennedy includes an 18-hole regulation course, a 9-hole regulation course, a 9-hole par-three course, and a lighted driving range with evening hours. There is also a miniature golf course for those junior putters. Arrange for junior, men's, and women's golf lessons, or reserve a tee time online.

WILLIS CASE GOLF COURSE

4999 Vrain St., 303/458-4877, www.denvergov.org/denvergolf

Map 7

Just north of the greater Highlands neighborhood and Regis University is the 18-hole regulation Willis Case Golf Course. The golf course is less than a 10-minute drive from downtown. While teeing up, take a look west at the spectacular view of the Rockies from this hilltop course. There is a pro shop and restaurant at Willis Case, but it's only a five-minute drive to some of the Highlands' most popular restaurants, too.

HIKING
Trails
BEAR CREEK LAKE PARK

15600 W. Morrison Rd., 303/697-6159, www.lakewood.org/bclp

HOURS: May-Sept. 6 a.m.-10 p.m., Mar.-Apr. and Oct. 7 a.m.-8 p.m., Feb.-Nov. 8 a.m.-6 p.m.

Map 7

There are several hiking trails within Bear Creek Lake Park, but my favorite is one that is a mix of paved and soft surfaces *and* gets you into the park for free. Simply start in Morrison and walk east along the creekside path and you will end up in Bear Creek Lake Park. In spring, there are meadows of wildflowers to enjoy, and in fall, leaves are golden and crunch underfoot as you wander. Pay attention to the signs that indicate who can be on certain trails—pedestrians, cyclists, and equestrians all have to share at times.

HIGH LINE CANAL

www.denverwater.org

HOURS: Daily 5 a.m.-11 p.m.

Map 7

The High Line Canal stretches for 66

miles south of Denver through suburbs like Englewood, Littleton, and Aurora—or from about Waterton Canyon to the Rocky Mountain Arsenal National Wildlife Refuge. This multiuse trail allows walking, bicycling, and horseback riding in different places along the trail. There are shady areas and chances to see wildlife or stop for a picnic, too.

LOOKOUT MOUNTAIN NATURE CENTER & PRESERVE

910 Colorow Rd., Golden, 720/497-7600, http://jeffco.us

HOURS: Preserve is open daily 8 A.M.-dusk; Nature Center is open Tues.-Sun. 10 A.M.-4 P.M., in summer Tues.-Fri. 10 A.M.-4 P.M., Sat.-Sun. 9 A.M.-5 P.M.

Map 7

The Lookout Mountain Nature Center & Preserve offers a simple, limited hike around the property, but with spectacular views of the city. There is often wildlife to see, and the center itself is a handy amenity, especially with little kids or if the weather is not great. The historic Boettcher family summer house is nice to tour, when it is not being used for weddings or other private events.

TRADING POST TRAIL AT RED ROCKS PARK & AMPHITHEATRE

18300 W. Alameda Pkwy., Morrison, 303/697-4939, www.redrocksonline.com

HOURS: May-Sept. Daily 8 A.M.-7 P.M., Oct.-Apr. Daily 9 A.M.-4 P.M., depending on shows

Map 7

The Trading Post Trail at Red Rocks is only 1.4 miles of easy hiking, but the terrain is not smooth, so wear proper shoes. Also, keep in mind the elevation is 6,280 feet above sea level. Depending on the season and time of day, there's a good chance you will spot wildlife such as deer or snakes while hiking. And don't forget about the stairs in the amphitheater, which are commonly used by runners for an intense workout when there are no concerts.

WILLOW CREEK TRAIL

Roxborough State Park, 4751 Roxborough Dr., Littleton, 303/973-3959, http://parks.state.co.us/parks

Map 7

Trails at Roxborough State Park range from very easy and flat to moderate with significant elevation gain. The 1.4-mile Willow Creek Trail is special for its more abundant wildflowers and wildlife, such as deer and birds. The wildflowers peak in late spring, just as things begin to really heat up for the summer season. Like the other trails here, the Willow Creek Trailhead is at the park's visitors center. The trail starts out in thick scrub oak, but also has some shadeless spots as it opens up. The best times to see the red rock formations are early in the morning or at dusk.

Resources
DENVER ADVENTURES

303/984-6151, www.denveradventures.com

Denver Adventures offers expert guides to take you on a hike anywhere along the Front Range. The $89 half-day price and $149 full-day price (prices are per person, but group rates are also available) include door-to-door transportation, snacks or lunch and a drink, and, of course, an expert guide. Hikes can be as easy or challenging as you choose (or have time for). Be aware that the weather can change quickly and your hike could be cancelled at the last minute. Denver Adventures has services beyond hiking, too, including mountain biking, snowshoeing, rock climbing, and more.

KAYAKING
Parks
CONFLUENCE PARK

15th St. between Platte and Little Raven Sts., www.denvergov.org

Map 3

The South Platte River through Confluence Park has been slightly manipulated to create an exciting white-water park with Class II–III

ARTS AND LEISURE

OUTDOOR RECREATION INFORMATION CENTER

Inside the **REI flagship store** (1416 Platte St., 303/756-3100, www.rei.com, Mon.-Fri. 10 A.M.-9 P.M., Sat. 10 A.M.-7 P.M., Sun. 10 A.M.-6 P.M.) at Confluence Park is a small counter adjacent to the bookstore called ORIC, for **Outdoor Recreation Information Center** (www.oriconline. org). Have a question about where to go and explore? This is the place to go for free advice, maps, and brochures. ORIC is partnered with a long list of official organizations, including the U.S. Forest Service, Colorado Division of Wildlife, Colorado State Parks, and more. There are also maps and books for sale.

Resources
CONFLUENCE KAYAKS

2373 15th St., 303/433-3676, www.confluencekayaks.com
HOURS: Mon.-Thurs. 10 A.M.-6 P.M., Fri. 10 A.M.-7 P.M., Sat. 10 A.M.-6 P.M., Sun. noon-5 P.M.
Map 3

Whether you're looking for advice and gear to head up to the white water of the mountains, or just interested in a quick lesson steps away on the South Platte River, Confluence Kayaks is the place to go. If you are in Commons Park or Confluence Park during the warm months, chances are you will spot a few kayakers either in the chutes or dripping wet as they walk back to Confluence Kayaks to return their rented boat. Pool and lake lessons are taught at other locations, and private instruction is also available.

SWIMMING
Pools and Parks
ELDORADO SPRINGS POOL

294 Artesian Dr., 303/499-9640, www.eldoradosprings.com
HOURS: Sat. before Memorial Day-Labor Day Daily 10 A.M.-6 P.M.
COST: $9 adult, $6 child and senior
Map 7

When things heat up in the summer with temperatures over 100°F in the city, run for the hills and the Eldorado Springs Pool. The water in the pool is always on the chilly side, no matter how hot the day is. This historic artesian spring-fed pool is pretty basic, with a large slide and diving board, but the scenery is to die for. There is a small snack bar with outdoor tables next to the rushing creek waters.

rapids, depending on the flow. From behind REI to just below 20th Street, there are 13 drops in 1.5 miles of river. Don't be shy about your kayaking skills here, though, because bridges hover right over the chutes, making this as popular a spot to watch boaters as it is to boat. Also be careful with those rollovers, as the water quality is highly questionable.

UNION CHUTES

Santa Fe Blvd. and Union Ave.
Map 7

From Chatfield Reservoir, there are 17 miles of artificially constructed rapids along the South Platte River, and one of the parks with seven drops is Union Chutes. Rapids at Union Chutes range from Class II to Class III, and can be pretty tricky when the water is high. The water is suitable for both kayaks and canoes. Even though you are in the thick of the city, it feels like wilderness here and there, with thick groves of trees and green spaces.

PIRATE'S COVE

1225 W. Belleview Ave., Englewood, 303/762-COVE (303/762-2683), www.piratescovecolorado.com
HOURS: Summer daily 10 A.M.-6 P.M.

Confluence Park attracts recreationists in the shadow of the downtown skyline.

COST: $8-9.25 day-use fee
Map 7

South of downtown Denver in the suburb of Englewood is a water park worth the drive. Pirate's Cove, part of the city of Englewood's Parks and Recreation Department, includes a 35-foot slide tower with three slides, a lazy river, a lap pool, giant splash buckets, and cabana areas to dry off and have a snack. This place can get very busy, so plan accordingly and arrive as early as possible in the day.

Resources
DENVER PARKS AND RECREATION
303/458-4795, www.denvergov.org/swimmingpools
The city's Parks and Recreation department oversees the maintenance of dozens of pools, including 16 outdoor pools. By going to the website, you can locate a pool near you and get schedules. Some favorites are the pool at Congress Park and the Stapleton pools.

WINTER ACTIVITIES
Cross-Country Skiing and Snowshoeing
BARR LAKE
13401 Piccadilly Rd., Brighton, 303/659-6005, http://parks.state.co.us/parks
Map 7

If there is enough snow and frigid days to follow, it's possible to just head over to Washington Park or City Park and strap on the cross-country skis for a good, quick workout close to home or the hotel. But in Denver, the sun usually melts the snow within hours, so it's best to drive a little ways outside of the urban heat zone for some winter schussing. Barr Lake is less than a 30-minute drive from downtown, with a view of the snow-capped Front Range to the west. The flatter terrain here includes an 8.8-mile trail around the lake and the one-mile Prairie Welcome Trail. The trails are not groomed. The lake does not completely freeze over in all places, so it's best to avoid walking across it.

Ice Fishing
BARR LAKE
13401 Piccadilly Rd., Brighton, 303/659-6005, http://parks.state.co.us/parks
Map 7
Although the whole lake does not freeze over, portions of Barr Lake are used for ice fishing in the winter months. The lake is stocked with rainbow trout, walleye, channel catfish, and smallmouth and largemouth bass. Note that there is no fishing allowed in the wildlife refuge area. Be sure to call ahead or check the website for the most current conditions at the lake.

EVERGREEN LAKE
29614 Upper Bear Creek Rd., Evergreen, 303/512-9300 or 303/674-0532, www.evergreenrecreation.com
Map 7
Much like ice skating at Evergreen Lake, ice fishing opportunities depend wholly on the

ARTS AND LEISURE

COURTESY OF VISIT DENVER

current weather conditions and just how cold the winter season is. The lake is periodically stocked with rainbow trout and tiger muskie, and you can check with the Colorado Division of Wildlife (http://wildlife.state.co.us/fishing) for the most recent stocking dates. A fishing license is required for ice fishing. Always call ahead for the most current conditions.

Ice Skating
EVERGREEN LAKE

29614 Upper Bear Creek Rd., Evergreen, 303/512-9300 or 303/674-0532, www.evergreenrecreation.com
HOURS: Call ahead
COST: $4.50 adult, $4 child and senior, $3 skate rental
Map 7

It's as pretty as a postcard or an old Hollywood movie at Evergreen Lake, with snow on the nearby trees and skaters gliding across the frozen surface. At least 30 minutes from downtown, Evergreen Lake is worth the drive for the mountain scenery. The skating season is roughly from mid-December through mid-March and completely depends on if the weather stays cold enough for the 40-acre lake to stay solidly frozen. The Lake House serves as a warming hut with a fireplace inside.

JOY BURNS ARENA AT UNIVERSITY OF DENVER

2201 E. Asbury Ave., 303/871-3904, www.recreation.du.edu/ice
HOURS: Check the website calendar or call to find out public skate times for each day as they change often.
COST: $6 adult, $5 child, $4 senior, $3 skate rental
Map 7

Between figure skating and hockey practice, there's room for public lessons and public skate time on the rink at the University of Denver campus southeast of downtown. This 150-seat rink got a major upgrade in 2008, when the base underneath the ice was changed from sand to concrete to make for overall smoother conditions. The indoor arena is open year-round.

SOUTHWEST RINK AT SKYLINE PARK

1701 Arapahoe St., www.downtowndenver.org
HOURS: Mid-Nov.-mid.-Feb.
COST: Free, $2 skate rentals
Map 1

Sponsored by Southwest Airlines, the Southwest Rink at Skyline Park has become an annual holiday tradition for many Denver families (including mine!). Skating downtown from about Thanksgiving through Valentine's Day is a great way to enjoy seeing the city all dressed up for the season. The rink is located at the base of the D&F tower, where there is a small, outdoor pizza restaurant and bar. Families, couples, experts, and novices all come out to slip, slide, and glide around the small rink during winter.

Sledding
🇨 COMMONS PARK

15th and Little Raven Sts., 720/913-1311, www.denvergov.org
HOURS: Daily 5 A.M.-11 P.M.
Map 3

Depending on your perspective, Denver has been blessed or cursed with some blizzards in recent years. Sure, the roads were a nightmare of icy potholes, but it made for great urban sledding conditions and a chance for residents to sample what's within walking distance of their homes. One of the more popular sled slides was in Commons Park, where different sides of the hill provided a variety of speeds and chutes for all ages. For those who aren't close enough to walk and don't want to drive on winter roads, Commons Park is just a short walk from the light rail station behind Union Station.

STAPLETON CENTRAL PARK

Martin Luther King and Central Park Blvds., 303/355-9600, www.stapletondenver.com
Map 7

The flat eastern plains were once the ideal setting for long, smooth airport runways. But as the former Stapleton Airport site has evolved into a new neighborhood, it's full of surprises that include a giant sledding hill in Central Park. Adjacent to the playground, the 30-foot hill was created with snow and speed in mind. It's quickly become a favorite place for sledders who come from beyond the immediate Stapleton community on the snowiest days.

BIRD-WATCHING
BARR LAKE
13401 Piccadilly Rd., Brighton, 303/659-6005, http://parks.state.co.us/parks

`Map 7`

Over 300 bird species have been spotted at Barr Lake, with an ever-changing population on view between migratory birds and resident birds. While there are little bluebirds, warblers, and finches, there are also pelicans, bald eagles, and sandhill cranes. Stop in at the Nature Center to get a bird checklist and find out which birds are likely to be there during your visit.

TAI CHI AND YOGA AT THE GARDENS

On Tuesdays mornings in the summer months, the **Denver Botanic Gardens** (1005 York St., 720/865-3500, www.botanicgardens.org) open extra early at 7 A.M. for fitness walks and tai chi classes. The cost is $8 for members of the Denver Botanic Gardens, and $10 for non-members.

The **Tai Chi Project** (www.taichidenver.com) starts classes at 7:15 A.M. in the amphitheater. Tai chi is an ancient Chinese practice that is sort of like a meditation in motion; it's a system of exercises done with very deliberate movements.

On Thursdays mornings, it's **sunrise yoga,** specifically Vinyasa yoga for all levels. Costs and times are the same as the tai chi classes.

ROCKY MOUNTAIN ARSENAL NATIONAL WILDLIFE REFUGE
Havana St. and E. 56th Ave., Commerce City, 303/289-0930, www.fws.gov/rockymountainarsenal

HOURS: Tues.-Wed. and Sat.-Sun. 6 A.M.-6 P.M. (tours)

`Map 7`

You can get in some peaceful bird-watching on the way to or from Denver International Airport at the Rocky Mountain Arsenal National Wildlife Refuge, where about 300 bird species have been seen. A bird checklist from the visitors center lists when to see each species of bird, or whether it's incredibly unlikely to see a sandpiper in these parts (though it's not unheard-of). The list also highlights which birds are frequently seen—starlings, Great Blue Herons (except in winter), kingfishers, and hundreds more. Verify that the Arsenal is open before heading out; they sometimes close for long remediation projects.

CLIMBING
ELDORADO CANYON STATE PARK
9 Kneale Rd., Eldorado Springs, 303/494-3943, www.parks.state.co.us/parks

`Map 7`

Eldorado Canyon is just outside of Boulder and still a reasonable drive from Denver, especially if you take Highway 93 up and bypass Boulder completely. The canyon is a draw for rock climbers from all over the world, and the people who want to just hang out and watch them—there is usually a small crowd of spectators along the road craning their necks for a look up. There are over 500 technical climbing routes in the park, though some areas are occasionally closed during nesting season for the many birds of prey that call these rocks home.

REI
1416 Platte St., 303/756-3100, www.rei.com

HOURS: Sat.-Sun. 10 A.M.-4 P.M.

ARTS AND LEISURE

COURTESY OF VISIT DENVER

The 47-foot Pinnacle at REI lets people practice their rock climbing skills.

COST: $10 non-members, free for members' first climb, $5 all additional climbs

Map 3

The REI Denver Flagship Pinnacle is a 47-foot imitation of the actual sandstone climbing rocks further west of town. The pinnacle is a 6,400-square-foot surface of hand-sculpted formations, including hand- and footholds instead of bolts. REI offers classes for beginners, women, kids, and more with a schedule that changes monthly. (Classes are for REI members, but it's easy to join.) While most of the people who scale this monolith are serious about climbing, it's become a favorite snapshot spot with people paying to climb just high enough for that "Look at me!" moment.

HORSEBACK RIDING
BEAR CREEK LAKE PARK

15600 W. Morrison Rd., Lakewood, 303/697-9666, www.bearcreekstablescolorado.com

HOURS: Apr.-Oct. 9 A.M.-6 P.M.

COST: $40-75

Map 7

Horseback riding is another fun way to see the beauty of the foothills on the west edge of Denver. Families can plan a day of riding at the Bear Creek Lake Park, where there are miles of trails to explore on guided horses. Those lucky enough to own their own horses can also use the trails, and there is a warm-up arena, too.

CHATFIELD STATE PARK

11500 N. Roxborough Park Rd., Littleton, 303/933-3636, www.painthorsestables.net

HOURS: May 15-Sept. 15 daily 9 A.M.-6 P.M., call for winter hours

COST: $35-68, plus state-park pass fee

Map 7

Horseback rides are available by the hour at Chatfield State Park for all ages and levels of expertise. Reservations are required, and there is a two-horse minimum. There are also classes, lessons, and horse boarding available at Chatfield Stables. Because the entire Chatfield State Park area is popular for just about every kind of outdoor activity you can think of, there is a designated equestrian loop with only a few overlaps with bike and foot trails.

SKATEBOARDING
DENVER SKATEPARK

2205 19th St., www.denverskatepark.com

HOURS: Daily 5 A.M.-11 P.M.

COST: Free

Map 3

The largest free public skatepark in the country is the Denver Skatepark, on the northern edge of Commons Park just off the South Platte River. Its three acres (or 50,000 square feet) of concrete are meant to mimic an urban skate environment. The park includes a half-pipe, a 10-foot-deep "dog bowl," handrails, and a lot more features. Though helmets and pads are always recommended, they are not required by law at the skatepark. Check out the website to see photos of the park and links to other skateparks around the state.

TENNIS
GATES TENNIS CENTER
3300 E. Bayaud Ave., 303/355-4461,
www.gatestenniscenter.info
HOURS: Daily 7 A.M.-10 P.M.; check for open court hours
COST: $5-8
Map 6

Located just beyond the shops and mall of Cherry Creek is a 20-court, outdoor tennis center. There is an indoor pro shop and lounge. The center is open in the winter, but it's hit-or-miss based on current weather conditions. There are private lessons, group programs,

FINDING TENNIS COURTS

Denver Parks and Recreation (720/865-0690, www.denver.gov/recreation) oversees or owns over 100 tennis courts across the city. Go to the website to find out about youth tennis summer camps, and which parks have lighted courts and tournaments. **Washington Park, City Park,** and **Sloan's Lake Park** all have tennis courts that are available on a first-come, first-served basis.

adults mixers, and peewee classes all taught by professionals.

ARTS AND LEISURE

SHOPS

Shopping in Denver can be an all-day outing that includes a leisurely lunch and plenty of easy strolling. Whether you are looking for antiques, Western attire, a sexy dress, or the perfect shoes, there are a number of stores to check out. Heading out to do a little shopping is one of the best ways to experience Denver like a local.

Denver certainly has large malls with all the familiar stores, such as Cherry Creek Mall and the Denver Pavilions on the 16th Street Mall, but sprinkled around Denver's best neighborhoods are some appealing shopping districts, including tony Cherry Creek North, hip Highlands Square, and funky South Broadway. Each of these neighborhoods has a mixture of cafés and shops so people can wander from store to store browsing the goods, then grab a bite to eat and, once fortified, go back to spending.

In each neighborhood, the shops tend to represent the character of the area. On South Broadway near Ellsworth, it's about being original at the Fancy Tiger, where up-and-coming designers sell their latest creations, or find a mix of vintage and new duds at Decade. In Cherry Creek North, you can find beautiful clothes at Max, Garbarini, or Lawrence Covell, so you can dress to impress. The best cowboy boots, shirts, and other Western-style clothing and accessories are mostly found in LoDo at Rockmount Ranch Wear and at Cry Baby Ranch in Larimer Square. The Highlands has a mix of shops, with stunning flowers at the

© LARIMER SQUARE

HIGHLIGHTS

There are too many fabulous fabrics to choose from at Fancy Tiger Crafts.

◖ Best Craft Store: Fancy Tiger Crafts is like "Etsy Live" with inspiring fabrics, classes, patterns, and more for the crafty and wannabe-crafty (page 164).

◖ Best Independent Bookstore: The **Tattered Cover Book Store** is one of the country's most well-known independent bookstores. With three locations to choose from, there's always a chance to stop in and browse (page 167).

◖ Best Music Shop: Twist & Shout offers a huge selection and regular live music performances (page 167).

◖ Best Women's Bargain Boutique: It's hard to find anything over $50 at **Inspyre Boutique,** where simple and sexy tops and dresses can fit any body and budget (page 171).

◖ Best Lingerie Shop: If you're looking for the best-fitting bra or a sexy gift, the excellent staff at **Le Soutien** can help (page 172).

◖ Best Discount Designer Duds: The **Max** outlet store features big markdowns on designer clothes by Prada, Chloé, Diane von Furstenberg, Jimmy Choo, and many more (page 172).

◖ Best Cowgirl Gift Shop: Cry Baby Ranch is the shop for cowgirls with attitude and style. You can find a multitude of kitschy Western-themed gifts here, as well as boots for men and women, and cute children's clothing (page 173).

◖ Best Cowboy Shirts: Rockmount Ranch Wear is the inventor of the snap-front cowboy shirt and a favorite of rock stars who like a Western look. The shop's T-shirts are pretty cool, too (page 173).

◖ Best Place to Find a Gift: No matter what the season, the **Artisan Center** is always busy with gift-hunters looking for anything from jewelry to dishes to scarves (page 174).

◖ Best Made-by-Locals Store: Go to the **I Heart Denver Store** for items designed and made by Denverites (page 175).

◖ Best Specialty Food Store: The aroma hits you before setting foot inside **Savory Spice.** Peruse hundreds of jars of spices and herbs before selecting your favorite to take home (page 185).

Perfect Petal; toys, gear, and clothes for the wee ones at Real Baby; and accessories to accent an outfit in any season at Kismet. Even the museums in Golden Triangle, Capitol Hill, and along Santa Fe Drive offer great shopping opportunities in their gift shops.

Arts and Crafts

CERAMICS IN THE CITY

1912 Pearl St., 303/200-0461,
www.ceramicsinthecity.com

HOURS: Mon.-Sat. 11 A.M.-9 P.M., Sun. noon-6 P.M.

Map 1

Sure, you'll end up paying three times what you would if you just bought a mug or a plate already painted, but it's so fun to personalize one! Ceramics in the City in the Uptown neighborhood is so popular that sometimes you have to make reservations to get a table. (No, there is no alcohol or food served here.) Adults and children come to make keepsakes and special gifts. The staff is friendly and patient

with people of all ages and ability levels. Plan ahead—it can take several days before your piece gets fired and is available for pick up.

THE COLORADO BEAD COMPANY

1245 E. Colfax Ave., 303/861-6823,
www.thecoloradobeadco.com

HOURS: Mon.-Thurs. 11 A.M.-7 P.M., Sat.-Sun.
11 A.M.-6 P.M.

Map 4

Beads of every texture, shape, origin, and style can be found at The Colorado Bead Company. It's even more than beads—there are gemstones, pearls, pendants, and all the tools one needs to make his or her own beautiful jewelry. Beading is for every generation, so there are options for kids' and adults' beading parties here, as well as classes for those who want their bead projects to appear a tad more sophisticated.

◖ FANCY TIGER CRAFTS

59 Broadway, 303/733-3855, www.fancytiger.com

HOURS: Mon.-Sat. 10 A.M.-7 P.M., Sun. noon-6 P.M.
(Tues. open until 9 P.M.)

Map 2

Sewing one's own clothes is fashionable again, and it doesn't get any more hip than Fancy Tiger Crafts, where adults and children can take classes to learn about knitting, sewing, felting, fashion design, and a lot more creative stuff. The raw materials for sale here include organic cotton fabrics by the yard, and organic yarn made from hemp, llama, and cotton. After picking a pattern and a cute printed fabric, head across the street to Fancy Tiger Clothing to buy clothes made by Fancy Tiger students and alums, as well as more mainstream designers.

COURTESY OF FANCY TIGER

Fancy Tiger is a crafter's paradise.

In 2012, Fancy Tiger Crafts moved just about a block away from their original location, which means more room for classes, events, and, of course, fabrics!

KOZO FINE ART MATERIALS

10 E. Ellsworth Ave., 303/733-2730,
www.kozofineartmaterials.com
HOURS: Mon.-Sat. 10 A.M.-6:30 P.M., Sun. noon-5 P.M.
Map 2

Kozo Fine Art Materials is for people who want to either buy unique handmade papers from around the world or have the chance to work with such fragile papyrus. The vibrant papers are beautiful and seem like works of art that should just remain on display, untouched. The supplies here are for bookmaking, printing presses, painting, and drawing. Check out the monthly class schedule that can range from bookmaking to Japanese papermaking and other paper-related crafts.

WILD YARNS

3450 W. 32nd Ave., 303/433-3762, www.wildyarns.com
HOURS: Tues.-Fri. 10 A.M.-7 P.M., Sat. 10 A.M.-5 P.M., Sun. noon-5 P.M.
Map 5

You might have already walked right by Wild Yarns and not even realized it was there. This little shop is tucked up a walkway next to another Highlands Square business, and must rely on word-of-mouth for people just to find it. But once they do find it, it's a reward for knitters. Opened in 2011, Wild Yarns has a friendly, helpful staff and regular classes for beginning to more advanced knitters. For those of us novice knitters, the idea of "local" yarn is as foreign as purling, but the name Wild Yarns is actually a clue to the fact that this shop specializes in Western-produced yarns. Sign up to learn how to knit a purse, socks, blankets, and much more.

Baby and Children's Clothing

THE GIGGLING GREEN BEAN

3929 Tennyson St., 720/988-3725,
www.the-giggling-green-bean.com
HOURS: Mon.-Fri. 11 A.M.-5 P.M., Sat. 10 A.M.-5 P.M., Sun. noon-4 P.M.
Map 5

The operative word in this shop's name is "Green," as in environmentally friendly baby gear. Cloth diapers? Check. Wooden toys? Check. Organic cotton onesies? Check. Plus all the other stuff needed by pregnant mamas, new mamas, toddlers, and so on. Located along vibrant Tennyson Street in the Berkeley neighborhood of greater Highlands, this is a fun store to browse and keep coming back to.

LITTLE ME'S

3000 E. 3rd Ave., Ste. 14, 303/322-6222,
www.littlemes.com
HOURS: Mon.-Sat. 10 A.M.-6 P.M., Sun. noon-5 P.M.
Map 6

Like some kids I know, a lot of personality in a small package is how I would describe Little Me's. This small boutique is for your favorite budding fashionita—from infant to tween. There are designer jeans, dresses, accessories, and all those stylish items you never knew you needed until you saw them here. Brands include Chaser, Rowdy, Sprout, Knuckleheads, Dxtreme Thermals, with new arrivals seasonally.

NEST

2808 E. 6th Ave., 720/287-1372, www.nestdenver.com
HOURS: Mon.-Sat. 10 A.M.-6 P.M., Sun. noon-4 P.M.
Map 6

From infants to eight-year-olds, Nest can dress your boy or girl fashionably without breaking the bank. Every time I am in this shop, the

SHOPS

COURTESY OF KELLY DOLAN AND WILD YARNS

Find local and regional yarns at Wild Yarns.

racks are full to bursting with the latest collections from Tea, Petit Bateau, Splendid, Ella Moos, and Mimi & Magee—and that's just the clothes. There is also a small selection of infant and toddler shoes, hair accessories, and toys for the little ones. A second location in Larimer Square (1408 Larimer St., Ste. 102, 303/534-1974) has less inventory and only goes up to five-year-olds, but still carries the same brands.

REAL BABY
3600 W. 32nd Ave., 303/477-2229,
www.realbabyinc.com
HOURS: Mon.-Sat. 10 A.M.-7 P.M., Sun. 11 A.M.-5 P.M.
Map 5

Founded and owned by parents in the Highlands neighborhood, Real Baby is the real deal when looking for everything from hip and casual maternity clothes to baby clothes and toddler furniture, toys, and books. A *Thomas the Tank Engine* table set up in the book and toy area makes it easy for parents to keep shopping while junior

is busy playing nearby. Don't rush through here; there are books for grown-ups about babies and kids, CDs for the whole family to enjoy, and body care products for moms and babes, all tucked into cubby shelves lining the wall.

TALULAH JONES
1122 E. 17th Ave., 303/832-1230, www.talulahonline.com
HOURS: Mon.-Fri. 10 A.M.-6 P.M., Sat. 10 A.M.-5 P.M., Sun. 11 A.M.-4 P.M.
Map 4

Talulah Jones is a little shop of girly and kids' treasures. The well-stocked inventory of stationery, soaps, jewelry, handbags, scarves, toys, books, and children's clothing takes some patient digging through to find that just-right item. The largest area of the two-room store is devoted to kids, with a few things set out for playing with as moms burrow through a basket of musical instruments or wiggle toys. While there are many small, independent labels here, there are also more recognizable items, such as the Calico Critters line of toys.

Books and Music

CAPITOL HILL BOOKS

300 E. Colfax Ave., 303/837-0700,
www.capitolhillbooks.com
HOURS: Mon.-Sat. 10 A.M.-6 P.M., Sun. 11 A.M.-5 P.M.

`Map 4`

Capitol Hill Books is a simple, old-fashioned bookstore with that musty smell and overflowing bookshelves stuffed with a wide variety of books. Though there are a few rare and antiquated books for sale here, this is a general bookstore with various paperbacks and hardbacks available. Located on the block just behind the State Capitol Building, Capitol Hill Books is easy walking distance from anywhere in downtown or Capitol Hill. This is a mellow place to spend a few hours just browsing the stacks.

THE HERMITAGE BOOKSHOP

290 Fillmore St., 303/388-6811,
www.hermitagebooks.com
HOURS: Mon.-Fri. 10 A.M.-5:30 P.M., Sat. 10 A.M.-5 P.M.

`Map 6`

For those in search of first editions and rare books, the Hermitage is the best place to go in search of everything from military history to children's books to Western Americana. Just below the sidewalk-level storefronts of Cherry Creek North, the Hermitage is designed for comfortable study of its many texts, with sofas, leather chairs, and coffee tables set up between the bookshelves. It's best to settle in and leisurely browse the inventory of 35,000 titles.

☾ TATTERED COVER BOOK STORE

2526 E. Colfax Ave., 303/322-7727,
www.tatteredcover.com
HOURS: Mon.-Thurs. 7 A.M.-10 P.M., Fri. 7 A.M.-11 P.M., Sat. 9 A.M.-11 P.M., Sun. 9 A.M.-6 P.M.

`Map 4`

Denver's beloved independent bookstore has three large locations: LoDo, Colfax Avenue, and the

suburb of Highlands Ranch. In 2006, the Tattered Cover closed its four-story store in Cherry Creek and relocated to the historic Lowenstein Theater on Colfax Avenue the same year. The new layout is completely unique—with bookshelves where theater seats used to be—and takes some getting used to. Each store has thousands of books and periodicals, as well as a coffee shop and special events space for book readings and signings. Check the Tattered Cover website or get on the mailing list to stay up-to-date on visiting authors, book signings, and more. The LoDo location can be found at 1628 16th Street at Wynkoop Street (303/436-1070), and the Highlands Ranch store is at 9315 Dorcester Street in the Highlands Ranch Town Center (303/470-7050).

☾ TWIST & SHOUT

2508 E. Colfax Ave., 303/722-1943,
www.twistandshout.com
HOURS: Mon.-Sat. 10 A.M.-10 P.M., Sun. 10 A.M.-8 P.M.

`Map 4`

Hands down, Twist & Shout is Denver's favorite independent music store. The store has joined the Tattered Cover Book Store at the Lowenstein Theater complex on Colfax Avenue, and it's better than ever. Shoppers can hang out and comfortably listen to tunes before purchasing, and the sales staff is always helpful and knowledgeable, or can find someone who knows even more. There are frequently free live music performances at the store, so check the website often to see if your favorite band is playing.

WAX TRAX RECORDS

638 E. 13th Ave., 303/831-7246,
www.waxtraxrecords.com
HOURS: Mon.-Thurs. 10 A.M.-7 P.M., Fri.-Sat. 10 A.M.-8 P.M., Sun. 10 A.M.-7 P.M.

`Map 4`

That's right, records—as in vinyl. For anyone

SHOPS

© STEVE CRECELIUS, COURTESY OF VISIT DENVER

The Tattered Cover Book Store has three Denver-area locations.

who still has a record player and not enough music to play on it, Wax Trax is the place to go for rare 45s and LPs. The stock is not completely vintage; the shop carries CDs and DVDs to round out more recent decades of music. This is the original Wax Trax—started by the owners of the more famous Chicago store and then bought and basically preserved by new owners way back in the 1970s.

Clothing and Accessories for Men

EMAGE

1620 Platte St., 720/855-8297,
www.emagenetwork.com
HOURS: Mon.-Sat. 11 A.M.-9 P.M., Sun. noon-8 P.M.
Map 3

Mostly full of teen to thirtysomething males, Emage is located just a couple of blocks from the Denver Skatepark with the purpose of outfitting anyone who likes to skateboard and snowboard. It also sells skateboards, snowboards, and all the parts and accessories needed for either sport. Emage has a good selection of shoes for the complete look, with Adidas, Nike, and Vans.

LAWRENCE COVELL

225 Steele St., 303/320-1023,
www.lawrencecovell.com
HOURS: Mon.-Sat. 10 A.M.-6 P.M.
Map 6

What started as a custom leather-goods shop in nearby Boulder in the 1960s has evolved into one of the country's best shops for a sophisticated and discriminating clientele. While the store sells both men's and women's clothing, this is the place for men who can afford to shop in style but aren't sure what that style is. Personal shopping and wardrobe consultation are available, with the owners as experts to help the most fashion-challenged. What man doesn't look his best in a Kiton suit and necktie or a Jil Sander shirt?

METROBOOM

1550 Platte St., 303/477-9700, www.metroboom.com
HOURS: Tues.-Fri. 10 A.M.-7 P.M., Sat. 10 A.M.-6 P.M., closed Sun.
Map 3

The concept at Metroboom is styling and grooming, from hair products to clothes and shoes. The look here is not metrosexual, but hip and urban and definitely male. There are jeans that fit just right, cowboy boots or loafers, button-down shirts with a bit of pattern, and cool T-shirts. Brands include Johnny Max, English Laundry, and Pistol Pete. In the grooming department, choose from American Crew, Pangea Organics, or Metroboom's own line.

PLAYERS

1501 Wazee St., 303/752-9377,
www.playersclothing.com
HOURS: Mon.-Fri. 10 A.M.-6 P.M., Sat. 10 A.M.-5:30 P.M., closed Sun.
Map 3

In the heart of LoDo, somewhere between Coors Field and the Pepsi Center, is the aptly named Players clothing store for men. The clientele here is not made up of sports fanatics, but men who live and work in the neighborhood and favor the "business casual" look. It's not quite "casual Friday," but more spiffy, with cashmere sweaters and brushed-cotton shirts. Look for familiar lines such as Cole Haan shoes, Tommy Bahama, Hiltl, and Remy.

TROUT'S AMERICAN SPORTSWEAR

1077 S. Gaylord St., 303/733-3983, www.trouts.net
HOURS: Mon.-Fri. 10 A.M.-6 P.M., Sat. 10 A.M.-5:30 P.M., Sun. 11 A.M.-4 P.M.
Map 6

Men's casual sportswear lines are found at Trout's among the shops and restaurants on Old South Gaylord Street in the Washington Park neighborhood. Men who like Cole Haan footwear and the colorful prints and simple khakis of designers like Tommy Bahama and Bills Khakis will enjoy outfitting themselves at Trout's. Imagine a well-dressed man on a long vacation—that's the idea for Trout's clientele.

SIDEWALK SALES

Every summer, the merchants of Cherry Creek North hold a four-day-long sidewalk sale that draws thousands of shoppers hungry for a deal. Officials with Cherry Creek North say that in January, people are already beginning to call to find out the specific dates for the sale, along with other pertinent information. The long-held tradition includes 320 shops, restaurants, and galleries in the 16-block neighborhood. The dates change annually to make it a four-day weekend, and shops are typically open during their regular business hours. However, anyone who wants to avoid the crowds is welcome to stop by the day before the official sale begins and see if there are any early markdowns. Go to www.cherrycreeknorth.com for the latest dates and information.

The last weekend in July, the businesses in Highlands Square host the "Sip N' Save" Sidewalk Sale, where customers are invited to enjoy refreshing beverages and stroll from shop to shop looking for great deals. Go to http://highlands-square.com for more information.

Clothing and Accessories for Women

THE BELLE ON COTTAGE HILL
4322 W. 35th Ave., 303/947-7063
HOURS: Tues.-Sat. 10 A.M.-3 P.M., closed Sun. and Mon.
Map 5

What started as a local designer, MargoBelle, selling aprons, skirts, and handbags at local farmers' markets has become a charming little shop. The store does emphasize locally made items beyond MargoBelle—there are also paintings, accessories, furniture, and other cute odd and ends. The hours here reflect the fact that it is owned by local moms who need to be there when school gets out. But if you can only make it at night, come over on a First Friday of every month and do your shopping then (5 P.M.–9 P.M.).

COMMON ERA
1543 Platte St., 303/433-4633,
www.mycommonera.com
HOURS: Mon.-Sat. 11 A.M.-7 P.M., Sun. noon-5 P.M.
Map 3

Looking for something new, but don't want to spend more than $50? Go straight to Common Era, where there are racks of colorful simple-but-sexy dresses, tops, and tees to choose from

at very reasonable prices. The styles are so versatile here that they can appeal to both a teenage girl and her mother. Don't be scared off if you happen by in October, when the store gets a bit over-the-top for Halloween, with crazy platform shoes, wigs, and other themed attire—by Thanksgiving they are back to normal.

DECADE
56 S. Broadway, 303/733-2288
HOURS: Mon.-Sat. 11 A.M.-6 P.M., Sun. noon-5 P.M.
Map 2

Wander past the retro home decor items, tempting toiletries, adorable baby gifts, and the fat store cat at Decade to find a women's boutique. This is a mix of new and used clothing, with lacy to modern styles in jeans, T-shirts, skirts, and lingerie. There is a small section for men, but Decade is really all about femininity. Locally made jewelry is also for sale at the front counter. Decade is the perfect place to find a little something girly to wear out for a casual evening—and not at an astronomical price.

DRAGONFLY
3615 W. 32nd Ave., 303/433-6331

HOURS: Mon.-Sat. 10:30 A.M.-6:30 P.M., Sun. 11 A.M.-5 P.M.

Map 5

When women need a new outfit or top with jeans for a girls' night out or a date with someone special, Dragonfly should be a first stop. Small designers to larger, established brands are carried here. Check out Tart Collections, Velvet, Harper Clothing, SOLD Design Lab, Ella Moss, Trina Turk, and lots more. Right next door to Strut, complete the look with a new pair of shoes.

ECCENTRICITY
290 Fillmore St., 303/388-8877, www.eccentricity.com
HOURS: Mon.-Fri. 10:30 A.M.-5:30 P.M., Sat. 10:30 A.M.-5 P.M., closed Sun.

Map 6

Eccentricity is the kind of shop someone might walk right by, except for that great, eye-catching jacket or sweater hanging in the window that is simply irresistible. This is one of the shops where, at first glance, it seems there isn't a lot in stock, but the genius is that Eccentricity has carefully selected the cream of the crop. With Lucchese cowboy boots and colorful sweaters and shawls, this is the place to piece together that urban Southwestern look.

GARBARINI
3003 E. 3rd Ave., Ste. D, 303/333-8686, www.garbarinishop.com
HOURS: Mon.-Sat. 10 A.M.-6 P.M., Sun. noon-5 P.M.

Map 6

Many years ago, Terri Garbarini started a small shoe store, which has since expanded to a one-stop shop for women's fashion. While there are still very fine shoes to be found at this store, there are also heaps of sexy women's fashions to choose from. Garbarini stays on the cutting edge of the latest styles, and the store is always crammed full of options—from flirty Nicole Miller dresses to sexy Rebecca Beeson T-shirts. The sales staff is knowledgeable, helpful, and honest when it comes to helping you put together an outfit or find that perfect-fitting pair of jeans.

INSPYRE BOUTIQUE
2021 W. 32nd Ave., 303/718-2645, www.inspyreboutique.com
HOURS: Mon.-Sat. 11 A.M.-8 P.M., Sun. 11 A.M.-6 P.M.

Map 5

Here is cute and affordable women's clothing. The concept at this boutique is to keep prices under $50 as much as possible. The emphasis at Inspyre is on women, and the window displays of sexy and colorful dresses make it appear as if the boutique is just for the fairer sex, but gentlemen are welcome and might find jeans or a hip T-shirt. These are not household brand names, but when you find that perfect summer dress or sexy top, who cares? It's always better to wear something more original, anyway.

JIL CAPPUCCIO & SEWN
18 S. Broadway, 303/832-1493, www.jilcappuccio.com
HOURS: Mon.-Sat. 11 A.M.-6 P.M., Sun. 11 A.M.-5 P.M.

Map 2

In 2012, Jil Cappucio moved her tiny shop of one-of-a-kind clothing for men, women, and children over to the strip of trendiness along South Broadway. No longer a namesake shop, the sign out front simply reads, "SEWN," in large, colorful letters. Obviously, with the designer and seamstress working in sight—Jil Cappucio has been known to work on her latest designs right in the shop—SEWN sells one-of-a-kind items. Cappuccio's dresses and pajamas are all roomy and colorful pieces, with a few little ones for children, and she makes men's shirts, too. The shop also carries items from other local designers, including very lovely knitwear by Pearl. And with this expanded store, customers will find more local designers of everything from soap to pillows.

KISMET

3640 W. 32nd Ave., 303/477-3378,
www.kismetaccesories.com
HOURS: Tues.-Sat. 10:30 A.M.-6:30 P.M., Sun.-Mon.
11 A.M.-5 P.M.

`Map 5`

Looking for that perfect colorful scarf, a stylish summer hat (or winter one), or just some unique jewelry? Kismet is my personal fave for these items, but they also have sweet little dresses, tops, handbags, belts, shoes. In the heart of Highlands Square, Kismet is a must-see part of the shopping experience in the neighborhood. The store has two other locations in the greater metro area, so check the website for details.

(LE SOUTIEN

246 Milwaukee St., 303/377-0515, www.lesoutien.com
HOURS: Mon.-Fri. 10 A.M.-6 P.M., Sat. 10 A.M.-5 P.M.,
closed Sun.

`Map 6`

No appointment is necessary for a personal bra fitting at Le Soutien, where customers can select from only the best lingerie lines—Chantelle, Simone Perele, and Cosabella, to name a few. Just like all fashion, lingerie has seasons, so there are new choices in spring and fall in different colors and styles. Le Soutien also has swimwear, which needs to fit all those same areas just as perfectly, if not better.

(MAX

264 Detroit St., 303/321-4949, www.maxfashion.com
HOURS: Mon.-Sat. 10 A.M.-6 P.M., Sun. noon-5 P.M.

`Map 6`

Long considered a high watermark of women's fashion in Denver, Max is the store to visit for the woman who needs an extra special dress, skirt, or outfit. At any one of Max's stores, a customer may be helped by the owner himself, Max Martinez. Max and his staff know women, and how to dress them properly in the best styles. Look for Stella McCartney, Chloé,

Prada, Thakoon, Versace, and many other fabulous designers. Finances pinched? Head down to the lower level for the Max outlet store, with lower prices on the same hot designers. Hours differ for the outlet store, so call ahead.

SOL

248 Detroit St., 303/394-1060, www.sollingerie.com
HOURS: Mon.-Sat. 10 A.M.-6 P.M., closed Sun.

`Map 6`

Finding a good, bra-fitting expert like those at SOL (short for "Store of Lingerie") in Cherry Creek North is just as important as finding a good hairdresser. Once a woman has been properly fitted for a bra, there's no going back to guessing sizes on her own. Sexy, lacy, comfortable, and practical are all found at SOL in the form of thongs, panties, bras, camisoles, and pajamas, including slinky sleepwear and loungewear from SOL's own line.

SOUS LE LIT

1550 Platte St., 303/455-1622, www.souslelit.com
HOURS: Mon.-Sat. 10 A.M.-6 P.M., Sun. noon-5 P.M.

`Map 3`

Opened in 2009, Sous le Lit joined the growing hip and popular strip of shops along Platte Street, with lesser-known designers for women to choose from. In this small shop space, there are shoes, hats, dresses, jeans, tops, and jewelry. Even though Sous Le Lit started with just shoes and accessories, without physically expanding its space, the business grew the offerings for customers. The service here is always friendly and not overbearing.

STARLET

3450 W. 32nd Ave., 303/433-7827,
www.shopstarlet.com
HOURS: Mon.-Sat. 11 A.M.-6 P.M., Sun. 11 A.M.-5 P.M.

`Map 5`

Crammed with colorful accessories, from hats to necklaces to sunglasses and purses, Starlet is an accessory shop for all tastes. There is a second location in the SoBo neighborhood at 26 Broadway, which is equally tiny. Starlet is a terrific place to find that last-minute hostess gift for a girlfriend who is so hard to shop for. There is more than a hint of vintage in the items at Starlet, which makes them even more special.

Cowboy Boots and Western Accessories

◖ CRY BABY RANCH

1421 Larimer St., 303/623-3979,
www.crybabyranch.com

HOURS: Mon.-Fri. 10 A.M.-7 P.M., Sat. 10 A.M.-6 P.M., Sun. noon-5 P.M.

Map 3

Cry Baby Ranch is an unusual hybrid of kitschy Western everything with a dash of bohemian style in the form of cute kids' clothes and women's shirts. The specialty here is the West—Western shirts; cowboy boots for men, women, kids, and even babies; home decor; jewelry; and a whole lot of other stuff that no one ever knows they need until they see it here. Look for Annie Oakley action figures, Boss Lady toiletries, state of Colorado pillows, and books galore for grown-ups and kids.

◖ ROCKMOUNT RANCH WEAR

1626 Wazee St., 303/629-7777, www.rockmount.com

HOURS: Mon.-Fri. 8 A.M.-6 P.M., Sat. 10 A.M.-6 P.M., Sun. 11 A.M.-4 P.M.

Map 3

Rockmount Ranch Wear is famous for a lot of things: the founder and owner, affectionately called "Papa Jack," who worked daily at

© STEVE CRECELIUS, COURTESY OF VISIT DENVER

Rockmount Ranch Wear sells cowboy shirts for all ages.

the store until he died in 2008 at 107 years old; the original snap-front cowboy shirts; the celebrities and rock stars who have bought many of Rockmount's ornate Western shirts; and the legacy of being in business in the same historic building since 1946. This is part office, part store, part museum. Don't think you can carry off a Western shirt? No problem, as one of Denver's best souvenirs is a Rockmount T-shirt featuring a bucking bronco rider in men's, women's, and children's sizes and styles.

Gifts

◀ ARTISAN CENTER

2757 E. 3rd Ave., 303/333-1201, www. artisancenterdenver.com

HOURS: Mon.-Sat. 10 A.M.-5:30 P.M., Sun. noon-5 P.M.

Map 6

The Artisan Center is a can't-miss store for people who like precious gifty items or are looking for the perfect present. Outside the store, there are colorful wind chimes or garden items, and inside, it's a plethora of trinkets. There are baby clothes, soaps, candles, jewelry, dishes, scarves, rugs, cards, and little bowls of even tinier things, like matchbox shrines. It seems like there is never a season when this store is not busy with customers carefully selecting just the right treasure-and they've been doing it since 1977. The Artisan Center also offers free and lovely gift wrapping.

CREATOR MUNDI

2910 E. 3rd Ave., 303/322-1901, www.creatormundi. com

HOURS: Mon.-Fri. 10 A.M.-5 P.M., Sat. 10 A.M.-4 P.M., Sun. 1-4 P.M., note that hours change frequently, so call ahead

Map 6

When a gift needs to have a sacred meaning, the best place to find it is Creator Mundi in Cherry Creek North. The shop is essentially decorated with many religious objects, with crosses hanging on the walls and angels set atop tables alongside candles and jewelry. Creator Mundi seems to represent most faiths; Native American and Catholic icons, books, cards, and other items all share space here.

5 GREEN BOXES

1596 S. Pearl St., 303/777-2331, www.5greenboxes. com

HOURS: Mon.-Sat. 10 A.M.-6 P.M., Sun. noon-5 P.M.

Map 6

Really two stores, 5 Green Boxes' locations are one block apart and have slightly different concepts. The original, what is called the "Little

Find whimsical gifts for all ages at 5 Green Boxes.

© MINDY SINK

SHOPS

CULTURAL GIFTING

Shopping for the person who doesn't really need anything? Try a cultural institution gift shop for something unexpected and unusual. The **Denver Art Museum** (100 W. 14th Ave. Pkwy., 720/865-5000, www.denverartmuseum.org) has two gift shops, one in each wing. In the Frederic C. Hamilton Building, the museum is a large shop with about twice the amount of inventory as the smaller store in the North Building. Both have jewelry, children's books and toys about art and artists, stationery, and items related to current exhibits.

At the **Denver Botanic Gardens** (1005 York St., 720/865-3500, www.botanicgardens.org) you'll find gifts with a green theme—rosebud soaps, tulip lollipops, books on gardening, and pretty note cards.

For things with a Latin flair, try the **Museo de Las Americas** (861 Santa Fe Dr., 303/571-4401, www.museo.org). It's a great place to get Day of the Dead ornaments, too.

If it's design and decorative arts that interest you, go straight to the **Kirkland Museum of Fine & Decorative Art** (1311 Pearl St., 303/832-8576, www.kirklandmuseum.org) to buy one-of-a-kind ceramics by Colorado artists or items such as a scarf featuring Vance Kirkland's own artwork.

And don't forget the **History Colorado Center** (1300 Broadway, 303/866-3682, www.historycoloradocenter.org) gift shop for unique books about city and state history and to pick up some miniature Big Blue Bears.

Store," is chock-full of knickknacks that include pretty little shoes, colorful scarves, jewelry, and more. The "Big Store" at 1705 South Pearl Street (303/282-5481) offers home decor items, including its own line of upholstered chairs (very shabby chic) and footstools. Need a wool three-tiered wedding cake? This is the place.

I HEART DENVER STORE
500 16th St., 303/720-9069, http://iheartdenver.info
HOURS: Mon.-Sat. 10 a.m.-9 p.m., Sun. 11 a.m.-6 p.m.
Map 1

When I first heard about this shop, I could not figure out where it was because I did not believe it was in a mall. A store all about the local in a place all about the franchise? This is almost like an art gallery that celebrates the city, with locally made and designed crafts and clothes. The goal is to support creative entrepreneurs through sales at the store. Even for window shoppers and browsers, it's an impressive selection of what's made in Denver.

MORE FLOWERS
2501 15th St., 303/477-0947, www.moreflowers.com
HOURS: Call ahead
Map 5

More Flowers is not your typical florist shop. It feels more like a wholesale floral business, but customers are certainly welcome to buy flowers by the stem or bouquet. The best way to order from More Flowers is to give them your price range (warning: the delivery minimum price is $50), let the experts do their thing, and have the jaw-droppingly gorgeous arrangement delivered to your loved one. With much of the foliage stripped away, there is a lot packed into each vase, always with a surprising color combination.

NATIVE AMERICAN TRADING COMPANY
213 W. 13th Ave., 303/534-0771,
www.nativeamericantradingco.com
HOURS: Tues.-Fri. 10 a.m.-5 p.m., Sat. 11 a.m.-4 p.m., First Fridays 5-9 p.m., closed Sun. and Mon.
Map 2

Part art gallery, part jewelry and curio shop, the Native American Trading Company is a

SHOPS

place to find unique Southwestern and Native American wares. Only one block from the Denver Art Museum and across the street from the Byers-Evans House, the store is in a 1906 mission-style townhome. It's easy to walk into the Trading Company for a quick visit, and end up staying an hour or more looking at artwork and listening to the owners' stories of their relationships with the various artists and artisans who they represent.

OLD MAP GALLERY

1550 Wynkoop St., 303/296-7725,
www.oldmapgallery.com
HOURS: Mon.-Sat. 10 A.M.-5 P.M., closed Sun.
Map 3

The Old Map Gallery caters to serious map collectors and experts, and for the rest of us, it's a fascinating peek into the world of cartography and a shop to find a unique piece of artwork or a gift for someone obsessed with a specific place.

The I Heart Denver Store shows off locally made wares.

Along with antique maps featuring countries, oceans, celestial bodies, and food and wine, there are very affordable current maps for sale.

THE PERFECT PETAL

3600 W. 32nd Ave., 303/480-0966,
www.theperfectpetal.com
HOURS: Mon.-Sat. 9 A.M.-8 P.M., Sun. 11 A.M.-5 P.M.
Map 5

Considered one of Denver's top floral shops, the Perfect Petal is also a charming boutique in the heart of Highlands Square. It's really one of those very girly shops with cute stationery, antique jewelry, cookbooks, candles, and other sweet-smelling and -looking goods. The flowers are up some steps in the rear of the store and can be sold by the stem or made into creative and unusual arrangements.

POME

1071 S. Gaylord St., 303/722-2900,
www.pomedenver.com
HOURS: Mon. 10:30 A.M.-5 P.M., Tues.-Sat. 10 A.M.-6 P.M., Sun. 10:30 A.M.-4 P.M.
Map 6

While waiting for a table at Devil's Food Bakery in Washington Park, wander over to Pome to look for handsome baby gifts or other treasures created by a local designer. Pome has a little of everything, from kitchen aprons to drawer pulls and things for babies and toddlers. The store almost feels as if you're in a very cute flea market booth. Pome is often voted Denver's top boutique in local surveys.

REJUVANEST

1550 Platte St., 303/455-1504, www.rejuvanest.com
HOURS: Mon.-Sat. 10 A.M.-6 P.M., Sun. noon-5 P.M.
Map 3

Personally, I like a gift shop that doesn't smell like a candle shop at the mall. Rejuvanest is that quintessential gift shop that does, indeed, have scented candles, but pleasant ones, tucked in here and there between cute baby clothes,

COURTESY OF SAMUEL SCHIMEK/I HEART DENVER

linens, sexy lingerie, bath salts, plush robes, and a little jewelry. It sounds like a strange mix, but trust me, it all works together and the shop is filled with irresistible luxuries.

THE STATIONERY COMPANY

2818 E. 6th Ave., 303/388-1133,
www.stationerycompany.com
HOURS: Mon.-Fri. 10 A.M.-6 P.M., Sat. 10 A.M.-5 P.M., closed Sun.

Map 6

Even with the rise in postage rates and increasing use of email, there is still room in the world for old-fashioned stationery. At The Stationery Company, the owner and her excellent staff are there to help pick out wedding and birth announcement cards, or just let customers browse the shelves of greeting cards, boxes of stationery, and other odds and ends, such as baby blankets and books, wrapping paper, toiletries, and clocks.

WORDSHOP

3180 Meade St., 303/477-9673,
www.wordshopdenver.com
HOURS: Tues.-Sat. 11 A.M.-6 P.M., Sun. noon-5 P.M., closed Mon., or by appt.

Map 5

A card for any occasion can be found at Wordshop, especially if you tell the helpful owner as much as you can about who you are buying the card for. In addition to the birthday, anniversary, get well, and humorous anytime cards, there are invitations and announcements to choose from. The store is a bit difficult for first-time visitors to find; it's tucked in around the corner from the storefronts on 32nd Avenue.

Health and Beauty

ARTEMISIA & RUE

70 Broadway, 303/484-8982,
www.artemisiaandrue.com
HOURS: Mon.-Sat. 10 A.M.-6 P.M., Sun. noon-6 P.M.

Map 2

Opened in 2011, Artemisia & Rue is a place for herbal healing, as well as a scented showroom of herbs, elixirs, and tinctures. There is a separate clinic for herbal and massage healing, with a focus on women's reproductive health, as well as a naturopathic doctor and certified master herbalist on staff. Check the online schedule for free classes featuring beneficial herbs and how to use them. Once a year during Mother's Day, the shop also sells fresh garden plants.

EDIT EURO SPA

159 Adams St., 303/377-1617, www.editeurospa.com
HOURS: Mon-Sat. 9 A.M.-5:30 P.M., closed Sun.

Map 6

Just a block or so away from the busy sidewalks of the Cherry Creek North shopping district is the calm oasis of fabulous skin care at Edit Euro Spa. In a two-story Victorian house, rooms have been transformed into miniature day spas where the city's best facials and waxing are done. One look at the owner's gorgeous skin and anyone will be sold on the services and products at Edit. To combat Colorado's dry climate and harsh sunshine, be sure to check out the hydrating treatments and skin care line.

TALLGRASS SPA

997 Upper Bear Creek Rd., Evergreen, 303/670-4444,
www.tallgrassspa.com
HOURS: Mon.-Wed. 8:30 A.M.-7:30 P.M., Thurs.-Fri. 8:30 A.M.-8:30 P.M., Sat. 8:30 A.M.-6:30 P.M., Sun. 10 A.M.-6:30 P.M.

Map 7

To truly relax and unwind, one must first get out of town and head to the spa. Tallgrass Spa in Evergreen is about 30 minutes from downtown and is an ideal retreat for pampering. This is an Aveda spa and salon, which means everything from the scented candles to the massage oils are Aveda products. Set in the foothills, Tallgrass is a great place to bond with girlfriends for the day or spend a special day with your sweetie. In this dry climate, don't miss "the quencher" treatment, meant to rehydrate the face, hair, and hands.

WOODHOUSE DAY SPA

941 E. 17th Ave., 303/813-8488,
www.denver.woodhousespas.com

HOURS: Mon.-Wed. 9 A.M.-7 P.M., Thurs.-Sun. 9 A.M.-8 P.M.

Map 4

Woodhouse Day Spa has quickly become a favorite for spa treatments, according to several local surveys. Nothing has been overlooked at Woodhouse, including attention to male clients, for whom there is a menu of services ranging from massage to facials. A day at the spa would take over six hours to enjoy with various manicures, pedicures, and "refreshers." The location in a stunning, old home along 17th Avenue is ideal for people who are staying downtown and don't want to travel too far to a spa.

Home Decor and Furnishings

DJUNA

899 N. Broadway, 303/355-3522, www.djuna.com
HOURS: Mon.-Sat. 10 A.M.-5 P.M., closed Sun.

Map 2

It's always so tempting to flop into one of the overstuffed sofas or chairs at Djuna and just hang out, taking in the richly hued variety of rugs, mirrors, pillows, throws, and other furnishings artfully crammed together in the store. Many of the beds and other furniture are custom-made for Djuna. On the one hand, Djuna is a store for people with large homes to decorate right down to the last detail; on the other hand, there are some wonderful linens and fabrics that appeal to smaller budgets and spaces.

FIREFLY FURNISHINGS

2445 E. 3rd Ave., 303/333-4463,
www.fireflyfurnishings.com
HOURS: Sun.-Mon. 11 A.M.-5 P.M., Tues.-Sat. 10 A.M.-6 P.M.

Map 6

Babies and kids need to have stylish furniture in their bedrooms, too. Firefly Furnishings makes setting up a nursery fun, with the latest styles in coordinating colors for a rocker, crib, mobile, and other gear. Furnishings available here and in the online store are for rooms for children of all ages, not just infants.

HAZEL & DEWEY

70 S. Broadway, 303/777-1500,
http://hazel-dewey.com
HOURS: Mon.-Fri. 11 A.M.-7 P.M., Sat. 11 A.M.-6 P.M., Sun. noon-5 P.M.

Map 2

A new addition to the South Broadway shops is Hazel & Dewey, with a yummy variety of kitchenwares that are artfully arranged in this clean space. It was voted Denver's Best Kitchen store by *Westword* magazine in 2012. This is the place for Helvetica-character cookie cutters, cast-iron tea kettles, and other perfect housewarming or hostess gifts.

HW HOME

199 Clayton Ln., 303/394-9222, www.hwhome.com
HOURS: Mon.-Thurs. 10 A.M.-6 P.M., Fri.-Sat. 10 A.M.-7 P.M., Sun. 11 A.M.-5 P.M.

Map 6

At first glance, HW Home appears to be an

upscale chain furniture store, but in fact, it is a locally owned shop with three locations in Colorado. What makes this store fabulous is its ability to put it all together so it looks meant to be, and maybe even like you did it yourself. It's not straight from a catalog cookie-cutter style, and emphasizes top-notch designs for living rooms, bedrooms, and dining rooms.

MOD LIVIN'
5327 E. Colfax Ave., 720/941-9292, www.modlivin.com
HOURS: Mon.-Sat. 10 A.M.-5:30 P.M., Sun. noon-5 P.M.
`Map 7`

Mid-century modern and contemporary modern furniture and accessories fill the huge space of Mod Livin' in Denver's Park Hill neighborhood. Just about every room in the house—and outside of the house, for those with patio space—can be filled with chairs, tables, beds, lights, benches, and more from this store. Even babies and kids can start out in stylishly modern surroundings, thanks to Mod Livin'. Look for Alessi, Modernica, Eames, and other designers throughout the large space or on the website.

REVAMPT
2601 E. 3rd Ave., 720/536-5644,
www.revamptgoods.com
HOURS: Mon.-Sat. 10 A.M.-6:30 P.M., closed Sun.
`Map 6`

Beyond eco- and green shopping is recycled, or "revampt," goods that have found a second life as some useful home furnishing or decor. Skateboards are now earrings, cabins are now trunks, bike rims and sprockets are now side tables, silverware has become napkin rings, barrels are turned into one-of-a-kind chairs, and the list of seemingly improbably transformations goes on. It's a mysterious treasure hunt of "What do you think it was before?", as well as a shopping trip.

Z MODERN
1132 N. Speer Blvd., 303/298-8432, www.zmodern.com
HOURS: Tues.-Sat. 11 A.M.-6 P.M., closed Sun. and Mon.
`Map 2`

Z Modern is for people with modern tastes that go beyond mid-century revival pieces. There's a deeper story behind each piece of furniture or lighting that's worth hearing. (What's up with that pistol lamp?) Well-known designers such as Kartell, Herman Miller, and Philippe Starck are available at Z Modern. Check out the "Do Hit" chair, which comes with its own sledgehammer so the new owner can demolish the metal piece to his or her liking. Two doors down from Z Modern is Zeitgeist Modern Furniture Classics, which has the same address and phone number as Z Modern. Both stores are owned by Randy Roberts, who is usually found in Zeitgeist, more of a vintage store.

SHOPS

Open-Air Markets

CHERRY CREEK FRESH MARKET

N. Cherry Creek Dr. at University Blvd., 303/442-1817, www.coloradofreshmarkets.com

HOURS: May-Oct. Sat. 8 A.M.-1 P.M., plus June-Sept. Wed. 9 A.M.-1 P.M.

Map 6

The Cherry Creek Fresh Market is very popular on Saturday mornings in summer, when more fresh produce and flowers are available weekly from farms around the state. It's a chance to meet the people growing your food, and hear the stories of farm life. Check out the website to see what's in season and expected soon at the market. Colorado specialties include apples, peaches, and Rocky Ford melons.

OLD SOUTH PEARL STREET FARMERS MARKET

S. Pearl St. between E. Florida and Iowa Aves., www.oldsouthpearlstreet.com

HOURS: June-Oct. Sun. 9 A.M.-1 P.M.

Map 6

Smaller than the Cherry Creek Fresh Market, the Old South Pearl Street Farmers Market is utterly charming. The market is set right on the blocked-off street, which is lined with restaurants open for breakfast and brunch, and shops set to open shortly. Because this tends to be a quieter event, it's easy to chat with the farmers and learn more about where the produce is grown and maybe even how to best prepare it.

© MINDY SINK

The Old South Pearl Street Farmers Market sells fresh produce.

Outdoor and Fitness Gear and Apparel

GO LITE

1535 Platte St., 303/477-0547, www.golite.com

HOURS: Mon.-Sat. 10 A.M.-8 P.M., Sun. 10 A.M.-6 P.M.

`Map 3`

Founded in Boulder, Colorado, in 1998, Go Lite has become a small, Western chain of outdoor-gear stores that specialize in, you guessed it, lightweight clothing and gear. The idea is to do "more with less," and enjoy your hiking, camping, and other outdoor adventures without being unnecessarily weighed down by the bulk of your stuff. Over the years, Go Lite's gear has won many awards; the store has garnered media recognition for its sleeping bags, packs, and clothes. This location opened in 2012 and carries clothing for both men and women.

PATAGONIA

1431 15th St., 303/446-9500, www.patagonia.com

HOURS: Mon.-Sat. 10 A.M.-7 P.M., Sun. 11 A.M.-5 P.M.

`Map 3`

On the ground floor of the historic Studebaker building, and only two blocks from Larimer Square, is a Patagonia store that offer men's, women's, and children's clothing, and just a small amount of gear. The children's section includes a Lego table and other toys, and there is a small—one chair—reading area for grown-ups to pass the time. Patagonia seems to generally inspire brand devotion in its customers, and this store is certainly a destination for those types. The parking around here is not easy.

REI

1416 Platte St., 303/756-3100, www.rei.com

HOURS: Mon.-Fri. 10 A.M.-9 P.M., Sat. 10 A.M.-7 P.M., Sun. 10 A.M.-6 P.M.

`Map 3`

This is the REI Denver flagship store and it definitely stands out from other locations. REI occupies a historic tramway building right along the South Platte River. The enormous space has a 37-foot climbing pinnacle and there are multiple levels selling clothing, gear, shoes, and outdoor equipment. There is also a small bookstore and a huge map selection. Up on the children's level, parents can let kids romp in the indoor playground near the sale merchandise. Equipment rental is also available here.

WILDERNESS EXCHANGE UNLIMITED

2401 15th St., 303/964-0708, www.wildernessexchangeunlimited.com

HOURS: Mon.-Fri. 11 A.M.-8 P.M., Sat. 10 A.M.-7 P.M., Sun. 11 A.M.-6 P.M.

`Map 3`

Outdoor-gear bargain hunters head to the Wilderness Exchange, about one block from the REI flagship store near Confluence Park. The store has a small but regularly refreshed inventory of men's and women's clothing, tents, sleeping bags, and shoes, which are all appropriate to the current season. The Wilderness Exchange buys and trades used outdoor gear at this location, and merchandise includes those used items as well as manufacturer's overstock, discontinued items, and slightly damaged items.

Pet Supplies and Grooming

DOG SAVVY BOUTIQUE & SPA

1402 Larimer St., 303/623-5200, www.dogsavvy.com
HOURS: Mon.-Fri. 10 A.M.-7 P.M., Sat. 10 A.M.-6 P.M., Sun.
11 A.M.-5 P.M.
Map 3

Denver is a dog town, not a cow town. And all those pooches need stuff—their own clothes, manicurists, beds with fresh linens, and personalized dishes. Dog Savvy is ready to meet all these doggie needs and more. Seriously—your canine can get a blueberry facial. There are also more basic items available, such as canned food, leashes, and collars. In the heart of Larimer Square, Dog Savvy includes an outdoor patio where dogs and their owners can enjoy the weather and do a little people- and animal-watching on the busy street.

MOUTHFULS

4224 Tennyson St., 720/855-7505, www.mouthfuls.net
HOURS: Mon.-Fri. 10 A.M.-6 P.M., Sat. 9 A.M.-5 P.M., Sun.
10 A.M.-4 P.M.
Map 5

Not so long ago, a pet store was a place to buy pets. Now they are boutiques to bring pets to for an outing and a nibble of a tasty, handmade treat. Mouthfuls is just such an over-the-top pet store, which certainly sells the requisite dog and cat food—including a full baker's display case of cupcakes, donuts, and other treats just for the pooch—but also lots of clothes for dogs, toys for cats and dogs, and breath mints for animals. There is always a dog here, either trying on clothes (or having them tried on) or in residence greeting customers.

ZEN DOG

2401 15th St., 303/744-7067, www.zendogonline.com
HOURS: Mon.-Fri. 10:30 A.M.-6 P.M., Sat.-Sun.
10:30 A.M.-5 P.M.
Map 3

This neighborhood is teeming with dogs, dogs, and more dogs! So it makes sense to have a boutique for man's best friend—and a few cats, too. Depending on which day you stop in, you might be greeted by the owner's four pooches or no canines at all. Zen Dog has it all—food, treats, leashes, clothes, literature, and lots and lots of toys.

Shoes

STRUT

3611 W. 32nd Ave., 303/477-3361, www.strutdenver.com
HOURS: Sun.-Mon. 11 A.M.-4 P.M., Tues.-Sat.
10 A.M.-6 P.M.,
Map 5

Looking for that shoe that you can't find anywhere else in Denver? Strut probably has it. Miss Sixty, Butter, Ted Baker, and a dozen more shoe brands can be found at Strut, with styles ranging from elegant sandals and flats to knock-out heels. Strut is a handbag and accessories store to boot—find Rebecca Norman hoops, Foxy Originals matching necklaces and earrings, and other jeweled surprises. The knowledgeable sales staff can help find a great-looking but still comfortable pair of women's shoes.

TRUE LOVE SHOES & ACCESSORIES

42 Broadway, 303/860-8783, www.trueloveshoes.com
HOURS: Daily 11 A.M.-7 P.M.
Map 2

What do women love more than shoes? Affordable shoes, of course! The whole idea at

True Love is for women to find a fabulous new pair of shoes, and still be able to afford a second pair. Colorful, sparkly, feminine, flats, wedges, heels, and on it goes with a selection of stylish shoes for women in every season. And what makes this shoe store even more unusual is that all of their products are vegan.

Shopping Centers and Districts

Although the original, distinct ethnic character of different Denver neighborhoods has long since disappeared, there are unique styles and personalities for many shopping districts and centers throughout the city. Some of these areas—such as Cherry Creek North and Highlands Square—have annual sales and large festivals that are worth checking out.

CHERRY CREEK MALL

3000 E. 1st Ave., 303/388-3900,
www.shopcherrycreek.com
HOURS: Mon.-Sat. 10 A.M.-9 P.M., Sun. 11 A.M.-6 P.M.
Map 6

Cherry Creek Mall is the counterpoint to Cherry Creek North, drawing lots of shoppers to its anchor stores like Nordstrom, Saks, Neiman Marcus, and Macy's. The other 160-plus stores include Tiffany & Co., Burberry, and Calvin Klein. There is a movie theater on the second level, and the restaurants inside the mall tend to be fast food, with pizza, ice cream, and cookies. The most popular place in the mall is a free play area with giant foam pieces of breakfast food for babies and young children to climb on. At Christmastime, the lines for Santa Claus at Cherry Creek are some of the longest in the city. Outside of the mall are additional stores and restaurants generally considered part of the mall, such as **Elway's Restaurant** (2500 E. 1st Ave., 303/399-5353, www.elways.com). Parking at the mall is free and shaded.

CHERRY CREEK NORTH

Bounded by 1st Ave. to Adams St. to the north, over to 3rd Ave. to the west, and Josephine St. to the south
Map 6

Cherry Creek North has long had a reputation for being a shopping district for the well-to-do, and it does not disappoint in this regard. Located across from the Cherry Creek Mall, the Cherry Creek North shopping district is known for the locally owned shops that have been here for decades. As boutiques have become vogue again in contrast to malls, national stores have begun to rent space in Cherry Creek North rather than in the mall and some have the appearance of being one of the local shops. Around every corner is another shop for every occasion—menswear, womenswear, gifts, art, and more.

COLORADO MILLS MALL

14500 W. Colfax Ave., Lakewood, 303/384-3000,
www.coloradomills.com
HOURS: Mon.-Sat. 10 A.M.-9 P.M., Sun. 11 A.M.-6 P.M.
Map 7

Located in the western suburb of Lakewood, Colorado Mills is the nearest outlet mall to downtown, with big names like Neiman Marcus Last Call, The Gap Outlet Store, Gymboree Outlet, and many more. There are play areas for kids of various ages and a large food court in the center of the mall, as well as a United Artists movie theater. Although this is an outlet mall, the best bargains are still found on the sale racks in just about every store.

The Denver Pavilions shopping center is on the 16th Street Mall.

© STEVE CRECELIUS, COURTESY OF VISIT DENVER

DENVER PAVILIONS

500 16th St., 303/260-6000, www.denverpavilions.com
HOURS: Mon.-Sat. 10 A.M.-9 P.M., Sun. 11 A.M.-6 P.M.
Map 1

Right in the heart of downtown is an open-air mall with all of the usual stores and restaurants, including a Virgin Megastore, Banana Republic, The Gap, Barnes & Noble, Hard Rock Café, and Corner Bakery Café. On the third level is a United Artists movie theater and a Lucky Strike Lanes, as well as Jazz at Jack's. The mall opened in 1998 and gave the 16th Street pedestrian strip a much-needed boost, as old department stores had long since vacated, often leaving empty storefronts. The Pavilions hosts weekly farmers markets, live music, and an annual arts festival.

HIGHLANDS SQUARE

Bounded by Julian St. to Meade St. along 32nd Ave.
Map 5

The heart of the greater Highlands neighborhood is Highlands Square. Just like Larimer Square in LoDo, there is no actual square here, but rather a cluster of businesses for a few blocks. What makes this an appealing place to shop is the range of goods—gifts for expecting parents or their little ones at **Real Baby**, women's apparel at **Dragonfly** with shoes at **Strut** next door, and accessories at **Kismet,** right across the street. Book lovers can unwind at **Westside Books,** and the **Perfect Petal** has flowers and an assortment of gifts perfect for housewarmings. When the shopping is done, grab a bite at **Bang!** or a cup of coffee at **Common Grounds,** or perhaps a cocktail at the **Coral Room.**

LODO

Bounded by Wynkoop St. to the west, 14th Ave. to the south, Lawrence St. to the east, and 20th St. to the north
Map 3

When it comes to shopping in LoDo, Larimer Square is the indisputable center of the universe, with restaurants and shops tightly packed into this historic block. These are mostly locally owned boutiques with distinctly Denver style, such as **Cry Baby Ranch.** Beyond Larimer Square, the shops are more random and include anything from **Patagonia** to the historic **Rockmount Ranch Wear.** Check the calendar to see if any of your favorite authors will be speaking and signing books at the **Tattered Cover Book Store** in this neighborhood, too.

OLD SOUTH PEARL STREET

S. Pearl St. between Buchtel Blvd. and E. Iowa Ave.
`Map 6`

With the light rail train making a stop just a couple of blocks from South Pearl Street, this historic neighborhood has fresh appeal as a place to go for dining and shopping without having to find good parking. The shops here include bookstores, art galleries, gift shops,

and clothing retailers. There are also plenty of good restaurants and coffee shops for making a day of it.

SOBO

Along S. Broadway from Ellsworth to Bayaud Aves.
`Map 2`

Hipster alert! SoBo is short for South Broadway, part of what was once Denver's own Miracle Mile of commerce. While the neighborhood has had some ups and downs in its history, things are on the upswing with a new energy and thriving businesses of all kinds that attract a mostly young and hip crowd. **Fancy Tiger** is both a fabric shop and retail store for local designers—like a slice of Etsy. Somewhere between vintage shops and places like **True Love Shoes** and **Starlet,** you can truly dress yourself like a rock star when shopping SoBo.

Specialty Foods

🄲 SAVORY SPICE

1537 Platte St., 720/283-2232,
www.savoryspiceshop.com
HOURS: Mon.-Fri. 10 A.M.-6 P.M., Sat. 10 A.M.-5 P.M., Sun. 11 A.M.-4 P.M.
`Map 3`

It's a genius idea: packaging spices in an appealing and original way. The spices and blends at Savory Spice are cleverly named after local geographical highlights, such as rivers, canyons, 14,000-foot peaks, and even neighborhoods. Of course, there are also familiar herbs and spices, such as cinnamon, ginger, paprika, and so much more, but within each of these, there are myriad choices: origin, organic or not, whole or ground. It's hard to resist this shop when the spice scents waft out the door for a half a block or so. What has become a successful franchise business in at least seven

different states, all started here in this cute, little shop.

ST. KILLIAN'S CHEESE SHOP

3211 Lowell Blvd., 303/477-0374,
www.stkillianscheeseshop.com
HOURS: Mon. 1-6 P.M., closed Tues., Wed.-Sat. 11 A.M.-7 P.M., Sun. noon-5 P.M.
`Map 5`

The selection at St. Killian's keeps growing, though the shop has remained the same size. Choosing cheese can be as daunting as finding the right wine—it requires a bit of knowledge and expertise. The owners of St. Killian's are happy to let customers sample the cheese, and they explain the flavors and origins of each oh-so-patiently. It's the perfect place to pick up a picnic lunch with salamis and cheese, along with bread from the **Denver Bread Company** down the street (3200 Irving St., 303/455-7194, http://thedenverbreadcompany.com, Sun.–Fri. 10 A.M.–6 P.M., Sat. 9 A.M.–5 P.M.). Pick up a bottle of wine from next door at Mondo Vino (3601 W. 32nd Ave., 303/458-3858, www.mondovino.net, Mon.–Thurs. 10:30 A.M.–10 P.M., Fri.–Sat. 10:30 A.M.–11 P.M., Sun. noon–8 P.M.), and it's a meal.

SUGARLICIOUS

3000 E. 3rd Ave., 303/388-8650, http://sugarliciouscandy.com

HOURS: Mon.-Sat. 10 A.M.-6 P.M., Sun. noon-5 P.M.

Map 6

It's wall-to-wall candy at Sugarlicious. Grab a handful of jelly beans, get a couple of old-fashioned candy bars, or order a gift basket—it can all be done here. The amount of sweets in one place is mind-boggling. Prefer your candy personalized? No problem! Sugarlicious does it on short notice. Only eat Nunu Chocolates from NY? This shop has them. Or just like Sockerbit from Sweden? You won't go hungry here.

Toys

KAZOO & COMPANY

2930 E. 2nd Ave., 303/322-0973, www.kazootoys.com
HOURS: Mon.-Fri. 10 A.M.-8 P.M., Sat. 10 A.M.-5:30 P.M., Sun. noon-5 P.M.

Map 6

Whether it's for an educational item, a soft rattle for baby, puzzles, Legos, books, or any other toy, Kazoo is the perennial favorite. This is a store that remembers that kids continue to learn through playing well past the toddler years. Even when just browsing, let the little ones play here with any number of toys set up just for that purpose. There's even a "Made in the USA" section for shoppers who prefer not to buy toys made in China since the lead-paint scare. For gifts, take advantage of the wonderful complimentary gift wrapping.

WIZARD'S CHEST

230 Fillmore St., 303/321-4304, www.wizardschest.com
HOURS: Mon.-Fri. 10 A.M.-7 P.M., Sat.-Sun. 10 A.M.-5:30 P.M.

Map 6

As much for adults as kids, the Wizard's Chest is a year-round toy store, but it is *the* place to go for Halloween costumes every fall. With its faux castle storefront, the Wizard's Chest practically screams playful to passersby. The name is also a clue to the many magic tricks available here—cards, prankster items, kits, and DVDs. Ask any of the helpful sales staff to point you in the direction of the toy you seek, whether it be stuffed animals or dolls, novelty items, action figures, science experiments, or those wacky costumes.

ANTIQUES ROW

South Broadway has long been a haven for antiques lovers, with shops shoulder to shoulder for several blocks of this busy boulevard. It's a curious mix of antiques as each store has its own specialty from books to dishes to dolls to furniture and everything in between. To get started, either put on some walking shoes and go door to door, or visit www.antique-row.com to find a list of the establishments.

In the midst of all of this is the ARC Thrift Store, one of the city's busiest thrift stores with a lot of turnover in merchandise. The store receives tons of donations at its back door year-round; it's a bargain hunter's dream.

While the whole strip has seemed antiquated for many years, it's about to get a shot in the arm with new development. For decades, as people drove down this section of South Broadway, the first thing they'd see was the Gates Rubber Plant, a large manufacturing site that sat vacant for many years. However, it's on the verge of becoming the city's newest infill project, with plans for residences, movie theaters, restaurants, and shops. With an emphasis on mass transit to the new, mixed-use urban neighborhood, South Broadway's antiques row will be that much more accessible.

Vintage and Used Clothing

BABAREEBA THEN & NOW
3629 W. 32nd Ave., 303/458-5712
HOURS: Sun.-Wed. 11:30 A.M.-5:30 P.M., Thurs.-Sat. 10:30 A.M.-7 P.M.
Map 5

At Highlands Square's only vintage shop, the notion is of "recycled" clothes, not used. True vintage women's clothing is seamlessly blended with newer styles meant to coordinate here, making the 1960s and the 2000s a perfect match. The owner seems to prefer dresses and casual wear to business attire when she is buying (or recycling) clothes to sell in the shop. In addition to apparel, there are shoes, handbags, and all kinds of accessories.

BOSS UNLIMITED
10 S. Broadway, 303/871-0373, www.bossvintage.com
HOURS: Mon.-Sat. 11 A.M.-6 P.M., Sun. noon-5 P.M.
Map 2

One of Denver's oldest vintage apparel stores, Boss Unlimited could dress the entire family with clothes for Mom, Dad, and the kids. Boss is pretty much a traditional vintage store, with racks stuffed with clothes from every decade

and some more costumey than others. There are also shoes, handbags, and the store's own line, Daredevil, with a rockabilly theme on screen-printed T-shirts and jackets. Veterans of South Broadway shops may be confused at first, since Boss took over the space of longtime vintage favorite All American Vogue, which has closed.

BUFFALO EXCHANGE
230 E. 13th Ave., 303/866-0165, www.buffaloexchange.com
HOURS: Mon.-Sat. 11 A.M.-7 P.M., Sun. noon-6 P.M.
Map 4

It seems there is a Buffalo Exchange in every town now, or at least in every town with a college or university in it. This Capitol Hill store is dependable; its skillful buyers, with good to wild taste, regularly buy new used items that make thrift shopping fun. While many of the clothes and shoes here are vintage and evoke a bygone era of fashion, some are recently used items from the mall, available here at a discount. Check the website for locations elsewhere, too.

DEJA BLUE

303 University Blvd., 303/996-5668,
www.goodwilldenver.org/dejablue

HOURS: Mon.-Sat. 10 A.M.-6 P.M., Sun. 11 A.M.-6 P.M.

`Map 6`

In a first for Goodwill Industries of Denver, Deja Blue is a boutique that features only gently used high-end fashions and accessories. Your wallet and your conscience will like shopping here. The store opened in March 2012, and it is not a donation site, but the proceeds from sales here go to Goodwill programs. Deja Blue also features repurposed fixtures and displays.

PERPETUAL CLOTHING

2027 32nd Ave., 303/953-0816,
www.perpetualclothingdenver.com

HOURS: Mon.-Sat. 11 A.M.-7 P.M., Sun. noon-6 P.M.

`Map 5`

Mannequins in the window of Perpetual Clothing are always styled so well that it is hard to believe this is a resale boutique. The owner is very selective about what she will take from sellers, and while this might aggravate someone trying to make a few dollars off of his or her closet clutter, it's good news for shoppers who can dependably find modern looks for good prices.

HOTELS

Whether you're visiting Denver for business or pleasure, you'll find there is an accommodation to meet the needs of every kind of traveler. While downtown is certainly geared towards executives and conventioneers, with hotels like the Hyatt Regency and Marriott City Center, Denver's most luxurious and elegant hotels are sprinkled throughout the city's historic districts. Hotels such as the Brown Palace, the Oxford, and the Teatro are not only wonderful places to stay overnight, but are also home to some of the city's top-notch restaurants and bars.

Hotels like the Monaco and the Magnolia have made wonderful use of historic buildings in downtown, as have bed-and-breakfasts in Capitol Hill and City Park, where spectacularly restored mansions now offer regal and comfortable rooms for romantic getaways or business travel.

Most of Denver's accommodations are within walking distance of many recommended sights, shops, restaurants, bars, nightclubs, and recreational areas. According to the Downtown Denver Partnership, there are 8,400 hotel rooms in downtown, and metro-wide, there are 42,000 hotel rooms.

When Denver International Airport opened on the plains northeast of the city in the 1990s, the nearest hotels were still located near the old Stapleton Airport a few miles east of downtown. Stapleton is now a large infill community and its hotels managed to survive. Currently, both the Stapleton and the Denver

HOTELS

HIGHLIGHTS

The Brown Palace Hotel is one of Denver's premier hotels.

(**Best Overall:** The **Brown Palace Hotel** has it all—history, elegance, restaurants, and a spa (page 191).

(**Best Deal:** The **Comfort Inn** is connected to the Brown Palace Hotel by a skybridge, pro-viding easy access to all that the Brown Palace offers at more affordable prices (page 191).

(**Best Theme Hotel:** Pretend you're Austin Powers or dare to go on the "scary" 13th floor at **The Curtis** theme hotel (page 192).

(**Best Hotel for Business Travelers:** The **Denver Marriott Residence Inn City Center** understands business needs like no other hotel in Denver (page 192).

(**Best Mix of Locals and Travelers:** With residences and hotels rooms in the same build-ing, the **Four Seasons Hotel Denver** lets vis-itors feel like locals and locals live like welcome guests (page 193).

(**Best Luxury Hotel:** The wonderfully ap-pointed **Hotel Teatro** treats everyone like roy-alty—even guests' pets (page 194).

(**Best Bedtime Snack:** The **Magnolia Hotel** stands out with its complimentary bed-time cookies-and-milk buffet (page 194).

(**Best Hipster Hotel:** The **Jet Hotel** is the place to see and be seen in the city (page 197).

(**Most Romantic Hotel:** Plan ahead with a reasonable romantic weekend package at **The Oxford Hotel** (page 197).

(**Most LGBT-Friendly Hotel:** The **Capitol Hill Mansion Bed and Breakfast Inn** is the most romantic and friendly place for gay and lesbian couples to stay (page 198).

International Airport areas provide a selection of brand-new or refurbished hotels nearby, typi-cally offering free shuttle service to the airport.

Even if you're not checking in, many of Denver's hotels are a great destination for an evening out. Stop by the Cruise Room in the Oxford Hotel for a cocktail, go up to the Peaks Lounge in the Hyatt Regency for a breathtak-ing view of the Rockies, or dine at Restaurant Kevin Taylor in the Hotel Teatro before going next door to enjoy a night at the theater.

CHOOSING A HOTEL

Certainly anyone coming to Denver for a convention has the best pick of rooms within walking distance of the Colorado Convention Center, as well as many wonderful restaurants and sights. The selection of hotels downtown goes from standard to luxury in just a few blocks, and any business traveler could take in a show, dine at a four-star restaurant, and do a little shopping without ever driving.

Budget travelers will have the toughest time

PRICE KEY

- $ Under $150
- $$ $150-250
- $$$ Over $250

finding a decent, affordable room that is very close to the action of the city's sports venues, bars, restaurants, and nightclubs. The options include hostels and a couple of hotels that overlook downtown from the eastern edge of the Highlands neighborhood.

Bed-and-breakfasts in the Capitol Hill neighborhood give visitors the best chance to experience life like a local in an area next door to historic homes and a few apartment buildings. Capitol Hill is also close enough to downtown for walking to the sights there.

Heading east from the city's center, there is a strip of hotels along Quebec Street where the old airport, Stapleton, used to be. The airport is gone now and the area is essentially a suburb, so while this is not walking distance from downtown, there are parks and restaurants nearby.

For a more complete listing of hotels in Denver and the nearby foothills, check out www.denver.org/hotels. This is the Visit Denver website (the Convention and Visitors Bureau), where you can search for a hotel by name, location, or type of lodging.

The rates in this chapter are based on double occupancy in the high season (summer).

Downtown   Map 1

BROWN PALACE HOTEL $$$

321 17th St., 303/297-3111, www.brownpalace.com

Since first opening its doors in 1892, the Brown Palace Hotel has been a symbol of lodging elegance and luxury in Denver. The triangular building has a beautiful stained-glass eight-story atrium where visitors can enjoy cocktails or English tea service while listening to the sounds of live piano music. The 230 rooms range from standard to suites and remodeled presidential suites (so named for the many presidents who stayed in them, such as Eisenhower, Roosevelt, and Reagan). The Brown is just a short walk from the State Capitol Building, the Denver Art Museum, and many other sights. Or stay in and enjoy the hotel's spa and salon, award-winning restaurants, and cigar bar.

COMFORT INN $$

401 17th St., 303/296-0400,
www.denvercomfortinn.com

Enjoy some of the amenities of staying at the Brown Palace while lodging at the more affordable Comfort Inn just across the street. The two hotels are connected by a skybridge, which allows easy access to the Brown's restaurants, shops, and spa. Guests at the Comfort Inn can also order room service from the Brown. The 231-room Comfort Inn is just one block from the 16th Street Mall and the shops and restaurants along this promenade, and it's an easy walk from the Colorado Convention Center.

COURTYARD BY MARRIOTT DENVER DOWNTOWN $$

934 16th St., 303/571-1114, www.marriott.com

The Courtyard by Marriott Denver Downtown is right on the 16th Street Mall and just down the street from the Denver Performing Arts Complex. This Marriott hotel has 177 rooms and a nice restaurant, the Rialto Café, which has patio seating on the mall itself. Being near the Colorado Convention Center, the hotel is ready for business travelers, too, with desks and free high-speed Internet access. This is a

HOTELS

pet-free and smoke-free hotel. Parking is tricky at the Courtyard, which offers $20-per-day valet parking. The hotel will also recommend nearby parking lots with various rates.

CROWNE PLAZA DENVER DOWNTOWN HOTEL ❸❸

1450 Glenarm Pl., 303/573-1450 or 877/227-6963, www.hoteldenver.net

A recent, multi-million dollar renovation has made the Crowne Plaza Denver Downtown Hotel more appealing than ever. Given its central location to many of the city's most desirable sights, restaurants, and the convention center, the Crowne Plaza seems to have it all. In addition to the 332 guestrooms and 32 suites, there is a rooftop swimming pool and expanded fitness center.

💢 THE CURTIS ❸❸

1405 Curtis St., 303/571-0300, www.thecurtis.com

Guests need a sense of humor and playfulness

FAB FOR FUN

In 1964, the Beatles were an international sensation, and the band's tour of the United States included a concert date at Red Rocks Amphitheatre. The lads from Liverpool had to sleep somewhere before the big show, and they chose the **Brown Palace Hotel** (321 17th St., 303/297-3111, www.brownpalace.com). Word got out and the hotel was besieged with young female job applicants who suddenly wanted to be hotel maids.

Since John, Paul, George, and Ringo stayed in the suite that is now named after the band, the hotel has been remodeled and the only clue to the room's history is a small plaque.

Nonetheless, true fans could make a nostalgic summer weekend of it by staying in the Beatles Suite at the Brown and driving up to the Red Rocks Amphitheatre (www.redrocksonline.com) to see 1964, the Beatles tribute band.

to truly enjoy the Curtis and its whimsical touches. The hotel is located across the street from the Denver Center for the Performing Arts and one block from the convention center, so it caters to a spectrum of theater types and business travelers, with an emphasis on youthful attitude. The common areas are themed, from Austin Powers to Elvis (whose voices can also be ordered for wake-up calls), but the 326 rooms are simple and contemporary with modern amenities. An entire floor of rooms is dedicated to travelers with pets.

💢 DENVER MARRIOTT RESIDENCE INN CITY CENTER ❸❸

1725 Champa St., 303/296-3444 or 800/331-3131, www.marriott.com

The 14-story Denver Marriott Residence Inn City Center features the 229 studio and one-bedroom guest suites ($169–439) that include full kitchens, with separate living areas in the one-bedroom suites. There is both wired and wireless Internet access throughout the hotel, in rooms as well as in the lobby and business center. After a hectic day of meetings, head up to the eigth floor and enjoy the rooftop hot tub for a relaxing soak amid the city lights.

EMBASSY SUITES DENVER-DOWNTOWN/CONVENTION CENTER ❸❸

1420 Stout St., 303/592-1000, http://embassysuites1.hilton.com

Opened in late 2010, the Embassy Suites Denver-Downtown/Convention Center is taking full advantage of its proximity across the street from the Colorado Convention Center. There are 400 rooms, plus meeting and banquet space. And the best part: daily, complimentary, cooked-to-order breakfast and a nightly Manager's Reception in the atrium. But it's not exclusive to business travelers—this hotel boasts family-friendly amenities that include a children's menu, cribs, and playpens.

FOUR SEASONS HOTEL DENVER $$$

1111 14th St., 303/389-3000,
www.fourseasons.com/denver

Not just a new addition to Denver's hotels, the Four Seasons Hotel Denver is new to the city's skyline, with it's spike atop 45 stories of residences and guestrooms. This unique combination of travelers and locals means that you might be swimming next to a Denverite in the third-story pool, or mixing it up with conventioneers in the hotel's spa. The Edge Restaurant just off the grand lobby feels elegant for dinner and casual for lunch. What you see is what you get here—the photos on the website accurately show the terrific views of downtown and the mountains, as well as the luxurious decor.

GRAND HYATT DENVER $$$

1750 Welton St., 303/295-1234,
www.granddenver.hyatt.com

One of the larger downtown hotels is the Grand Hyatt Denver, with 512 rooms. Like other downtown hotels, the Grand Hyatt is walking distance to the Colorado Convention Center, the 16th Street Mall, and numerous sights, restaurants, and other attractions. The hotel entrance is uniquely found in an alleyway between buildings. The valet parking fee is $28 daily, or there are other parking lots and garages nearby for self-parking. Enjoy a game of tennis on the hotel's mini-resort rooftop or swim in the indoor pool.

THE GREGORY INN $$

2500 Arapahoe St., 303/295-6570,
www.gregoryinn.com

The Gregory Inn is walking distance from Coors Field and many restaurants, bars, and

HOTELS

COURTESY OF THE GREGORY INN

Beyond LoDo, find the homey comfort of The Gregory Inn.

sights in LoDo, though it is located in Curtis Park, a historic neighborhood of beautiful old homes in various states of renovation. There are eight rooms, plus a more private carriage house, in this meticulously reconstructed home, where decks and a lovely veranda provide additional leisure space. In addition to all of the antiques, the rooms here have more modern touches, with jetted whirlpool tubs, cable TV, and wireless Internet access. Walking in this neighborhood is not advisable at night.

HAMPTON/HOMEWOOD SUITES HOTELS IN DOWNTOWN DENVER

550 15th St., 303/623-5900 for Hampton Inn & Suites, 303-534-7800 for Homewood Suites by Hilton, www.denverdowntownconventioncentersuites. hamptoninn.com, www.denverdowntownconventioncenter. homewoodsuites.com

Denver's first "combo hotel" was set to open in April 2013. Inside this single 13-story building there are two distinctive hotels—two lobbies, two front desks, unique decor for each, different kitchens for each, and 302 rooms to choose from in total. The name says it all—it's about proximity for convention-goers here. Amenities will include an indoor pool, a gym, complimentary hi-speed Internet access, and complimentary breakfast.

HOTEL MONACO ❸❸

1717 Champa St., 303/296-1717 or 800/990-1303, www.monaco-denver.com

Freshly renovated in spring 2012, the Hotel Monaco (part of the Kimpton Hotels chain) now has a playful Western design to welcome guests. It's been named to *Travel + Leisure*'s 2012 list of the 500 World's Best Hotels, and *U.S. News*'s 2012 Best Hotels in Denver. In addition to 189 guestrooms, there is a 24-hour fitness room available to guests, an Aveda Spa and Salon, and Panzano, a restaurant featuring Italian fare. The hotel is proudly pet-friendly

(there is a goldfish swimming in its own bowl in each guestroom), though the evening wine hour is best for just pet owners.

☕ HOTEL TEATRO ❸❸❸

1100 14th St., 303/228-1100, www.hotelteatro.com

As Denver's boutique luxury hotel, the Hotel Teatro never disappoints with its excellent service, comfortable rooms (with Frette linens), and award-winning restaurant. The hotel is named for its proximity to the Denver Center for the Performing Arts theater complex across the street, and the lobby is decorated with photographs and costumes of past productions. Amenities at the 110-room Teatro include complimentary transportation in a Cadillac Escalade anywhere in downtown, Godiva chocolates with turndown service, and many perks for pets.

HYATT REGENCY DENVER AT THE COLORADO CONVENTION CENTER ❸❸❸

650 15th St., 303/436-1234, www.denverregency.hyatt.com

Paired with the Colorado Convention Center, the Hyatt Regency was built and opened in 2005 to welcome business travelers to Denver. The 1,110 spacious rooms and suites afford mountain and city views, as does the hotel's Peaks Lounge on the 27th floor. Floor-to-ceiling windows in the hotel's restaurant Altitude, as well as the Strata Bar, offer city views from a lower level. The state-of-the-art hotel features ergonomic chairs at workstations, high-speed wireless Internet access, individual climate control, and the low-tech option of being able to open the windows in guest rooms.

☕ MAGNOLIA HOTEL ❸❸

818 17th St., 303/607-9000, www.magnoliahoteldenver.com

The 13-story Magnolia Hotel is in a luxuriously remodeled 1906 bank building with 246

PET-FRIENDLY HOTELS

A handful of hotels in Denver not only allow pets but cater to four-legged guests as much as their owners.

The **Hotel Teatro** in LoDo allows pets—mostly just dogs, after some bad experiences with parrots—at no extra charge in select rooms. The pooches can be walked by hotel staff or get a personal pet-sitter, and canine spa appointments can also be arranged for anything from massages to manicures. All dogs staying at the Teatro receive a dog bone-shaped tag with the hotel's contact information to put on their collars. In 2012, the Teatro began offering dog wardrobe options for a variety of services.

Cherry Creek's **JW Marriott** does not charge extra for pets either, and the hotel welcomes canines with a treat at check-in and their own blanket and pillow to use during their stay. The concierge is able to tell guests the best dog-walking trails nearby.

The **Hotel Monaco** has a Cocker Spaniel named Tulo (after Colorado Rockies' shortstop Troy Tulowitzki) ready to greet guests in the lobby and provides goldfish on demand for any room. People traveling with their dogs or cats will be provided pet dishes and beds, a pooper scooper with a walking map of the area, and dog-sitting services are available for an additional fee.

In Capitol Hill, the **Holiday Chalet** does charge a $5 per day cleaning fee for all pets, but given that the owners black lab is on the premises it's a very dog-friendly place. Pet-sitting and -walking services are available on request.

HOTELS

guest rooms and suites. With its proximity to the convention center and the city's business district, the Magnolia caters to guests who appreciate high-speed Internet access and a conference room. Harry's Bar and the billiards room offer places to wind down before calling it a night. Don't forget to stop by the Club Room for the complimentary bedtime cookies-and-milk buffet.

MARRIOTT CITY CENTER ❸❸

1701 California St., 303/297-1300, www.marriott.com

With nearly half of their 600-plus rooms designed for business travelers, the Marriott City Center definitely has a niche clientele. It is a three-block walk from the convention center and has over 25,000 square feet of meeting space, along with a full-service business center. The hotel also attracts leisure travelers, and has laundry and babysitting services available for families. The Marriott City Center has a fitness center and pool, but spa services are at other nearby locations.

MELBOURNE HOTEL AND INTERNATIONAL HOSTEL ❸

607 22nd St., 303/292-6386, www.denverhostel.com

With an entrance in the rear of the Los Paisanos bus station, the Melbourne Hotel and International Hostel is clearly for the budget-minded traveler who wants to be walking distance from all that downtown has to offer. Dorm rates start at $16 for members in the five dorm rooms (not including $3 sheet rental) with a total of 22 beds, and go up to $52 for a double, with two beds in one of the 11 private rooms. The rooms are typically clean, and include refrigerators and ceiling fans (no a/c). There is free Wi-Fi available, too.

QUEEN ANNE BED AND BREAKFAST INN ❸❸

2147 Tremont Pl., 303/296-6666, www.queenannebnb.com

Between the skyscrapers of downtown and the historic homes of the Five Points neighborhood is one of the most charming blocks in Denver, home to the Queen Anne Bed and Breakfast Inn. The inn is made up of two separate,

© RON STARR

Soak up the view of the Rocky Mountains while soaking in a tub at The Ritz-Carlton.

late-1800s Victorian houses, connected only by a large backyard and patio area. Typically, bed-and-breakfasts are not the preferred lodging of business travelers, but because the Queen Anne is so close to downtown (as well as many restaurants and sights), it attracts business travelers as well as tourists on a romantic getaway.

THE RITZ-CARLTON $$$

1881 Curtis St., 303/312-3800, www.ritzcarlton.com
With the largest standard guest rooms in downtown, The Ritz-Carlton is a plushy place to stay, either as an extravagant stopover after a week of skiing and snowboarding, or while on a business trip. The hotel's 202 rooms all have marble bathrooms with two sinks and separate, oversized bathtubs for soaking, as well as 37-inch flat-screen TVs. Two years in a row, The Ritz-Carlton Denver received the AAA Five-Diamond Award—making it the first hotel in Denver to get the prestigious designation. Guests dine at the award-winning Elway's, a

popular steakhouse owned by NFL Hall of Fame quarterback, John Elway. The completely renovated, former Embassy Suites building also offers guests access to the adjacent Forza fitness center, co-owned and designed by Denver Nuggets trainer Steve Hess.

SHERATON DENVER DOWNTOWN HOTEL $$

1550 Court Pl., 303/893-3333 or 800/325-3535, www.sheratondenverdowntown.com
After a $70 million renovation, the former Adam's Mark Hotel was transformed into the Sheraton Denver Downtown Hotel. where it anchors the east end of the 16th Street Pedestrian Mall. A portion of the 1,231 rooms and 82 suites are in the I. M. Pei–designed building. Features include an outdoor heated pool, a fitness center, and a selection of sexy and comfortable restaurants on the ground floor with windows to watch the world go by along the mall.

COURTESY OF THE SHERATON DENVER DOWNTOWN HOTEL

HOTELS

The Sheraton Denver Downtown Hotel has an outdoor pool that is open all year.

LoDo and Platte River Valley Map 3

◖ JET HOTEL ❸❸

1612 Wazee St., 303/572-3300, www.thejethotel.com

In 2008, the Jet Hotel (formerly Luna) got a total makeover—from the 18 guest rooms to the lobby/lounge. The Jet Hotel caters to "urban business travelers," which means people who appreciate a nightclub vibe and look. Below the lobby is a VIP bar with bottle service, and in the rear of the hotel is the Asian/Japanese fusion restaurant XO. Thursday through Saturday, the lobby is packed with beautiful people drinking cocktails and enjoying the loud music.

◖ THE OXFORD HOTEL ❸❸❸

1600 17th St., 303/628-5400,
www.theoxfordhotel.com

The renovated historic Oxford Hotel is no longer relying on guests who are interested in Victorian charm alone; it is also meeting the needs of busy executives. In 1891, Union Station was a thriving transportation hub for the Rockies, and all those train travelers needed a classy place to rest. The Oxford was designed by Frank Edbrooke, who also designed the Brown Palace Hotel at the opposite end of 17th Street. The 80 rooms are still appointed with lovely antiques, but also include high-speed Internet access and dual phone lines. Stop in the Cruise Room for a cocktail before walking to other bars and restaurants throughout LoDo.

SPRINGHILL SUITES BY MARRIOTT ❸❸

1190 Auraria Pkwy., 888/236-2427,
www.marriott.com/hotels

Instead of rating a hotel online, visitors to Springhill Suites by Marriott can rest assured that the employees here will be graded on everything they do. Opened in summer 2012, and one of only 10 college student–operated hotels in the country—and the only one in an urban setting—Springhill Suites is on the Metropolitan State University of Denver campus. Approximately 80 percent of the staff is students, as part of the school's hospitality program. There are 150 guestrooms, meeting space, and more.

UNION STATION
1701 Wynkoop St.

Construction was beginning at Denver's historic Union Station to create a boutique hotel within the building. The hotel will be affiliated with the Oxford Hotel, one block away. It is projected that the hotel would open in the spring of 2014.

WESTIN TABOR CENTER $$
1672 Lawrence St., 303/572-9100,
www.starwoodhotels.com

For loyal Westin clients, the Westin Tabor Center will not disappoint, with its signature Heavenly Bed and Heavenly Bath, as well as some rooms with views of the Rocky Mountains. The hotel's location can't be beat; it is right off the 16th Street Mall, around the corner from Lannie's Clocktower Cabaret, and just a couple of blocks from historic Larimer Square, with several restaurants, shops, and nightclubs. A fun feature at this Westin are the *Runner's World* magazine maps that provide three- and five-mile jogging and walking routes from the hotel. With 430 rooms, this is one of Denver's larger hotels.

Capitol Hill and City Park   Map 4

ADAGIO BED AND BREAKFAST $$
1430 Race St., 303/370-6911 or 800/533-4640,
www.adagiobb.com

The Adagio is a bed-and-breakfast with a musical theme; each of the six rooms is named after a different composer, such as the Copland Suite and the Vivaldi Room. This pink-and-white Victorian building is located just off of busy Colfax Avenue, abutted on one side by the Walgreens parking lot and on the other by a private patio and garden. It is walking distance from the Denver Botanic Gardens, the Tattered Cover Book Store, and a few good restaurants.

BURNSLEY HOTEL $$
1000 Grant St., 303/830-1000, www.burnsley.com

A former high-rise apartment building, the Burnsley is now an all-suite hotel with 80 suites bigger than many New York City apartments. In the 1960s, the apartment building was converted into a hotel and jazz club, and though it was sold and fully remodeled since that time (more than once), the music lives on.

Every Friday and Saturday night, there is live entertainment in the lounge, with soulful singing and piano music. Sights such as the Denver Art Museum, Molly Brown House Museum, and State Capitol Building are just steps away from the Burnsley.

◖ CAPITOL HILL MANSION
BED AND BREAKFAST INN $$
1207 Pennsylvania St., 800/839-9329,
www.capitolhillmansion.com

Back in the day, when Molly Brown was in residence just a few blocks away, Capitol Hill was a neighborhood of stately mansions with views of the Rocky Mountains. While it's more crowded with apartments and office buildings now, inns like the Capitol Hill Mansion offer guests an opportunity to experience life in that bygone era, with a few modern touches. Meet your fellow guests over a gourmet breakfast each morning or during a two-hour beverage meet and greet with the innkeeper and others. The eight-room inn makes a point of

the historic Capitol Hill Mansion Bed and Breakfast Inn

HOTELS

found at The Holiday Chalet, but that's not a bad thing. This 1896 restored brownstone with 10 guestrooms has a homey style and feel, with lacey curtains, flowery bedspreads, and antiques throughout. When not busy whipping up a gourmet breakfast and running the chalet, the owner is also a fashion designer whose clothing and jewelry can be found in the She She Boutique. The Holiday Chalet is pet-friendly, and the owner's dog is there to greet guests.

welcoming families and gay and lesbian guests, as well as business travelers.

CASTLE MARNE
BED AND BREAKFAST INN $$

1572 Race St., 303/331-0621, www.castlemarne.com
Located on an unexpectedly peaceful street between the bars and restaurants of Colfax Avenue and 17th Street, Castle Marne Bed and Breakfast Inn offers a unique stay in the middle of the city. The 1889 mansion has nine antique-filled rooms, and original woodwork and artifacts are on display in the parlor and dining room, where tea service is held daily. The presidential suite in the distinctive turret includes a solarium, fireplace, and private balcony.

THE HOLIDAY CHALET $

1820 E. Colfax Ave., 303/437-8245,
www.theholidaychalet.com
The flip side of modern accommodations is

THE PATTERSON INN $$

428 E. 11th Ave., 303/831-4307, www.pattersoninn.com
Historically known as the Croke-Patterson-Campbell Mansion, The Patterson Inn has a reputation as a haunted house. Built in 1891 from sandstone blocks, this castle-like building has been used as offices and apartments over the years, and has now been converted into nine guestrooms that highlight many of the original features, such as the hand-carved oak stairway and stained-glass windows. The rumors of ghosts began in the 1970s and surely will be part of the allure for some guests. The mansion was bought by architects and transformed into the inn in 2012. Breakfast is included in the room rate.

WARWICK HOTEL $$

1776 Grant St., 303/861-2000,
www.warwickdenver.com
While certainly not unique to Denver, the Warwick Hotel's outstanding reputation is upheld here. The 219 large rooms and suites were remodeled in 2000 and include marble bathrooms and European antique furniture, with ample room for sitting on comfortable chairs and couches. Amenities include a fitness room with views of the city, a heated rooftop pool that is open year-round, and dining at the inviting Randolph's restaurant, with outdoor patio seating for warmer days and indoor tables near the hearth in winter.

Rumor has it the Patterson Inn is haunted.

Highlands

Map 5

HAMPTON INN & SUITES $

2728 Zuni St., 303/455-4588, www.hamptoninn.com
There are limited lodging options within the Highlands neighborhood. Located on the eastern edge of Highlands and perched on a hill overlooking downtown, the Hampton Inn & Suites is a relative bargain compared to many of the hotels right in downtown. The 62 hotel rooms and public areas are pretty basic, with both smoking and nonsmoking options. Just off the top of an I-25 exit ramp, the hotel is convenient for road-weary travelers.

LUMBER BARON INN & GARDENS $$

2555 W. 37th Ave., 303/477-8205,
http://web.mac.com/lumberbaron/
The Highlands neighborhood is brimming with exquisite turn-of-the-20th-century homes, but perhaps none is more special than the 8,500-square-foot Lumber Baron Inn. The inn is something of a special events center, hosting weddings and murder mystery dinners in the third-floor ballroom, as well as bed-and-breakfast guests. Each of the five, well-appointed rooms has a whirlpool tub and free Wi-Fi. The inn is walking distance from some good restaurants, and is only a mile from the sights of downtown. A spacious garden with flowering trees and seating areas make it more inviting in the spring and summer.

MARRIOTT RESIDENCE INN $$

2777 Zuni St., 303/458-5318, www.marriott.com
The Marriott Residence Inn is situated on the eastern edge of the Highlands neighborhood, making it walking distance from Invesco Field at Mile High, the Pepsi Center, and all downtown restaurants, shops, and parks. Hemmed

in by a couple of busy streets and a gas station, the hotel's location is a bit odd, but the entire property is fenced in and in a world of its own, with 189 rooms available. Rates are generally $179–209, with a penthouse suite for $299 during the high season (summer).

Cherry Creek   Map 6

INN AT CHERRY CREEK $$
233 Clayton St., 303/377-8577,
www.innatcherrycreek.com

There is reasonably affordable lodging to be found in Cherry Creek North, within easy walking distance of the neighborhood's specialty shops and restaurants. The Inn at Cherry Creek has 35 rooms plus two corporate residences available. The rooms and suites vary in size and amenities, and those with terraces are the most appealing. All rooms include free high-speed Internet access; only some have LCD flat-screen TVs. Limited parking is offered to guests for an additional fee ($10 per night).

JW MARRIOTT $$$
150 Clayton Ln., 303/316-2700,
www.jwmarriottdenver.com

After years as a drop-in destination neighborhood, Cherry Creek has finally made itself into a vacation destination with the addition of the 196-room JW Marriott on the rim of the Cherry Creek North shopping district. This luxury hotel includes suites with surprising views of the Rocky Mountains to the west. Second Home Kitchen + Bar, the hotel's restaurant, has the feel of rustic elegance, with stone walls and polished wood ceilings. Bring the family for pajama brunch on weekends or chill out on the patio with fireplace year-round. The perks extend to canine guests, with special pet-friendly services available.

Luxury awaits at the JW Marriott in Cherry Creek North.

Greater Denver Map 7

HOTELS

DOUBLETREE HOTEL ❸❸

3203 Quebec St., 303/321-3333,
www.denver.doubletree.com

The Doubletree Hotel is halfway between Denver International Airport and downtown, and offers free shuttle service between the airport and hotel (which takes about 25 minutes). There is also complimentary shuttle service to the Shops at Northfield. In addition to the hotel's 560 rooms, there is a business center and a fitness center for all guests. Other amenities include a heated indoor pool and an outdoor whirlpool tub. The Hilton Honors rewards program is applied here.

EMBASSY SUITES ❸❸

7001 Yampa St., 303/574-3000,
http://embassysuites1.hilton.com

The Embassy Suites is one of the closest hotels to Denver International Airport, just six miles away. The hotel has 174 two-room suites spread out on six floors surrounding a six-story atrium. There is free parking for guests and complimentary transportation to the airport. Embassy Suites is a full-service hotel with fitness and business amenities, such as a pool, a fitness center, and meeting rooms.

LOEWS DENVER HOTEL ❸❸❸

4150 E. Mississippi Ave., 303/782-9300 or
800/345-9172, www.loewshotels.com

This beautiful hotel is a bit off the beaten track, just southeast of the Cherry Creek shopping district. Everything about the hotel is Italian, including its restaurant, Tuscany. There are 183 rooms, including 17 suites, many with gorgeous views and all with luxurious sheets, bathrobes, and towels. The hotel makes a point of welcoming guests who aren't paying the bill—children and pets—with special kids' menus and games and toys available,

and a long list of amenities for dogs. (There is a one-time $25 pet fee.)

RED LION HOTEL ❸

4040 Quebec St., 303/321-6666,
www.redlion.rdln.com

When Denver International Airport (DIA) opened up in the 1990s, the hotels across the road from the closed Stapleton Airport remained open. Eventually, new hotels began popping up closer to DIA, but today, Stapleton is an infill community; now the area is booming with malls and housing, and the old hotels are getting much-needed face-lifts. The 298-room Red Lion Hotel is a great example of this—renovations were completed in 2008. Halfway between downtown and the airport, with complimentary shuttle service to DIA, the Red Lion is a good bargain.

THE TIMBERS HOTEL ❸❸

4411 Peoria St., 303/373-1444 or 800/844-9404,
www.thetimbersdenver.com

One of many hotels near Denver International Airport, The Timbers Hotel sets itself apart with an inviting Western ambience, including antique Colorado maps and cowboy decor. Of the 127 rooms, executive and one-bedroom suites include a full kitchen in a separate living area. The hotel offers free transportation to the airport, as well as complimentary transportation within a five-mile radius of the hotel. (Sorry, that doesn't quite reach downtown.) Guests also have access to the 24-hour business center and fitness center.

WESTIN WESTMINSTER ❸❸

10600 Westminster Blvd., Westminster, 303/410-5000,
www.westindenverboulder.com

Between Denver and Boulder are a couple of

HOTELS

COURTESY OF THE WESTIN WESTMINSTER

Get a little closer to the Rocky Mountains at the Westin Westminster.

suburbs, including Westminster, that drivers pass through along Highway 36. The Westin Westminster rises up off the floor of former farmlands as you drive west to Boulder. The hotel has 369 rooms, many with views of the Rocky Mountains to the west. Check the website for many good offers on rooms. It is most convenient to have a car if you choose to stay at this hotel, so you can drive up to the mountains or into downtown Denver.

EXCURSIONS FROM DENVER

There are many worthwhile excursions from Denver that are within a two-hour drive of the city. No matter how far you've come to visit Denver, after a few days of looking at the Rocky Mountains from afar, it's worth traveling just an hour or so to visit the dramatic splendor of Rocky Mountain National Park. Historic towns, religious architecture, mountain peaks, funky college towns, and ski resorts are also a relatively quick drive away—depending on the weather, of course.

The city of Golden is close enough to feel like an outlying suburb of Denver, but it has a character all its own that makes a visit feel like a little vacation.

If you're in the mood for a walk in the mountains followed by a sophisticated dinner afterwards, the college town of Boulder, hugging the foothills of the Rocky Mountains, is for you. In Boulder, you will find numerous hiking and biking trails within the foothills, gourmet restaurants, and an array of shops along the open-air Pearl Street Mall. The University of Colorado campus includes many historic and scientific buildings of interest. The Eldora Mountain Ski Resort is not far from Boulder, and some Boulder hotels offer ski package deals with Eldora.

If Victorian-era buildings and history are your thing—and you don't mind squeezing past dozens of modern mega-casinos to see a bit of quaint, mining-town history—head up to Central City and Blackhawk, where casinos

COURTESY VISIT ESTES PARK

HIGHLIGHTS

The Great Stupa of Dharmakaya is a rare example of Asian architecture in the Rocky Mountains.

COURTESY THE SHAMBHALA MOUNTAIN CENTER

◖ **Best Park to Begin a Hike:** Boulder's **Chautauqua** has a historic theater used for summer music festivals, a restaurant, a playground, and cabins, and is also the starting point for dozens of stellar hikes (page 213).

◖ **Best Get-Smart Hike:** The **National Center for Atmospheric Research** has many scientific displays inside, but also offers the Walter Orr Roberts Weather Trail with signs that tell about local weather (page 213).

◖ **Best Opera Venue:** The **Central City Opera House** is both a historical attraction and an excellent place to see a performance (page 223).

◖ **Most Refreshing Hike:** The **Bluebird Lake Trail** on the south end of Rocky Mountain National Park passes by Ouzel Falls, Ouzel Lake, Calypso Cascades, and Bluebird Lake. Although it can be a difficult hike, it is the perfect respite from a hot summer day in the city (page 226).

◖ **Best Red Rocks:** Whether you choose to see **Garden of the Gods** near Colorado Springs on foot, by car, on horseback, or by mountain bike, you will be awed by the natural beauty (page 231).

◖ **Best Free Drinks:** The **Mineral Springs** in Manitou Springs trickle from decorative spigots and fountains around the historic town. Anyone can bring a cup or bottle and drink as much of the potentially healing waters as desired (page 237).

◖ **Best Cross-Country Skiing: Devil's Thumb Ranch,** just 15 minutes outside of Winter Park Ski Resort, is a gorgeous and peaceful valley exclusively for cross-country skiing and snowshoeing in winter (page 240).

◖ **Best Alpine Garden:** Billed as the highest botanical garden in the world, the **Betty Ford Alpine Gardens** in Vail are a beautiful example of what grows, blooms, and thrives at a high altitude (page 242).

◖ **Best of the Old West:** Ride a historic trolley car and see historic homes in Fort Collins's celebrated **Old Town** (page 247).

◖ **Most Unique Architecture:** No matter what your religion, **The Great Stupa of Dharmakaya** shrine at the Shambhala Mountain Center is worth the hike (page 251).

now dominate but some vintage charm remains, particularly at the Central City Opera House.

It's been called the crown jewel of Colorado, and Rocky Mountain National Park never fails to impress in any season. Nature really puts on a show in and around this stunning park, where there are easy waterfall or wildflower hikes for beginners, 14,000 peaks for experts to climb, or just scenery to take in driving along Trail Ridge Road. Chances are good that you will

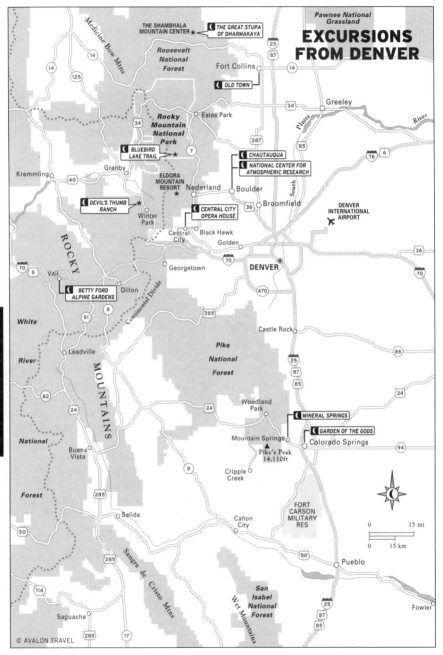

EXCURSIONS
FROM DENVER

spot an elk—even one just wandering through the park's gateway town, Estes Park—and other wildlife throughout the park.

The world-renowned ski slopes of Vail are just under a two-hour drive from Denver. As the small towns along the Vail Valley have grown, so have the year-round activities that now include fly-fishing, golf, zip-lining, and a walk through the world's highest botanic gardens, the Betty Ford Alpine Gardens.

Denver's own Winter Park Ski Resort is great for downhill skiing that isn't too far of a drive from downtown Denver, and there is also a fabulous cross-country and snowshoe resort nearby at Devil's Thumb Ranch.

South of Denver is the state's second-largest city, Colorado Springs, where you can check out the Colorado Springs Fine Arts Center and Cheyenne Mountain Zoo, and you should not miss the Garden of the Gods. Delightful Manitou Springs is just west of downtown Colorado Springs and, being closer to Pikes Peak, includes the Cog Railway as one route up the famous mountain. Manitou Springs has several intriguing historical sights—from mineral spring fountains to the Miramont Castle Museum.

While each of these destinations could make for a long weekend vacation or more, they are close enough to just sample as part of a visit to Denver.

PLANNING YOUR TIME

How much time you choose to spend at any of these destinations depends on what you want to do—there are historic sites, recreational activities, and many other attractions in each. While these places are all relatively close to Denver, they are in opposite directions along the Front Range, so it's not practical to do more than one in a day.

Whether you choose Winter Park Ski Resort, Eldora Mountain Ski Resort, or drive even farther to Vail, you can still be back in Denver for dinner after a day on the slopes. There are summer activities at each of the resorts and in the surrounding towns, and lodging rates are much lower than in the winter high season.

Golden is the closest destination from downtown, and has easy access to hiking or snowshoe trails depending on the season. The small town has more museums and sights than can be seen all in one day.

At less than 30 miles away, Boulder is close enough to zip up to for a quick meal, but has enough to offer to make a day of it. Central City and Blackhawk are of more interest in the summer during opera season—especially true if you are not going there to gamble. They are only a 30-minute drive from downtown. You can drive through these old mining towns en route to Rocky Mountain National Park, and come back through Boulder.

It's not possible to see all of the sights in both Colorado Springs and Manitou Springs in one day, so it's best to just pick one or two things to do in the area, or plan a whole weekend to see and do more. Though there is bus service from Denver, it's ideal if you have your own car to visit these towns, which are about a one-hour drive from downtown.

Make an excursion within an excursion by going to the Great Stupa of Dharmakaya at the Shambhala Mountain Center northwest of Fort Collins. It is a place for quiet contemplation, though it is like a small village. Fort Collins itself is a quiet college town with a charming downtown that invites visitors to have a relaxing lunch and a stroll among the shops in the historic buildings.

When venturing out during winter months, get the latest road conditions from the Colorado Department of Transportation at www.cotrip.org or by dialing 511. At the same time that it's dry and sunny in Denver, there can be near-blizzard conditions and closed mountain passes. Remember, if you are going to pursue any recreational activities solo, be sure to always tell someone else where you are headed and when you plan to return.

Golden

With the western suburbs sprawling out, the town of Golden feels like a corner of Denver and not a separate destination at only a 15-minute drive from downtown. However, this historic town was briefly the first capital of the Colorado Territory from 1862 to 1867, when it was called Golden City (now it's the City of Golden). Home to the Colorado School of Mines, Golden has museums, restaurants, creekside paths, and close access to the foothills. A day in Golden can feel like a little vacation from Colorado's capital.

SIGHTS
Astor House Museum
The Astor House Museum (822 12th St., 303/278-3557, www.goldenhistory.org, Tues.–Sat. 10 A.M.–4:30 P.M., Sun. noon–4:30 P.M.

summer hours, check back for Nov. 1–April 30 Tues.–Sat. 11 A.M.–4:30 P.M., Sun. noon–4:30 P.M., $3 age 6 and over) was a rooming and boarding house from the time it was built in 1867 until 1971. Today, visitors can walk through the furnished rooms, take in the view, and imagine a time when it was a luxury to take a hot bath in a tub for a mere $0.25.

Bradford Washburn American Mountaineering Museum
The country's only museum devoted to the culture, technology, and history of mountaineering is right in downtown Golden at the Bradford Washburn American Mountaineering Museum (710 10th St., 303/996-2755, www.mountaineeringmuseum.org, Mon., Wed.–Thurs. 9 A.M.–6 P.M., Tues. 9 A.M.–7 P.M., Fri.

© BOB PEARCE, COURTESY CITY OF GOLDEN

A giant welcome sign greets visitors to Golden, just west of Denver.

9 A.M.–4 P.M., Sat. noon–5 P.M., $5 adult, $1 child under 12). Inside, visitors will see a rare scale model of Mount Everest, experience interactive exhibits on Colorado's highest mountains and what it's like to sleep on a mountain face, and learn more about many famous mountain climbers.

Clear Creek History Park

Not all museums are indoors, and the Clear Creek History Park (11th and Arapahoe Sts., www.goldenhistory.org, buildings open Tues.–Sat. 10 A.M.–5 P.M., Sun. noon–4 P.M., park is always open) can be seen year-round, just one block off the main street in downtown. The park is made up of a reconstructed ranch that was moved here in the 1990s. It includes a schoolhouse, cabins, a blacksmith shop, and more.

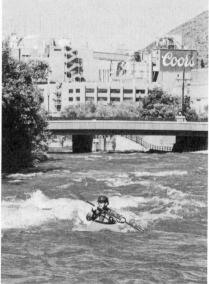

A kayaker paddles in Clear Creek near the MillerCoors Brewery.

© STAN OBERT, COURTESY OF VISIT DENVER

Colorado School of Mines

The Colorado School of Mines campus (1500 Illinois St., 303/273-3000, www.mines.edu) is relatively small, but just the right size for Golden. The campus has some attractive historic buildings, such as the Guggenheim Building that was home to the school's first Geology Museum. Today, the **Geology Museum** (1310 Maple St., 303/273-3815, www.mines.edu/geology_museum, Mon.–Sat. 9 A.M.–4 P.M., Sun. noon–4 P.M.) is two levels filled with rocks, fossils, and gemstones from all over the world—and beyond, since it has a moon rock and meteorites on display. Learn more about the mining history that helped to found this town.

Foothills Art Center

On the perimeter of the School of Mines campus are two historic buildings—a former church and a former home—that house the Foothills Art Center (809 15th St., 303/279-3922, www.foothillsartcenter.org, Mon.–Sat. 10 A.M.–5 P.M., Sun. 1–5 P.M., $5 adult, $3 senior, additional costs for special exhibits), which draws surprisingly big names to this small town. In the spring of 2012, the center hosted an exhibit of work by glass artist Dale Chihuly, and it has watercolor shows and sculpture exhibits annually.

Golden Brewery Tour

Founded in 1873, the Coors Brewing Company (13th and Ford Sts., 303/277-2337, www.millercoors.com/golden-brewery-tour.aspx, Thurs.–Mon. 10 A.M.–4 P.M., Sun. noon–4 P.M.)—now MillerCoors—has been making beer and showing off how it's done right here in Golden. The tour ends with sampling some of the beers, so a valid ID is required. Be sure to call ahead for current hours and holiday closures.

Golden History Center

For a small town, Golden has a lot of varied history, and one can learn about it all at the Golden History Center (923 10th St., 303/278-3557, www.goldenhistory.org, Tues.–Sat. 10 A.M.–5 P.M., Sun. noon–4 P.M., $3 age 6 and over). Learn about dinosaurs, mining, pioneers, and beer.

Lookout Mountain Nature Center & Preserve

Not exactly in Golden, but worth the drive (or bicycle ride, for the extremely fit) is the Lookout Mountain Nature Center & Preserve (910 Colorow Rd., 720/497-7600, www.jeffco.us, Tues.–Sun. 10 A.M.–4 P.M., in summer Tues.–Fri. 10 A.M.–4 P.M., Sat.–Sun. 9 A.M.–5 P.M.), with grand views of the Queen City of the Plains far below. The land was once owned by the prominent Boettcher family of Denver, and its summer home remains on the property near the nature center and along one of the hiking trails here.

Rocky Mountain Quilt Museum

Quilts truly are works of art, and the Rocky Mountain Quilt Museum (1213 Washington Ave., 303/277-0377, https://rmqm.org, Mon.–Sat. 10 A.M.–4 P.M., call ahead for Sunday hours, $6 adult, $5 senior, $4 student, free for child under 5) hosts marvelous exhibits showing off quilters' skills. The museum looks like a storefront, and does have a cute gift shop right inside the front door, so people often walk right by when they are looking for it.

RESTAURANTS

Certainly you can make a day of it in Golden and dine out for every meal at a different local place. Playing off the town's history is the **Old Capitol Grill** (1122 Washington Ave., 303/279-6390, www.oldcapitolgrill.com, Sun.–Thurs. 11 A.M.–8:30 P.M., Fri.–Sat. 11 A.M.–9:30 P.M., $13–25) located in the old capitol building,

where the first legislature sessions were held. Come in for sandwiches at lunchtime or steak for dinner. To learn about a completely different history from another part of the world, walk over to the **Sherpa House Restaurant & Cultural Center** (1518 Washington Ave., 303/278-7939, www.ussherpahouse. com, Mon.–Sat. 11 A.M.–2:30 P.M., daily 5–10 P.M., $9–13). Here you can taste authentic Himalayan cuisine while learning about Sherpa culture, Tibet, and Nepal. The **Table Mountain Inn Grill & Cantina** (1310 Washington Ave., 303/277-9898, www.tablemountaininn.com, Mon.–Fri. 6:30 A.M.–3 P.M. and 4:30–10 P.M., Sat.–Sun. 7:30 A.M.–2 P.M. and 4:30–10 P.M., $12–23) has Southwestern cuisine inspired by its Santa Fe–like architecture and decor. If the weather is cooperating, go for a patio creekside table at the **Bridgewater Grill** (800 11th St., 303/279-2010, www.bridgewatergrill.com, Mon.–Thurs. 6:30 A.M.–9 P.M., Fri. 6:30 A.M.–10 P.M., Sat. 7 A.M.–10 P.M., Sun. 7 A.M.–9 P.M., $9–28), where they have breakfast, lunch, and dinner. For dessert (or anytime), the Golden Sweets shop (1299 Washington Ave., www.golden-sweets.com, 303/271-1191, Sun.–Thurs. 11 A.M.–7 P.M., Fri.–Sat. 11 A.M.–9 P.M.) has ice cream, taffy, chocolates, and this key lime bar on a stick that is divine.

RECREATION

Golden feels like Denver's backyard, and for residents here, it is! Hiking trails are very close to downtown Golden.

Some popular trails for hikers are the **Matthews/Winters Park** trails (1103 County Hwy. 93, 303/271-5925, http://jeffco.us/openspace). A basic understanding of geologic formations is helpful as you go to explore this foothills area, where the plains meet the hogbacks before the mountains rise up. For a hike with views of Red Rocks Park and the city, take about a 10-minute drive from downtown on I-70 West and get off at exit 259. From the parking lot, begin the 6.5-mile loop up to the top of the hogback for the best views. The hike is moderately difficult and the trail is used by mountain bikers, as well. Bring a hat, since this trail does not provide much shade.

Rawhide Loop at **White Ranch Open Space Park** (25303 Belcher Hill Rd., 303/271-5925, http://jeffco.us/openspace) is just outside the town of Golden and has several trails to choose from. The Rawhide Trail is a 4.8-mile loop that goes through forest and grassy plains. The trail is shared with mountain bikers and possibly some wildlife, including deer, mountain lions, and bears.

For winter fun in the foothills, try snowshoeing or cross-country skiing at **Golden Gate Canyon State Park** (92 Crawford Gulch Rd., 303/582-3707, http://parks.state.co.us/parks). This park is accessible via County Highway 93. All trails in Golden Gate Canyon State Park can be used for snowshoeing and cross-country skiing, and on the website is a list of the best trails and where conditions tend to be consistently good, with less wind or melt-off. The site also provides helpful detailed directions to each trailhead.

Right in town is some fun for kayakers at the Clear Creek Whitewater Park (1201 10th St., 303/384-8133, www.cityofgolden.net). Built in 1998, the Clear Creek Whitewater Park in downtown Golden is designed for canoeing and kayaking. The park includes a stretch of flat water, giant boulders to steer around, drop offs, and fast-moving eddies. There are roughly seven city blocks of whitewater fun. The park is used for many championship events during the year, and can also be rented for private functions.

For those who just want to cool off, head over to **Splash Aquatics Park** (3151 Illinois St., 303/277-8700, www.splashingolden.com, daily 10 A.M.–6:30 P.M. in summer, $3–8.50 day-use fee). The littlest children will enjoy the spray fountain, beach sand area, and smaller,

slippery slides. Older kids and their grown-ups are sure to have a blast on the two huge, curly slides and getting splashed by the very giant bucket of water. Splash is about a 10-minute drive from downtown. Go early on the hottest days, as this place gets jammed.

SHOPS

Every one of the sights listed for Golden has a unique gift shop for finding that special item from Colorado. Along Washington Avenue, there are a variety of local stores in which to browse. If you're planning a hike, go to **Vital Outdoors** (1224 Washington Ave., 303/215-1644, www.vitaloutdoors.com, Mon.–Sat. 10 A.M.–8 P.M., Sun. 10 A.M.–5 P.M.) to get gear for the whole family. The store's helpful staff might also have some insider tips on hikes. If you're looking for a bargain, go over to the **Sports Mine** (801B 14th St., 303/216-1040, www.thesportsmine.com, Mon.–Sat. 10 A.M.–5 P.M., Sun. noon–5 P.M.) where they have consignment sports gear at a discount. If you are inspired by what you see at the Rocky Mountain Quilt Museum, shop for supplies at the **Golden Quilt Company** (1108 Washington Ave., 303/277-0717, www.goldenquiltcompany.com, Mon.–Sat. 10 A.M.–5:30 P.M., Sun. noon–4 P.M.).

HOTELS

Being so close to Denver, it is completely practical to spend a day in Golden and rest your head back in the Mile-High City. However, Golden does have some lovely hotels for those making a weekend of it here.

The **Table Mountain Inn** (1310 Washington Ave., 303/277-9898, www.tablemountaininn.com, $169–249) is one of the most distinctive buildings in downtown with its Southwestern architecture. Many of the rooms have beautiful views of the mesas and foothills from the balconies.

The **Golden Hotel** (800 11th St.,

303/279-0100, www.thegoldenhotel.com, $129–299) is right on both Clear Creek and Washington Avenues, making it possible to walk to nearly every sight and shop mentioned.

PRACTICALITIES
Tourism Office

Stop by or call the **Golden Visitors Center** (1010 Washington Ave., 303/279-3113, www.goldenvisitorsbureau.com, Mon.–Fri. 8:30 A.M.–5 P.M., Sat. 10 A.M.–4 P.M., closed Sun.) to learn more about the activities, art,

history, and other interesting things to see and do in this charming town.

Getting There

From downtown, you can either take 6th Avenue, which turns into a highway as you drive west, and turn off at 19th Street to get to downtown Golden, or take I-70 West to the exit for Highway 58, and then take the Washington Avenue exit. It's even close enough to ride your bike! The Golden Visitors Center has detailed directions for the bike route.

Boulder

Sitting at the base of the purple Rocky Mountains with the dramatic flatirons jutting above, the city of Boulder is breathtakingly scenic and invites the most committed couch potato to get outside and be active. While the city's 30,000 acres of open space and hundreds of miles of trails for hiking, biking, and jogging are a big attraction, there is plenty to see, do, and eat in this busy college town. Though Boulder's reputation as a home to eco-minded, rock-climbing vegetarians is not totally inaccurate, there is much more going on here, with impressive regional-fare restaurants, a hip art scene, and nationally significant scientific research organizations.

SIGHTS
Boulder Dushanbe Teahouse

Thanks to a sister-city partnership, Boulder has the unique Dushanbe Teahouse (1770 13th St., 303/442-4993, www.boulderteahouse.com, daily 8 A.M.–9 P.M.), just a couple of blocks from the Pearl Street Mall. It took three years for artisans in Tajikistan (formerly Persia) to create the hand-carved and hand-painted ceiling, columns, and ceramic tiles of the building before it was sent to the United States in the 1990s. The rose garden out front and the

creekside location compliment the delicate architecture inside. It's worth stopping by just to gawk, but the teahouse is also a full-service restaurant and offers an extensive tea menu.

Boulder Museum of Contemporary Art

A couple of blocks from the Pearl Street Mall, the Boulder Museum of Contemporary Art (1750 13th St., 303/443-2122, www.bmoca. org, Tues.–Fri. 11 A.M.–5 P.M., Sat.–Sun. 11 A.M.–4 P.M., $5 adult, $4 senior and student, free for child under 12) is in a great location next to the Dushanbe Teahouse and Boulder Creek. The museum includes three galleries and a small black-box theater where regional, national, and international contemporary visual and performing arts are showcased year-round. This is also a popular venue for special events, so be sure to check the schedule before stopping by, or make it a point to be here during the **Boulder County Farmers' Market** Saturday mornings or Wednesday evenings in the summer (www.boulderfarmers.org).

Celestial Seasonings

It's hard to remember a time when herbal tea was a cutting-edge health food concept, but back in the 1960s, a group of tea radicals began picking fresh herbs in the nearby Rocky Mountains and bagging them dried for sale in health food stores. Now Celestial Seasonings (4600 Sleepytime Dr., 303/530-5300, www. celestialseasonings.com) is a household name and visitors can take free daily tours to watch the millions of tea bags roll off the assembly line. Tours are on the hour Monday–Saturday, 10 A.M.–4 P.M., and Sunday, 11 A.M.–3 P.M. There is also a gift shop and café at the company's campus in the suburb of Gunbarrel, northeast of Boulder.

C Chautauqua

It's not just that Chautauqua (Colorado Chautauqua Association, 900 Baseline Rd., 303/442-3282, www.chautauqua.com) is a beautiful gateway to the broad meadow of Bluebell Shelter and other well-worn hiking trails that can lead up to the flatirons; with its historic auditorium, cabins, and dining hall, it's also a relaxed setting for wonderful events like the Silent Film Festival and the Colorado Music Festival each summer. In addition to the natural attributes, the park includes a large playground and grassy area perfect for playing Frisbee, enjoying a picnic, or sunbathing. Located on 26 acres leased from the city, Chautauqua was part of the nationwide Chautauqua Movement, an effort to provide cultural and educational programs in the summer.

The Dairy Center for the Arts

It took decades to secure funding to turn the old Watts-Hardy Dairy into a cultural facility, but once the transformation was complete in 1992, it became an instant success. The Dairy Center for the Arts (2590 Walnut St., 303/440-7826, www.thedairy.org, gallery hours Mon.–Tues. 9 A.M.–5 P.M., Wed.–Fri. 9 A.M.–8:30 P.M., Sat.–Sun. 1–8:30 P.M., also open during live performances and film screenings; box office hours Mon.–Fri. 1–5 P.M. and one hour prior to shows) is home to three art galleries, two theaters, a performance space, and classrooms for ballet. The place is humming with creative energy, as all art forms are practiced or displayed here throughout the year. Many of the events at The Dairy are free.

Leanin' Tree Museum and Sculpture Garden of Western Art

What started as a small greeting-card business featuring Western scenes on holiday cards evolved into such a successful empire that the founder amassed a large art collection from his favorite Western artists. The Leanin' Tree Museum and Sculpture Garden of Western Art (6055 Longbow Dr., 303/530-1442, www.leanintreemuseum.com, Mon.–Fri. 8 A.M.–5 P.M., Sat.–Sun. 10 A.M.–5 P.M., free) is founder Edward P. Trumble's private collection of bronze sculptures and paintings of cowboys and Western landscapes.

C National Center for Atmospheric Research

If you drive into Boulder from the east, the mountains grab your attention as you head west. But then you begin to wonder about the distinctive building just below those magnificent rocks. It's the National Center for Atmospheric Research (1850 Table Mesa Dr., 303/497-1000, www.ncar.ucar.edu, Mon.–Fri. 8 A.M.–5 P.M., Sat.–Sun. and holidays 9 A.M.–4 P.M.), a federal research center that studies all aspects of weather. There is a lot of important and fascinating work going on here daily, but the building and its surroundings have a reputation and history all their own. The center was designed by renowned architect I. M. Pei, whose 1960s' design was influenced by Native American cliff dwellings in southern Colorado and the dramatic rocks above the site. The building was immortalized in Woody Allen's film *Sleeper.* Free guided tours

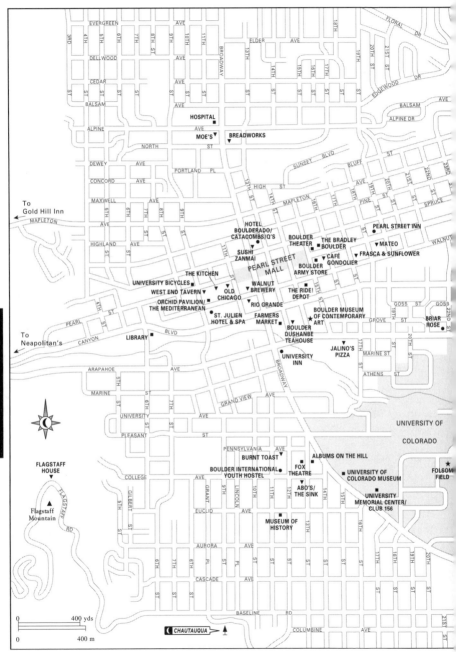

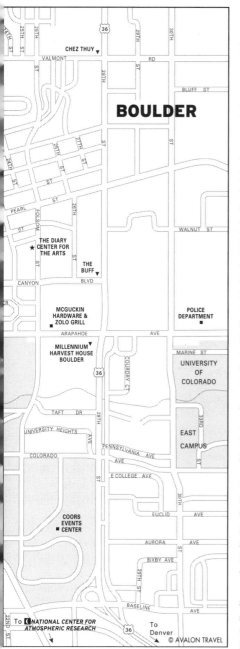

are offered daily at noon, and there's a gift shop and art gallery inside the building. Outside, you can walk the **Walter Orr Roberts Weather Trail** to learn about local weather and take in the view of the city below. Organized group tours require reservations, but audio tours and self-guided tours are available anytime the center is open.

Pearl Street Mall

The Pearl Street Mall (Downtown Boulder Inc., 303/449-3774, www.boulderdowntown.org) started as a 1970s' antidote to the indoor mall and has become more than a shopping destination since. It extends along Pearl Street between 10th and 15th Streets, but with shops and restaurants trickling off for several blocks in either direction—it now feels like the "Pearl Street Mall Area." In the summer, entertainers hang out on each block—often in front of the courthouse—performing magic tricks, fire-eating, singing songs, making balloon animals, and doing other weird, unexpected things to the delight of throngs of people. In addition to shops like **Boulder Bookstore** (Mon.–Sat. 10 A.M.–10 P.M., Sun. 10 A.M.–8 P.M.) and **Peppercorn** (Mon.–Thurs. 10 A.M.–6 P.M., Fri. 10 A.M.–7 P.M., Sat. 10 A.M.–6 P.M., Sun. 11 A.M.–5 P.M.), there are also carts set up selling hats, sunglasses, and such.

University of Colorado

Sure, most people on the University of Colorado campus (CU, 914 Broadway, Boulder, 303/492-1411, www.colorado.edu) are either students or their visiting parents or professors. But this is a place open to the public, and it's worth a stop for anyone.

The university was founded in 1876, the same year that Colorado became a state, and there were a mere 44 students. Now the school is like a small town, with over 30,000 students arriving each fall. While

2008 © UNIVERSITY CORPORATION FOR ATMOSPHERIC RESEARCH

The National Center for Atmospheric Research is housed in a famous I.M. Pei-designed building.

the misbehaviors of partying students and a few sports team members have made headlines, it is actually a very well-regarded school academically, with four Nobel laureates on staff and seven MacArthur fellows. Prestigious annual events such as the **Colorado Shakespeare Festival** (www.coloradoshakes.org) and the **Conference on World Affairs** are held on the campus.

To learn more about the history of the campus, start with the **Heritage Center** (1600 Pleasant St., Old Main 3rd Fl., 303/492-6329, www.cuheritage.org, Mon.–Fri. 10 A.M.–4 P.M.), where you can get an overview of the school's early history, learn about "CU in Space," read the roster of distinguished alumni (most of whom have buildings named after them on the campus), and see the trophies in the CU Athletics Gallery. There is also the **University of Colorado Museum of Natural History** (303/492-6892, http://cumuseum.

colorado.edu), which is very child-friendly, with permanent dinosaur collections and changing exhibits that feature everything from meteorites to Inuit culture.

The University Memorial Center is the hub of the campus with the **Alferd Packer Grill** and other restaurants, a bowling alley, and a bookstore. The halls of the center have become like a small fair or mall, with tables often set up where you can buy sweaters, T-shirts, or phone cards.

Fiske Planetarium (303/492-5002, http://fiske.colorado.edu, Mon.–Fri. 9 A.M.–4 P.M., admission varies per event) has star and laser shows with different themes, such as Perseus and Andromeda or Pink Floyd. You can't miss the white dome of the **Sommers Bausch Observatory** (303/492-6732, http://lyra.colorado.edu/sbo); it's open to the public with free stargazing through the telescopes on Friday night and during other special events.

RESTAURANTS

Boulder has become a foodie town, with menus at various restaurants that feature the bounty of local produce and meats from nearby farms and ranches. My lunch favorite (though it's also open for dinner) is **The Kitchen** (1039 Pearl St., 303/544-5973, www.thekitchencafe.com, Mon.–Fri. 11 A.M.–3 P.M. for lunch, 3–5:30 P.M. for community hour; Sun.–Mon. 5:30–9 P.M. and Tues.–Sat. 5:30–10 P.M.for dinner, $12–30). The Kitchen made a name for itself by being "green" in a variety of ways—using wind power, recycling grease—and because of its delicious food. Check out the giant blackboard to see the list of local purveyors who grow the food you eat. The menu changes daily.

It's a special night out to dine at **Frasca** (1738 Pearl St., 303/442-6966, www.frascafoodandwine.com, Mon.–Sat. 5:30 P.M.–close, $28–36), where the menu is based on the cuisine of the Fruili region of Italy. Frasca also emphasizes using local sources for its Italian dishes. Reservations are recommended.

Black Cat Bistro (1964 Pearl St., 303/440-5500, www.blackcatboulder.com, Mon.–Sat. 5:30 P.M.–close, $16–24) doesn't have quite the same buzz as The Kitchen or Frasca, but it's popular with locals who appreciate the simple, organic fare made into unexpected dishes like "Juxtaposition of Duck" with lavender honey or "Blue Crab, Hot and Cold." Black Cat offers a few tasting menus (including vegetarian or vegan) also paired with wines.

The ultimate in fine dining has long been the **Flagstaff House** (1138 Flagstaff Dr., 303/442-4640, www.flagstaffhouse.com, Mon.–Fri. and Sun. 6–10 P.M., Sat. 5–10 P.M., $32–76). Everything will make you swoon—the view, the food, the wine. This family-owned gem is one of the country's premier dining experiences, and well worth the drive up the twisting mountain road.

On the other end of the spectrum is the casual **Mountain Sun Pub & Brewery** (1535 Pearl St., 303/546-0886, www.mountainsunpub.com, Mon.–Sat. 11:30 A.M.–1 A.M., Sun. noon–1 A.M., $5–7), just off the Pearl Street Mall to the east. Mountain Sun has a groovy kind of reggae vibe with tasty burgers and lots of vegetarian options. Stacks of games for kids and adults make this a family-friendly place.

One of the best burger restaurants in Colorado has a place in Boulder; it's **Larkburger** (2525 Arapahoe St., 303/444-1487, www.larkburger.com), with yummy burgers and to-die-for truffle parmesan fries. And right next door is another favorite, **Cuba Cuba Sandwicheria** (2525 Arapahoe St., 303/442-1143, www.cubacubasandwicheria.com), with a lunch version of what's on the menu at their original restaurant in Denver, Cuba Cuba Café & Bar.

The **Dushanbe Teahouse** (1770 13th St., 303/442-4993, www.boulderteahouse.com, daily 8 A.M.–9 P.M., $12–18) is worth seeing in itself, but is also a great place for a meal. The breakfast, lunch, and dinner menus are all fairly simple, but with a strange mix of cultures—Tajikistan (the birthplace of the teahouse) *plov* (a traditional beef rice dish), Indian tikka masala, and pizza are all offered.

NIGHTLIFE

In a college town with a reputation for wild parties, there is no shortage of places to go for a drink after dark. The two main parts of town for nightlife are The Pearl Street Mall and The Hill. **The West End Tavern** (926 Pearl St., 303/444-3535, www.thewestendtavern.com, daily 11:30 A.M.–10 P.M.) has a very appealing rooftop deck with a view of the mountains and is perfect for happy hour and watching the sunset. There is live music on Tuesday nights.

The Walnut Brewery (1123 Walnut St., 303/447-1345, www.rockbottomrestaurantsinc.com, daily 11 A.M.–midnight) can be a bit loud, especially during happy hour or on weekends, but that's part of the boisterous fun at this bar. The beers have names that reference local places, like Indian Peaks Pale Ale and Devil's Thumb Stout.

At the **Hotel Boulderado,** the **Corner Bar** (2115 13th St., 303/442-4880, www.qsboulder.com, Mon.–Fri. 11:30 A.M.–11:30 P.M., Sat.–Sun. 11 A.M.–11:30 P.M.) is a nice place to sit inside or out on the patio for a little people-watching while enjoying a cocktail.

The **Absinthe House** (1109 Walnut St., 303/443-8600, www.boulderabsinthehouse.com) claims to have the "largest selection of genuine absinthe of any bar in North America." Another feature is a rooftop bar with a view of the flatirons.

In the summer, check the schedule at **Chautauqua** (900 Baseline Rd., 303/440-3776, www.chautauqua.com) for concerts and silent movies held in the historic building. The **Boulder Outdoor Cinema** (1750 13th St., 855/262-9324, www.boulderoutdoorcinema.com, check website for summer calendar, showtimes 7:30 P.M.) also has evening fun down by the creek and behind the **Boulder Museum of Contemporary Art.**

FESTIVALS AND EVENTS

Even non-runners have heard of the Bolder Boulder (www.bolderboulder.com), an annual 10K that takes over the town on Memorial Day and has become one of the largest road races in the world. Over the same weekend is a three-day event that seems to grow each year, the **Boulder Creek Festival** (www.bceproductions.com), with multiple stages for live music, activity areas for kids, hundreds of vendors, and, best of all, a huge rubber ducky race in the creek.

RECREATION

What makes Boulder so appealing is easy access to the great outdoors, where you can simply start running, biking, or hiking right out the front door.

Chautauqua (900 Baseline Rd., www.

bouldercolorado.gov) is a great place to start for hikes of varying length and difficulty. Go to the **Ranger Cottage** near the entrance of the park (Mon.–Fri. 9 A.M.–4 P.M., Sat.–Sun. 8 A.M.–6 P.M.) for park maps, brochures, and expert advice from the staff. **Royal Arch,** a natural arch that you reach on an easy and rewarding hike, is less than a mile one-way and offers a great view. This is also a starting point to reach the base of the three flatirons, which can be climbed, too.

For a bit steeper climb, **Gregory Canyon** is pretty and thick with trees before opening up for beautiful views. Go to the www.bouldercolorado.gov website for trail maps, closures, where dogs and bikes are allowed, and other helpful information.

Known for rock climbing and natural springs, **Eldorado Canyon State Park** (303/494-3943, www.parks.state.co.us/parks) is also a lovely place for hikes. It is just about 10 miles south of Boulder, so it's reachable by bike or car. There is a fee of around $3–8 to enter the park on foot or in a car. Trail maps should be available at the entry station.

Mountain biking is allowed in Eldorado Canyon, and there are 43 miles of trails around town, too. Again, the website www.bouldercolorado.gov provides trail maps and tips for riders. The popular **Greenbelt Plateau Trail** offers a chance to see a bit of wildlife, including birds, and probably some equestrians. It's an easy ride on the plains below the foothills and connects to other trails.

Cycling on paved roads and trails is nice along **Boulder Creek,** where the path stretches out east of town to Cherryvale Road from its starting point in the foothills at Fourmile Canyon. The trail is very popular and there are speed-limit signs on this seven-mile path.

There are a few options for cooling off in Boulder on a hot summer day. First, the **Boulder Reservoir** (5100 51st St., 303/441-3468, www.bouldercolorado.gov) east of town is Boulder's version of a beach. It's a shadeless, sandy park along the water, and fun in the summer for sailboating, swimming, fishing, or just floating. Boulder Creek is used for kayaking and tubing, but be aware of the rough conditions before trying either activity. The creek is very choppy in spots with large rocks.

If you just want to hang out with the little ones and enjoy a playground, the best options are **Chautauqua** (900 Baseline Rd.), where there is a playground and large grassy field; **Scott Carpenter Park** (30th and Arapahoe Sts., 303/441-3427, www.bouldercolorado. gov), which has a large outdoor pool, skatepark, and playground; and **Eben G. Fine** (3rd and Arapahoe Sts., www.bouldercolorado.gov), with a playground, picnic spots, and a chance to wade into the creek.

SHOPS

As the Pearl Street Mall has grown and changed over the years, **The Peppercorn** (1235 Pearl St., 303/449-5847, www.peppercorn.com, Mon.– Thurs. 10 A.M.–6 P.M., Fri. 10 A.M.–7 P.M., Sat. 10 A.M.–6 P.M., Sun. 11 A.M.–5 P.M.) has remained and grown considerably itself. Peppercorn calls itself a "home" store, but it's overall a kitchen store with cookbooks, dishes, flatware, and the like. In the front of the store are featured Colorado products and books.

Another longtime staple and anchor on the west end of the mall is **The Boulder Bookstore** (1107 Pearl St., 303/447-2074, www.boulderbookstore.net, Mon.–Sat. 10 A.M.–10 P.M., Sun. 10 A.M.–8 P.M.), with many floors of books (children's, travel, cooking, science fiction, and much more) and magazines, as well as a popular coffee shop.

Off the east end of the mall is the **Boulder Army Store** (1545 Pearl St., 303/442-7616, http://boulderarmystore.com, Mon.– Fri. 9 A.M.–7 P.M., Sat. 9 A.M.–6 P.M., Sun. 10 A.M.–6 P.M.), with a curious mix of seemingly everything, from Swiss Army watches to camping gear and jeans. It's a longtime favorite of every Boulderite I know.

Into the Wind (1408 Pearl St., 303/449-5356, www.intothewind.com, June–Dec. Mon.–Sat. 10 A.M.–9 P.M., Sun. 10 A.M.–6 P.M., Jan.–May daily 10 A.M.–6 P.M.) is a kite store that also has a large selection of toys for all ages. Given the high winds along the Front Range, there is often a chance to go fly a kite in Boulder. Another favorite is **Grandrabbit's Toy Shoppe** (2525 Arapahoe St., 303/443-0780, www. grtoys.com, Mon.–Sat. 9:30 A.M.–7 P.M., Sun. 10 A.M.–5 P.M.), with a big selection of books, games, and dolls.

Women who like Prada, Bottega Veneta, Missoni, and other high-end designers are sure to find something special and sophisticated at **Max** (1177 Walnut St., 303/449-9200, www. maxfashion.com, Mon.–Sat. 10 A.M.–6 P.M., Sun. noon–5 P.M.). For more casual clothes (and prices), **Starr's Clothing & Shoe Company** (1630 Pearl St., 303/442-3056, www.starrsclothingco.com, Mon.–Fri. 10 A.M.–8 P.M., Sat. 10 A.M.–7 P.M., Sun. 11 A.M.–6 P.M.) has a huge selection of Levi's and cute tops, dresses, and skirts.

During growing season (late spring– fall), don't miss the weekly **Boulder County Farmers Market** (1900 13th St., 303/910-2236, www.boulderfarmers.org, Sat. and Wed. mornings), the largest and most popular farmers market in the area.

HOTELS

The Victorian architecture and decor make the **Hotel Boulderado** (2115 13th St., 303/442-4344, www.boulderado.com) timeless and always appealing for a comfortable night's stay. It's one block off the Pearl Street Mall and walking distance to many recommended restaurants and shops. Rates range from $239 for a queen to $399 for the Presidential Suite. **Q's Restaurant** (303/442-4880, www.qsboulder. com, Mon.–Fri. 6:30 A.M.–2 P.M. and 5–10 P.M.,

Sat.–Sun. 7 A.M.–2 P.M. and 5–10 P.M.), on the ground floor of the Boulderado, is a great place for brunch with family or for a business lunch.

One of Boulder's newest hotels is the swanky **St. Julien Hotel and Spa** (900 Walnut St., 720/406-9696, www.stjulien.com), with over 200 rooms and suites. The St. Julien has aspirations to be an "eco-hotel" with zero waste. Rates range from $269–479 in the high season.

The **Boulder Outlook Hotel** (800 28th St., 303/443-3322, www.boulderoutlook.com, $79–179) is the city's first zero-waste hotel. It offers allergy-friendly rooms and has a chlorine-free pool and whirlpool tub. The hotel is close to the university, so it's most expensive during graduation in spring, when the city fills up.

The **Briar Rose Bed and Breakfast Inn** (2151 Arapahoe St., 303/442-3007, www.briar-rosebb.com, $134–219) is a very cute old house with eight rooms available between the main house and carriage house. Tea and organic breakfast are served daily and can be enjoyed outside in the sweet garden. The Briar Rose is close to the campus and Naropa University.

Some of the lodge rooms and cottages at **Chautauqua** (900 Baseline Rd., 303/442-3282, www.chautauqua.com) are available for nightly rental year-round. Cottage rates range from $122–319 per night, lodge rates range from $1,155–1,275 per night for the entire eight-bedroom facility, and from mid-June–mid-August, nightly rentals are available at the Columbine Lodge and offers cheaper rooms for $75–126 as opposed to renting a whole cabin. Keep in mind that there is no air-conditioning in some of the cabins and daily housekeeping is not offered.

PRACTICALITIES
Tourist Office
The Boulder Convention and Visitors Bureau is located at 2440 Pearl Street, but can also be reached at 303/442-2911 or www.bouldercolo-radousa.com.

Media
The city's major daily newspaper is the *Boulder Daily Camera* (www.dailycamera.com). There's also the *Colorado Daily* (www.coloradodaily.com), a free, small, tabloid-style paper found all over town. The town's "alternative" newspaper is the *Boulder Weekly* (www.boulderweekly.com), with long feature stories and weekly events. The glossy *Boulder Magazine* (www.getboulder.com) offers lots of suggestions for fun activities in the area.

Getting There
Boulder is an easy, 30-mile highway drive west from Denver. The most common route is to take Highway 36 from I-25, and a handful of exits will point out how to get to the University of Colorado campus or other locales. Another route is to take I-70 to Highway 6 to Golden, and then head north on Highway 93 to Boulder, where the highway turns into Broadway. While this is a more scenic drive closer to the foothills—there is not much development this close to the old Rocky Flats Nuclear Weapons Facility—the road is not safe during high winds. The RTD (Regional Transportation District) has bus service several times a day from downtown Denver to downtown Boulder (www.rtd-denver.com for schedules and fares).

Getting Around
It's possible to ride the bus into Boulder and enjoy much of what the city has to offer without a car. There is also the Boulder Transit Center (14th and Walnut Sts., 303/229-6000), where many buses originate. Look for the affordable, around-town buses and their silly names like "Leap," "Hop," "Skip," "Dash," and so on. Bike paths along Boulder Creek and designated bike lanes on most city streets make it easy to navigate Boulder on two wheels. Rental bikes are available through B-cycle (http://boulder.bcycle.com).

Eldora Mountain Resort

The closest ski resort to Denver is Eldora Mountain Resort. Only an hour's drive from Denver, Eldora offers more time on the mountain than driving there and back—and there's regular bus service from Boulder directly to the resort. The motto on the resort's website is, "Friends Don't Let Friends Drive I-70," in reference to the highway that leads to most other ski resorts in Colorado. The drive up to the resort takes you through the quirky town of Nederland, which is worth a stop for a meal or a look around. But considering the resort's proximity to Denver and Boulder, you can keep your hotel room or just have dinner back at home later.

SIGHTS
The Carousel of Happiness

It might sound like a place just for kids, but adults might have an appreciation for the work that went into creating The Carousel of Happiness (20 Lakeview Dr., 303/258-3457, www.carouselofhappiness.org, daily 10 A.M.–8 P.M.). The carousel itself (the part that makes it go round and round) is restored from 1910, but the wooden animals for riding are all original works of folk art that took over two decades to carve. The people here are very friendly and love to see the joy children get from riding a merry-go-round.

RESTAURANTS

There is very casual food service at Eldora, with pizza, chili, burgers, and beer and hot chocolate.

If you're driving back to Denver on Highway 72, consider stopping at the **Wondervu Café** (33492 Hwy. 72, 303/642-7197, www.wondervucafe.com, Oct. 1–May 31 Tues.–Thurs. 11 A.M.–9 P.M., Fri.–Sun. 9 A.M.–9 P.M.; June 1–Sept. 30 Tues.–Wed. 11 A.M.–9 P.M.,

Thurs.–Sat. 9 A.M.–10 P.M., Sun. 9 A.M.–9 P.M., closed Mon., $5–15) for chips and salsa and big, sloppy burritos.

In Nederland, the **New Moon Bakery & Café** (1 W. 1st St., 303/258-3569, http://newmoonbakery.com, Mon.–Fri. 6:30 A.M.–5 P.M., Sat.–Sun. 7 A.M.–5 P.M.) is good for breakfast or lunch with freshly made pastries, sandwiches, and hot coffee.

FESTIVALS AND EVENTS

Bredo Morsteol passed away in his native Norway in 1989, and was subsequently brought to the United States to be a subject of cryonics (a scientific method used to freeze people until they can be brought back to life somehow). Eventually, Mr. Morsteol's body ended up in his grandson's Nederland storage shed, where he is still repacked in dry ice regularly. At first, locals were aghast when they learned of the frozen dead guy, but for nearly 10 years, they have been hosting **Frozen Dead Guy Days** (www.frozendeadguydays.org). The event includes a parade with people in mock coffins. It's all in good fun in a macabre sort of way, and you can buy a Frozen Dead Guy T-shirt, hat, or tote bag.

RECREATION

For people who are really into skiing, Eldora is considered a beginners' resort—great news for all the beginners and non-experts out there!

There are 12 lifts in all at Eldora Mountain Resort (2861 Eldora Ski Rd., Ste. 140, 303/440-8700, www.eldora.com, lift tickets $10–72), where the peak elevation is 10,800 feet. There are adult and child lessons offered daily during ski season. Eldora does have some challenging and expert runs, including the Corona Bowl, a double-black-diamond. There are four terrain parks for snowboarders, and

PEAK-TO-PEAK BYWAY

If you just want to enjoy the scenery at your own pace with lots of stops or none at all, hit the Peak-to-Peak Byway between Estes Park and Blackhawk. The 55-mile designated scenic byway lies along the eastern flank of the Continental Divide and includes glimpses of several peaks: Mount Meeker (13,911 feet), Longs Peak (14,256 feet), Ouzel Peak (12,716 feet), and Pawnee Peak (12,943 feet). You get the idea: You're driving from peak to peak, or at least in the peaks' long shadows.

The most popular time of year to do this drive is in the fall, in mid- to late September, when the leaves of the many aspen trees are turning bright gold, orange, and red. It's a picturesque drive or ride on a bike, as the road's wide shoulders have room for both cars and bicycles.

From Denver, take Highway 6 to Highway 119, which merges with Highway 72 (and becomes Highway 72), until it becomes Highway 7 before entering Estes Park. You will drive through Blackhawk, Nederland, and Allenspark before reaching Rocky Mountain National Park. The drive takes at least two hours, but you can always return on a different, more direct route.

ski- and snowboard-equipment rental is available for all ages and abilities.

Just a short walk across the parking lot from the downhill runs is **Eldora's Nordic Center,** which rents cross-country and telemark skis and snowshoes. There are group or private lessons, but the bargains are in the packages that include instruction and rental.

Snowshoers and cross-country skiers with their own gear can use the Jenny Creek Trail for free—it's a U.S. Forest Service access trail that winds around parts of the resort and runs.

SHOPS

Eldora Mountain Sports (2775 Canyon Blvd., 303/440-8700, www.eldora.com) is located down in Boulder; you can purchase lift tickets or season passes and some gear before driving up the mountain.

HOTELS

Check the Eldora website (www.eldora.com) to find lodging options such as a "Boulder Ski Escape" package deal, with hotel and lift tickets included.

Between Boulder and Eldora is a sweet little lodge, **The Alps Boulder Canyon Inn** (38619 Boulder Canyon Dr., 303/444-5445, www.alpsinn.com, $99–274), which hugs the side of the mountain at a bend in the road. There are spa services, private patios, and whirlpool tubs in most rooms.

One of the nearest hotels to the ski resort is the **Sundance Lodge** (23492 Hwy. 119, Nederland, 303/258-3797, www.sundancelodge.com, $89–99). While "lodge" is perhaps a bit too grand a word here, it has clean and cozy rooms.

PRACTICALITIES
Tourism Office

You can check in with the **Boulder Convention and Visitors Bureau** (2440 Pearl St., 303/442-2911, www.bouldercoloradousa.com) for more information about the Eldora Mountain Resort and surrounding area, or contact the **Nederland Chamber of Commerce and Visitor Center** (1st St. and Hwy. 119, 303/258-3936, www.nederlandchamber.org).

Visitor Center

On the drive up to the ski resort, stop in at the **Nederland Visitor Center** (1st St. and Hwy. 119, 303/258-3936, www.nederlandchamber.org, May–Oct. daily 9 A.M.–5 P.M.) to get maps of the area and learn about what this hippie mountain town has become famous for— Bredo Morsteol, a frozen dead guy.

Getting There

From Denver, take I-70 West to Golden, then follow Highway 93 to Highway 72 until it meets with Highway 119; or take I-25 North to Highway 36 through Boulder; then follow signs to the resort. There is regular bus service from Boulder to the resort (303/299-6000, www.rtd-denver.com).

Central City and Blackhawk

If you want to see the well-preserved remains of two precious mining towns that date back to the gold rush days of the 1860s, you should not miss Central City and Blackhawk. During those heady times, this area was dubbed "the richest square mile on Earth," and gorgeous buildings like the Central City Opera House and the Teller House were built. Today, it's a gold rush of a different sort; with dozens of large casinos here, the towns have become a mecca for gamblers. Though the casinos were mostly welcomed by the townspeople to provide much-needed revenue for maintaining the historic structures, these garish additions to the quaint towns can be a bit jarring and depressing. If you have no interest in gambling, then just come for the opera during the summer.

SIGHTS

◖ Central City Opera House

Arguably the main historical attraction between the two gaming towns is the Central City Opera House (124 Eureka St., Central City, 303/292-6500, www.centralcityopera. org). The opera house was built in 1878, as riches were being dug out of the nearby mines daily and people wanted to celebrate their newfound wealth with the most decadent buildings. When the bottom dropped out on the silver boom, the opera house was closed. In 1932, it was refurbished and reopened with a performance of *Camille* starring Lillian Gish. Central City Opera House has been putting on shows ever since, and it is the oldest surviving opera house in Colorado. Three different operas are staged each summer-festival season. There are tours of this National Historic Landmark stone building and the trompe l'oeil murals in the summer. Over 100 opera houses were built in Colorado between 1860 and 1920, and the Central City Opera House is one of only 13 still in use.

Teller House

Next door to the Central City Opera House is the once-spectacular Teller House (120 Eureka St., 303/582-0600, www.ktrg.net). Originally a hotel, the Teller House has sadly lost much of its historical integrity over the years, as it was temporarily turned into a casino. The building hails from 1872, and the famous "face on the barroom floor" was not painted until 1932. The mysterious woman's visage remains and is seen on tours during opera season. There is a restaurant in the building during opera season only.

Gilpin County Historical Society Museum

To learn about the gold and silver rush and the people who prospered or lost it all (or most of their fortunes) in these parts, stop in the Gilpin County Historical Society Museum (228 High St., Central City, 303/582-5283, www.gilpinhistory.org, Memorial Day–Labor Day daily 10 A.M.–4 P.M., or by appt. in off-season). The historical society also provides the Opera House and Teller House tours.

EXCURSIONS FROM DENVER

© MARK KIRYLUK

The Central City Opera House attracts crowds each summer.

Hidee Mine Tours

Once you have learned about the riches pulled from the earth here, take a mine tour to see exactly how it was done. There are a handful to choose from, including those at the Hidee Mine (MM 6.3 Central City Pkwy., 720/548-0343, www.hideegoldmine.com, Thurs.–Sun. in summer, tours between 10 A.M.–4 P.M., $12–18, gold panning is extra), which sits at the heart of the Glory Hole area in the "Richest Square Mile on Earth." This is cash only; no credit cards accepted.

Mountain City Historic Park

In Blackhawk, 12 Victorian and Gothic homes were relocated to make way for the mega-casinos; they now make up the Mountain City Historic Park (Gregory St., Blackhawk, 303/582-5221). The homes were moved here and renovated with the intention of turning them into shops, but for now, the collection of them makes for a free wander through history.

The most architecturally important home is the **Lace House,** so named for its intricate wooden trim.

RECREATION

A good arm-workout is what you get at the slot machines in these limited-stakes gaming towns. Poker, blackjack, and slots are what you'll find, no matter how grand the casino is. There are dozens of casinos to choose from, each with various amenities.

The Gilpin Casino (111 Main St., Blackhawk, 303/582-1133, www.thegilpincasino.com, daily 8 A.M.–2 A.M.) was one of the first casinos to open in 1992, after gambling was legalized. There are 450 slot machines and table games.

Central City's largest casino is the **Reserve Casino & Hotel** (321 Gregory St., Central City, 303/582-0800, www.reservecasinohotel.com, daily 24 hours) with live entertainment, a dance floor, 700 or so slot machines, and a few card tables. There are also 118 hotel rooms and complimentary parking.

RESTAURANTS

During opera season, **Kevin Taylor's Rouge at the Teller House** and **The Face Bar Restaurant** (140 Eureka St., Central City, 303/582-0600, performance days 11:30 A.M.–10 P.M., $26–35) are open for lunch and dinner on opera performance days only. Offering fine and casual dining, it's that rare restaurant in town not affiliated with a casino. Reservations are recommended.

Much more casual is **Dostal Alley Brewpub & Casino** (1 Dostal Alley, Central City, 303/582-1610, Mon.–Thurs. 10 A.M.–2 A.M., Fri.–Sat. 24 hours, $10–20), in a simple historic building where pizzas and fresh root beer are served alongside slot machines. There is free parking available behind the restaurant and casino.

The **Ardore Tuscan Steakhouse** (Reserve Casino, 321 Gregory St., Central City, 303/582-0800, www.reservecasino.com, Fri.–Sun. 4:30–10:30 P.M., $16–24) is an upscale option that is also very popular; reservations are recommended. If you don't have a reservation, you may end up at **Market Street** for pizza, sandwiches, coffee, or other casual fare (daily 8 A.M.–11 P.M.) at the same casino.

Visitors to Blackhawk can try the **White Buffalo Grille** (240 Main St., Blackhawk, 303/582-6375, www.thelodgecasino.com, Sun.–Thurs. 5–9 P.M., Fri.–Sat. 5–10:30 P.M., $19–40); the restaurant is situated inside a bridge with views of the mountains.

SHOPS

There are very few independent shops left in Central City or Blackhawk, as most storefronts sit empty or were swallowed whole by expanding casinos. **Bevie Sue's Emporium** (115 Main St., Central City, 303/582-5524, daily 8:30 A.M.–4:30 P.M.) sells Victorian-era hats and estate jewelry.

HOTELS

With both the casinos and the opera drawing visitors to the towns, the hotels are vying for those tourist dollars, and many offer lodging discounts. A short walk from the action—but a world away—is the **Hooper Homestead** (210 Hooper St., Central City, 303/582-5828, www.hooperhomestead.com, $100–300), a small bed-and-breakfast, which is a step back in time in terms of decor.

In Blackhawk, the **Chase Creek Bed and Breakfast** (250 Chase St., 303/582-3550, www.chasecreekinn.com, $95–195) is a historic home that was relocated from the busy town center to make way for bigger casinos. Somewhat secluded, it's still walking distance to downtown.

PRACTICALITIES
Tourist Office

The **Central City Visitor Center** at 103 Eureka Street is open daily and can be reached from 10 A.M.–6 P.M. and can be reached at 303/582-3345. You can also try www.centralcitycolorado.us, or go to **City Hall** (141 Nevada St., Central City, 303/582-5251, Mon.–Fri. 8 A.M.–5 P.M.). For Blackhawk, go to either www.blackhawkcolorado.com or www.cityofblackhawk.org and find some online casino deals.

Getting There

There has been a lot work and money invested in making the twisting, turning mountain drive to these gaming towns more safe and desirable. It's about a 40-minute drive from Denver, going up either I-70 West or Highway 119, following the signs. There are numerous bus and limo services that go directly to the casinos. The Blackhawk/Central City Convention and Visitors Bureau website, www.visitbhcc.com, provides directions from your own address, as well as current road conditions.

Rocky Mountain National Park

At any time of the year, Rocky Mountain National Park, northwest of Denver, is absolutely dazzling. In summer, take a longer hike and be rewarded by the sight of a stunning waterfall; in the fall, come to hear the huge elk bugling and see the spectacular aspen trees changing colors; in the winter, snowshoe or cross-country ski to, and around, a handful of pristine lakes; in the spring, drive or walk among the wildflowers blooming and catch glimpses of wildlife, including bighorn sheep, cougars, moose, and bears. Among the 60 peaks that are over 12,000 feet high, the more adventurous types can attempt a hike to the top of 14,259-foot Longs Peak.

RECREATION

The sights in Rocky Mountain National Park are inextricably meshed with recreation of some sort, and you can see a lot of the park just by driving. There are trails for every hiking interest and ability somewhere in the 416 square miles of wilderness in Rocky Mountain National Park. You can go to www.nps.gov/romo for details on hiking in the park.

Trail Ridge Road

Trail Ridge Road goes from Estes Park, on the east side of the national park, up and over the Continental Divide to the park's west side and the town of Grand Lake. This is the highest continuous paved road in North America, peaking at 12,183 feet. On this 48-mile scenic drive, you'll go through lush forest and the treeless alpine tundra, where the **Alpine Visitors Center** (www.nps.gov, May 23–Oct. 8, daily 9 A.M.–5 P.M., weather permitting), at 11,796 feet, has small exhibits about plant and animal life from the area, along with rangers to answer your questions. The road is generally

open from Memorial Day to mid-October, depending on snowfall.

Hikes

There are 30 miles of the 3,100-mile **Continental Divide National Scenic Trail** within Rocky Mountain National Park. Check with park rangers to find out about the current conditions on this montane and sub-alpine stretch of scenic trails.

EMERALD LAKE, DREAM LAKE, AND NYMPH LAKE LOOP

A personal favorite that is popular for both hiking in summer and snowshoeing in winter is the 1.8-mile loop to Emerald Lake, Dream Lake, and Nymph Lake. If you go in June or July, you are likely to see wildflowers on the 6.4-mile round-trip hike to **Bridal Veil Falls.**

◀ BLUEBIRD LAKE TRAIL

A more difficult hike is on Bluebird Lake Trail to Ouzel Falls, Ouzel Lake, Calypso Cascades, and Bluebird Lake. It sounds odd to include a hike through a fire-damaged forest, but the reality is that the new growth and wildflowers are thriving in this recovering landscape. There are many waterfalls along the way, so you can choose to go just halfway and still see some amazing scenery.

LONGS PEAK

Talk to park rangers before attempting a hike up Longs Peak, which has an elevation gain of over 5,000 feet in eight miles. The peak stands at a majestic 14,259 feet and can be seen outside of Rocky Mountain National Park or from many other locales within the park. This is a technical climb, even on the "easiest" routes up, and people have died trying to reach the summit.

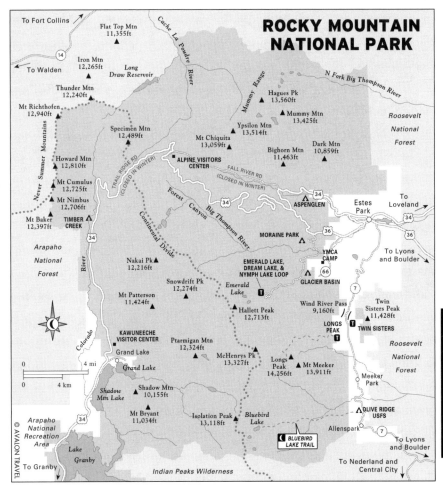

Always check with rangers (970/586-1206) for the very latest conditions on the peak.

Fishing

There are dozens of lakes in the park where fishing is allowed, but you will need to check in at a visitors center to find out which are currently open and fully stocked. For tours and lessons, contact **Estes Angler** (338 W. Riverside Dr., Estes Park, 970/586-2110, www.estesangler.com, daily 9 A.M.–5 P.M.).

Horseback Riding

Horseback riding is permitted within the park on about 260 miles of trails. There are two stables in the park, **Moraine Park Stables** (970/586-2327, www.sombrero.com, rates start at $50/person) and **Glacier Creek Stables** (May–Sept. 970/586-3244, www.sombrero.com, rates start at $50/person), and two in Estes Park, **Aspen Lodge Stables** (970/577-3448, www.aspenlodgehorseback.com, rates range from $35–$220) and **Sombrero Ranch**

COURTESY VISIT ESTES PARK

The Estes Park Aerial Tramway takes people from Estes Park to the top of Prospect Mountain.

Stables (1895 Big Thompson Ave., Estes Park, 970/586-4577, www.sombrero.com, daily 8 A.M.–5 P.M., rates are $35/person for one hour, $50/person for two hours, $65/person for three hours, $75/person for four hours), which has hourly rides on private ranch and national forest land. The National Park site, www.nps.gov/romo, has lists of horseback riding rules and recommended trails.

Rock Climbing

For information about rock climbing in the park, or to sign up for a guided climbing trip, contact the **Colorado Mountain School** (351 Moraine Ave., Estes Park, 970/586-5758 or 800/836-4008, www.totalclimbing.com, summer only Mon.–Fri. 8 A.M.–5 P.M.).

Estes Park Aerial Tramway

If you don't want to do much besides look at this glorious place, take the Estes Park Aerial Tramway (420 Riverside Dr., Estes Park, 970/586-3675, www.estestram.com, daily 9 A.M.–6 P.M. in summer, $8–12), which takes you to the 8,896-foot peak of Prospect Mountain and provides views of Longs Peak and the Continental Divide.

RESTAURANTS

There are limited fine dining options in Estes Park, but **Cascades Restaurant** (333 Wonderview Ave., 970/586-3371, www.stanleyhotel.com, daily 7 A.M.–10 P.M., $18–35) at the Stanley Hotel has a nice wine and beer list to accompany its Colorado game specials. Outside seating is especially pleasant in the summer.

The Dunraven Inn (2470 State Hwy. 66, 970/480-0396, www.dunraveninn.com, daily 4–9 P.M., $12–34) has hearty Italian food, steaks, seafood, and a children's menu. The **Sweet Basilico Café** (430 Prospect Village Rd., 970/586-3899, www.sweetbasilico.com, Mon.–Fri. 11 A.M.–10 P.M., Sat.–Sun. 11:30 A.M.–10 P.M. in summer; Wed.–Fri. 11 A.M.–9 P.M., SAT.–SUN. 11:30 A.M.–9 P.M. in winter, $10–18) serves yummy pizza and Italian dishes.

Mexican food is a favorite option before or after a day of hiking. Creekside, there is **Ed's Cantina & Grill** (390 E. Elkhorn Ave., 970/586-2919, www.edscantina.com, daily 11 A.M.–close; breakfast Fri.–Sun. 7 A.M.–11 A.M. in summer, Sat.–Sun. 7 A.M.–11 A.M. in winter, $7–15).

For a caffeine and Internet fix (free Wi-Fi), stop in at the **Notchtop Bakery and Café** (459 E. Wonderview Ave., 970/586-0272, daily 7 A.M.–5 P.M., $6–9), which also serves breakfast and lunch.

SHOPS

People often joke that when it comes to shopping in a gateway town like Estes Park, it is limited to fudge shops and T-shirt stores. There is some truth to this, and there are a fair amount of gift stores with carved wood artwork and wind chimes, too. These all make for pleasant window shopping as you stroll along the town's main street and across the creek in places.

For practical purposes, the **Estes Park Mountain Shop** (2050 Big Thompson Ave., 970/586-6548, www.estesparkmountainshop. com, daily 8 A.M.–9 P.M.) has not only outdoor gear for sale and rental; it is also a place to register for guided fishing, hiking, and rock climbing. Also try **Kirk's Fly Shop** (230 E. Elkhorn Ave., 970/577-0790, http://kirksflyshop.com, daily 7 A.M.–7 P.M. in summer, check for off-season hours) for guided tours in the area, as well as gear for any kind of excursion into the park.

HOTELS AND CAMPING

The most famous hotel in Estes Park is the **Stanley Hotel** (333 Wonderview Ave., 970/586-3371, www.stanleyhotel.com, $239–750) for its association with the horror movie *The Shining*. However, the movie was filmed at other hotels, too, so the interior is not the same as the movie. The hotel does have a grand view of the town and the park.

The **Estes Park Resort** (1700 Big Thompson Ave., 970/577-6400, www.estesparkresort.com, $169–279) on the northern edge of Lake Estes has views of Longs Peak from some of its comfortable rooms and wraparound decks.

Affordable lodging for large groups or families is available in the lodges and cabins of the **YMCA of the Rockies/Estes Park Center** (2515 Tunnel Rd., 970/586-3341, www. ymcarockies.org, $74–349 per season and group size). Winter and summer activities are available on the property.

There are five drive-in campgrounds and over 200 other campsites in the park. For information and reservations, call 970/586-1206, 888/448-1474, or 877/444-6777, or go to www.nps.gov/romo. Backcountry camping in the park requires a permit; call 970/586-1242.

PRACTICALITIES

For more information on the town of Estes Park, go to the **Estes Park Visitors Center** (500 Big Thompson Ave., 970/577-9900 or 800/443-7837, www.estesparkcvb.com, Mon.–Sat. 9 A.M.–5 P.M., Sun. 10 A.M.–4 P.M.). You can download a visitor's guide from the website or have one mailed to you. Of course, in addition to lodging and dining information for Estes Park, the visitors center has brochures and can answer questions about the park.

There are three visitors centers on east entrances to the park; all have the same phone number and website (970/586-1206, www. nps.gov/romo). The Beaver Meadows Visitor Center (Rte. 36, 3 miles from Estes Park, daily 8 A.M.–9 P.M.) has restrooms, maps, a 20-minute film about the park shown throughout the day, and rangers who can answer questions. The Fall River Visitor Center (Rte. 34, 5 miles from Estes Park, check for seasonal hours) has hands-on nature exhibits, restrooms, and helpful rangers. The Moraine Park Visitor Center and Museum (off Bear Lake Rd., 1.5 miles from the Beaver Meadows park entrance, check for seasonal hours) includes a half-mile nature trail.

Getting There

From Denver, you can either take I-25 north to exit 243 through Longmont, and then take State Highway 66 to Lyons to merge with Highway 36 into Estes Park; or, from I-25, get on Highway 36 to Boulder and stay on the road as it passes through town and on to Lyons and then Estes Park. Another option is the Peak-to-Peak Scenic Byway, which starts in the town of Blackhawk on State Highway 119.

EXCURSIONS FROM DENVER

COURTESY VISIT ESTES PARK

The Stanley Hotel overlooks the town of Estes Park, with views into Rocky Mountain National Park.

It takes at least one hour to drive to the park from downtown Denver (longer if you take a scenic route).

From Denver International Airport, Estes Park Shuttle (970/586-5151, www.estesparkshuttle.com) offers at least three rides a day for $45 one-way and $85 round-trip.

Getting Around

There can be traffic jams in the park during the busy summer months, and even in the fall, when the elk are more visible and the leaves are changing color. There is free shuttle bus service within the park in spring, summer, and fall. For more information about bus schedules, check www.nps.gov/romo or call 970/586-1206. Always check with the park for the latest road conditions because the high elevations can have dramatically different weather than the lower elevations.

Colorado Springs

Colorado Springs is the second-largest city in the state and has a hodge-podge identity unto itself. The largest employer in Colorado Springs is the military, with the Fort Carson United States Army base, the United States Air Force Academy, and the North American Aerospace Defense Command (NORAD). Tourism comes in as the third-largest industry (behind high-tech), bringing in over $1.2 billion annually with an estimated five to six million visitors to the area.

SIGHTS
◖ Garden of the Gods

Before it was named Garden of the Gods by white settlers, Native American tribes made annual pilgrimages to the area of beautiful red rocks that stand up so distinctly against the green mountain slopes. By 1871, Colorado Springs was being laid out nearby as a resort destination. The Garden of the Gods (1805 N. 30th St., 719/634-6666, www.gardenofgods.com) remains the top tourist attraction around, with an estimated two million visitors each year.

Like many other sensational natural wonders in the area, Garden of the Gods has been tinkered with too much and has a heavy theme-park atmosphere that can be a big turn-off. There are bus tours, not one but three gift shops, and Native American dances for lunchtime entertainment. That said, you can take a number of easy hiking trails to escape the crowds (some trails also allow mountain biking and horseback riding) and appreciate the 1,350-acre park.

Stop in at the **Visitor and Nature Center** (1805 N. 30th St., Colorado Springs, 719/634-6666, www.gardenofgods.com, Memorial Weekend–Labor Day daily 8 A.M.–8 P.M., Labor Day–Memorial Weekend daily 9 A.M.–5 P.M.)

to learn more about the geology of the rocks and the plants and critters that dwell here. Visiting the park is free year-round, but there are fees for guided tours and special programs.

Colorado Springs Fine Arts Center

The Colorado Springs Fine Arts Center (30 W. Dale St., 719/634-5583, www.csfineartscenter. org, Tues.–Sun. 10 A.M.–5 P.M., $8.50–10) is a wonderful little museum that has an impressive permanent collection (with art from John Singer Sargent to Fritz Scholder to many more familiar names) and intriguing temporary exhibits. In the Lane Family Gallery, the hand-blown glass creations of artist Dale Chihuly are shown alongside Native American artworks—blankets and baskets—that influenced his work. Also look for Chihuly chandeliers elsewhere in the center.

The art deco building with Southwestern flair was designed in 1936 by Santa Fe architect John Gaw Meem. On the west end of the building is **Café 36** (719/477-4377, Tues.–Sun. 11 A.M.–1:30 P.M., reservations recommended). The outdoor patio is a terrific place for a special lunch with a view of Pikes Peak.

Group tours are available and advance reservations are needed. Free weekend tours start at 2 P.M. and no reservations are required.

Cheyenne Mountain Zoo

What sets the Cheyenne Mountain Zoo (4250 Cheyenne Mountain Zoo Rd., 719/633-9925, www.cmzoo.org, daily 9 A.M.–6 P.M. in summer, daily 9 A.M.–5 P.M. off-season, free admission for children age 2 and under year-round, May 1–Labor Day adults $17.25, children (ages 3–11) $12.25, seniors (65+) $15.25, military adults $14.25, military child $9.25; Labor Day–April 30 adults $14.25, children (ages

The Colorado Springs Fine Arts Center has permanent and temporary collections.

© PHILLIP SPEARS

3–11) $10.25, seniors (65+) $12.25, military adults $11.25, military child $7.25) apart from other zoos is its elevation of 6,800 feet above sea level and the large giraffe herd that lives and breeds here. The zoo's setting in the foothills beyond the Broadmoor Hotel gives the zoo a natural feeling, to some extent.

Zoo founder Spencer Penrose was great friends with humorist Will Rogers. After Mr. Rogers died in 1935, Mr. Penrose built the **The Will Rogers Shrine of the Sun** to honor his friend. Visitors to the zoo can go inside and take in the views from the top deck of the five-story shrine at over 8,000 feet above sea level.

There's the usual assortment of zoo creatures—lions, elephants, meerkats, and a lot more—but the giraffes are very popular, so the zoo sells special crackers that can be fed directly to them by guests. There is also a carousel and open-air chairlift ride that tours the entire zoo.

United States Air Force Academy

Depending on the current U.S. security color code, visitors are generally welcome at the **United States Air Force Academy** campus (2346 Academy Dr., 719/333-2025, www. usafa.af.mil), where one of the highlights is the **Cadet Chapel** (Mon.–Sat. 9 A.M.–5 P.M., Sun. 1–5 P.M.) for its unique architecture and all-faiths house of worship model.

RESTAURANTS

If you can really splurge, **Charles Court** (1 Lake Ave., 719/577-5733, www.broadmoor. com/charles-court.php, dinner Thurs.–Mon. 5–9 P.M., breakfast daily 7 A.M.–10 P.M., $22–44) in **The Broadmoor** is a wonderful restaurant with dishes that highlight local ingredients, such as Colorado lamb and beef and San Luis Valley quinoa. The menu can change nightly and there is a dress code. There are eight restaurants to choose from at The

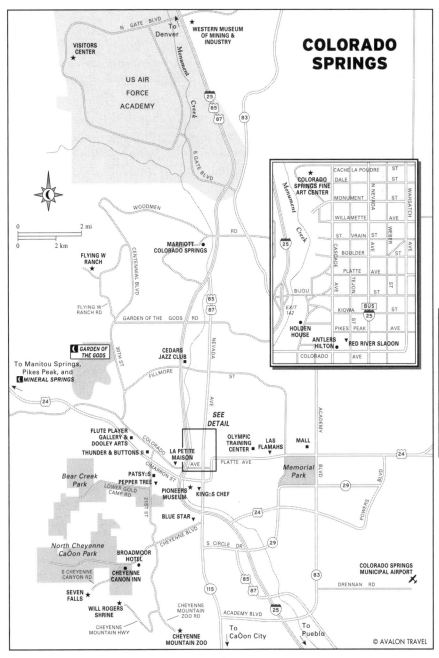

© AVALON TRAVEL

the Cadet Chapel at the U.S. Air Force Academy in Colorado Springs

© RICH GRANT, COURTESY OF VISIT DENVER

Broadmoor, so perhaps there is one with a different menu, price range, or location with more appeal for you.

The **Phantom Canyon Brewing Company** (2 E. Pikes Peak Ave., 719/635-2800, www.phantomcanyon.com, daily 11 A.M.–close, $12–25) is a sister brewpub to the iconic LoDo **Wynkoop Brewery.** Like the Wynkoop, the Phantom Canyon Brewing Company is located in a historic building in downtown and has a second floor devoted to billiards. This is standard pub food for lunch or dinner, but dependably good, with fresh beer on tap.

In about the same price range as the Phantom Canyon Brewing Company is the **Ritz Grill** (15 S. Tejon St., 719/635-8484, www.ritzgrill.com, Mon.–Fri. 11:30 A.M.–2 A.M., Sat. noon–close, Sun. 11 A.M.close, $13–27), with a sophisticated art deco look and a late-night menu that makes it a local favorite. Check the website for live music nights, too.

NIGHTLIFE

There's definitely a country-and-western scene in Colorado Springs. A good place to kick up your heels is **Cowboys** (25 N. Tejon St., 719/596-1212, www.cowboyscs.com, Wed.–Thurs. 5 P.M.–2 A.M., Fri.–Sun. 4 P.M.–2 A.M., no cover), where there is live music and dancing (lessons on Sunday).

On the west side of town is **Motif** (2432 Cucharras St., 719/635-5635, http://motifwest.com, May–Oct. Thurs.–Sat. 4 P.M.–midnight; Nov.–April Thurs.–Sat. 5 P.M.–midnight, closed Sun.–Wed.), which has live jazz music featuring local musicians. Look for the bamboo fence as signage is lacking for Motif.

RECREATION

While you can just drive through **Garden of the Gods** (1805 N. 30th St., 719/634-6666, www.gardenofgods.com), there are also 15 miles of trails for hiking. The visitors center has maps of designated hiking, biking, and horseback riding areas. It is also the meeting point for the free guided nature walks (daily 10 A.M. and 2 P.M.). Rock climbing is allowed in the park, but check in at the visitors center first to read over the regulations. For horseback riding, contact **Academy Riding Stables** at 719/633-5667 or go to www.academyridingstables.com (daily 8:30 A.M.–4:30 P.M.).

The **North Cheyenne Cañon Park** is a 1,600-acre park that includes natural waterfalls and wildlife (especially hummingbirds) and the **Starsmore Discovery Center** (2120 S. Cheyenne Cañon Rd., 719/385-6086, www.springsgov.com) for kids and adults. Hands-on nature exhibits, a climbing wall, and a gift shop are all at the center. Call ahead for seasonal hours and program offerings. The center is a good place to pick up trail maps and find out more about the park.

Check the city's website, www.springsgov.com, for a complete list of city parks, trails, and open spaces.

SHOPS

Started in 1899 by Artus Van Briggle and world renowned for art nouveau styles with a silky matte glaze, the gallery **Van Briggle Pottery** (1024 S. Tejon St., 719/633-7729, www.vanbriggle.com, Mon.–Sat. 9 A.M.–5 P.M.) has distinctive pottery pieces in the permanent collections at the Smithsonian and the Metropolitan Museum of Art in New York. The studio has continued to produce classic Van Briggle pottery as well as new original works, including decorative tile.

Just northwest of downtown is historic **Old Colorado City** (24th through 27th Sts. along West Colorado Ave., www.shopoldcoloradocity.com), which was a town during the early gold rush days before Colorado Springs was developed. Now it's a few blocks of specialty shops, art galleries, and antique stores mixed in with some restaurants and bars. To schedule a tour, call 719/636-1225 or visit www.occhs.org.

HOTELS

There's a reason that you have likely heard of **The Broadmoor** (1 Lake Ave., 719/577-5775 or 800/634-7711, www.broadmoor.com, $270–445)—it's a remarkable luxury hotel that has been around since the early 1900s. The Broadmoor is a destination in itself, not just a place to stay for a night. Set at the base of Cheyenne Mountain, the large, pink, Mediterranean-style hotel opened in 1918 and was meant to capture the luxury of Asian and European designs seen by the owners in their travels. The numbers can tell the story here: There are 700 rooms and suites, 18 restaurants, 3,000 acres with meticulously landscaped grounds, eight tennis courts, three golf courses, three swimming pools, and a spa, and that's not all. On the website, you can sign up for special offer alerts or find a package deal.

In downtown, the **Antlers Hilton Colorado Springs** (4 S. Cascade Ave., 719/955-5600, www.antlers.com, $179–369) is certainly popular with business travelers, but it is also a convenient location for seeing the sights. West-side rooms have views of Pikes Peak.

For accommodations with a homier feel, the **Holden House** (1102 W. Pikes Peak Ave., 719/471-3980, www.holdenhouse.com, $145–165) has five roomy suites available near downtown. It's your typical bed-and-breakfast, with floral prints everywhere, overstuffed chairs and sofas, and lots of antiques throughout the turn-of-the-20th-century Victorian home.

PRACTICALITIES
Tourism Office

Stop by the **Experience Colorado Springs at Pikes Peak Visitor Center** (515 S. Cascade Ave., 719/635-7506, www.visitcos.com, Mon.–Fri. 8:30 A.M.–4:30 P.M.) for maps and brochures of the area. The city's website, www.springsgov.com, is also helpful.

Getting There

From Denver, take I-25 south about 60 miles and look for signs to the various sights or downtown. You can fly directly in and out of Colorado Springs (www.flycos.com) on many major airlines. **The Front Range Express** (719/636-3739 or 877/425-3739, www.frontrangeexpress.com) is a commuter bus service between Denver and Colorado Springs with multiple ride options daily.

Media

The *Colorado Springs Gazette* (www.gazette. com) is the city's main newspaper, with listings of the latest local happenings. There is also the alternative weekly the *Independent* (www.csindy.com).

Getting Around

There are two bus options to get around Colorado Springs. One is a free shuttle for downtown only called Dash, and the other is the citywide Mountain Metropolitan Transit system. Go to www.springsgov.com and follow the links to get the latest schedules.

Manitou Springs

It's been called a "Hippie Mayberry," and Manitou Springs is certainly an appealing blend of historic allure and New Age trappings. Manitou Springs is a gateway to Pikes Peak, as well as to the Garden of the Gods. On a clear day, the view from the 14,110-foot peak is incredible—and even inspired the lyrics for "America the Beautiful." There is enough to see and do in Manitou Springs to fill a weekend or make for a worthwhile afternoon away from Denver.

SIGHTS
Cave of the Winds

If you have ever been curious about caves, but too timid to crawl around in the dark, then maybe Cave of the Winds (Hwy. 24, 719/685-5444, http://caveofthewinds.com, daily 9 a.m.–9 p.m. in summer, daily 10 a.m.–5 p.m. in winter, $9–24) is just right. Guided tours of the cave are well-lit with wide walkways and handrails, and visitors can clearly see stalagmites, stalactites, and limestone caverns. This Discovery Tour takes 45 minutes and is offered daily every 30 minutes. The Lantern Tour is for the slightly more adventurous spelunker and it takes twice as long, with some stooping and less light. Overall, it can be a fun experience for school-age children.

Cave of the Winds was "discovered" by two brothers in the late 1800s. Today, it is a tourist trap—an enormous gift shop cleverly conceals the cave entrance. There is a pretty incredible view of the canyons below from the gift shop deck, which is equipped with binoculars. Cave of the Winds is about a five-minute drive from Manitou Springs.

Manitou Cliff Dwellings Preserve and Museums

Right off the bat, you should know that the Manitou Cliff Dwellings (Hwy. 24, 719/685-5242, www.cliffdwellingsmuseum.com, $9.50 adult, $7.50 child, free for child 6 and under, $8.50 senior) were relocated from somewhere else, and some of the buildings here are reproductions. The good news is that this lack of authenticity means more access to the entire site, unlike truly preserved cliff dwellings in southwestern Colorado. There are self-guided tours of the site and a lack of "do not touch" signs, as the effort here is to educate people about Native American cultures. Hours change seasonally; call ahead for current times.

◀ Mineral Springs

Free for all ages and types, some of the best attractions in Manitou Springs are the springs themselves, which are made conveniently available in decorative fountains around the historic downtown. Stop in at the **Manitou Springs Chamber of Commerce and Visitors Bureau** (354 Manitou Ave., 719/685-5089 or 800/642-2567, www.manitousprings.org, Mon.–Fri. 8:30 A.M.–5 P.M., Sat.–Sun. 9 A.M.–4 P.M.), where you will be given a small, plastic souvenir cup for sampling the spring waters, a map of the various springs, and a detailed list of the health benefits of the mineral spring water. I'm not sure why or how, but the water at each of the springs has a completely different taste, some far less palatable than others. There are also guided tours available with reservations in the summer.

Miramont Castle Museum

Tucked into the town's historic district is a large castle that was constructed as a private home for a French priest and his mother in 1895. Miramont Castle Museum (9 Capitol Hill Ave., 719/685-1011, www.miramontcastle.org, call for seasonal hours, $8 adult, $5 child, free for child 5 and under, $7 senior) is an amalgam of architectural styles with 46 odd-shaped rooms. The castle has had many uses over the years—sanitarium, apartments—and is now filled with furniture and curiosities of the Victorian era.

Pikes Peak

Pikes Peak is not only the state's most famous "fourteener" (a mountain peak that stands over 14,000 feet high); it is the second most-visited peak in the world. Over the years, people seem to have come up with every conceivable way to experience or ascend this mountain (all for a fee, unless you are fit enough to hike up). The

© GEORGE BURBA | DREAMSTIME.COM

The Manitou Springs train runs over the top of Pikes Peak.

360-degree panorama from the top is simply spectacular.

Just up a narrow road from downtown Manitou Springs, the **Pikes Peak Cog Railway** (515 Ruxton Rd., 719/685-5401, www.cograil-way.com) slowly chugs train cars up the side of the mountain through forests and out to the barren mountaintop—and gift and donut shop. The trip is a little over three hours, and there are health warnings and restrictions because of the altitude and heights. Rates are $19–35, and there are several trips daily year-round.

Pikes Peak also has its own toll road. It's 19 miles of curvy mountain driving that is only paved for about half the distance, then gravel the last nine miles. Every summer, the **Pikes Peak International Hill Climb** (719/685-4400, www.ppihc.com) takes place on this seemingly dangerous road.

Barr Trail is the route for hikers to get to the 14,110 peak, and this, too, inspires an annual event with the Pikes Peak Marathon in August.

For more information on Pikes Peak, visit www.springsgov.com.

RESTAURANTS

Adam's Mountain Café (934 Manitou Ave., 719/685-1430 or 719/685-4370, www.ad-amsmountain.com, daily 8 A.M.–3 P.M., Tues.–Sat. 5–9 P.M.; closed Mon. Oct.–Apr., $8–22) is a homey-feeling restaurant with lots of vegetarian options. They are kid-friendly and have a nice creekside patio where diners can watch other tourists sample the waters of Cheyenne Spring.

The Cliff House (306 Cañon Ave., 719/685-3000 or 888/212-7000, www.thecliffhouse.com, daily 6:30–10:30 A.M., 11:30 A.M.–2:30 P.M., 5:30–9 P.M., $20–35) is open for breakfast, lunch, and dinner with a separate (cheaper) Veranda menu available in the summer months for dining outside the main dining room. The huge wine list is impressive, and one of the four staff sommeliers can help you make

the right choice to accompany the Colorado bass or grilled venison.

Another fine dining option is the **Briarhurst Manor Estate** (404 Manitou Ave., 719/685-1864 or 877/685-1448, www.briarhurst.com, daily 5–8:30 P.M., $20–45), which was the home of Manitou Springs's founder, Dr. William Bell. The pink, sandstone, tudor-style house is open for dinner nightly and entrées feature Colorado lamb and deer. Call ahead to verify Monday and Tuesday hours in the fall and winter.

A guidebook from the visitors center has a complete listing of the town's restaurants, and most places are within easy walking distance of lodgings and other eateries.

RECREATION

For a moderately difficult hike, try the seven-mile **Waldo Canyon Loop** that follows Waldo Creek. You can also mountain bike this trail, or might be sharing it with mountain bikers. The trailhead is two miles past the Cave of the Winds exit off Highway 24. This area was affected by a wildfire in 2012. Check with the Forest Service for current trail conditions at www.fs.usda.gov.

SHOPS

Shopping in Manitou Springs means the usual tourist candy stores, T-shirt shops, and art galleries, but then it gets more interesting with the themed stores. There is the **Hemp Store** (2 Ruxton Ave., 719/685-1189, www.toddshempstore.com, Mon.–Tues. 11 A.M.–6 P.M., Wed. 2–6 P.M., Thurs.–Sun. 11 A.M.–6 P.M.), with a variety of things made from the fiber, and **Nature of Things Chain Saw Art** (347 Manitou Ave., 719/685-0171, www.nature-ofthingschainsawart.com), with lots of wooden sculptures and demonstrations available.

Not a store but worth a look is **Rockey's Storybook Art Studio** (10–12 Cañon Ave., 719/685-9076, hours vary), where artist and local legend C. H. Rockey displays his sculptures and works on an intricately illustrated storybook.

HOTELS

Listed on the National Register of Historic Places, the **Cliff House at Pikes Peak** (306 Cañon Ave., 719/685-3000 or 888/212-7000, www.thecliffhouse.com, $129–409) is a blend of historic integrity and modern amenities since a fire damaged much of the interior in the 1980s. The 54 guestrooms and suites include "celebrity rooms" named after former guests, such as Clark Gable and Teddy Roosevelt.

The Two Sisters Inn (10 Otoe Pl., 719/685-9684, www.twosisinn.com, $79–155) is a little pink house that has bedrooms in the main house (with private or shared bathrooms) and a private guest house out back in the garden. The rates are reasonable and the service attentive.

PRACTICALITIES
Tourist Office

Take Highway 24 to Manitou Avenue and the

Manitou Springs Chamber of Commerce and Visitors Bureau (354 Manitou Ave., 719/685-5089 or 800/642-2567, www.manitousprings. org, Mon.–Fri. 8:30 A.M.–5 P.M., Sat.–Sun. 9 A.M.–4 P.M.) will be on your right before you actually enter the town. There are more brochures than you will ever need and a helpful staff to answer questions and make suggestions.

Getting There

From Denver, take I-25 south just past the exit for downtown Colorado Springs and exit on Cimarron Street (which becomes Highway 24) or Colorado Avenue. The drive takes about one hour and 15 minutes from downtown Denver, but try to avoid rush-hour gridlock in Colorado Springs.

Getting Around

Manitou Springs is small enough for walking around to see the historic buildings and springs. Keep in mind that it is at a higher elevation than Denver and has many inclined streets.

Winter Park Ski Resort

The downside to skiing or snowboarding in Colorado is getting to the resorts and back, given road conditions and traffic along I-70 in winter. Winter Park Ski Resort is one of the closer resorts to Denver, and it is owned by the city of Denver and managed by Intrawest. The small town of Winter Park is to the west of the ski area. There are over 2,000 acres to ski and 134 runs on three mountains here. In addition, transportation is available to nearby Devil's Thumb Ranch, the state's only resort devoted to cross-country skiing and snowshoeing.

RECREATION

Visitors come to **Winter Park Ski Resort** (85 Parsenn Rd., Winter Park, 303/316-1564,

www.winterparkresort.com, Nov.–April Mon.–Fri. 9 A.M.–4 P.M., Sat.–Sun. 8:30 A.M.–4 P.M.) to be active in some form or another, mostly in the winter when it gets crowded on the mountain, but also in the summer when snowshoe trails become perfect for hikers and mountain bikers.

Winter Park is best known for Mary Jane, which is actually made up of three mountains: Parsenn Bowl, Vasquez Cirque, and Mary Jane. Each mountain has its own reputation: Mary Jane is all about the bumps or moguls; Vasquez Cirque has backcountry conditions and super-steep runs; and Parsenn Bowl tops out at over 12,000 feet, with tree runs and open space all the way down the mountain. Mary Jane (named after a onetime madam who lived and worked in a nearby town) has a triple chairlift. The other mountains at Winter Park are Vasquez Ridge and Winter Park. The resort's 300-plus inches of snow each winter are enhanced, thanks to snowmaking machines, and an opening before Thanksgiving is practically guaranteed.

For those not quite ready for the four-plus-mile runs of Mary Jane or even the gentler runs of Vasquez Ridge, there is ski school for children and adults, along with equipment rental. The **National Sports Center for the Disabled** (33 Parsenn Rd., Winter Park, 970/726-1518, www.nscd.org) is based at the Winter Park Ski Resort, where anyone with a disability can participate in therapeutic recreation programs from skiing to golf.

Snowshoeing is a winter activity that attracts more people every year, given its no-skill-needed appeal and the low cost of necessary gear and equipment. Just across Highway 40 from the resort is the **Bonfils-Stanton Nature Trail,** which is an easy hike in winter or summer and partially wheelchair accessible.

The **Trestle Bike Park** (85 Parsenn Rd., Winter Park, 970/726-1675, www.trestlebikepark.com, Season pass is $259, adult full day ticket is $39 for 9:30 A.M.–5 P.M., adult half day is $34 for 1:30 P.M.–5 P.M.) is a good place for novice mountain bikers to start. Equipment rental, lessons, and clinics are all available, but it can get expensive with the added cost of lift tickets. There are hundreds of miles of mountain bike trails in the area that are mostly free to use. Download a free copy of the *Mountain Bike and Trail Guide* at www.winterparkguide.com.

Pole Creek Golf Club (6827 County Rd. 51, 970/887-9195, www.polecreekgolf.com, fees $48–99 depending on season, time of day, number of holes, age, and day of the week) has 27 holes total in three nine-hole courses accented with great views of the surrounding mountains.

To find out more about fishing, horseback riding, rafting, and more outdoor activities in the Winter Park area year-round, visit www.visitgrandcounty.com, www.playwinterpark.com, or www.winterparkguide.com to request a free visitors guide.

◖ Devil's Thumb Ranch

Devil's Thumb (3530 County Rd. 83, Tabernash, 970/726-5632, www.devilsthumbranch.com) is exclusively for cross-country skiers and snowshoers; there are no lift lines or lift ticket prices, but there are groomed trails to explore in a rather peaceful valley.

Come summertime, Winter Park Resort has turned itself into a destination for anglers, golfers, and mountain bikers. Start with Colorado's longest **Alpine Slide** (800/729-7907, www.winterparkresort.com, daily 10 A.M.–5 P.M. in summer, $15 adults, $6 children age 5 and under), where a chairlift brings people up to the top, and plastic sleds with wheels whirl them 3,000 feet down a 610-foot vertical drop.

RESTAURANTS

It's not like people drive out of their way to dine in Winter Park, where "regional cuisine" means food from another region. Stick to the basics, like **Deno's Mountain Bistro** (78911 Hwy. 40, 970/726-5332, http://denoswp.com, daily 11:30 A.M.–2 A.M., $13–36) for burgers, pizza, and steaks.

The corny, faux Swiss Alps decor of the Gasthaus Eichler hotel is a clue to what is on the menu at its **Gasthaus Eichler Restaurant** (78786 Hwy. 40, 970/726-5133, www.gasthauseichler.com, daily 11:30 A.M.–2 P.M. and 5–9 P.M., $12–29). There is classic cheese fondue, schnitzels, goulash, and steaks and burgers.

The Ranch House at Devil's Thumb (3530 County Rd. 83, Tabernash, 970/726-5633, www.devilsthumbranch.com, Wed.–Sun. 5–9 P.M., hours vary by season) is very

Western chic in a historic homestead building. The menu is more upscale, but there are simple burgers and salads, too. Reservations are recommended. **Heck's** is the more casual restaurant in the main lodge building (3530 County Rd. 83, Tabernash, 970/726-7013, www.devilsthumbranch.com, Sun.–Thurs. 7:30 A.M.–9 P.M., Fri.–Sat. 7:30 A.M.–10 P.M.) with soaring ceilings and impressive views. The food at Heck's is hearty fare, like bison meatloaf, lasagna, and ribs—because cross-country skiing makes a person very hungry!

SHOPS

In downtown Winter Park, there is a simple pedestrian-friendly mall, **Cooper Creek Square** (47 Cooper Creek Way, 970/726-8891, www.coopercreeksquare.com), with a variety of shops, restaurants, and places to buy or rent gear and equipment for every recreational possibility.

HOTELS

If you are purely interested in location, the **Winter Park Mountain Lodge** (81669 Hwy. 40, 866/726-4211, www.winterparkhotel.com, $124–550) is right across the road from the ski resort. There are basic rooms and suites with in-room whirlpool tubs, in addition to an indoor swimming pool and hot tubs.

There is also the **Vintage Resort Hotel & Conference Center** (100 Winter Park Dr., 800/472-7017, www.vintagehotel.com, $300–600), which has a ski lodge feel with high ceilings and fireplaces in some suites.

Devil's Thumb Ranch (3530 County Rd. 83, Tabernash, 970/726-5632, www.devilsthumbranch.com, $110–1,500) has three different types of lodging: The Bunkhouse is the most

affordable and is located a couple of miles down the road from the main facilities; the Lodge has 52 rooms, many with fireplaces and to-die-for bathrooms with copper bathtubs; and 16 cabins of various sizes are available for a solo stay or getting the family together.

PRACTICALITIES
Tourism Office

The **Winter Park-Fraser Valley Chamber of Commerce and Visitor Center** is located in downtown Winter Park at 78841 Highway 40, and can be reached by phone at 970/726-4221 or 800/903-7275. The website is www.playwinterpark.com; free visitors guides are mailed on request.

Media

Though Winter Park has only 700 residents, there is a local newspaper, the *Sky-Hi Daily News* (www.skyhidailynews.com).

Getting There
DRIVING

From Denver, take I-70 West to U.S. Highway 40 and over Berthoud Pass to Winter Park. **Powderhound Transportation** (970/455-4315, www.ridethepowder.com, $56.25 one-way from or to airport, $225 round-trip) provides shuttle service.

Getting Around

It's possible to walk from the ski resort to the town, but chances are you will need to put your gear in storage or lug it along. The resort provides shuttle service to town during peak ski months, so check www.allwinterpark.com for the latest schedules, or call **The Lift Resort Shuttle** at 970/726-4163.

Vail

Vail is a town that is still young enough to be finding itself. This is a company town, known for its exceptional ski conditions and luxury accommodations, but it has been turning itself into a year-round destination as well. Located along either side of I-70 in a mountain valley, Vail enjoys increased allure due to its proximity to smaller towns to the west, such as Edwards and Minturn, that don't make it into guidebooks but that are part of the scene. It's all becoming part of the greater Vail Valley and giving visitors and locals more to do.

SIGHTS
◖ Betty Ford Alpine Gardens
Billing itself as the world's highest botanic garden at 8,200 feet, the Betty Ford Alpine

Gardens (183 Gore Creek Dr., 970/476-0103, www.bettyfordalpinegardens.org, daily dawn–dusk, free) make for pleasant walks through well-maintained grounds that display plants thriving at high altitude. Former president Gerald Ford and his wife, Betty, maintained a home in Vail, and many buildings are named after Mr. Ford in the town. (And no, the Gore Mountain Range and nearby Gore Creek are *not* named after former vice president Al Gore.)

Colorado Ski Museum
The Colorado Ski Museum (231 S. Frontage Rd., 970/476-1876, www.skimuseum.net, seasonal hours vary, free) is in an odd location on the third floor of the Vail Village Parking Garage, but it's worth a visit to learn about the

The picturesque ski town of Vail has appeal in any season.

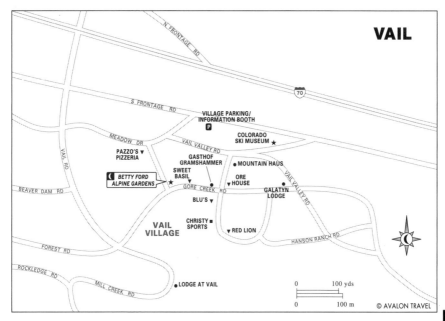

state's long skiing history. Photographs, old clothing and equipment, and timelines of skiing history make for an interesting lesson about this popular sport. Who knew that mail—not to mention provisions to small outposts and even the Word of God—was delivered by determined early skiers in the 1880s?

RESTAURANTS

If you came to Vail to ski, chances are that you will eat not far from your last run—maybe on the top of the mountain or down at the base. There is a variety of upscale dining and greasy carbs just about everywhere. Be sure to check the *Vail Daily* newspaper for two-for-one specials at many local restaurants.

Larkspur (458 Vail Valley Dr., 970/479-8050, www.larkspurvail.com, daily noon–10 P.M., $27–45) is an outstanding restaurant right in the heart of things at the base of the Golden Peak Ski Area. The lunch and dinner menus change weekly based on the availability

of seasonal ingredients for making this creative cuisine. During ski season, the same owner runs the neighboring Market with fresh sandwiches, pastries, and coffee starting with breakfast.

If you do want to drive, Larkspur's owner has also started **Larkburger** (105 Edwards Village Blvd., Edwards, 970/926-9336, www.larkburger.com, daily 11 A.M.–9 P.M., $5–7), which is like a gourmet In-N-Out Burger. I just have one thing to say: truffle fries. It's worth the 15-minute drive from Vail.

The Red Lion Inn (304 Bridge St., 970/476-7676, www.theredlion.com, daily 11 A.M.–close, $10–27) is a local institution in a bit of a time warp. They are open for lunch and dinner, serving burgers, barbecue, and salads, all in ample portions.

Ignore the not-so-glamorous setting and dig into some mouthwatering, tangy barbecue at **Moe's Original BBQ** (675 W. Lionshead Cir., 970/479-7888, www.moesoriginalbbq.com, daily 11 A.M.–9 P.M., $8–12), which relocated to Vail from Alabama. **Vendetta's Italian Restaurant** (225 Wall St., 970/476-1305, www.vendettasvail.com, daily 11 A.M.–2 A.M., $18–32) has affordable pizza and a nice patio for dining outside in the summer. It has been voted the best local's bar in Vail by the, er, locals.

RECREATION

The reason Vail is on the map at all is because of the incredible skiing, with almost 200 trails over 5,289 acres and a mountain peak of 11,500 feet. What makes Vail so appealing is that there is something for every skill level and activity—downhill skiing, snowshoeing, snowboarding... and that's just in the winter. To find out more about year-round activities, lift ticket prices, gondola and chairlift rides, mountain biking, hiking, ski lessons (offered in many languages), and more, go to www.vail.com or call 800/805-2457.

Even though the terrain makes for a challenging course, golf is still popular in Vail, such as at the **Vail Golf Club** (1778 Vail Valley Dr., Vail, 970/479-2260, www.vailgolfclub.net or www.vailrec.com, daily 6:30 A.M.–dusk, $25–107 depending on number of holes, season, walking or with cart, age, and time of day), with a stunning 18-hole course at 8,200 feet, where golf balls supposedly fly 10 percent farther than at lower elevations.

In the summer, **Gore Creek Fly Fisherman** (970/476-3296, www.gorecreekflyfisherman.com) offers free casting lessons every day at 10:30 A.M. at their four locations, as well as guided fishing trips arranged in advance.

If you are seeking the latest adventure craze, try **Zip Adventures** (4098 Colorado 131, Wolcott, 970/926-9470, www.zipadventures.com), where, for $125, you zoom (or zip) down a cable seeing the canyon scenery at a high speed. There is a bit of hiking involved.

COLORADO MUSIC FESTIVALS

Colorado scenery inspires people to write songs and make music—from Katharine Lee Bates, who wrote "America the Beautiful" after seeing Pikes Peak, to John Denver's "Rocky Mountain High." The purple mountains, quaking aspen leaves, and remarkable heights all make a great setting for music festivals, too.

The annual **Bravo! Vail Valley Music Festival** (877/812-5700, www.vailmusicfestival.org) holds several concerts late June through early August in a variety of locations. Visiting jazz and philharmonic orchestras play in private residences, churches, the Gerald R. Ford Amphitheater in Vail, and the Vilar Performing Arts Center in Beaver Creek.

In Boulder, there's the **Colorado Music Festival** (303/449-1397, www.coloradomusicfest.org) held at the historic Chautauqua Auditorium with visiting musicians from around the world. The music festival usually runs from mid-June to early August, with two to four concerts weekly and special family and kids' programs.

In January, the one-of-a-kind **MahlerFest** (www.mahlerfest.org) is held in Boulder to celebrate the life and work of Gustav Mahler through seminars, recitals, and concerts.

To find out about music festivals throughout the state, go to www.coloradomusic.org/festivals.

SHOPS

There is as much shopping as skiing going on in Vail, with many familiar stores, but also a few one-of-a-kind shops that represent the culture of the area.

The Golden Bear (286 Bridge St., 970/476-4082, www.thegoldenbear.com, daily 10 A.M.–6 P.M., open until 8 P.M. in winter) has been around almost as long as the town of

Vail selling its iconic jewelry, as well as clothing and other accessories.

Axel's (201 Gore Creek Dr., 970/476-7625, http://axelsltd.com, daily 10 A.M.–8 P.M.) is another local shopping institution that features leather goods—cowboy boots, belts—and very decorative belt buckles and tailored clothes for men and women.

Going for that Nordic look? Check out **The Swedish Clog Cabin** (500 E. Lionshead Mall, 970/476-8083, www.tessaclogs.com, Mon.–Sat. 10 A.M.–8 P.M., Sun. 10 A.M.–6 P.M.), where the specialty is imported clogs that are hand-painted locally. And there is just about everything else imported from Sweden, including food, books, and clothes.

Throughout Vail, there are many sportswear and sports equipment stores, such as **Pepi Sports** (231 Bridge St., 970/476-5202, www.pepisports.com, Nov.—mid-April daily 8 A.M.–9 P.M., mid-April–June daily 10 A.M.–6 P.M., July–Oct. daily 9 A.M.–8 P.M.), which has men's and women's gear and equipment for rent. For off-season visitors, there is also bike rental here.

HOTELS

Vail and the surrounding villages are home to some world-class hotels that each has its own unique appeal, depending on location to the slopes and other natural amenities.

The Westin Riverfront Resort & Spa at Beaver Creek Mountain (126 Riverfront Ln., 970/790-6000, www.westinriverfront-beavercreek.com, $879–2,299) has over 200 luxurious rooms and suites that are conveniently located next door to the **Riverfront Gondola,** which operates during the winter to get them onto Beaver Creek Mountain. Check into the **Spa Anjali** (126 Riverfront Ln., 970/790-3020, http://spaanjali.com) for a day of relaxation or enjoy breathtaking mountain views from the outdoor pool. Dine at **Cima** (126 Riverfront Ln., 970/790-5500, www.

westinriverfrontbeavercreek.com, Mon.–Sat. breakfast 7 A.M.–10:30 A.M., lunch 11:30 A.M.–2:30 P.M., happy hour 2:30–6 P.M., dinner 6–9:30 P.M., Sun. brunch 9 A.M.–2:30 P.M., dinner 6–9:30 P.M.; note that hours change seasonally so always call ahead to verify) for any meal of the day, and if the weather is accommodating, eat out on the terrace near one of the firepits.

Four Seasons Resort Vail (1 Vail Rd., 970/477-8600, www.fourseasons.com/vail, $560–6,275) has 121 rooms and suites and 10 residential units that are also rented out. In summer, mountain bike rental is available here and there is easy access to local hiking trails. In winter, take advantage of the ski concierge and shuttles. Year round, enjoy the heated outdoor pool on site. With two restaurants, a fireside lounge, and room service, you never have to leave the property to eat.

The Arrabelle at Vail Square (675 Lionshead Pl., 970/754-7777, http://arrabelle.rockresorts.com, $600–1,200 for rooms or suites) is on the Vail Square in Lionshead. The Arrabelle has 62 rooms and 25 one-to-five-bedroom condominiums, and it is walking distance from shops, restaurants, and an ice skating rink.

Also in Lionshead is the **Antlers at Vail** (680 W. Lionshead Pl., 970/476-2471 or 800/843-8245, www.antlersvail.com) with 87 condominiums just steps from the **Vail Gondola** (660 W. Lionshead Pl., Vail, www.vail.com, 970/476-9090, hours change seasonally). The rates here vary tremendously depending on the time of year—the same studio/one bath that goes for $240 per night in the summer and early fall fetches $785 per night during the winter holidays. A larger unit with four bedrooms and four baths during the holidays goes for $2,725 per night.

A great resource for accommodations is www.vail.net, where you can check "Last Minute Specials" and "Lodging Specials." Also, plan ahead because there are advance discounts offered at many hotels, especially in the off-season (late spring through early fall).

PRACTICALITIES
Tourism Office
Stop by or contact the **Vail Valley Partnership Chamber and Tourism Bureau** (101 Fawcett Rd., Ste. 240, Avon, 970/476-1000, www.visitvailvalley.com, Mon.–Fri. 8 A.M.–5 P.M.) with questions about Vail and the entire Eagle County corridor. It's about a 10-minute drive on the highway from downtown Vail.

Media
The *Vail Daily* (www.vaildaily.com) is the main newspaper here, with plenty of tips and coupons for discounts. It also has more in-depth articles with reviews of local restaurants.

Getting There
From Denver, just hop on I-70 and head west for 120 miles. In the winter, the traffic and road conditions can be dicey, sometimes making the two-hour drive take much longer. Check in at www.cotrip.org or dial 511 for the latest road conditions.

The **Vail/Eagle County Airport** (219 Eldon Wilson Dr., Gypsum, 970/524-9490 or 877/204-7881, www.eaglecounty.us/airport) is a 30-minute drive from Vail and has year-round service from major airlines that fly in from around the country. There are several car rental agencies based at the airport.

From Denver International Airport, **Colorado Mountain Express** (970/926-9800 or 800/525-6363, www.coloradomountain-express.com) provides shuttle service to the Vail Valley. There is service from downtown Denver.

Getting Around
The **ECO Transit System** (970/328-3520, www.eaglecounty.us) has bus service that serves the greater Vail Valley. There is a good bike trail system, too, which is quite scenic.

Fort Collins

North of Denver by about 60 miles is the college town of Fort Collins. As the home of the Colorado State University campus, and positioned close to the foothills, Fort Collins can seem a bit like Boulder. Yet it is unique in that the university was founded as an agricultural college and the city's roots are in agriculture, specifically sugar beets. The fourth-largest city in Colorado, Fort Collins has consistently been named as one of the best places to live in the United States by *Money* Magazine.

SIGHTS
Colorado State University
Opened in 1879 as the Colorado Agricultural College, Colorado State University is the flagship of the state university system. The school may be best known today for its veterinary medicine degree, though it has doctoral degrees in 40 fields of study. If you can time your visit right, you will be able to see the campus's **Trial Gardens** (www.flowertrials.colostate.edu) in full bloom. Between May and October, this display shows off the college's horticultural research.

The campus's **Oval** is a large green space surrounded by American elm trees in the center of the campus surrounded by American elm trees and shows off the historic buildings of the school. It's more than just a favorite gathering place for students—President Barack Obama gave a 2008 campaign speech here.

The **Curfman Gallery** (Lory Student Center, www.curfman.colostate.edu, Mon.–Thurs.

9 A.M.–9 P.M., Fri. 9 A.M.–9:30 P.M., Sat. noon–4 P.M.) shows off local artists' work, as well as that of national and international artists. **The University Center for the Arts** (1400 Remington St., www.colostate.edu) in the old high school houses performance spaces and two museums, the **University Art Museum** (1400 Remington St., Ft. Collins, 970/491-1989, www.artmuseum.colostate.edu, Tues.–Sat. 11 A.M.–7 P.M., closed Sun.–Mon.) and the **Avenir Museum of Design and Merchandising** (216 E. Lake St., Ft. Collins, 970/491-6648, www.dm.cahs.colostate.edu, Mon.–Wed. 11 A.M.–6 P.M., Thurs. 11 A.M.–8 P.M., Fri. 11 A.M.–6 P.M., closed Sat.–Sun.).

Fort Collins Museum of Art

In a historic post office building in the city's charming Old Town area is the Fort Collins Museum of Art (201 S. College Ave., 970/482-2787, http://ftmca.org, Wed.–Fri.,

10 A.M.–5 P.M., Sat.–Sun. noon–5 P.M., closed Mon. and Tues., $3–6), which hosts an interesting variety of shows throughout each year. Past exhibits have included works by Marc Chagall, Ansel Adams, local artists, and themed group shows. Just outside of the building on the Oak Street Plaza is a public art sculpture, "Confluence," by artist Lawrence Argent, who also created the "I See What You Mean" (aka The Big Blue Bear) sculpture in Denver.

◖ Old Town

If you have ever been to and liked Disneyland's Main Street, U.S.A., then you are going to love Fort Collins, because the theme park was modeled on this downtown. The Old Town section (www.downtownfortcollins.com) is made up of 23 historic buildings, enhanced by a broad and well-landscaped College Avenue in the middle of it, with public art and fountains alongside

A vintage trolley car runs through downtown Fort Collins.

restaurant patios. Shops, galleries, a hotel, a museum, and brewpubs can all be found here. Wait, what was that about restaurants? Yes, there are over 80 restaurants in this historic district. Speaking of historic, there is even a historic trolley car to ride and see the historic homes that lie just to the west of downtown.

RESTAURANTS

Much like Denver, Fort Collins has developed a large and reputable brewery community, with a variety of brewpubs to choose from—for touring or just having a drink. **New Belgium Brewing Company, Inc.** (500 Linden St., 970/221-0524, www.newbelgium.com, Tues.– Sat. 10 A.M.–6 P.M., closed Mon. and Tues.) is home of the Fat Tire ale. Stop in for a sip or reserve a spot on a tour. **Odell Brewing Company** (800 Lincoln St., 970/498-9070, www.odell-brewing.com, taproom only Mon.–Thurs. 11 A.M.–6 P.M., Fri.–Sat. 11 A.M.–7 P.M.; free tours Mon.–Sat. 1 P.M., 2 P.M., and 3 P.M.) has award-winning beers (India Pale Ale anyone?) available for sampling. If you want a bite to eat with your beer, go to **Coopersmith's Pub & Brewing** (5 Old Town Square, 970/498-0483, http://coopersmithspub.com, Sun.–Thurs. 11 A.M.–11 P.M., Fri.–Sat. 11 A.M.–midnight, $8–20), where they have a pub, billiards, and brewery tours by appointment.

Much like the legacy of John Elway in Denver, former Colorado State University Rams' football coach Sonny Lubick is a local legend, celebrity, and namesake restaurant owner. **Sonny Lubick Steakhouse** (115 S. College Ave., 970/484-9200, www.sonnylubicksteahouse.com, Mon.–Thurs. 4–10 P.M., Fri.–Sat. 11 A.M.–midnight, Sun. 4–10 P.M., $12–46) draws people in the mood for an upscale steak dinner—or those interested in its connection to the local football team.

The **Silver Grill Café** (218 Walnut St., 970/484-4656, www.silvergrill.com, daily 6:30 A.M.–2 P.M., $4–9) is a local favorite for hearty and affordable breakfasts that start with giant cinnamon rolls. Also on the menu are omelets, breakfast burritos, steak and eggs, biscuits and gravy, and more.

Family owned since 1979 is **Bisetti's Ristorante** (120 S. College Ave., 970/493-0086, www.bisettis.com, Sun.–Thurs. 11 A.M.–9 P.M., Fri.–Sat. 11 A.M.–10 P.M., $12–18), with traditional Italian entrées and excellent service.

NIGHTLIFE

Fort Collins isn't exactly known for its nightlife scene. The **Aggie Theatre** (204 S. College Ave., 970/482-8300, www.aggietheatre.com) is a tiny venue with big-name acts, such as Reverend Horton Heat and Blues Traveler. It's a college-town crowd here.

For a more sophisticated experience, head over to **Ace Gillett's Lounge** (239 S. College Ave., 970/449-4797, www.acegilletts.com, Mon.–Sat. 4 P.M.–2 A.M., Sun. 4 P.M.–midnight) in (or more like under) the **Armstrong Hotel** (970/484-3883, www.thearmstronghotel.com), where there is music four nights a week, and fine dining and cocktails every night.

Elliot's Martini Bar (234 Linden St., 970/472-9802, http://elliotsmartinibar.com, Mon.–Sat. 4:30 P.M.–2 A.M., Sun. 8 P.M.–2 A.M.) has a seasonally changing menu of classic and original martinis...and "dessertinis." "Mikhail's Cousin is in Town" is one of the bar's creative martinis, and "Naked in the Woods" is a dessertini.

RECREATION

When it comes to enjoying the great outdoors, there is something for every age, ability, and interest level—from river rafting to hot air ballooning and much more in between.

Find a trail for bicycling, walking, jogging, or even skating at www.fcgov.com, where you can learn which trails go through town or along

Downtown Fort Collins has lots of shops and restaurants.

creeks, and what their distances are. A favorite local hiking trail is **Greyrock Mountain Trail** (www.fs.fed.us/r2/arnf), which is about a 20-mile drive outside of town in the **Arapaho and Roosevelt National Forests and Pawnee National Grassland** area. The hike is seven miles round-trip and considered moderate to strenuous. Get there early as this popular trail's parking lot fills up fast.

The Outdoor Recreation tab on the Fort Collins Convention & Visitors Bureau website (www.visitftcollins.com) provides links to several white-water rafting companies that service the Poudre River. Here you will also find information about fly-fishing, horseback riding, the three different options for hot air ballooning, and activities for every season in and around Fort Collins.

SHOPS

The shops in Old Town are a fun mix of outdoor gear, city hipsters, and local crafts. And a handful of the shops here also have locations in Denver.

For fashion lovers, stop by **Kansas City Kitty** (136 N. College Ave, 970/482-5845, www.kckitty.com, Mon.–Fri. 11 A.M.–6 P.M., Sat. 11 A.M.–7 P.M., Sun. noon–5 P.M.) and check out everything, from Japanese denim brand One Green Elephant to local designers and Kansas City Kitty's own line. **Cira Ltd.** (21 Old Town Square, 970/494-0410, Mon.–Thurs. 10 A.M.–8 P.M., Fri.–Sat. 10 A.M.–9 P.M., Sun. 11 A.M.–7 P.M.) has fashions that appeal to college-age women who like to dress up on weekends in something sheer and slinky. **Solemates** (172 N. College Ave., 970/472-1460, http://solematesinc.com, Mon.–Sat. 10 A.M.–7 P.M., Sun. noon–5 P.M.) has shoe lovers covered with the latest in heels, wedges, sandals, and boots from designers such as Kate Spade, Michael Kors, Frye, Diane von Furstenberg, and more. Of course, the perfect shoes need a matching handbag, and Solemates also sells accessories.

The Cupboard (152 S. College Ave., 970/493-8585, http://thecupboard.net, Mon.–Fri. 9:30 A.M.–8 P.M., Sat. 9:30 A.M.–6 P.M., Sun. noon–5 P.M.) is a large kitchen supply shop where you can sign up for cooking lessons with local chefs.

Yes, it appears there are a lot of tchotchkes at **Trimble Court Artisans** (118 Trimble Ct., 970/221-0051, www.trimblecourt.com, Mon.–Sat. 10 A.M.–8 P.M., Sun. noon–6 P.M.), but they are the wares of local artists and craftspeople. The shop is filled to the brim with pottery, photography, paintings, and all kinds of knick-knacks for the home.

HOTELS

There is a limited supply of non-chain lodging in Fort Collins. The **Armstrong Hotel** (259 S. College Ave., 970/484-3883, www.thearmstronghotel.com, $129–220) is a renovated historic hotel in Old Town with 43 rooms and suites that have an eclectic mix of vintage and modern furnishings, set off by bright colors on the walls and in other accents. The central location makes it easy to walk to shops, restaurants, and the campus.

The other options for locally owned lodgings in this central location are bed-and-breakfasts. The **Inn at City Park** (1734 W. Mountain Ave., 970/672-4725, www.innatcitypark.com, $125–175) is in a residential neighborhood about a mile from Old Town in a country-like setting.

The **Edwards House Bed & Breakfast** (402 W. Mountain Ave., 970/493-9191, http://edwardshouse.com, $99–175) has eight rooms named after people who were significant to the history of Fort Collins.

PRACTICALITIES
Tourist Office

The **Fort Collins Convention & Visitors Bureau** is located at 19 Old Town Square, and can be reached at 970/232-3840 or 800/274-3678 (Mon.–Fri. 8:30 A.M.–5 P.M., Sat.–Sun. 11 A.M.–5 P.M.). The bureau's website (www.visitftcollins.com) has a current events calendar and you can request a free guide to the area, as well.

Media

The Rocky Mountain Collegian (www.collegian.com) is a student-run daily or weekly newspaper available online and in print.

Getting There

From Denver, take I-25 north for 60 miles to the exits for Fort Collins and follow them west to your specific destination. From Denver International Airport, there is **Super Shuttle** (970/482-0505, www.supershuttle.com) service to Fort Collins, specifically the Colorado State University campus and a few hotels in the area.

Getting Around

Within Fort Collins, there is **Transfort Bus Service** (970/221-6620, www.fcgov.com/transfort) to get around town. The **Fort Collins Bike Library** (13 Old Town Sq., Ft. Collins, 970/419-1050 and 222 La Porte Ave., Ft. Collins, 970/221-2453, www.fcbikelibrary.org, seasonal hours Thurs. 10 A.M.–3 P.M., Fri.–Sun. 10 A.M.–5 P.M., call ahead for fall and winter hours) provides bike rental around town for a reasonable fee. The "library" also provides maps for self-guided, themed tours around Fort Collins. More of a tourist attraction than real transportation that takes you from one destination to another is the **Fort Collins Municipal Railway**'s trolley car (1801 W. Mountain Ave., Ft. Collins, 970/224-5372, www.fortnet.org/trolley, May–Sept. Sat.–Sun. noon–5 P.M., closed Oct.–April). The antique trolley does a three-mile round-trip between downtown and City Park on weekends in the summer months.

VICINTY OF FORT COLLINS
◀ The Great Stupa
of Dharmakaya

The **Shambhala Mountain Center** (4921 County Rd., Ste. 68-C, 970/881-2184, www.shambhalamountain.org) is not just for Buddhists or followers of the Dalai Lama, but anyone curious about religious architecture. The Great Stupa of Dharmakaya is one of the largest examples of sacred Buddhist architecture in North America, and it's open to the public. There are programs offered year-round here, including yoga and massage, as well as access to recreational activities in nearby wilderness areas. The greater Poudre Canyon and Red Feather Lakes area offers a huge variety of outdoor activities, such as horseback riding, canoeing, river rafting, and fishing, or an opportunity to relax and watch the sunset while the abundant wildlife wanders by.

There is pretty much one major attraction here, and it's the Great Stupa of Dharmakaya, which was consecrated in a 10-day ceremony in 2001. The Buddhist shrine houses a very large gold statue of Buddha. The word "stupa" refers to the outer 108-foot-tall building, which is symbolically painted white and other bright colors to symbolize the body of the Buddha. All around the building are other statues and "mandalas," or patterns that represent the universe. Unlike typical stupas that are sealed shut, this one allows public visitation on the first floor, where pillows and chairs are available for peaceful meditation. The stupa holds the ashes of Chogyam Trungpa Rinpoche, a Tibetan exile who founded the Naropa University in Boulder and the Rocky Mountain Shambhala Center where the shrine now sits. Past visitors have included the Dalai Lama and rock star Sting.

The Great Stupa of Dharmakaya is open to visitors daily, 9 A.M.–6 P.M., but is sometimes closed for special events. Public tours are available on weekends at 2 P.M., and group tours can be arranged in advance. An $8–10 donation is suggested for visiting the stupa. Once you have parked, head to the visitors center to register and get a map. It's at least a 20-minute hike up a gravel path to the stupa at more than 8,000 feet above sea level, so be sure to bring water and wear comfortable shoes and sun protection.

Because the Shambhala Mountain Center is used for many large conferences, its dining facilities are set up to accommodate hundreds of people at one sitting. There are two indoor dining halls, an outdoor dining tent, and picnic tables outside. Three meals per day are included with lodging. If you're just visiting for the day, lunch is served 12:30–1:30 P.M. for $10 per person.

The 500-acre Shambhala Mountain Center is mostly wilderness, with 12 miles of hiking trails, a local garden, and access to the activities at nearby Red Feather Lakes. The center offers a number of programs, mostly in the summer, for children and those interested in yoga, meditation, Buddhism, and more.

The center is adjacent to the **Red Feather Lakes, Roosevelt National Forest,** and **La Poudre River,** where white-water river rafting, horseback riding, and fly-fishing are all available for experts or beginners. The Shambhala Mountain Center recommends the website www.coloradomountainvacation.com to find links to outfitters nearby.

The range of lodging available at the Shambhala Mountain Center goes from tents to luxurious suites, with tents adding 350 spaces in summer.

From June through September, **platform tents** can be rented for $69 (double) to $79 (single) per night. The tents are scattered about the property, some close to the dining halls and gift shop, others higher up in the trees and a bit of a walk. Guests must use shared public restrooms while staying in the tents. **Red Feather Lodge** is a group of four cabins with a shared bathhouse that is removed from the core of the community, but still within walking distance of the dining and meeting facilities. Rates are $69–90, depending on the cabin—one called Earth is set up like a dormitory, and the others have five double rooms each. The rooms at **Ridgen Lodge** and **Shambhala Lodge** are more like traditional hotel rooms, with private baths in some rooms (but not all), desks, public phones, and Internet access. Rates start at $99 and go up to $199.

The center is a little more than a two-hour drive northwest from Denver. If you are flying in to Denver International Airport, shuttle service is available, but advance reservations are required for the **Shamrock Airport Express** (970/482-0505, www.rideshamrock.com), which drops you off at the Fort Collins Hilton (where the Shambhala Shuttle will pick you up). The **Shambhala Shuttle** (970/881-2184, ext. 298, smcshuttle@shambhalamountain.org) costs $80 (round-trip) and requires a minimum two weeks' advance reservation and careful timing for arrival and departure.

BACKGROUND

The Setting

As the Mile-High City, Denver is automatically associated with its elevation and those hundreds of mountain peaks to the west. But the city is located on the high plains to the east, about 12 miles east of the foothills of the Rocky Mountains. This eastern expanse is called the Front Range of the Rockies.

Denver is a little bit of both mountains and plains, and the core neighborhoods vary greatly from floodplains to hills overlooking the city and everything in between.

Shaped by its location as a gateway city to the towns and beauty that lie to the west in the Rocky Mountains and as a hub of the entire region, Denver has a natural appeal all its own.

GEOGRAPHY AND CLIMATE

The word "plains" suggests flatland or lowland, but in reality, the land is more dynamic than that, with the plains east of Denver at an even higher elevation. This actually causes the waters of Cherry Creek to flow northwest, unlike rivers that run south and east from the mountains. From a different perspective, Denver is at the western edge of the plains, not the eastern side of the mountains.

Denver is not a lush city, despite the waterways running through it and numerous reservoirs on the outskirts of the city. This is a high desert climate, with a history of minimal precipitation and relying on irrigation. The average annual rainfall in Denver is 15.47 inches, and average annual snowfall is 59.6 inches. The summers are dry and can be quite hot—though statistics put the average high at 88.1°F in July, it frequently climbs into the 100s. Denver has more annual days of sunshine than coastal places like San Diego, and typically, a couple inches of snowfall will melt off within a few days. Winters can be quite chilly, with average January lows at 16.9°F, but snowfall varies significantly: Some years, there's little snow all season, but every few years, it seems the city is paralyzed by a blizzard.

Because those blizzards garner a lot of national headlines, people mistakenly believe that Denver has such severe storms every winter. It's a paradox for officials: Because such snowstorms are unusual, they are not adequately prepared with enough plows and staff, yet the city does need to be prepared for such emergencies. It can be bad publicity for the city, but is usually good news for the ski resorts.

ENVIRONMENTAL ISSUES

Growth is a double-edged sword for Denver, and always has been, resulting in two prominent environmental issues: air pollution and water use.

Since the city's earliest days, there have been struggles to divert enough clean water to supply the city—and now the greater metro area, which consists of seven counties. There needs to first be a certain percentage of precipitation at the highest points in the mountains, where rivers and streams are fed by rain and snow each year. Most of the rivers actually head west from the Continental Divide, and what is flowing east doesn't simply end in Denver, but keeps heading south through other parched

states to the distant ocean. One source of water is brought "uphill" over the Continental Divide to provide water to Denver and its suburbs. Water laws and rights are complicated issues that have become more prominent during drought years, such as 2002. That was the year that Denver Water began mandatory water-use rules and even created water "police" who fined people for watering their grass at the wrong time. The strict, hit-them-in-the-wallet restrictions did decrease water use by billions of gallons, but as growth continues along with the naturally arid conditions, conservation efforts are an ongoing part of life in Denver.

While taking fewer showers or living with a yellow lawn turned out to be acceptable conservation measures for residents, helping to reduce air pollution and the city's notorious "brown cloud" is another challenge.

Once upon a time, Denver had a streetcar system that was done away with to make way for the almighty automobile. As the population boomed between 1960 and 1980, the number of cars on the freshly built highways and roads also exploded. It wasn't until the 1980s that auto emission tests became mandatory here. Cars weren't the only source contributing to the smog (or "smaze," as some called it), and trash burning was prohibited. Coal-burning power plants have had to cut their emissions and wood-burning fireplaces are nearly obsolete, with restrictions on days that they can be used. The fact that Denver lies in a river basin between the plains and the mountains means that the fine particles of pollution—whether from road sand or carbon monoxide emissions or smoke—are going to settle in the air in this low spot.

The brown cloud is not gone, and it can obscure views from the city or of the city itself when approaching it, but there is more and more emphasis on alternative transportation in Denver and beyond to possibly reduce the haze and pollution. Residents and visitors alike

FLOODS AND FIRE

For all the talk of Denver being so arid, water has dramatically shaped the city.

As the first settlements at the confluence of Cherry Creek and the Platte River were being built, Native Americans warned the white men that flooding was a risk. But before they could be proved right, a fire broke out in 1863, when drunken revelers knocked over a lamp. The simple wood-frame structures were engulfed in flames and most of the city's business district was lost. Though precious supplies were gone, the buildings were quickly rebuilt–this time with brick.

Brick, however, was no help a year later, when Cherry Creek became a raging torrent of water after heavy spring rains. Lives, buildings, livestock, and much more were lost, but people kept rebuilding, even in the floodplain. There were many more floods until the 1950s, when the Army Corps of Engineers built the Cherry Creek Dam.

In 1965, the relatively tame South Platte River became swollen with rainwater and crashed through bridges and property, causing $300 million in damage. The floodwaters were full of the refuse that was freely dumped in the river, including items as big as refrigerators. This disaster led to the Platte Redevelopment Committee, which over the next decade turned the waterways into a greenbelt and a growing source of civic pride.

are encouraged to ride bikes, take the light rail trains or buses, or simply walk instead of driving. The city often struggles to stay in compliance with Environmental Protection Agency standards and has to keep finding ways to reduce air pollution.

History

To learn Denver's history is to wonder how there came to be a city in this place at all.

The Laramie Treaty of 1851 had conceded this land to the Arapaho and Cheyenne tribes, but that agreement was pretty much ignored when prospectors found flecks of gold in the Platte River in 1858. Others had come through this stretch before, only to categorize it as a "desolate wasteland" and keep on going. Though there wasn't really a fortune to be found in the waters near the confluence of the Cherry Creek and the Platte River, prospectors set up their town on the banks. General William Larimer of Kansas put some sticks on a nearby hill to make his claim, which later became Denver.

Denver is that rare city that was not built up along a road, railroad, or navigable body water. There were initially three towns, but in 1859, a shared barrel of whiskey was all it took for the two smaller towns to be convinced to become part of Denver. Even the naming of the city was a bit of a bumble, when local leaders strove to impress territorial governor James Denver, who lived in Kansas, by naming the city after him, but he had already retired and never came to Denver.

As the first Denver City was established with cabins and tents set up at what is now Confluence Park, Native Americans were edged out—often in violent and bloody confrontations. There is evidence that people had used the same spot as an ancient hunting ground as many as 11,000 years ago. The new settlers and members of the Cheyenne and Arapaho tribes clashed, and a new treaty was drawn up in 1861 that gave Denver to the United States.

In those early years, Denver was the "Wild

AFRICAN AMERICAN HISTORY IN DENVER

Certainly African Americans who came to Denver in the early days were subject to racism, segregation, and violence like that seen in other parts of the country, but many lived somewhat prosperous lives and had a lasting impact on the city and state.

In the 1860s, sons of abolitionist Frederick Douglass were part of the effort to successfully oppose Colorado statehood on the grounds that the proposed constitution denied African Americans the right to vote.

Justina L. Ford was the first female African American doctor licensed to practice in Colorado, and even as late as the 1950s, was the only female African American doctor in the state.

Barney Ford was a fugitive slave when he came to Denver in the 1860s and began to build a small business empire that included a barbershop, restaurant, and hotel. His financial success helped make him a prominent advocate for African American rights in Denver. A stained-glass portrait of Mr. Ford can be seen in the Colorado State Capitol Building, and there is the Barney Ford House Museum in Breckenridge, Colorado.

West," with saloons, brothels, and lawlessness. Once gold was found in the mountains, the town was briefly left practically deserted. But rather than fold up, the city established itself as a supply center for the thousands flocking to the newest gold discoveries in the nearby mountains, and the mountains' harsh winters sometimes drove people to the more hospitable Denver weather. The population in Denver was only 3,500 in 1866, one year before it was named the state capital. The town weathered devastating fires and floods, but there were always those optimists who saw the potential for Denver to be more than a dusty frontier town.

It was a shock then, when Cheyenne, Wyoming, 100 miles north, was selected to be a stop on the transcontinental railroad. In other towns, the loss of the railroad may have been the last word, and the place could have easily become a ghost town. Instead, a spur was built to the railroad, and this saved Denver. With new millionaires from the mining boom ready to flaunt their wealth, mansions, elegant hotels, and opera houses were built, making Denver more attractive to tourists, businesses, and people who wanted to relocate. The railroad lines were key to bringing all those people, as well as freight, to the city.

The city continued to find ways to reinvent itself, as industries such as mining, ranching, and agriculture, then the federal government, developed in the area. The cow town reputation came about during the many years that huge stockyards did a lot of business not far from downtown. By inviting the federal government to set up bases and weapons-making facilities, Denver gained importance nationally as well as regionally.

DENVER'S HISTORIC BUILDINGS PRESERVED

By the 1960s, there was growing concern among some Denverites about the demolition of many historic homes, buildings, and whole neighborhoods. The protests were led in large part by Dana Crawford and other like-minded women, such as future congresswoman Patricia Schroeder, who took on developers with plans to tear down all of Larimer Square. The Daniels and Fisher Tower on 16th Street was also saved, but many other buildings were lost to the wrecking ball. The original town of Auraria, founded at the same time as Denver and eventually incorporated into the city, was demolished even though it was a Latino enclave. The land—about 20 city blocks—was used to make way for the Auraria college campus.

In 1970, the organization Historic Denver was formed and the Molly Brown House was successfully saved and restored. It was just the first of many important preservation projects

in Denver, and the stories of many of those salvaged edifices are found in Historic Denver's series of small paperback books. The books serve as neighborhood guides or thematic tours of landmarks such as churches. Places like the Molly Brown House Museum and the Colorado History Museum sell the books, or they can be found at www.historicdenver.org.

Another preservationist managed to save that most valuable asset: the mountain view. Helen Millet Arndt, founder of the Denver Landmark Preservation Committee, conducted a survey that revealed that locals thought the mountain backdrop was what made their city special. In 1968, city council passed the Mountain View Preservation ordinance, thanks to Arndt and her supporters. This has prevented building that might obstruct the mountain view from the state capitol and numerous parks.

Government

When Denver was selected over New York City to be the host for the 2008 Democratic National Convention (100 years after first hosting the convention), it was as if the city was finally being recognized as sophisticated and full of potential. The West itself has been emerging as a significant force in national elections, and the "Mile-High City" is positioned as the hub of this relatively new political power region.

A lot changed since Denver hosted the Democratic National Convention in 1908, but then again, not so much. Back then, civic leaders and citizens were eager to show the world just how cosmopolitan the "Queen City" was.

Never mind that the state and many surrounding Western states have long been conservative strongholds; Colorado's governors and Denver's mayors have alternated between Republicans and Democrats.

Denver's first mayor was John C. Moore

(1859–1861), back when Denver was part of the Jefferson Territory. Charles A. Cook was elected mayor in 1861, after the area became Colorado Territory. As the city grew, some mayors were more effective and memorable than others at improving local services and infrastructure. In 1904, Robert W. Speer was elected mayor for the first time (he was elected again in 1916) and established the City Beautiful programs, the beginning of transforming an often dirty and rough town that had caused at least one visitor to remark that it was more "plain than Queenly" (in reference to the city's nickname, Queen City of the Plains). Speer's beautification efforts remain some of the city's jewels today—-the tree-lined Cherry Creek, Civic Center Park, improved city parks, and increased acreage of the parks.

A rather unseemly period in Denver's mayoral past was during the connection between

MAYORS AND BEER

There might be a connection between serving the fine citizens of the Mile-High City a nice cold ale and getting yourself elected to the city's highest office.

Joseph E. Bates, who served two terms as Denver's mayor from 1872 to 1873, and again from 1885 to 1887, also owned the Denver City Brewing Company.

John W. Hickenlooper was a co-founder of the Wynkoop Brewing Company and was first elected mayor in 2003, then again to a second term in 2007. The Denver City Brewing Company is long gone, but the Wynkoop is open seven days a week and sometimes Governor Hickenlooper still stops by.

Benjamin F. Stapleton, who was elected to his first term in 1923, and the Ku Klux Klan. At the time, many prominent citizens were affiliated with the Klan, and Stapleton aligned himself with them to gain votes. Stapleton's popularity outlived the prominence of the Klan, though, and he was re-elected many times, even after abandoning the group's leaders.

In the 1980s, Denver was hit hard by the oil bust, and then some setbacks for high-tech companies. In the 1990s, Denver began to pull itself back up by the bootstraps and find its niche, thanks in part to the vision of its mayors.

Denver's first Latino mayor, Federico Pena, was sworn in to office in 1983. Pena not only weathered the fiscal storms of the era, but also found ways to reinvest in the city; he initiated the new Denver International Airport plans and a major league baseball team. Wellington Webb became Denver's first African American mayor in 1991, and during two terms, he further shaped the city into what it is today, with expansion of the park system and completion of the airport.

Through the 1990s, old warehouses became lofts and art galleries, historic buildings were transformed into charming blocks of sophisticated shops and restaurants, and Coors Field was built for the Colorado Rockies baseball team. Denver became more appealing and growth soared.

As lower downtown (LoDo) was on the cusp of becoming a draw, onetime geologist John W. Hickenlooper co-founded the Wynkoop Brewing Company across from Union Station. Years later, he raised his public profile when he fought over the naming of the new football stadium, insisting that "Mile High" remain part of the name even when naming rights were sold to the highest bidder. He became Denver's 43rd mayor in 2003, and was part of bringing the Democratic National Convention to the city in 2008. Hickenlooper was elected Governor of Colorado in 2010, and Michael Hancock was elected to be Denver's Mayor in 2011.

Economy

Denver's economic history is one of struggles and reinvention, as the city has weathered dramatic ups and downs through the years.

From the time it was just a tent city of hopeful prospectors, Denver's financial future was uncertain. At that time, the goal was to keep attracting people to the city to build more and spend more, making it bigger and better all the time. Mining quickly turned out to be the first bust for the city, as the gold found near Confluence Park was just placer gold and the real treasures were up in the mountains where Leadville, Central City, and Blackhawk were then founded. Denver transformed into a supply town for the mountain miners and catered to this crowd with saloons and brothels as well as mundane supplies.

After building a spur to the transcontinental railroad line, Denver began to change rapidly—adding hundreds of new citizens daily and bringing the population from less than 5,000 in 1870 to over 35,000 in 1880.

By the late 1800s, Denver was attracting not only new residents, but tourists and new businesses. (Denver also gained a reputation for being healthy, as the dry, thin air helped tuberculosis patients. Sanatoriums were built to care for the thousands who came for a cure—including future mayor Robert Speer.) The city brimmed with pride over one of the earliest telephone systems and electric street light systems, and luxurious mansions and hotels were built to show off the wealth pouring into this evolving frontier town.

By the turn of the 20th century, as gold and silver prices crashed, it became clear that Denver needed a more diverse economy. Instead of booming, Denver began to slowly build an economy reliant on a variety of industries, such as agriculture and manufacturing.

Yet when World War I began, silver was valuable again and long-closed mines were reopened as the precious metal once more provided a boom to the local economy. But the post-war years and the Great Depression hit Denver hard, and it wasn't until state and federal governments provided some relief that things began to turn around for the better.

Next, civic leaders lured the federal government to Denver, with the large affordable tracts of land perfect for army bases and weapons manufacturing. In the next several years, the federal government established Lowry Air Force Base east of the city, Rocky Mountain Arsenal, Fitzsimmons Army Hospital, and many other sites. There was even a shipbuilding plant for the army. The end of the war meant that many of those facilities became useful for research, so the thousands of jobs were not lost.

After the war, Denver went through yet another boom cycle, as soldiers from the local bases and others made the city their home. Between 1945 and 1983, over one million people settled in the metro Denver area. New highways were built to loop the growing suburbs to each other and downtown.

The 1970s were a time of urban renewal and uplift for the downtown skyline, as many oil and gas companies headquartered their offices in Denver. Skyscrapers were added while historic preservationists fought to maintain the integrity of some of the city's original structures.

All the growth wasn't so appealing to everyone. Richard Lamm ran for governor—and won—on an anti-growth platform. Lamm famously (or infamously, depending on your perspective) fought off hosting the 1976 Winter Olympics, citing a concern for how the environment would be affected in the long run. Though the state and Lamm have long been ridiculed for not embracing the opportunity

© STEVE CRECELIUS, COURTESY OF VISIT DENVER

Downtown Denver's 16th Street Mall is one of the city's main tourist attractions.

to host the Olympics, concerns about growth remain today.

By the 1980s, the city went through yet another bust cycle when oil prices fell. Denver had some of the highest office-vacancy rates in the nation, and people left the city in search of work in other states.

Once again, transportation was the answer, this time in the form of the new Denver International Airport that was built and opened in the 1990s. Population has continued to grow, and projections are for more people to be lured to the Mile-High City in the coming years.

In 2008, the Brookings Institute, a Washington DC think tank, released a report stating that Denver is at the center of one of the West's five "mountain mega" regions that will see intense growth in coming decades. The report predicts that the Front Range area will add 2.6 million people over the next 32 years. In essence, the area—with Denver as the hub—is becoming more crowded and more economically and politically significant, and that trend is going to continue.

Beyond the federal scientific research facilities and offices in the Denver metro area, many companies have a strong presence here as well. Colorado has the second-largest aerospace economy in the country, with companies such as Ball Aerospace, Lockheed Martin, and Raytheon all here. Other significant industries include aviation, bioscience, financial services, information technology services, and energy. Various cultural entities in Denver are also a significant part of the modern economy, serving as just one of the qualities that attract tourists to the Mile-High City year-round.

At 150 years old in 2008, Denver celebrated its sesquicentennial and its place as the country's 21st-largest metropolitan area.

To learn more about business and business development in the Denver area, go to the Metro Denver Economic Development Corporation website, www.metrodenver.org.

People and Culture

Though there have been a few moments in history when Denver struggled to just maintain its population, for the most part, the city's growth has increased year after year. In the 1990s, Denver's own population—not including the greater metro area—surpassed 500,000 for the first time. In 2006, the population in Denver was 566,974, a 2.4 percent increase over the 2000 census figures. As of 2010, statistics showed 2.8 million people in the greater metro area that surrounds and includes Denver. That growth is expected to reach close to 3.8 million by 2030.

Since the 1800s, Denver attracted people of many ethnic backgrounds—Italians, Germans, Latinos, African Americans, and many others. While traces of some early immigrant and ethnic communities remain today, Denver is not like Chicago or San Francisco with its distinctive ethnic neighborhoods. Census figures show that in the greater metro area, white and African American populations have decreased slightly, and the Latino population has increased between 2000 and 2006.

People move to Denver for many reasons, but a big one is access to the great outdoors and the mild climate. Even if they don't want to play sports, Denverites enthusiastically support no fewer than eight professional sports teams and other minor league teams, including the Denver Broncos football team, the Colorado Avalanche hockey team, the Denver Nuggets basketball team, and the Colorado Rockies baseball team. This could have something to do with the fact that the population is statistically young, with a median age of 35.5, compared to the national average of 36.4, with slightly more men than women.

Metro Denver is ranked third out of all U.S. states for the percentage of residents with a bachelor's degree or higher. This translates to having one of the most highly educated workforces in the nation, and a higher-than-average household income.

The Arts

When Denver was barely a town of any sort, one of the first businesses was a theater. Denver's cultural landscape has been growing ever since, and in recent years, the arts have all been heavily invested in as a way to make the city more desirable and progressive.

A study by the Colorado Business Committee for the Arts determined that "culture in metro Denver generated $1.46 billion in economic activity in 2009, with 11.2 million people attending cultural events." In other words, culture is big business in Denver, which creates jobs—in 2009, Scientific & Cultural Facilities District organizations employed 8,718 people, an increase of 7 percent from 2007—and generates huge tax revenues: $18.4 million in 2009. A similar study in 2005 also found that for every $1 of cultural spending, there is $1.32 spent at other businesses.

Attendance at cultural events even tops attendance at Denver's biggest sporting events, though certainly a large percentage of people consider sports to be culture, too.

Of course, tourists are an important part of the equation. The Colorado Business Committee for the Arts found that in 2005, 2.4 million people came to Denver to experience the cultural attractions—and spent $334 million to boot.

Culture in Denver is wide-ranging—from

DENVER CELEBRITIES

John Denver is perhaps associated with the Mile-High City more than any other celebrity, thanks to his adopted name (he was born Henry John Deutschendorf Jr. in New Mexico) and most famous song, "Rocky Mountain High," but before his untimely death in 1997, he was a longtime resident of Aspen, Colorado, and never lived in Denver.

There are, however, many well-known people who were either born in Denver, lived here for a time, or made their mark here.

ACTORS

- Tim Allen
- Roseanne Barr
- Don Cheadle
- Douglas Fairbanks
- Pam Grier
- Harold Lloyd
- Hattie McDaniel
- Bill Murray
- Jan-Michael Vincent
- AnnaSophia Robb

ARTISTS AND WRITERS

- Stan Brakhage
- Neal Cassady
- Ted Conover
- Thomas Hornsby Ferril
- Jack Kerouac
- Cleo Parker Robinson
- Vance Kirkland
- Mondo Guerra

SINGERS AND MUSICIANS

- Philip Bailey
- Judy Collins
- Diane Reeves
- Jill Sobule
- India.Arie

POLITICIANS AND MORE

- Madeleine Albright
- Chauncey Billups
- Molly Brown
- John Elway
- Condoleeza Rice

the Colorado Symphony Orchestra to Opera Colorado, from the Colorado Ballet to Cleo Parker Robinson Dance, from the Denver Performing Arts Complex to El Centro Su Teatro, from jazz and blues to indie rock, from funky art galleries to museums designed by world-famous architects, and so much more. The city's public art collection includes approximately 300 works of art on display, and there are over 160 music venues in the Mile-High City—including city-owned Red Rocks Amphitheatre.

The Denver Center for the Performing Arts is a remarkable facility, billing itself as the "multifaceted entertainment hub of the West," with 11 performance venues in a four-block complex. In addition to the theaters, the complex is also home to the National Theatre Conservatory and the National Center for Voice and Speech.

To learn more about arts in Denver, including music, film, public art, literature, and much more, visit www.denvergov.org/artculturefilm, where you'll find over a dozen links to websites with more extensive information on the city's cultural gems.

In addition to the various cultural organizations and sites, there are annual events that

READY FOR MORE CLOSE-UPS

Denver and many other parts of Colorado have appeared in hundreds of films over the years. However, both the city and the state want, rather desperately, to lure more television and movie productions here. The Office of Film Television & Media (formerly the Colorado Film Commission, www.coloradofilm.org) is offering new incentives for those who choose to film here—cold, hard cash in the form of rebates. The city of Denver mentions its "film-friendly" attitude on its website www.denvergov.org/film, which also includes many helpful links to film societies and schools and lists the many economic benefits to being part of the trillion-dollar film industry.

Maybe you've seen Denver in a few well-known films already: Clint Eastwood's *Every Which Way But Loose* (1978), Woody Allen's *Sleeper* (1973), *About Schmidt* (2002) with Jack Nicholson, *Around the World In 80 Days* (1956), *Die Hard 2* (2002) with Bruce Willis, *Dumb and Dumber* (1994) with Jim Carrey, and *10 Things to Do in Denver When You're Dead* (1995) with Andy Garcia.

Although the television show *Dynasty* was about a Denver family, the show was not filmed in Colorado. However, *Perry Mason* was filmed in Denver for a few years.

honor or celebrate aspects of the arts. Doors Open Denver is a free, two-day event with tours of the city's architectural highlights; One Book, One Denver is a sort of citywide book club for which a single book is chosen to be read and discussed in public forums for the year; The Cherry Creek Arts Festival is a summer festival that showcases local and national artists; and the city hosted its first international art biennial in 2010.

WRITERS

Denver is also associated with many famous names—particularly authors. Although in *On the Road,* Jack Kerouac expresses more affection for his Denverite pal, Neal Casssady, than the city itself, his imprint was left on the city where there are now lofts bearing the writer's name. Journalist and poet Eugene Field lived and worked in Denver for just a few years; a statute of the characters Wynken, Blynken, and Nod from his best-known poem is on display in Washington Park and a local library is named after him. Thomas Hornsby Ferril was a Denver native and writer who was named Colorado Poet Laureate in 1979. In 1996, City Park's largest lake was named Ferril Lake in

honor of the man, and his former, two-story Victorian house in Capitol Hill has served as home to a handful of arts organizations, most recently to the Lighthouse Writers Workshop (www.lighthousewriters.org).

POETRY

For a brief time, Denver could afford its own poet laureate. In 2004, Mayor John Hickenlooper appointed the city's first poet laureate. In 2006, Chris Ransick was named Denver's Poet Laureate and he served until 2010, when budget cuts ended the program. April is National Poetry Month and in Denver, there have been local workshops, readings, and other events. The Poetry in Motion program, which partners public transportation with poems, means that on over 800 buses, there are lines of poetry on large signs. Budget cuts have sidelined many of these programs, but there is hope they will return in a better economy.

MUSIC

A more prominent part of Denver's cultural scene is music—from classic to contemporary. The Colorado Symphony Orchestra is the region's only full-time orchestra, with

WALT WHITMAN

Denver has attracted and bred literary greats who have expressed their feelings about the city in their writings. Perhaps none expressed such great adoration as Walt Whitman, who visited in the fall of 1879 and wrote of his newfound love in *Specimen Days in America* (publisher Scott W. London, 1887):

In due time we reach Denver,
which city I fall in love with from
the first, and have that feeling
confirm'd, the longer I stay there.

Whitman also wrote that of all the many cities he had visited east of the Mississippi, Denver was the place where he was rather breathlessly captivated.

...newcomer to Denver as I am, and threading its streets, breathing its air, warm'd by its sunshine, and having what there is of its human as well as aerial ozone flash'd upon me now for only three or four days, I am very much like a man feels sometimes toward certain people he meets with, and warms to, and hardly knows why. I, too, can hardly tell why, but as I enter'd the city in the slight haze of a late September afternoon, and have breath'd its air, and slept well o' nights, and have roam'd or rode leisurely, and watch'd the comers and goers at the hotels, and absorb'd the climatic magnetism of this curiously attractive region, there has steadily grown upon me a feeling of affection for the spot, which, sudden as it is, has become so definite and strong that I must put it on record. So much for my feeling toward the Queen city of the plains and peaks, where she sits in her delicious rare atmosphere, over 5,000 feet above sea-level, irrigated by mountain streams, one way looking east over prairies for a thousand miles, and having the other westward, in constant view by day draped in their violet haze mountaintops innumerable.

many of their concerts held at Denver's Boettcher Concert Hall; Opera Colorado features three operas each season at the splendid Ellie Caulkins Opera House; from the 1920s through the 1950s, Denver's Five Points neighborhood was considered the "Jazz mecca" of the American West and legendary performers like Billie Holliday and Duke Ellington performed here. Today, Denver has several hip jazz clubs and the annual Five Points Jazz & Blues Festival captures the best of then and now. Beyond these venerable events, there are music festivals just getting a toehold, such as the Mile High Music Festival, with several stages and superstar bands, and the Denver Day of Rock, which is a multi-stage event. Of course, on any night of the week, there is live music playing at some club or bar in Denver to suit any musical preference.

ESSENTIALS

Getting There and Around

AIRPORT

It's hard to believe, but **Denver International Airport** (DIA, 303/342-2000, www.flydenver. com) is the largest international airport in the country in physical size, and the fourth-largest international airport in the world in physical size. Denver International Airport opened in 1995 to a combination of fanfare and ridicule (that state-of-the-art baggage system never did work), but its distinctive white-peaked roof has become a symbol of the city—and copied in smaller versions. The airport is 25 miles from downtown Denver, and like most airports these days, it's a mall of sorts, too (look for Tamales by La Casita and Dazbog Coffee). In addition to the shops and restaurants, the airport offers free Wi-Fi (call 800/986-2703 for technical support) and has a U.S. Post Office (Level 6, Jeppesen Terminal, closed Sun.), a USO Center (303/342-6876), a Jewish and Christian Interfaith Chapel, and an Islamic Masjid, all open 24 hours per day. Security wait lines can be miserable; try the line leading to Concourse A, then take the elevator to the trains to reach other concourses. Starting in 2012, the airport began a multi-million dollar redevelopment project to

COURTESY OF VISIT DENVER

The architecture of the Denver International Airport echoes the mountain peaks in the distance.

include a Westin hotel on site and light rail train service from the airport. The improvements are scheduled for completion by 2015.

DIA is served by most major domestic airlines; Frontier Airlines (303/371-7000 or 800/432-1359, www.frontierairlines.com) is based in Denver. Southwest Airlines (800/435-9792, www.southwest.com) has provided some good, low airfare competition, especially since United Airlines' (800/864-8331, www.united.com) low-cost carrier, Ted, fizzled and left the market. American Airlines (800/433-7300, www.aa.com) has many flights daily to and from DIA. International airlines that serve DIA include Aeromexico, Air Canada, British Airways, Icelandair, and Lufthansa.

Be sure to note your baggage claim number and location, as there are baggage claim carousels on both sides of the terminal, east and west.

It's typically a $55 flat rate to take a cab to or from DIA to downtown. Bus service is the cheapest transportation at $9 one-way or less for seniors, children, and advance purchases (RTD, 303/299-6000, www.rtd-denver.com). Shuttle vans are available at the airport to take passengers directly to destinations like Vail, Estes Park, and Boulder, and directly to downtown Denver hotels. **Colorado Mountain Express** (970/926-9800 or 800/525-6363, www.coloradomountainexpress.com) goes to Vail, Aspen, Keystone, and other ski towns; **Estes Park Shuttle** (970/586-5151, www.estesparkshuttle.com) costs $85 round-trip from the airport to Estes Park; and **Super Shuttle** (303/370-1300 or 800/258-3826, www.supershuttle.com) offers door-to-door service with discounts for ride shares. Contact the airport's **Ground Transportation Information Office** (Level 5, Jeppesen Terminal, 303/342-4059, daily 6:30 A.M.–11:30 P.M.) for additional information about services.

There are 10 rental car companies based at

DIA and each provides free shuttle service to its rental lot. The rental car agencies also have service counters in the Jeppeson Terminal, Level 5.

There is short- and long-term parking at DIA, and even valet parking for $30 per day. The closest garage parking is $21 per day or $2 per hour, and uncovered parking lots that are still walking distance from the terminal cost $11 per day or $1 per hour. The west-side parking lots seem to fill up faster than the east side. There are cheaper parking lots that require shuttle bus service to reach, and those cost $7 per day or $1 per hour.

TRAIN

Amtrak's California Zephyr (800/872-7245, www.amtrak.com) has arrivals and departures at Union Station. The route includes Emeryville, California; Salt Lake City, Utah; Omaha, Nebraska; and Chicago, Illinois.

Light rail trains (RTD, 303/299-6000, www.rtd-denver.com) that go from suburbs to downtown are packed at peak rush-hour times. There are plans to keep expanding the number of lines available, including providing service to the airport.

BUS

Denver's **Greyhound Bus Station** (1055 19th St., 303/293-6555, www.greyhound.com) is conveniently located downtown, within walking distance from hotels, car rental agencies, local bus depots, and Union Station.

To get around Denver and to and from its suburbs and other Front Range cities, use **RTD** (1600 Blake St., 303/299-6000, www.rtd-denver.com). The main terminal is in LoDo at 16th and Market Streets, where you can pick up schedules for just about every route. RTD provides bus service to and from the airport, Boulder, and many other towns in the greater metro area. City and regional buses are almost always equipped with bike racks in front.

Front Range Express (FREX, 719/636-3739 or 877/425-3739, www.frontrangeexpress.com) provides bus service to and from Colorado Springs, Castle Rock, and Monument south of Denver.

DRIVING

No matter where you are coming from by car, you'll end up on I-70 (east–west across the state) or I-25 (north–south across the state) to get to Denver. The most unpredictable part of the drive can be I-70 in the mountains, where icy roads, traffic accidents, and rock- and snow-slides have all closed the road at one time or another.

There are major car rental agencies at both the airport and downtown. Downtown, you can walk to **Avis** (1900 Broadway, 303/839-1280, www.avis.com, Mon.–Fri. 7 A.M.–6:30 P.M., Sat.–Sun. 7 A.M.–5 P.M.), **Enterprise Rent-A-Car** (351 Broadway, 303/575-0044, www.enterprise.com, Mon.–Fri. 7 A.M.–6 P.M., Sat. 9 A.M.–noon, closed Sun.), and **Budget Rent-A-Car** (1980 Broadway, 303/292-9341, www.budget.com, Mon.–Fri. 7 A.M.–6 P.M., Sat.–Sun. 7 A.M.–4 P.M.).

Like most midsize to large cities, Denver is plagued by gridlock on the highways that circle much of the city. Light rail trains did not do much to alleviate the rush-hour congestion, even though the trains are standing-room-only during rush hour. Fortunately, it is possible to get around the city on foot, bicycle, bus, or light rail, with limited expense and hassle.

Especially when you are doing any winter driving in the mountains, check road conditions first at www.coloradodot.info, or call 511, 303/639-1111, or 877/315-7623.

TAXIS

It's almost impossible to walk out to the curb of any Denver street and hail a cab. If you are downtown, go to the entrance of any hotel and

COURTESY OF VISIT DENVER

Cars head into the Rocky Mountains, just outside of Denver.

there is usually a small fleet of cabs waiting for a fare. Otherwise, you have to call and wait for the taxi to show up.

The most interesting thing to happen with Denver taxis is the transition to hybrid vehicles. **Metro Taxi** (303/333-3333, www.metrotaxidenver.com), the city's largest taxi company, began converting its fleet to hybrid-electric Toyota Prius cars in 2007, and **Yellow Cab** (303/777-7777, www.yellowtrans.com) added some hybrid vehicles in 2008. There is also **Freedom Cab** (303/444-4444, www.freedomcabs.com)—just look for the purple cars.

BIKING

Denver is an increasingly accommodating city for bicyclists, as two-wheeled transportation gets more support as an environmentally friendly alternative to cars. **Denver B-cycle** (http://denver.bcycle.com) debuted in 2010 and allows anyone to rent a bike and ride around the city for a small fee. Many city streets have bicycle lanes, biking paths are common, and city and regional buses (say, going to Boulder) have bike racks on the front so people can pedal to the bus stop, ride, then pedal on home or to the office.

Learn about bicycle ordinances, find bike maps, and get riding tips at www.denvergov.org/bikeprogram, or check out www.bikedenver.org, a bicycling advocacy group's blog. The **Denver Bicycle Touring Club** (www.dbtc.org) organizes group rides for members throughout Denver.

WHEELCHAIR ACCESS

There are five companies that offer wheelchair transportation service from DIA and elsewhere around Denver. RTD's **Access-a-Ride** (303/292-6560, www.rtd-denver.com) is for people who cannot board a wheelchair-equipped bus. Metro and regional RTD buses—including the free shuttles on the 16th Street Mall—are wheelchair accessible. Both

Denver B-cycle lets users rent bikes to get around town.

Metro Taxi (303/333-3333, www.metrotaxidenver.com) and **Yellow Cab** (303/777-7777, www.yellowtrans.com) have wheelchair-accessible vehicles available for passengers. **Dashabout** (800/720-3274) offers service from DIA with two–three days' advance notice; **Mobility Transport Services** (303/295-3900) requires 24-hour notice.

Conduct and Customs

GENERAL ETIQUETTE

New Yorkers often express surprise at how friendly people are in Denver, with total strangers smiling and saying hello as they pass on the street. This is also common when out walking or hiking in the mountains, where it's considered normal behavior for people to greet each other with a simple, "Hi, how's it going?" as they pass one another on a trail. It's a great icebreaker for the next question, "How much farther to the top?"

On busy urban pedestrian and bike paths, it is customary for the faster bicyclist to shout, "On your left!" (or something similar) as they approach slower cyclists or pedestrians from behind. Some paths are designated for only cyclists or pedestrians, and others are shared use.

Denver is more than halfway through a 10-year plan to end homelessness (www.denverroadhome.org). Throughout many popular sights in downtown Denver, such as Civic Center Park, and along the 16th Street Mall, there are often homeless people panhandling. In an effort to decrease this presence and help break the cycle of homelessness, the city has established places for donating money to be used by programs for those in need. Dozens of meters have been installed around downtown into which spare change can be deposited for such programs. The meters are distinguished by their red posts (as opposed to the silver posts of traditional meters) and bring in thousands of dollars annually that help provide services for the homeless. People are encouraged to donate their money there rather than give directly to panhandlers. In 2012, the city council approved a ban on camping in the city as a way to discourage homeless people from staying in city parks.

BUSINESS HOURS

For the most part, Denver shops open at 10 A.M. on weekdays and Saturday and not until noon on Sunday, with closing time anywhere from 5– 7 P.M. There are some exceptions, such as Rockmount Ranch Wear, which opens at the bright-and-early hour of 8 A.M. on weekdays.

Local art galleries tend to be closed on Sunday and Monday, and the Denver Art Museum is closed on Monday. Always call ahead to see if hours have recently changed; you may be pleasantly surprised to find the art gallery of your choice open all day on Monday.

Many Denver restaurants also take Monday off, but again, always call ahead to see if hours have changed. Typical kitchen closing time in Denver restaurants is about 10 P.M., and bars close up by 2 A.M. or earlier. If a restaurant has a bar, there is often a late-night menu to order from. Some bars prefer not to specify their closing times so that they can close up early on a slow night or maybe extend hours on a busier night.

SMOKING

Just like cities in other parts of the country, Denver has banned smoking indoors in public places. The Colorado Clean Indoor Air Act was passed in 2006 and took effect the same year. The Denver City Council has passed more specific ordinances, such as banning smoking outside of hospitals. It is not uncommon to see signs outside of some buildings asking smokers to stand a certain distance from a building entrance or exit. More common is the sight of restaurant and bar patios—or simply sidewalks in front of these establishments—filled with smokers in any kind of weather. The lone exception is cigar bars, such as the Churchill Bar in the Brown Palace Hotel, where cigar smoking is permitted. There are also designated smoking areas inside Denver International Airport.

LEAVE NO TRACE

The city of Denver has a Keep Denver Beautiful plan, which essentially promotes the message to not litter, period—anything from cigarette butts to food wrappers and drink containers. Littering is illegal and fines can add up to $1,000. For further information on this plan or to report littering, call the city's 311 hotline, email them at 311@ci.denver.co.us, or visit www.denvergov.org.

While Denver's laws apply to city streets as well as parks and bike paths, there are additional rules and customs to follow once you set off to explore the mountains.

For starters, always stay on designated trails or pathways to minimize impact on natural areas that make the area so appealing in the first place. You may even see signs that read, "Closed for Restoration" in areas that have been trampled by heavy use. It's also a good idea to stay on these designated trails—whether they are mere dirt footpaths or paved with concrete or asphalt—to prevent getting lost. As people try to explore true wilderness more and more, either by going out of bounds on a ski mountain or breaking their own trail on a summer hike, officials are becoming less patient and understanding because of the high cost of search and rescue. For this same reason, it's a good idea to always let someone know where you are headed when you go out for a run, bike ride, or hike.

Even if you are just going on a short day hike in the foothills, remember to "pack out what you pack in" and don't leave *any* waste. In some places, even city parks in the foothills of Boulder, you will find special garbage cans that are designed to keep animals (particularly bears) out, but otherwise you need to be prepared to carry out all garbage.

Because of the dry conditions, especially along the Front Range, be extremely cautious about making campfires. During intense drought seasons, fires of any kind are banned, so it's best to check with park rangers on the latest conditions and warnings in the specific park you are visiting. If fires are not banned, still use caution and only build a fire in an established campfire ring, being sure to put out the fire completely before leaving.

Wildlife and people interact more and more in the foothill communities where mountain lions, bears, deer, and elk will just show up in backyards and even on busy town streets. This is just a reminder that you should never feed wildlife—in the confines of a national park or in someone's backyard. State and national park visitors centers always have helpful information about how to react when you encounter wildlife, which is species-specific and depends on mating seasons. Use special care if you are with small children or dogs when hiking, as they are easier prey for hungry wildlife.

Wildlife and pets, especially dogs, are not a good mix. Be sure to verify if dogs are even allowed at the park you are visiting and what the leash laws are.

For more information, visit the Leave No Trace Center at www.lnt.org or call 303/442-8222.

Tips for Travelers

WHAT TO TAKE

Denver is as casual as the rest of America these days, so don't worry about bringing your formalwear unless you are coming for a black-tie event. Even the Brown Palace's stately Palace Arms Restaurant has given up its jacket-and-tie policy, though an evening gown and tuxedo would not look out of place in this setting. Jeans, slacks, T-shirts, sandals: It's all worn to church or a four-star restaurant.

Finally, a place to acceptably wear that bolo tie! Denver and a couple of other Western cities are about the only places I've seen officials—governors, mayors, and the like—donning cowboy boots, hats, and decorative bolo ties for work. If you've got one, throw it in the suitcase and drive up to The Fort for a Western dinner like no other.

You can easily buy the basics—hat, sunscreen, sunglasses, good walking or hiking shoes, thermal underwear—needed for any season in every neighborhood. A small backpack or other tote bag is handy to have for carrying extra water, sunscreen, and snacks on sightseeing walks or if you choose to hike in the nearby foothills.

TRAVELING WITH CHILDREN

There are many fun attractions and things to do with young kids in Denver and at the various excursions included in this book, but it's a good idea to ask about age limits at some museums and hotels. For example, the **Kirkland Museum** does not allow any children under the age of 13 with or without an adult, and children ages 13–17 must be accompanied by an adult. While the **Molly Brown House Museum** states that children are welcome, they are asked not to touch *anything,* and it's hardly fun for a toddler. (Grown-ups have to follow the same rules.)

Of course, the **Children's Museum** is

a perfect place to play with kids newborn through age eight, and the **Platte Valley Trolley** ride that makes a stop outside the museum is fun for adults and children. The **Denver Art Museum** has built in a variety of child-friendly activities in its permanent exhibits, as well as a small make-your-own-art area. At the **Denver Museum of Nature and Science,** kids can watch an IMAX movie on the enormous screen, see the stars and planets at the Gates Planetarium, watch volunteers clean off dinosaur bones, step inside replicas of original Native American homes, or pretend to be astronauts. **The Denver Zoo** appeals to children of any age who like animals. Check ahead to see what's on the schedule for families and kids at the **History Colorado Center** and the **Denver Public Library,** where there are different themes monthly.

Some of the best parks with playgrounds for kids include **Washington Park, Stapleton Central Park, Cheesman Park,** and **City Park,** and there is a playground at the **Children's Museum.** City Park also has paddleboats in the summer. In the winter, there is sledding at **Commons Park,** as well as **Stapleton Central Park.**

Sometimes kids just like to be outside where they can run free. My daughter loves going to the **Denver Botanic Gardens** and **Commons Park,** where there aren't any playgrounds.

Visit www.denverkids.com to find coupons for various classes and attractions.

GAY AND LESBIAN TRAVELERS

Denver seems to be a fairly supportive place for the gay, lesbian, bisexual, and transgender community, with many organizations, events, and businesses geared toward this population. In 2008, anti-discrimination laws were expanded to protect against discrimination based on sexual orientation in the workplace and beyond.

For more information on the local LGBT scene, check out the **Denver Gay and Lesbian Chamber of Commerce** (www.denverglc. com) or the **Gay, Lesbian, Bisexual and Transgender Community Center of Colorado** (www.glbtcolorado.org), which puts on the annual two-day Pridefest event. *Out Front Colorado* (www.outfrontcolorado.com) is a free biweekly paper available all over the city.

TRAVELERS WITH DISABILITIES

In addition to the transportation services for disabled travelers in Denver listed earlier in this chapter, there are many trails designed for and open to people in wheelchairs.

Rocky Mountain National Park has a handful of wheelchair-accessible trails that are as scenic as more challenging footpaths in the park. Go to www.nps.gov/romo for more detailed information on where to find these trailheads and what to expect on each trail.

For information on wheelchair-accessible trails and facilities at Colorado State Parks, go to http://parks.co.state.us or call 303/866-3437.

Nature-lovers in Denver can enjoy most of the **Denver Botanic Gardens** on their wide, smooth concrete pathways. The main Denver Botanic Gardens has complimentary wheelchairs available.

There is a theater group in Denver, the **Physically Handicapped Actors and Musical Artists League (PHAMALY),** that performs a few times a year in the Denver area and at the Denver Center for the Performing Arts. The group was formed in 1989, when physically disabled acting students became frustrated with the lack of parts available to them. Get the league's latest schedule at www.phamaly.org or call 303/575-0005.

TRAVELING WITH PETS

It's been noted more than once in this book that Denver is quite pet-friendly. Numerous hotels cater to dogs, including the **Hotel Teatro,**

Hotel Monaco, Loews, and the **JW Marriott** at Cherry Creek. Depending on the hotel, they will walk your dog for you or recommend the best places for you to take your dog on a walk, provide a menu for dogs, and display a list of spa services.

There is less love, however, in the public sector; in most public places, dogs are required to be on a leash and there are fines for not complying with this rule. The website www.eco-animal.com/dogfun lists off-leash dog parks for Denver and many other Colorado cities, with detailed directions, hours, and rules. People are also required to clean up after their dogs, and "dogi-pots" are conveniently located near popular parks and walkways for disposing of those little plastic baggies.

There is a small, enclosed area for pet exercise at Denver International Airport (www.flydenver.com), but keep in mind it is off of the main terminal and travelers must go through security again to get back to their concourse. Check the airport website for more detailed information on traveling with pets.

Health and Safety

HEALTH PRECAUTIONS

Whether just staying in the city or venturing up into the mountains, prevention is the key in warding off a few common local illnesses.

The altitude affects everyone differently and increases can be subtle, especially when driving or even hiking. Mild symptoms of fatigue, dizziness, headache, nausea, and nosebleeds can develop into a more serious illness. It's best to drink extra water and rest frequently. The body eventually acclimates to the decreased oxygen.

You're simply closer to the sun at high altitudes, so sunscreen (for lips, too) is a must, and hats and sunglasses are generally a good idea for adults and kids. Even on overcast days or on snowy slopes, you can get sunburned.

Bring your own water or water purification tablets with you while hiking, because you risk getting giardia from drinking infected river or lake water. This intestinal illness causes nausea, cramps, and diarrhea.

HOSPITALS

If you need to make a trip to the emergency room while in Denver, you are likely to end up at **Presbyterian/St. Luke's Medical Center** (1719 E. 19th Ave., 303/839-6000, www.pslmc.com); **Denver Health** (777 Bannock St., 303/436-6000, www.denverhealth.org), which serves the uninsured; or **Exempla Saint Joseph Hospital** (1835 Franklin St., 303/837-7111, www.exempla.org), all of which are downtown.

The Children's Hospital (13123 E. 16th Ave., or I-225 and 16th Ave., Aurora, 720/777-1234, www.thechildrenshospital.org) has relocated from its aging facility near downtown to Aurora, east of Denver. The hospital maintains emergency services at Exempla Saint Joseph Hospital and has care centers at a dozen other sites in the metro area.

The University of Colorado Hospital (www.uch.edu) is the state's academic hospital, with various specialties and locations around the city and state, including the central **Anschutz Medical Campus** (1635 Ursula St., Aurora, 720/848-2300) on the former Fitzsimmons Army Base.

PHARMACIES

A good concierge at your hotel should be able to direct you to the nearest pharmacy. On the 16th Street Mall, which is walking distance from many recommended downtown hotels, there is a **Walgreens** (801 16th St., 303/571-5314, www.walgreens.com) and a

Rite-Aid. There are other Walgreens locations in Highlands (2975 Federal Blvd., 303/433-8911), Capitol Hill (2000 E. Colfax Ave., 303/331-0917), and on South Broadway (120 S. Broadway, 303/722-0771).

Integrative or alternative pharmacies such as Pharmaca have not succeeded in the Denver market (though there are three Pharmaca locations in Boulder); for natural remedies, the best bet is to go to **Whole Foods** in Cherry Creek (2375 E. 1st Ave., 720/941-4100, www.wholefoodsmarket.com) or Capitol Hill (900 E. 11th Ave., 303/832-7701).

EMERGENCY SERVICES

For medical or fire emergencies, or to reach the police in an emergency, dial **911.** For issues that are not life threatening, contact the **Denver Police/Fire/Paramedics Communication Center** at 720/913-2000. **The Rocky Mountain Poison and Drug Center** can be reached at 303/739-1123 or 800/222-1222.

Metro Denver Crimestoppers can be reached at 720/913-7867.

For future reference, you can find emergency preparedness kits and contact lists at www.denvergov.org.

Communications and Media

PHONES

There are two area codes for Denver—303 and 720—used throughout the greater metro area. Always dial the entire 10-digit number, including the area code, even for local calls.

INTERNET SERVICES

There is free Wi-Fi available at various places all around Denver. All you need is a Wi-Fi-enabled laptop and you can surf the Internet from any bench or comfortable spot along the 16th Street Mall, where there is free Wi-Fi. All Denver Public Library locations have free Wi-Fi, as does the Cherry Creek North shopping district. The Colorado Convention Center, Denver International Airport, all Tattered Cover Book Store locations, and several local coffee shops offer free Wi-Fi. In some places, you will need to get a password from an employee or manager of the business before logging on.

MAIL SERVICES

There are post offices located in many Denver neighborhoods. In downtown, there is a post office on the edge of LoDo (951 20th St.).

Also downtown, you'll find a FedEx Kinko's

(555 17th St., 303/298-8610); there's another location in LoDo (1509 Blake St., 303/623-3500). If you call one branch, they can give you the address of another one close to you. The UPS Store (1550 Larimer St., 303/825-8060) in LoDo can also provide helpful information on locations around the city.

NEWSPAPERS AND PERIODICALS

Denver newspapers are not faring any better than those in other parts of the country. In 2009, the Pulitzer Prize–winning *Rocky Mountain News* (www.rockymountainnews.com) was shuttered. The *Denver Post* (www.denverpost.com) continues to print a daily newspaper, but there are regular layoffs and it has become steadily thinner.

Even though the physical size of the alternative weekly, *Westword* (www.westword.com), also keeps shrinking, the voice is still big and strong, thanks largely to longtime editor Patricia Calhoun, who knows Denver inside out. *Westword* magazine is free and can be picked up at businesses all over town. The weekly event listings can be really helpful when looking for something fun to do.

5280 Magazine (pronounced fifty-two eighty, www.5280.com) is a glossy monthly magazine that has a mix of serious news, restaurant reviews, and very popular "Best Of" issues on topics from food to doctors.

RADIO AND TELEVISION

Colorado Public Radio (KCFR, 90.1 FM, www.cpr.org) is the local news and information radio station, with original programming such as *Colorado Matters,* in addition to the National Public Radio and BBC programs aired throughout each day. Sister station KVOD (88.1 FM, www.kvod.org) plays classical music all day. Their websites provide the frequencies for picking up those stations in other Colorado locations. You can also pick up Boulder-based KGNU (88.5 FM in Boulder or 1390 AM in Denver, www.kgnu.org), an independent community radio station that offers some eclectic programming ranging from music to news. For jazz and blues music with knowledgeable deejays, there is jazz89 (89.3 FM, www.kuvo.org). All-talk stations include KHOW (630 AM, www.khow.com), with local favorites such as Peter Boyles and Tom Martino; KOA (850 AM, www.850koa.com), with shows that lean to the right from local Mike Rosen and Rush Limbaugh; and KNUS (710 AM, www.710knus.townhall.com), which has more news and talk.

Local news channels are Channel 2 (WB Network), Channel 4 (CBS affiliate), Channel 7 (ABC affiliate), Channel 9 (NBC affiliate), and Fox News (Channel 13 or 31). There are two PBS channels: Rocky Mountain PBS (KRMA, Channel 6) includes local shows like *Colorado State of Mind* and national ones like *The Newshour with Jim Lehrer;* and Colorado Public Television (KBDI, Channel 12) has a diverse program schedule with an emphasis on documentaries.

Information and Services

MAPS

Maps of Denver and beyond can be found at the VISIT DENVER (www.denver.org) Visitor Information Center in the 16th Street Mall (1600 California St., 303/892-1505).

You can also find maps, atlases, and gazettes at any **Tattered Cover Book Store** location (www.tatteredcover.com), or at office supply stores.

At the shuttle bus stops on each block of the 16th Street Mall, there are maps of downtown available for free. **VISIT DENVER, The Convention & Visitors Bureau** (www.denver. org) has maps of area attractions and accommodations available for download from its website.

TOURIST OFFICES

The Denver Metro Convention and Visitors Bureau has a public visitors center at 16th and California Streets, where you can pick up bags full of brochures and maps and ask lots of questions. They also have a visitors center at DIA.

The Colorado Tourism Office (www.colorado.com) has Colorado Welcome Centers located at several roadside spots around the state. The closest to Denver is in Morrison at Red Rocks Amphitheatre. You can also order a free vacation guide from the website.

The official state government website www.colorado.gov has a lot of helpful information, a place to ask questions, and resources for tourism, government, education, and more.

LIBRARIES

There are 23 library locations in the **Denver Public Library** (www.denverlibrary.org) system, many of them situated in small, historic buildings near parks and playgrounds. The central library was designed by architect Michael Graves, and this is where you will find the Western History and Genealogy Collections. All of the libraries host story times and events for kids, and the Smiley branch has a toy library for young children. Weekends include "Super Saturdays," when magicians, musicians, drummers, and storytellers entertain children for free. Every two months, the Denver Public Library puts out the *Fresh City Life* newsletter with a calendar of special events and classes (cooking, baking, knitting, reading club) that all share a common theme.

EDUCATION

The **University of Denver** (303/871-2000, www.du.edu) is the oldest independent university in the Rocky Mountain region, and is located southeast of downtown. The school has many prominent alumni, including Peter Coors of the Coors Brewing Company, former secretary of the interior Gale Norton, former secretary of state Condoleezza Rice, and many more familiar politicians and business CEOs. Two former Colorado governors are on the faculty at DU: Richard Lamm and Bill Owens.

The **University of Colorado at Denver** (www.cudenver.edu) has a presence on the Auraria campus in downtown, along with the **Metropolitan State College of Denver** (www.mscd.edu) and the **Community College of Denver** (www.ccd.edu). The Auraria campus is a commuter campus, with no campus housing and plenty of night classes for students continuing their education while working. The **University of Colorado Health Sciences Center** (www.uchsc.edu) is at 9th Avenue and Colorado Boulevard and on the Anschutz Medical Campus.

On the northern edge of the Highlands neighborhood is **Regis University** (www.regis.edu), a Colorado Jesuit university. The school has been here since 1877 and it's an attractive little campus with three specialty colleges.

RESOURCES

Suggested Reading

HISTORY AND GENERAL INFORMATION

Abbott, Carl, Stephen J. Leonard, and Thomas J. Noel. *Colorado: A History of the Centennial State,* 4th ed. Denver, CO: University Press of Colorado, 2005. Tom Noel, a history professor at the University of Colorado at Denver, is nicknamed Dr. Colorado for his bottomless well of knowledge on all things Denver and Colorado.

Brosnan, Kathleen A. *Uniting Mountain and Plain: Urbanization, Law and Environmental Change Along the Front Range.* Albuquerque, NM: University of New Mexico Press, 2002. This was the first book by University of Houston professor Kathleen Brosnan, who specializes in environment and Western history.

Goodstein, Phil. *Denver in Our Time: A People's History of the Mile High City.* Denver, CO: New Social Publications, 1999. Goodstein has written several books about Denver, most with a specific neighborhood or topic focus, but this one gives a more general overview.

Leonard, Stephen J., and Thomas J. Noel. *Denver: Mining Camp to Metropolis.* Denver, CO: University Press of Colorado, 1989. A precursor to the larger *Colorado: A History of the Centennial State* by the same authors, and just as packed with facts.

Stephens, Ronald J., and La Wanna M. Larson. *African Americans of Denver (Images of America: Colorado).* Mount Pleasant, SC: Arcadia Publishing, 2008. Learn more about the African Americans who came to Denver and Colorado and their impact on the city and state through the years. Author La Wanna M. Larson is the curator of the Black American West Museum.

Wyckoff, William. *Creating Colorado: The Making of a Western American Landscape, 1860–1940.* New Haven, CT: Yale University Press, 1999. Montana State University geography professor Wyckoff includes maps and historical photographs to illustrate his unique environmental telling of Colorado history.

TRAVEL GUIDES

Fielder, John. *John Fielder's Best of Colorado.* Boulder, CO: Westcliffe Publishers, 2002. John Fielder is a local photographer whose images make this hefty guidebook as interesting to look at as it is to read.

Irwin, Pamela, with David Irwin. *Colorado's Best Wildflower Hikes, Volume I: The Front Range.* Boulder, CO: Westcliffe Publishers, 1998. These wildflower hikes invite people of any fitness level to hike with a purpose.

Knopper, Steve. *Moon Colorado,* 8th ed. Berkeley, CA: Avalon Travel, 2012. More in-depth information about areas beyond Denver and how to get there.

Ryan, Sarah. *Moon Colorado Camping,* 4th ed. Berkeley, CA: Avalon Travel, 2011. Go beyond the skyscrapers of downtown Denver and get out under the stars for a few nights in a tent with the handy maps and insightful descriptions found in this book.

Walter, Claire. *Snowshoeing Colorado,* 2nd ed. Golden, CO: Fulcrum Publishing, 2000. For beginners and experts, a useful guide to snowshoeing trails around Colorado and many important tips about the popular sport.

Internet Resources

City of Denver
www.denvergov.org
The city's website is fairly easy to navigate and includes helpful options like "311" and signing up for street-sweeping-day parking alerts for residents. Look for the "Bike Maps" link to plan a two-wheeled excursion or route.

Colorado Local First
www.coloradolocalfirst.com
Do a search for a locally owned independent business in the directory and read reviews of listed businesses.

Colorado Tourism Office
www.colorado.com
If you are a resident and just want a "day-cation" or if you are coming for a longer stay, be sure to check out this website with vacation ideas and vacation values.

Denver Infill
www.denverinfill.com
Find out how Denver is growing *in* with infill projects where there were once industrial sites or parking lots.

Eat Drink Denver
http://eatdrinkdenver.com
Visit Denver's guide to the latest in eating and drinking in the Mile-High City.

5280
www.5280.com
5280 Magazine has monthly in-depth articles, plus regular "Top of the Town" issues with lists of favorite restaurants and more in Denver.

Gabby Gourmet
www.gabbygourmet.com
A radio show food critic now has a website with reviews, photos, and "find of the month" restaurant listings.

Greenprint Denver
www.greenprintdenver.org
An interesting look at the whole concept of a "sustainable city" and what plans are in the works to make Denver more "green."

The Intersection
http://the-intersection.blogspot.com
Denver street style captured in color photos and with a little commentary from local blogger Renee Mudd. A fun diversion to see if you agree or disagree with her fashion picks.

Metro Denver Economic Development Corporation
www.metrodenver.org
An affiliate of the Denver Metro Chamber of Commerce, the Metro Denver EDC has a lot of statistical data for the greater seven-county area. Request a Relocation Package and Guide

if you are a newcomer or relocating to the Denver area.

Regional Transportation District
www.rtd-denver.com
Not only can you find bus and light rail schedules and fare information, but the Regional Transportation District (RTD) website also has a trip-planning feature to help you figure out your mass-transit route.

State of Colorado
www.colorado.gov
What isn't on this website? You can get a hunting or fishing license, find out current weather, view maps, buy a state park pass, and much more.

VISIT DENVER, The Convention & Visitors Bureau
www.denver.org
This website is designed for tourists, locals, and yes, conventioneers. The site is loaded with facts, and helps with finding hotels, restaurants, and upcoming events.

Westword
www.westword.com
Find out about the latest events around town and check out the annual "Best Of" lists, as well as restaurant reviews.

Index

Restaurant Index

Nightlife Index

Shops Index

Hotels Index

www.moon.com

DESTINATIONS | ACTIVITIES | BLOGS | MAPS | BOOKS

MOON.COM is ready to help plan your next trip! Filled with fresh trip ideas and strategies, author interviews, informative travel blogs, a detailed map library, and descriptions of all the Moon guidebooks, Moon.com is all you need to get out and explore the world—or even places in your own backyard. While at Moon.com, sign up for our monthly e-newsletter for updates on new releases, travel tips, and expert advice from our on-the-go Moon authors. As always, when you travel with Moon, expect an experience that is uncommon and truly unique.

KEEP UP WITH MOON ON FACEBOOK AND TWITTER
JOIN THE MOON PHOTO GROUP ON FLICKR

MAP SYMBOLS

	Expressway	**C**	Highlight	✗	Airfield	⚓	Golf Course
	Primary Road	○	City/Town	✈	Airport	**P**	Parking Area
	Secondary Road	◉	State Capital	▲	Mountain	⬟	Archaeological Site
=======	Unpaved Road	⊛	National Capital	✛	Unique Natural Feature	⛪	Church
-------	Trail	★	Point of Interest				
············	Ferry	•	Accommodation	⭍	Waterfall	⛽	Gas Station
▬▬▬	Railroad	▼	Restaurant/Bar	⚑	Park	◌	Glacier
	Pedestrian Walkway	■	Other Location	⛾	Trailhead		Mangrove
⊞⊞⊞⊞	Stairs	⛐	Campground	⛷	Skiing Area		Reef
							Swamp

CONVERSION TABLES

$°C = (°F - 32) / 1.8$
$°F = (°C \times 1.8) + 32$
1 inch = 2.54 centimeters (cm)
1 foot = 0.304 meters (m)
1 yard = 0.914 meters
1 mile = 1.6093 kilometers (km)
1 km = 0.6214 miles
1 fathom = 1.8288 m
1 chain = 20.1168 m
1 furlong = 201.168 m
1 acre = 0.4047 hectares
1 sq km = 100 hectares
1 sq mile = 2.59 square km
1 ounce = 28.35 grams
1 pound = 0.4536 kilograms
1 short ton = 0.90718 metric ton
1 short ton = 2,000 pounds
1 long ton = 1.016 metric tons
1 long ton = 2,240 pounds
1 metric ton = 1,000 kilograms
1 quart = 0.94635 liters
1 US gallon = 3.7854 liters
1 Imperial gallon = 4.5459 liters
1 nautical mile = 1.852 km

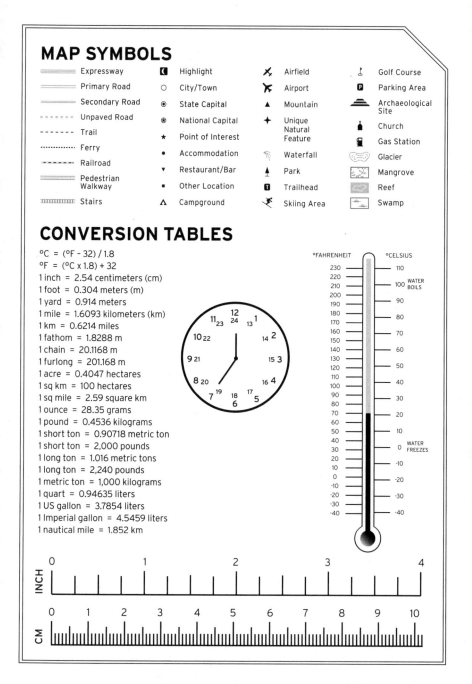

MOON DENVER

Avalon Travel
a member of the Perseus Books Group
1700 Fourth Street
Berkeley, CA 94710, USA
www.moon.com

Editor: Elizabeth Hollis Hansen
Series Manager: Erin Raber
Copy Editor: Beth Fitzer
Graphics Coordinator: Darren Alessi
Production Coordinator: Darren Alessi
Cover Designer: Darren Alessi
Map Editor: Albert Angulo
Cartographers: Kaitlin Jaffe, Chris Markiewicz,
    Lohnes + Wright, Kat Bennett

ISBN-13: 978-1-61238-290-6
ISSN: 1944-544X

Printing History
1st Edition – 2009
2nd Edition – May 2013
5 4 3 2 1

Text © 2013 by Mindy Sink.
Maps © 2013 by Avalon Travel.
All rights reserved.

Some photos and illustrations are used by permission
    and are the property of the original copyright
    owners.

Front cover photo: *The Broncos* by world-renowned
    sculptor Sergio Benvenuti, © Denver Broncos Team
    Photography
Title page photo: © Visit Denver, *I See What You
    Mean*, sculpture by Lawrence Argent.
Color interior photos: page 2 © Visit Denver; page 18
    (inset) © Rich Grant and Visit Denver, (bottom left)
    © Bob Ash and Visit Denver, (bottom right) © Todd
    Kreykes/123rf.com; page 20 © Visit Denver; page 22
    © Visit Denver; page 23 © Steve Crecelius and Visit
    Denver; page 24 Courtesy of the History Colorado.

Printed in Canada by Friesens

KEEPING CURRENT

If you have a favorite gem you'd like to see included in the next edition, or see anything
that needs updating, clarification, or correction, please drop us a line. Send your com-
ments via email to feedback@moon.com, or use the address above.